STUDIES IN RUSSIA AND EAST EUROPE
formerly Studies in Russian and East European History

Chairman of the Editorial Board: M. A. Branch, Director, School of Slavonic and East European Studies.

This series includes books on general, political, historical, economic social and cultural themes relating to Russia and East Europe written or edited by members of the School of Slavonic and East European Studies in the University of London, or by authors working in association with the School. Titles already published are listed below. Further titles are in preparation.

Phyllis Auty and Richard Clogg (*editors*)
BRITISH POLICY TOWARDS WARTIME RESISTANCE IN YUGOSLAVIA AND GREECE

Elisabeth Barker
BRITISH POLICY IN SOUTH-EAST EUROPE IN THE SECOND WORLD WAR

Roger Bartlett (*editor*)
LAND COMMUNE AND PEASANT COMMUNITY IN RUSSIA: Communal Forms in Imperial and Early Soviet Society

Roger Bartlett and Janet M. Hartley (*editors*)
RUSSIA IN THE AGE OF THE ENLIGHTENMENT: Essays for Isabel de Madariaga

Richard Clogg (*editor*)
THE MOVEMENT FOR GREEK INDEPENDENCE, 1770–1821: A COLLECTION OF DOCUMENTS

Olga Crisp
STUDIES IN THE RUSSIAN ECONOMY BEFORE 1914

John C. K. Daly
RUSSIAN SEAPOWER AND 'THE EASTERN QUESTION' 1827–41

Dennis Deletant and Harry Hanak (*editors*)
HISTORIANS AS NATION-BUILDERS: Central and South-East Europe

Richard Freeborn and Jane Grayson (*editors*)
IDEOLOGY IN RUSSIAN LITERATURE

Julian Graffy and Geoffrey A. Hosking (*editors*)
CULTURE AND THE MEDIA IN THE USSR TODAY

Jane Grayson and Faith Wigzell (*editors*)
NIKOLAY GOGOL: Text and Context

Hans Günther (*editor*)
THE CULTURE OF THE STALIN PERIOD

Harry Hanak (*editor*)
T. G. MASARYK (1850–1937)
Volume 3: Statesman and Cultural Force

Geoffrey A. Hosking (*editor*)
CHURCH, NATION AND STATE IN RUSSIA AND UKRAINE

Geoffrey A. Hosking and George F. Cushing (*editors*)
PERSPECTIVES ON LITERATURE AND SOCIETY IN EASTERN AND WESTERN EUROPE

D. G. Kirby (*editor*)
FINLAND AND RUSSIA, 1808–1920: DOCUMENTS

Michael Kirkwood (*editor*)
LANGUAGE PLANNING IN THE SOVIET UNION

Martin McCauley
THE RUSSIAN REVOLUTION AND THE SOVIET STATE, 1917–1921: DOCUMENTS (*editor*)

KHRUSHCHEV AND THE DEVELOPMENT OF SOVIET AGRICULTURE
COMMUNIST POWER IN EUROPE: 1944–1949 (*editor*)
MARXISM–LENINISM IN THE GERMAN DEMOCRATIC REPUBLIC: THE SOCIALIST UNITY PARTY (SED)
THE GERMAN DEMOCRATIC REPUBLIC SINCE 1945
KHRUSHCHEV AND KHRUSHCHEVISM (*editor*)
THE SOVIET UNION UNDER GORBACHEV (*editor*)
GORBACHEV AND PERESTROIKA (*editor*)

Martin McCauley and Stephen Carter (*editors*)
LEADERSHIP AND SUCCESSION IN THE SOVIET UNION, EASTERN EUROPE AND CHINA

Martin McCauley and Peter Waldron
THE EMERGENCE OF THE MODERN RUSSIAN STATE, 1856–61

Evan Mawdsley
THE RUSSIAN REVOLUTION AND THE BALTIC FLEET

László Péter and Robert B. Pynsent (*editors*)
INTELLECTUALS AND THE FUTURE IN THE HABSBURG MONARCHY, 1890–1914

Robert B. Pynsent (*editor*)
T. G. MASARYK (1850–1937) Volume 2: Thinker and Critic

MODERN SLOVAK PROSE: Fiction Since 1945 (*editor*)

Ian W. Roberts: NICHOLAS I AND THE RUSSIAN INTERVENTION IN HUNGARY

J. J. Tomiak (*editor*)
WESTERN PERSPECTIVES ON SOVIET EDUCATION IN THE 1980s

Stephen White and Alex Pravda (*editors*)
IDEOLOGY AND SOVIET POLITICS

Stanley B. Winters (*editor*)
T. G. MASARYK (1850–1937) Volume 1: Thinker and Politician

Alan Wood and R. A. French (*editors*)
THE DEVELOPMENT OF SIBERIA: People and Resources

Series Standing Order

If you would like to receive future titles in this series as they are published, you can make use of our standing order facility. To place a standing order please contact your bookseller or, in case of difficulty, write to us at the address below with your name and address and the name of the series. Please state with which title you wish to begin your standing order. (If you live outside the UK we may not have the rights for your area, in which case we will forward your order to the publisher concerned.)

Standing Order Service, Macmillan Distribution Ltd, Houndmills, Basingstoke, Hampshire, RG21 2XS, England.

NICHOLAS I AND THE RUSSIAN INTERVENTION IN HUNGARY

Ian W. Roberts
Honorary Visiting Fellow
School of Slavonic and East European Studies
University of London

M

MACMILLAN

in association with the
School of Slavonic and East European Studies
University of London

© Ian W. Roberts 1991

All rights reserved. No reproduction, copy or transmission
of this publication may be made without written permission.

No paragraph of this publication may be reproduced, copied or
transmitted save with written permission or in accordance with
the provisions of the Copyright, Designs and Patents Act 1988,
or under the terms of any licence permitting limited copying
issued by the Copyright Licensing Agency, 33–4 Alfred Place,
London WC1E 7DP.

Any person who does any unauthorised act in relation to
this publication may be liable to criminal prosecution and
civil claims for damages.

First published 1991

Published by
MACMILLAN ACADEMIC AND PROFESSIONAL LTD
Houndmills, Basingstoke, Hampshire RG21 2XS
and London
Companies and representatives
throughout the world

Typeset by Wessex Typesetters
(Division of The Eastern Press Ltd)
Frome, Somerset

Printed in Hong Kong

British Library Cataloguing in Publication Data
Roberts, Ian W.
Nicholas I and the Russian
intervention in Hungary
1. Hungary. Invasion by Russia,
1849
i. Title
943.9′042
ISBN 0–333–515978

For Pamela and Catherine

Contents

Acknowledgements	viii
Preface	ix
List of Illustrations and Maps	x
A Note on Dates, Place-names and Spelling	xi

Part I: The Prelude to the Intervention

	Introduction	3
1	Russian Reaction to the Revolutions of 1848	8
2	The Russian Intervention in the Danubian Principalities	36
3	The October Revolution in Vienna and its Aftermath	58
4	The Russian Intervention in Transylvania and its Consequences	77
5	The Russian Decision to Intervene in Hungary	99

Part II: The Intervention

6	Russian Preparations for War	121
7	The First Half of the Campaign	143
8	The Second Half of the Campaign	165
9	After the Surrender	185
10	The Aftermath of the Intervention	205
	Conclusion	224
	Notes	230
	Select Bibliography	276
	Index	286

Acknowledgements

The author and publishers wish to thank the following who have kindly given permission for the use of material held by them:

Her Majesty the Queen for gracious permission to quote from the letters of Queen Victoria and Prince Albert in the Royal Archives, Windsor.

The British Library for permission to quote from the Aberdeen Papers.

The Public Record Office for permission to quote from the Bloomfield, Canning and Russell Papers and other material.

The Trustees of the Broadland Archives Trust for permission to include extracts from the Palmerston Papers held by the University of Southampton.

The University of Durham for permission to quote from the Ponsonby Papers.

Baring Brothers and Company for permission to quote from material held by their own archives and the Northbrook Papers.

The Austrian State Archives for permission to quote from the Diary of Buol–Schauenstein and other material.

The State Archives of Denmark for permission to quote from material in their possession.

The State Archives of Sweden for permission to quote from material in their possession.

Preface

The present work is an attempt to give an account of Russian foreign policy during the revolutionary years 1848 and 1849 which culminated in Nicholas I's decision to respond to the appeal of Francis Joseph for aid in restoring order in Hungary. It is based on a study of material from diplomatic archives (published and unpublished) and makes extensive use of the memoirs written by Russian officers who took part in the campaign in 1849.

I owe a special debt to Professor Michael Branch, the Director of the School of Slavonic and East European Studies in the University of London, who appointed me an Honorary Visiting Fellow at the School in 1985. I am also grateful to the Leverhulme Trust for making me an award in the same year which assisted me with the expenses of my research and enabled me to visit Helsinki and Vienna.

I should also like to thank the staff of the State Archives in Vienna and the Slavonic Library of the University Library in Helsinki for their assistance during my visits in 1985 and for answering many enquiries from me since that date. The staff of the British Library, the London Library and the Library of the School of Slavonic and East European Studies have been unfailingly helpful, especially Mrs Gyenes, who assisted me in obtaining material from libraries in the Soviet Union and Eastern Europe through the Inter-Library Loan Scheme. The staff of the Public Record Office at Kew and the other archives I have used, which are listed in the acknowledgements, also did much to assist me to find the material used in this book.

Finally, I must thank Professor G. F. Cushing and the late Professor Hugh Seton-Watson, both of whom encouraged me to undertake the task of writing this book and gave me the benefit of their profound knowledge of East European and Russian history.

I. W. Roberts

List of Plates

1. Emperor Nicholas I of Russia (anonymous painting, 1856)
2. Emperor Francis Joseph of Austria (Bildarchiv Österreich)
3. Prince Alfred Windischgraetz (School of Slavonic and East European Studies, University of London)
4. Count Karl von Buol-Schauenstein (SSEES, University of London)
5. Prince Felix Schwarzenberg (Bildarchiv Österreich)
6. General Julius Haynau (SSEES, University of London)
7. Lajos Kossuth (The Mansell Collection)
8. General Artúr Görgey (SSEES, University of London)
9. General György Klapka (SSEES, University of London)
10. General Józef Bem (SSEES, University of London)
11. General Henryk Dembiński (Hulton-Deutsch Collection)
12. Count Karl V. Nesselrode (SSEES, University of London)
13. Field Marshal Ivan F. Paskevich (Hulton-Deutsch Collection)
14. Count Pavel I. Medem (Source unknown)
15. General Aleksandr O. Duhamel (SSEES, University of London)
16. General Aleksandr N. Lüders (SSEES, University of London)
17. General Fyodor V. Rüdiger (SSEES, University of London)

ACKNOWLEDGEMENTS

I am grateful to the above-named institutions for permission to reproduce paintings and drawings in their possession. The publishers have made every effort to locate the copyright owners of photographic material: in cases where we have not been able to do so, we will gladly put matters right at the earliest opportunity.

A Note on Dates, Place-names and Spelling

In order to avoid confusion all dates have been given in the New Style based on the Gregorian calendar, which was twelve days ahead of the Julian calendar used in Russia throughout the nineteenth century.

All place-names have been given in the form in use in the country in which the places are at present located, e.g. Bratislava in preference to the German Pressburg and Hungarian Pozsony. In a few cases, the form of the name which is more well-known in historical writing is given in brackets after the modern form e.g. Şiria (Világos).

Russian names have usually been transliterated direct from the Cyrillic alphabet, except where it seemed more appropriate to use the original form of the name of a person of foreign ancestry in Russian service, e.g. Duhamel instead of Dyugamel'.

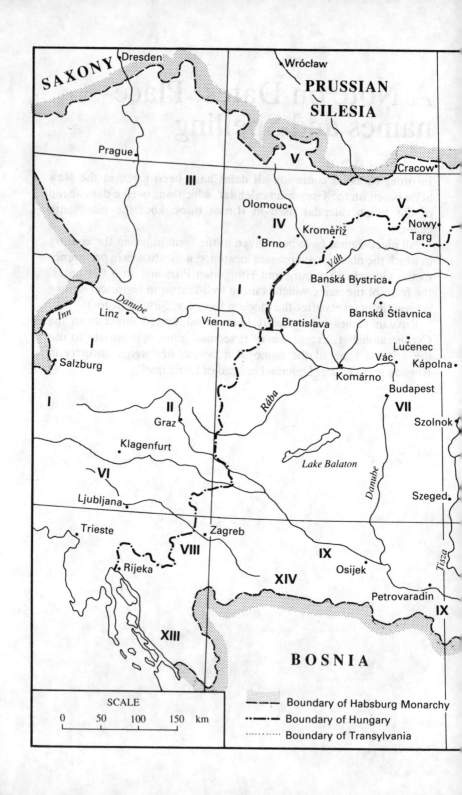

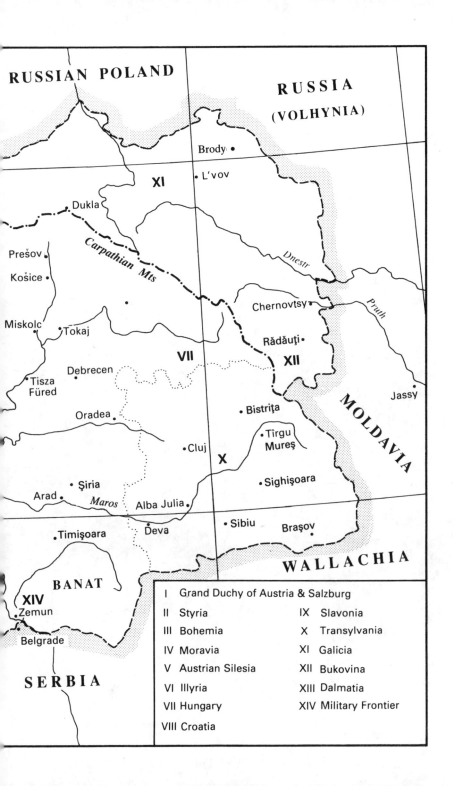

Part I
The Prelude to the Intervention

Introduction

'The fate of Hungary will largely influence the future condition of all Europe.' (Lord Aberdeen to Princess Lieven, 18 August 1849).[1] 'The fate and condition of Poland are now, as they have been for the last century, the key to the whole policy of Russia.' (*Edinburgh Review*, April 1847, vol. 222, p. 292).

The Russian intervention in Hungary in 1849 began on 17 June and ended on 13 August when the major part of the Hungarian army commanded by General Görgey surrendered to Field Marshal Paskevich, the Commander-in-Chief of the Russian army at Şiria (Világos in Hungarian). Although the campaign lasted only eight weeks, it made a deep impression on the rising middle class in western Europe and had far-reaching consequences for the future relationship between Russia and the Habsburg empire, which was never to be the same again. For Nicholas the intervention was the high point of his reign which was to end on a very different note in March 1855 during the Crimean War.

Nicholas succeeded to the Russian throne instead of his elder brother, the Grand Duke Constantine, the ruler of Russian Poland, who had earlier renounced his right of succession, in the aftermath of the unsuccessful Decembrist military revolt. The Tsar was never to forget the events which took place in Saint Petersburg on 26 December 1826 and the memories of that day would influence his actions for the rest of his life.[2] Nicholas' main interest in life was the Russian army and throughout his reign he was to reiterate that he would have much preferred to follow a military career rather than become the ruler of the Russian empire. He was the personification of an absolute monarch, and believed implicitly that he had been chosen by God to rule over his subjects. More German than Russian in his ancestry, he had lost his father at the age of five when the Emperor Paul was assassinated in Saint Petersburg in 1801 by a group of disaffected officers. His eldest brother Alexander I, who then succeeded to the throne, entrusted his education to their German mother, a Princess of Württemberg, and a group of tutors who brought Nicholas up during the Napoleonic wars in which he was too young to take part. Naturally straightforward and unwilling to compromise with his principles, he found it difficult to conceal his true feelings, but as the years went by, he was to gain the reputation of being a good actor and was able to exert considerable charm when necessary. As the young Queen Victoria wrote to her uncle King Leopold of Belgium after Nicholas' visit to Great Britain in 1844 to discuss the future of the Ottoman Empire, 'he is sincere, I am certain, *sincere* even in his most despotic acts, from a sense that this *is* the *only* way to govern.'[3]

Although the diplomatic correspondence of the period, both Russian and foreign, makes frequent reference to *'le cabinet russe'*, no such institution in the western sense existed in Russia at that time. The Council of State and the Council of Ministers were essentially advisory bodies which, in some instances, were called upon to implement decisions which had already been taken by the Tsar. Nicholas had regular meetings with his ministers individually and with the Military Council. The Commander-in-Chief of the Russian Army, Prince Paskevich, who replaced the Grand Duke Constantine as ruler of Russian Poland after his death from cholera in June 1831, also reported directly to the Tsar. Thus Nicholas acted as his own Prime Minister and his ministers were little more than the faithful executors of his decisions.

The cosmopolitan Count Nesselrode, whom Nicholas inherited as Minister of Foreign Affairs from Alexander I, was no exception to this rule. Disliked by the old Russian nobility because of his foreign ancestry, he was a model bureaucrat, industrious and hard-working, who sometimes persuaded the Tsar to have second thoughts and thus saved him from the consequences of some of his impulsive decisions.[4] While his admirers described him as *'un homme de bon conseil'*, his detractors scornfully referred to him as 'the mere head clerk of the Russian Ministry of Foreign Affairs'.[5]

At the beginning of Nicholas' reign, Russian foreign policy was dominated by three problems, two of which had their origin in the reign of Catherine the Great. These were the ultimate fate of the Ottoman Empire which had begun its long and slow process of decline; the consequences of the partition of Poland between Austria, Prussia and Russia at the end of the eighteenth century; and finally, the fear of the resurgence of revolutionary France under the leadership of a successor to Napoleon Bonaparte.

Nicholas began his reign by having to act against his instincts and make common cause with Great Britain and France in assisting the Greeks to establish an independent state, much to the dismay of Metternich and the Emperor Francis of Austria. He then fought a war with Persia which brought Russia further gains in the Caucasus.

Introduction

An attempt made at the beginning of his reign to reach a peaceful settlement with Turkey on outstanding problems failed and was followed by a long and costly war in 1828–9. Once again the Tsar's instinctive wish to occupy Constantinople had to give way to the more measured advice of a special committee he had established, which recommended that Russia's best interests would be served by the preservation of the Ottoman Empire and the solution of its problems in concert with the other European powers. The war was ended by the Treaty of Adrianople which consolidated Russia's hold on the mouth of the Danube and strengthened its influence in the Danubian Principalities and the Principality of Serbia.

1830 witnessed the outbreak of revolution in France and the advent to power of Louis Philippe, as well as a revolt in Belgium which led to the establishment of an independent state. Nicholas, who was always to regard Louis Philippe as a usurper, had no success in his efforts to create an alliance to suppress the revolutions in France and Belgium by a military intervention which would have involved the use of part of the Polish army. At the end of the year there was a revolt in Russian Poland and in January 1831 the Romanov dynasty was deposed. The Tsar, who had always been an unenthusiastic supporter of the Polish constitution granted by Alexander I after the Napoleonic wars, had no hesitation in using the Russian army to crush the Poles. Paskevich, who had played a prominent part in the campaigns in Persia and Turkey, replaced the previous commander Field Marshal Diebitsch, who died of cholera, and captured Warsaw on 8 September 1831. The revolution collapsed and the Polish leadership, which had been divided by internal dissensions, fled abroad, mainly to France, where its two main factions were to continue their efforts to foment revolution in their divided country and reunite it. Russian Poland lost its constitution and its own army, and retained only a small measure of administrative autonomy under the rule of Paskevich. From this time onwards Paskevich, whose friendship with Nicholas dated from the end of the Napoleonic wars, became an increasingly close confidant of the Tsar, who had served under him as a young brigade commander during the final years of the reign of Alexander I.

Immediately after the Polish revolt, Nicholas' attention was again engaged by the problems of the Ottoman Empire, when the first Egyptian–Turkish crisis occurred. In July 1833 he scored a notable success with the Treaty of Unkiar–Skelessi by which Russia and Turkey agreed to come to each other's aid in the event of attack.

But the Tsar had not forgotten the problems of western Europe, and after a vain attempt to involve Great Britain and France in reviving the alliance established by his elder brother after the Napoleonic wars, he found himself compelled to turn to Austria in his efforts to prevent the spread of liberal ideas. Austrian reservations about Russia's relationship with Turkey were temporarily set aside, while Nicholas was persuaded to overcome his innate suspicions of Metternich and Austrian policy.[6]

In September 1833 at a meeting between the elderly Emperor Francis and Nicholas in the Bohemian town of Mnichovo Hradiště (Muenchengraetz in German) a new alliance was formed in which Prussia was eventually to participate. Although the declared purpose of the alliance was to prevent a break-up of the Ottoman Empire, which would be detrimental to the interests of Austria and Russia, the three absolutist powers were equally united by their common purpose of opposing the French principle of non-intervention and preventing the reunification of a divided Poland. In the eyes of Great Britain and France, the new alliance concluded at Mnichovo Hradiště was nothing more than the revival of the Holy Alliance established after the Congress of Vienna; and as a result, Europe became divided into two opposing camps.

In 1839 the second Egyptian–Turkish crisis led to dissension between France and Great Britain of which Russia sought to take advantage. At one time it appeared that there would be war between France and Germany, but eventually the five great powers signed the Straits Convention in London in 1841 which closed the Bosphorus and Dardanelles to all foreign warships in peacetime. Nicholas' subsequent attempts to establish by personal diplomacy a special understanding with Great Britain about the future of the Ottoman Empire during his visit to London in June 1844 did not lead to the signing of any formal agreement, and was to be the cause of much misunderstanding in the period before the outbreak of the Crimean War.

In 1846 the attention of Austria, Prussia and Russia again focused on Poland when a revolt in Galicia and Cracow was suppressed by the combined military intervention of Austria and Russia. In the absence of any serious opposition by Great Britain and France, who were occupied with the affairs of Spain and Portugal, Prussia was reluctantly persuaded by Austria and Russia to agree to the suppression of the independent state of Cracow, created in 1815, which was incorporated into Austrian Galicia.

Introduction

The Tsar, who had always regarded Cracow as a thorn in his flesh, especially since the Polish revolt of 1830, was delighted that a further blow had been delivered to the cause of Polish independence. Nevertheless, as the decade of the 1840s drew to a close, Nicholas, who celebrated his fiftieth birthday in 1846, was becoming more and more uneasy about the state of the Russian alliance with Austria and Prussia.[7] On more than one occasion he was to express the view that it no longer consisted of three powers but one and a half.[8] By this the Tsar meant that he could no longer rely on his brother-in-law Frederick William IV of Prussia, who had succeeded to the throne in 1840 and was failing to stand up to liberal pressure. In addition, he had doubts about the ability of the Austrian Council of State, which ruled Austria during the reign of the successor to the Emperor Francis, the weak-minded Emperor Ferdinand, to keep the Habsburg empire together in the face of increasing restiveness among the nationalities and serious financial problems.[9] In short, by the end of 1847 Nicholas felt that Russia was the only member of the alliance which would be able to stand firm against the rising tide of liberalism and nationalism which was sweeping across the countries of Europe as they were gradually being transformed into modern industrial societies.

1 Russian Reaction to the Revolutions of 1848

The dawning of the fateful year of 1848 found Nicholas laid low with influenza accompanied by a high fever. Throughout Europe it had been a bitterly cold winter; in Saint Petersburg a piercing south-west wind which had sprung up in the previous December had kept the temperature down to 14° Fahrenheit. During the Tsar's illness his eldest son, Alexander, had deputised for him until he too fell ill. The indisposition of the Tsar and his heir made it even more difficult than usual for Nicholas' ministers to obtain approval for decrees and despatches sent to Russian missions abroad.

Even while he was bed-ridden Nicholas had found time to upbraid his brother-in-law, Frederick William IV of Prussia, about his experiments in constitutionalism, pointing out that Russia had been compelled to pay a heavy price in 1831 for Alexander I's unwise decision to give Russian Poland a constitution after the Napoleonic Wars.[1] On his return to work at the end of January he set down on paper his thoughts about the future of Europe in the year ahead, which he was convinced would be a momentous one. Predictably, he attributed the chief cause of Europe's problems to the decision by the Great Powers to recognise Louis Philippe as the lawful ruler of France after the overthrow of Charles X in 1830. The subsequent secession of Belgium from the United Kingdom of the Netherlands and the revolt in Russian Poland were the inevitable consequences of this action. While Russia had dealt firmly with the Poles, Prussia and Austria were now reaping the reward for their conciliatory behaviour towards their Polish subjects who were fostering unrest further afield in East Prussia and in Hungary. Indeed, Nicholas even believed that Polish emigrés had helped to stir up trouble in the universities of Germany. As for Great Britain, the passing of the Reform Bill of 1832 had dealt a mortal blow to the old order in that country and it was therefore hardly surprising that Great Britain was disposed to support the cause of revolution. For the immediate future Nicholas foresaw a continuation of unrest throughout Germany and Italy, as efforts were made to unify these countries with the consequence that Prussia and Austria could no longer be regarded by Russia as reliable allies.

On the basis of this gloomy analysis Nicholas then set down his guide lines on Russian foreign policy, which was to be based on two considerations, Russia's own interests and its obligations to its allies. During the Swiss crisis of 1847 Russia had only been able to lend moral support to its allies because the despatch of Russian troops to support the Roman Catholic cantons of the *Sonderbund* in their struggle against the Federal authority was not a practical proposition. For the same reason, Russia would not send troops to Italy in the event of war between Austria and Piedmont, unless France also attacked Austria, since that would probably cause a general European war. But if there were widespread disturbances throughout Germany which could not be brought under control, Russia would intervene in order to defend its own interests. For the time being Russia needed to do no more than observe the situation and prepare for all eventualities.[2]

While Nicholas faced the possible outbreak of trouble in 1848 with an apparent air of confidence, Metternich in Vienna was filled with foreboding about his ability to deal with the situation in Europe. In a letter to the King of Prussia he expressed the opinion that 1848 would clarify a number of matters.[3] Like Nicholas, he also composed a memorandum about future foreign policy, but after a long exposition of the causes of Europe's problems, he could only conclude that Austria, Prussia and Russia should remain united in the face of the trouble which lay ahead, in the hope that the smaller European states would rally to their cause.[4] Metternich was now sixty-seven years old, and as Lord Ponsonby, the British ambassador in Vienna, commented to Palmerston in a phrase from the boxing ring, Metternich would only fight verbal battles and would no longer 'come to the scratch' if he could help it.[5]

In fact, Metternich had good reason to be worried about Austria's ability to weather the coming storm, even although he had boasted to the Duke of Wellington the previous year that Austria was like a rock in the middle of a stormy sea. As a precautionary measure, the government had decided to increase the strength of the Austrian forces in Italy by 40 000 men. Unfortunately, Austrian finances (which had never fully recovered from the effects of the Napoleonic Wars) were in their usual parlous state. As a result of extensive borrowing the state debt had reached the huge total of 1131 million gulden (£113 million) by 1847. Furthermore, the silver reserves of the National Bank, which amounted to 20 million gulden (£2 million), were sufficient to cover only one-eighth of the total amount of paper money in circulation. To add to Austria's financial difficulties the foreign bankers who had been lending money had forbidden the printing of any more paper money.

Although there was a minor crisis in Austro–Russian relations caused by Austrian slowness in satisfying a Russian demand for the removal of a bishop from a monastery of Old Believers at Biala Krinitsa in Bukovina, Metternich was sure that the Tsar would be sympathetic to Austria's request for a loan of ready money. Accordingly on 20 January he wrote to Nesselrode, explaining that the money would be used for the additional military expenditure needed to enlarge the strength of the Austrian forces in Italy.[6] A secret emissary from the Austrian Ministry of Finance would, unknown to the Austrian mission in Saint Petersburg, travel to Russia to discuss the details of the transaction with the appropriate officials.[7]

The first disturbances of the year took place in Milan where the inhabitants protested about the Austrian tobacco monopoly. On 12 January much more serious disturbances took place in Palermo in Sicily. During the lengthy stay of his wife there at the end of 1845 Nicholas had spent some time in the Kingdom of the Two Sicilies and had made the acquaintance of Ferdinand II, later to become notorious as King 'Bomba'. By the end of the month the disturbances had spread from Sicily to Naples, and on 10 February Ferdinand was forced to grant a constitution which was, however, rejected by his subjects in Sicily. Despite pressure from Nesselrode, Nicholas declined to write to Ferdinand, and readily admitted to the British Ambassador in Saint Petersburg that reforms should have been carried out in Naples and Sicily long ago.[8] On 17 February the Grand Duke Leopold of Tuscany was forced to grant a constitution, and his example was followed on 4 March by King Charles Albert of Piedmont and on 14 March by the Pope in Rome.

As he surveyed the European scene, Nicholas was also moved to write to King Ludwig of Bavaria about the misrule of his son Otto in Greece. The death of King Christian VIII of Denmark at the end of January served as a reminder that there might be trouble in a country on which Russia relied to protect its trade through the Baltic. At the same time Nicholas was receiving alarming reports from the King of Württemberg, the father-in-law of his daughter Olga, about the uneasy situation in southern Germany, especially in Bavaria, where King Ludwig's infatuation with Lola Montez was causing considerable unrest.

But the month of March was to bring news of disturbances with far more serious implications for Russia. The first of these was the overthrow of Guizot in France, the abdication of Louis Philippe, the vain attempt to establish a regency until his grandson came of age, and the proclamation of a republic. On 3 March the first news of these events reached Saint Petersburg by the optical telegraph from Warsaw.[9] The information was rapidly confirmed the following day by an intercepted dispatch sent through the post to the French chargé d'affaires in Saint Petersburg. On Sunday 5 March Nicholas interrupted the dancing of a mazurka at a ball given by Alexander in the Anichkov Palace as the climax to the carnival celebrations with the announcement that a republic had been proclaimed in France. Nicholas considered that the usurper Louis Philippe had deserved his fate, and told some of his closest advisers who were at the ball that he had no intention of helping him to regain his throne.[10]

On 6 March the usual Monday meeting of the Council of State took place, but its proceedings were overshadowed by the news from France. Did the proclamation of a republic in France presage another 1789? Nicholas' first concern was with military preparations, and he was able to discuss these with Paskevich who was in Saint Petersburg on a visit from Warsaw.[11] The following day a decree was published calling up reserves of the army in order that it could be put on a war footing. A similar decree for the navy followed a few days later.[12] Several of Nicholas' advisers warned him that Russia could ill afford the extra military expenditure, but the Tsar was not to be deterred when it was a question of protecting Russia from the onslaught of revolution. On top of the loan to Austria of 6 million silver roubles (£960 000), he authorised the allocation of 7 million silver roubles (£1 200 000) for the increase in Russia's own military expenditure. It was expected that within three months Russia would have 450 000 men in the field.[13] Meanwhile Nicholas informed the French chargé d'affaires that although he would not recognise the new French government, he did not intend to interfere in French affairs as long as the treaties of 1815 were respected.[14] French citizens in Russia could leave if they wished, and his own representative in Paris was ordered to leave the country. No further visas were to be issued by the Russian consul in Paris without reference to Saint Petersburg.

Nicholas had long cherished the idea that a wall should be built round Russia, although he realised that this was a physical impossibility. Under the influence of Count Orlov, the Head of the Third Department (secret police), and other advisers, he was persuaded to agree to the establishment of a committee to tighten up censorship regulations and counter the influence of ideas from abroad. The committee was set up on 10 March and was reconstituted on 14 April (2 April o.s.). Its activities were to continue for the remainder of Nicholas' reign and were to usher in a period of repression in Russian literature and journalism.[15]

Nicholas' next thought was for his allies. Medem was ordered to return to Vienna and was informed of Nicholas' intention to leave Austria to deal with the disturbances in Italy, unless France decided to intervene. However, in order to ease Austria's burden, he was prepared to move one army corps up to the frontier of Galicia and even occupy the province if there was a recurrence of the disturbances of 1846. In addition, Nicholas was prepared to send a Russian officer to Vienna to co-ordinate Austrian and Russian military plans.[16]

Nor did Nicholas waste any time in writing to the King of Prussia about the need to defend Germany. He was uncertain whether France would try to invade Germany at once or would bide its time and seek to take advantage of any disturbances which might occur. He therefore proposed that Prussia should head an army in north Germany which would include the forces of Hanover, Saxony and Hesse, while Bavaria and Württemberg would lead an army in the south. Russian troops could, if required, be moved to the Polish frontier and would act as a reserve. Meanwhile the situation should be kept under review, since there was no question of attacking France.[17]

Although Nicholas had spoken wistfully of the Duke of Wellington as the leader of a new coalition against France, he realised that he was unlikely to gain any support from the British government for his plans. His ambassador in London, Baron Brunnow, had received the news from Paris before the Tsar and at once urged Britain to support his own country, along with Austria and Prussia, in keeping France in check.[18] Later in March he received from Nesselrode his instructions about asking Great Britain not to recognise the new French government which had been shown to Lord Bloomfield, the British ambassador in Saint Petersburg, before despatch.[19] Because of the time it had taken for the instructions to reach him it was too late for Brunnow to take effective action. The British government, although initially perturbed by the circular of 27 February issued by Lamartine, the new French Foreign Minister, about future French foreign policy and his meeting with a delegation from Ireland, had received a private assurance from him at the beginning of March, sent to the Duke of Wellington, that France only wished to defend the freedom of the peoples of Europe and would respect existing treaties. Even although the King of Holland might be fearful that France would invade Belgium, whose independence was of especial interest to Great Britain, the British government decided to take Lamartine's profession of good faith at its face value. On 28 March Palmerston wrote to the British ambassador in Saint Petersburg that Great Britain had decided to recognise the new régime in France in accordance with its usual practice.[20] Brunnow was doubtless disappointed that he had failed to achieve Nicholas' aim of non-recognition, but he could hardly have been surprised by the British decision. Even his great friend Sir Robert Peel, the former Tory Prime Minister, had warned him of the dangers of a war of principle over France and the necessity of recognising the new French government.[21]

Meanwhile the news of the events in Paris had spread throughout Europe, with devastating consequences for Nicholas' plans to rally his allies. In the Lower House of the Hungarian Diet, which had been meeting in Bratislava since November 1847, deadlock had been reached on the acceptance of a programme for reform. On 3 March Kossuth made a speech which called for the introduction of representative government in Hungary. When an account of this speech reached Vienna, the smouldering discontent of the population burst into flames and there were clashes between troops and demonstrators, many of whom were students. On 13 March Metternich resigned and fled the country. An imperial manifesto announced the abolition of censorship and promised the summoning of a National Assembly. The news of the disturbances in Vienna encouraged the Hungarian Diet to press their demands with the Emperor, and on 15 March a delegation from Bratislava arrived by steamer in Vienna where it was given a triumphant reception. On the same day there were demonstrations in Pest organised by the Hungarian radicals led by the poet Sándor Petőfi. He had already written of the Sicilian orange trees, about which Nicholas' wife was nostalgically dreaming in snow-bound Saint Petersburg, being covered with blood-red roses. The government in Vienna soon yielded to the Hungarian demands, and the events in Pest led to a lessening of opposition in the Upper House of the Hungarian Diet among the higher aristocracy to the reforms demanded by the lesser nobility in the Lower House. By the end of March the Emperor Ferdinand had accepted the 'Twelve Points' reform programme which later became known as the 'April Laws'. For practical purposes, Hungary had set off on the road which was to lead to the establishment of a virtually independent state, controlling its own defence, financial and foreign affairs.

Elsewhere in the Habsburg Empire there were disturbances and demands for reform, especially in Lombardy and Venetia. After five days' fighting Marshal Radetzky was forced to evacuate Milan on 23 March and withdraw his troops to the fortresses of the Quadrilateral (Mantua, Peschiera, Legnano and Verona). On 22 March a republic was proclaimed in Venice under the presidency of Daniele Manin who had been released from prison. On 23 March, in response to an appeal from the people of Milan, the King of Piedmont, after some hesitation about a possible French attempt to gain possession of Nice and Savoy, declared war on Austria and embarked on a campaign to unify Italy with the aid of troops from the Kingdom of the Two Sicilies and the Papal States. The upheaval in Italy was completed by the flight of the rulers of the states of Parma and Modena which were under Austrian domination.

The overthrow of Louis Philippe had given encouragement to the liberals throughout Germany, and by mid-March most German states, including Hanover, Saxony and Württemberg, had yielded to popular demands and introduced responsible government and granted civil liberties. In Bavaria King Ludwig abdicated on 20 March in favour of his son Maximilian after granting concessions earlier in the month.

Nor did Prussia escape the wave of disturbances spreading through Europe. The frail union of Rhineland liberals and Prussian landowners was broken when Frederick William IV yielded to liberal demands after disturbances in Berlin which had begun on 15 March. Three days later the King proclaimed the abolition of censorship, the summoning of a United Diet and the granting of a constitution. While Nicholas' wife wept in Saint Petersburg about her brother's behaviour, the King appeared in public wearing a sash in the newly-adopted German national colours of black, red and gold which the German radical poet Freiligrath believed to represent gunpowder, blood and flame. On 21 March the King made an historic statement that Prussia would merge into Germany, an announcement the significance of which was not to be lost on the German *Vorparlament* (preliminary parliament) when it met in Frankfurt at the end of the month. Finally, on 24 March the King promised a deputation from Russian Poland that he would reorganise the Grand Duchy of Posen.

Only in Sweden was there any news which pleased Nicholas. King Oskar had suppressed a minor disturbance in Stockholm and upheld the monarchical principle, an event on which Nicholas hastened to congratulate his fellow-monarch.[22]

The fall of Metternich was particularly disturbing for Nesselrode, who had fought hard for the maintenance of the Russian alliance with Austria against the sceptics in his own country. To the British ambassador he spoke of 'the failure of all his schemes and the destruction of all his political combinations'.[23] There could now be no question of granting Austria the promised loan, and on 22 March the Austrian officials who had arrived in Saint Petersburg to collect the money were officially informed of the reversal of the Tsar's decision and had to return to Vienna empty-handed.[24] In Warsaw Paskevich, who had received the news from Austria and Prussia while he was returning there from Saint Petersburg, reflected gloomily on the consequences for the defence of Russia as a result of the apparent loss of its two principal allies. But he was able to assure the Tsar that in Warsaw there were no disturbances.[25]

Despite the turmoil in western Europe, Nicholas saw no reason to change his plans for putting his forces on a full-scale state of readiness and being ready for all eventualities. But he felt that it was necessary to rally his own population to be ready to face the tide of revolution which was threatening to overwhelm Russia. On 21 March he instructed a senior official, Baron Korff, to prepare a draft manifesto. Four days later Korff was again summoned to the Tsar's presence and learnt that Nicholas had prepared his own draft which Korff was ordered to prepare for publication. The manifesto was signed the same evening, and printed and published on the following day, Sunday 26 March, when it was read out in all the churches in the Russian Empire.[26]

The language used by Nicholas in his manifesto was far from diplomatic. It began with a forthright declaration that Russia would resist any attempt at aggression by the forces of revolution which had spread through Europe up to the frontiers of Russia. It then called on the population of Russia to rally to the cause of Holy Russia and concluded with one of Nicholas' favourite quotations, 'God is with us! Take heed, ye nations, and submit, for God is with us!' As Nicholas explained to Paskevich, all he was trying to do was to make it clear that he would attack no-one, but would not allow anyone to attack Russia.[27]

Nesselrode and some of Nicholas' other advisers would almost certainly have preferred the manifesto not to have been published, but were sufficiently experienced to know that Nicholas could not be persuaded to change his mind at this time. Nevertheless, a few days later Nesselrode was able to arrange for the publication in the semi-official *Journal de Saint Pétersbourg* of an explanatory commentary on the manifesto which expressed Nicholas' sentiments in more diplomatic language.[28]

In deciding on further action, Nicholas' first thought was for the threat to Russian Poland. He was afraid that any disturbances in the Duchy of Posen and Galicia would spread from there to Russian Poland and Russia's Baltic and western provinces. Possibly under the influence of Count Benckendorff, the Russian military representative in Berlin, Nicholas was especially critical of the King of Prussia for agreeing to the release from prison of Mierostawski, one of the leaders of the Polish revolt of 1846.[29] Nicholas was also perturbed by the proposal of the liberally-minded Minister of Foreign Affairs in the new Prussian government that Prussia and France should join forces to restore the independence of Poland, an idea which the King of Württemberg claimed met with the approval of Lamartine.[30] Thus it appeared that there was a danger of war between Prussia and Russia over Poland, although Nicholas must have found it difficult to believe that his own friends and acquaintances in the Prussian army would be unfaithful to the tradition of Prussian and Russian military friendship which he had so carefully fostered throughout his reign. Nicholas' concern over the prospect of trouble in Galicia was equally great, and a warning was issued to Lebzeltern in Saint Petersburg that if Galicia tried to secede from the Habsburg empire, Nicholas would not hesitate to occupy it in the name of the Emperor Ferdinand.[31]

Paskevich shared Nicholas' concern about the threat to Russian Poland from the west and the south, and he began to make preparations for a possible invasion. Nicholas was happy to agree that the Russian troops already stationed in Poland should be reinforced, especially as the King of Prussia had requested this, but was adamant that no troops should cross the frontier without his permission.[32] When the Russian reserves who had been called up had joined their units, he intended that the Third Infantry Corps in Poland should be reinforced by the Second Infantry Corps from Lithuania which would be replaced, in its turn, by the First Infantry Corps. The Fourth Infantry Corps would be deployed in the western provinces of Volhynia and Podolia, from where it could move into Galicia if necessary. There was ample evidence of propaganda in these provinces fostered by the Polish emigration which was directed at the mixed civilian population of Poles and Ukrainians, and also at the army, which was enjoined to refuse to obey orders to put down any disturbances which might arise.³³ There were also reports of unrest in the Baltic provinces in the aftermath of the campaign to convert the non-Russian population to the Orthodox faith. In April Paskevich was to deal with a minor conspiracy in Warsaw which was, however, soon suppressed. Mindful of the fighting between peasants and landowners which had taken place in 1846, he forbade the further manufacture of scythes, large numbers of which were impounded and stored in the Russian fortresses in Poland.³⁴ Although Nicholas and Paskevich were taking all these precautions, neither of them seem to have believed that they would be faced with anything more serious than incursions by armed bands,³⁵ but it was obviously prudent to ensure that any attempt at revolt should be crushed and that every effort should be made to counter the effects of hostile propaganda among the civilian population and in the ranks of the army, where there were still members of the independent Polish army which had been disbanded after the suppression of the revolt of 1830.³⁶

At the end of March Prince Czartoryski, the leader of the aristocratic faction of the Polish emigration in Paris, and a group of his supporters, as well as members of the democratic faction of the Polish emigration from Brussels, arrived in Berlin. Baron Meyendorff, the Russian ambassador, persuaded the King not to see Czartoryski, and was assured that Prussia would not go to war with Russia over Poland. The same assurance was repeated to the visiting British diplomat Stratford Canning, who found the King complaining about his difficulties and the impossibility of removing his Minister of Foreign Affairs who was urging him to defend Polish interests.³⁷ The older officers in the Prussian army were bewildered by the situation, and General Dohna, who had served with the Russian army during the Napoleonic Wars, wrote from Kaliningrad to the Prussian ambassador in Saint Petersburg for advice. After consulting Nicholas, Rochow, the ambassador, assured Dohna and another senior officer, General Colomb, who was also highly regarded by Nicholas, that Russia did not intend to attack Prussia and that Prussian troops would always receive a warm welcome in Russia.³⁸ The Prussian military representative in Saint Petersburg also conveyed a message from Nicholas to General Prittwitz, the commander of the Prussian Guards in Berlin, who was congratulated on the efforts he had made to defend the cause of law and order during the recent disturbances in that city.³⁹

At the beginning of April both Meyendorff and Benckendorff were able to report that trouble had broken out in the Duchy of Posen between the Germans and the Poles, and on 3 April Frederick William IV ordered General Colomb to restore order. Meyendorff was confident that the problems of the Duchy were no longer a threat to Russia, but only an inconvenience.[40] At the same time Kiselev, the Russian chargé d'affaires in Paris, received an assurance from Lamartine that he had no intention of allowing France to become involved in war with Russia over the restoration of Polish independence, a war which, as he was to write later, would have been a crusade to conquer a sepulchre. Kiselev, who had decided not to obey Nicholas' order to leave France, was even able to report Lamartine's wish to improve relations with Russia, and a proposal that a senior French military officer should be sent to Saint Petersburg.[41] In mid-May Lamartine ceased to be Minister of Foreign Affairs, and although there was an outcry in the French Parliament about the fate of Poland, the new French Minister of Foreign Affairs, Bastide, continued his efforts to achieve a reconciliation with Russia by sending a new French diplomatic representative to Berlin with instructions to drop the Polish question.

The Polish question was also discussed with Great Britain. Palmerston had no hesitation in assuring the Russian ambassador in London that he did not wish to have a European war over Poland. In fact, Palmerston would have liked Poland to have had a constitution, a free press and an independent judiciary, but he appreciated the importance of Russia's neutrality and did not press the point in his conversations with Brunnow. In a private letter to Bloomfield he wrote that Britain would never do anything underhand in Polish affairs.[42] Nor could Nicholas resist the opportunity to make his point about the preservation of peace in Europe depending on Britain and Russia in additional letters addressed personally to Queen Victoria and Prince Albert.[43] It is ironic that there were those in Russia who shared Palmerston's views about giving Poland constitutional government, but their proposals were indignantly rejected by the Tsar's advisers.[44]

Baron Meyendorff's forecast about the unlikelihood of a war with Prussia over Poland proved to be correct. The efforts of General Colomb to restore order were successful and on 9 May Mierostawski was defeated. In subsequent negotiations, a new demarcation line for the Duchy of Posen was drawn up, and two-thirds of the province was admitted to the German Confederation with the right to send twelve deputies to the Frankfurt Parliament. However, there was one problem arising out of the troubles in Posen which was to occupy the Russian ambassador in Berlin for some weeks to come. This concerned the activities of the Russian emigré Mikhail Bakunin, who had been expelled from France at the end of 1847. In 1848 he appeared in Wróctaw and was accused by the Russians of having recruited two Poles for a mission to assassinate Nicholas. The matter was to drag on until September, requiring the vigorous intervention of the Prussian ambassador in Saint Petersburg with his own government before Bakunin was finally expelled from Prussia on 6 October.[45] He was to continue to play an active part in revolutionary activities for the rest of the year and in 1849.

The future organisation of the Duchy of Posen was not the only problem affecting the relationship between Prussia and Russia. More serious was the war which broke out between Prussia and Denmark over the future of the duchies of Schleswig and Holstein, which were linked to Denmark by dynastic ties and formed about two-fifths of the total population of Denmark. This problem was further complicated by the fact that Holstein, unlike Schleswig, formed part of the German Confederation and thus there was a clash between Danish and German national interests. In addition, there was the prospect of a succession problem when the childless King Frederick VII died, as the duchies followed the Salic law while Denmark accepted a female succession. The news of the revolution in France brought a demand from the Danish nationalists for the incorporation of Schleswig into Denmark, while the diets of Schleswig and Holstein demanded a new constitution and incorporation of Schleswig into the German Confederation. The rejection by the King of Denmark of these demands led to the setting-up of a provisional government at Kiel on 24 March, to which the Danes responded by sending troops into Schleswig. There followed an appeal by the provisional government for support from the Diet of the German Confederation. Besides recognising the new government and voting to admit Schleswig to membership of the Confederation, the Diet also called upon German governments to provide forces to support the Schleswig-Holsteiners in their struggle against Denmark. The King of Prussia had no choice but to agree to the Confederation's request and provided the bulk of the German force which, under the leadership of the Prussian General Wrangel, crossed the river Eider, the boundary between the two duchies on 23 April. By 2 May the German forces had advanced into Jutland, the mainland of Denmark.

Nicholas' immediate reaction to the Prussian action was one of further anger with Frederick William IV for supporting those who were rebelling against the authority of their lawful ruler. As a direct descendant of a member of the house of Holstein-Gottorp (his grandfather Peter III) Nicholas had a claim to the Danish throne, which Russia recognised by a treaty signed in 1773 as the link between Denmark and the duchies. Besides his wish to see Denmark remain in control of the entrance to the Baltic, Nicholas also viewed with misgiving the wider implications of Prussia possibly assuming the leadership of a unified Germany under a ruler who was proving unable to withstand the liberal pressures to which he was being subjected. Although Nicholas was to draw up contingency plans for a possible war with Prussia in the middle of May,[46] he was as anxious to avoid a war with Prussia on this issue, as he had been over the Duchy of Posen. The matter was of less importance to Russia than its preoccupations with Russian Poland and the Ottoman Empire, and it was desirable that the Russian army should not be diverted to other tasks. Nor did Nicholas wish to attempt to mediate on the problem, as public opinion in Germany was already hostile to Russia because of its refusal to allow the re-establishment of an independent Poland.[47] Fortunately for Nicholas, Great Britain was concerned about the danger of the port of Kiel being used as a naval base by a hostile power and Palmerston was willing to mediate, an offer which was perfectly acceptable to Nicholas. Besides this, the King of Sweden felt he had to support his fellow Scandinavian monarch and wrote to Nicholas about his disapproval of the Prussian and German action in occupying the duchies.[48]

Nicholas informed Frederick William IV that Russia could not tolerate the collapse of Denmark and its absorption into Germany. He hoped that the Prussians would withdraw their forces from Jutland.[49] Successive Danish envoys to Saint Petersburg seeking armed intervention and financial aid returned to Copenhagen empty-handed, since Nicholas did not wish to become involved in a dispute which could turn into a full-scale European war. As he put it in a brusque military fashion to the Ambassador of Württemberg at a troop review: 'All I want is the rear-guard not to become the advance guard'.[50] The Danes were advised to be conciliatory and make any concessions compatible with their own interests. Nevertheless, Nicholas agreed to allow part of the Baltic fleet to be used to assist Sweden to transport troops to Denmark should this be necessary. On 25 May the Third Division of the Baltic Fleet commanded by Rear-Admiral Epanchin set sail for Danish waters to await further orders.[51] Four days earlier the Grand Duke Constantine and Menshikov, the Minister for the Navy, had left Saint Petersburg to discuss any possible Russian naval involvement with the Swedish and Danish governments.[52] While the Prussians were more successful than the Danes on land, neither Prussia nor the German Confederation were able to prevent the Danes mounting a naval blockade. Eventually an armistice of seven months' duration was negotiated with the aid of the Swedes and was signed at Malmö on 26 August, without any reference to the Frankfurt Parliament which since mid-July had replaced the Diet of the German Confederation. Nicholas was exasperated by Danish and Prussian intransigence throughout the dispute and by the end of August his patience was becoming exhausted.[53] After the conclusion of the armistice Russia rejected a Danish proposal that the Russian ships should spend the winter months in a Danish harbour. The Third Division had been reinforced by the First Division on 4 August under Admiral A. P. Lazarev[54] and on receipt of the news of the armistice the Russians were ordered to return to port. In fact, serious outbreaks of cholera and scurvy had occurred among the crews of the ships, and Nicholas had no wish to advertise these shortcomings to the Danes during the winter months of enforced idleness.[55]

At first the Frankfurt Parliament voted to reject the armistice, but in the face of an increasing realisation of its powerlessness to influence the decisions of Austria and Prussia in military matters, it was persuaded largely owing to the influence of the Regent of Germany, Archduke John of Austria, to reverse its decision on 17 September.[56] This action led to an outbreak of violence in Frankfurt which had to be suppressed by the Austrian and Prussian forces stationed in the Confederation's garrison at Mainz. The violence was soon brought under control, but two members of the parliament were killed in the fighting.

Nicholas was not sorry about what had happened in Frankfurt. He was sceptical about the possibility of Germany becoming unified, and refused to receive a representative of the new central German authority created by the parliament. Convinced that Prussia no longer represented a serious military threat to Russia, his main concern as the autumn approached had become the achievement of a reduction in military expenditure, in order to ease his budget problems which were becoming increasingly serious.[57] He proposed to Paskevich that part of the First and Fourth Infantry Corps and most of the Sixth Infantry Corps, together with many of the cavalry and artillery reserves, should be sent on indefinite leave during the winter months.

However, a discussion with Benckendorff from Berlin at the end of August and reports of the activities of the Prussian Parliament convinced him that neither the King nor Prince William would be able to reassert their authority, despite the high morale of the Prussian army and the adherence to traditional Prussian values by the landowners in East Prussia.[58.]

In September Frederick William IV made use of Count Brassier, his ambassador in Sweden, to send an official request to Nicholas for aid in restoring order, especially if Prussia were to be attacked by France or the other German states while its army was engaged in Berlin. In fact, the Tsar did not believe that Prussia faced attack from abroad, but he was so convinced of Frederick William's inability to deal with the worsening internal situation that he decided to scrap his plans to reduce the size of the Russian forces during the winter months. In his reply to the King, he emphasised the necessity for the restoration of the 'old Prussia' which had existed in the reign of Frederick William III, while assuring his brother-in-law that Russian troops would come to his aid if a republic were to be proclaimed in Berlin.[59]

The internal situation in Prussia was to be restored later in the year, but meanwhile Nicholas' attention was being increasingly directed towards events in the Habsburg Empire, the fortunes of which he had been following with as much attention as those of his other ally. After the fall of Metternich and the resignation of the Archduke Ludwig from the Council of State, its other leading member, Count Kolowrat, headed the government for a short time until 4 April. He was then replaced by Count Ficquelmont, the new Minister of Foreign Affairs, who had originally been summoned from Milan to become the new Head of the Military Council. An experienced soldier and diplomat who had served as Austrian ambassador in Russia and had a Russian wife, Ficquelmont was well regarded by the Tsar. He was aware that Nicholas would be concerned about Austria's future and one of his first acts was to send a special envoy to Saint Petersburg to reassure both Nicholas and Nesselrode about the intentions of the new Austrian government. For this purpose he chose Count Thun-Hohenstein, the Austrian ambassador in Sweden, who had been on leave.

Metternich had already warned Ficquelmont that his new task would be far from easy and drew his attention to the part played by events in Hungary in causing the disturbances in Vienna. The same point was emphasised not only in Ficquelmont's instructions to Thun, but also in a letter to Nesselrode.⁶⁰ Thun reached Saint Petersburg at the end of March and was received by Nicholas without delay. The threat to the stability of the Habsburg Empire posed by Hungary had been mentioned by Fonton, the Russian chargé d'affaires in Vienna in his reports, and also figured prominently in a memorandum sent to the Tsar by the Russian poet and diplomat F. I. Tyutchev on 12 April.⁶¹ Thus Thun's remarks came as no surprise to Nicholas, who wished to know what the Austrian government intended to do about the demands of the various provinces for a more democratic form of government. With Russian Poland in mind, it was natural that Nicholas' first question to Thun should be about the future of Galicia and the possible revival of the free state of Cracow which had been annexed by Austria in 1846. His words on the subject were as unequivocal as they had been to the Austrian chargé d'affaires the previous month. If Galicia were allowed to become a centre of revolution, he would have no choice but to occupy it.⁶² Ficquelmont had assured Fonton some days earlier that the Austrian army would act in Galicia as it had done in Lombardy⁶³ and this assurance, together with a similar one given by Thun, seems to have convinced Nicholas that there was unlikely to be more than incursions by armed bands from that quarter.⁶⁴

Both Nicholas and Nesselrode dwelt on their anxieties about Prussia and events in the Duchy of Posen. Because of this possible source of disturbance on Russia's right flank, it was all the more important that Austria should protect Russia's left flank when, as seemed probable, a revolt began in Galicia.⁶⁵ The Austrians were only too conscious of the possibility of a recurrence of trouble in Galicia, and had made a point of abolishing forced labour in the province in March. The Hungarians, too, had proposed on 12 April that the Emperor Ferdinand should grant Galicia a constitution. For Nicholas, on the other hand, the events of March had meant the abandonment of the cautious attempts made by the Russian government to ease the lot of the peasants by the compilation of inventories of the holdings of the landowners in the western provinces. This retrograde step could only provide further fuel for the Polish emigrés in their efforts to incite the peasants to revolt and as a result, Nicholas instructed Paskevich to ensure that any attempts at revolt in Volhynia, Podolia and Kiev would be immediately crushed, using force if necessary. The Tsar's instructions were repeated in identical words to the Governor General of these provinces, D. G. Bibikov.⁶⁶ The Russian fears that there would be a revolt in Cracow proved to be correct, but on 26 April the Austrian forces were able to suppress it within a short space of time.

Although Nicholas did not change his mind about the despatch of Russian troops to Italy, he reacted swiftly to the King of Piedmont's declaration of war on Austria by breaking off diplomatic relations. In addition, the King's name was struck from the roll of the Russian army, and the name of a Russian light cavalry regiment which bore the King's name was changed.[67]

But the Russophile Ficquelmont was not destined to remain in charge of Austrian foreign affairs for long. On 25 April the Austrian cabinet, largely under the influence of Baron Pillersdorf, the Minister of the Interior, proclaimed a constitution with a limited franchise which was to apply to the German provinces, Bohemia, Moravia and Galicia. Its provisions satisfied the moderates, but not the students and radicals who demonstrated outside Ficquelmont's house. In the early hours of 4 May he resigned and was replaced by the liberal-minded Pillersdorf, whom Nesselrode was later to call a traitor. For Nicholas the departure of Ficquelmont was a further indication that the government was unable to control the radicals and their allies, the Polish emigrés. The Fourth Infantry Corps stationed in the western provinces was to be made ready to move into Galicia, if there was further trouble.[68] In due course Ficquelmont was to write to Nesselrode about the influence of the Poles in persuading the radicals that he was little better than a Russian agent, and predicted that only Russia would be able to save Europe from 'its furies and mistakes', as it had done after the failure of Napoleon's invasion of Russia in 1812.[69]

On 15 May there were more student demonstrations in Vienna, which led the government to agree to the establishment of a Constituent Assembly, elected by universal suffrage. Since Vienna now appeared to be in the hands of the radicals, the Emperor Ferdinand and his brother the Archduke Francis Charles, accompanied by their wives and various court officials, fled the capital for Innsbruck in the Tyrol on 17 May. In an attempt to curb the power of the radicals, the government decreed on 25 May that the Academic Legion, a student body, should be merged with the National Guard. The workers in Vienna decided to support the students rather than the government, and it seemed as if there would be further violence. The following day Pillersdorf yielded to popular demands and agreed to the establishment of a Committee of Public Safety, presided over by the radical Dr Fischhof. For the next three months the Austrian government was divided between Innsbruck and Vienna. The practical problems of continuing to run the administration were solved by appointing the Emperor's uncle, the Archduke John, as his representative in the capital, while Doblhoff, the Minister of Trade, acted as a liaison officer between ministers and the Emperor in Innsbruck. By the beginning of July the elections for the Constituent Assembly had taken place and Pillersdorf was in his turn replaced by Baron Wessenberg, who had replaced Ficquelmont as Minister of Foreign Affairs in May. A well-known liberal who had fallen foul of Metternich earlier in his career, he was disliked by the Tsar, but respected by Palmerston who congratulated him on his appointment, urging him to put an end to the war in Italy.[70] Palmerston's views were shared by Stratford Canning who, on his arrival in Vienna, had witnessed the demonstration against Ficquelmont, and was also in no doubt that constitutional government was the only solution to Austria's problems in keeping the Habsburg Empire in being.[71]

Nicholas considered that Ferdinand's decision to leave Vienna for the safety of Innsbruck where he was surrounded by loyal subjects was the correct one in the circumstances. His ambassador Medem, who had finally returned to Vienna after the fall of Metternich, had on his own initiative accepted the Emperor's invitation that members of the diplomatic corps should accompany him to Innsbruck. This decision met with the Tsar's approval, since the confused political situation in Austria had prevented the new Austrian ambassador, appointed before the fall of Metternich, from taking up his post, and the Russians were continuing to have to deal with the unimportant Lebzeltern. In any case, Nicholas believed that it was the duty of his ambassador to protect the interests of a fellow sovereign whenever possible.

Medem's closest diplomatic colleague throughout the Emperor's enforced stay in Innsbruck was the British ambassador, Lord Ponsonby, who had no love for the Hungarians or the French and was already apprehensive about the consequences for Anglo–Austrian relations of Palmerston's wish that Austria should abandon its possessions in northern Italy, a view in which he was fully supported by Queen Victoria and Prince Albert, who was beginning to play an increasingly important part in influencing the Queen on foreign affairs. On 19 June Medem handed the Emperor a personal letter from the Tsar, and informed him that he and Ponsonby had decided to ignore the request made by the Austrian Ministry of Foreign Affairs that members of the diplomatic corps should return to

Vienna.[72] As a result, both diplomats were to gain the confidence of the Empress and the Archduchess Sophie, who were the leading members of the court group which historians have christened the *camarilla*. They were to become privy to the plans being made to restore the authority of the Emperor throughout the Habsburg Empire, where much had been happening outside the capital.

In Hungary, the new government constituted on the basis of the April Laws, headed by Count Lajos Batthyańy, began to carry out its task. The Prime Minister had been forced to include the radically-minded Lajos Kossuth, who was far from popular with his colleagues, especially the liberal aristocrat Count Széchenyi. Appointed Minister of Finance, Kossuth used the post to embarrass the central administration in Vienna in its efforts to deal with the Empire's financial problems by arguments about the share of the national debt which should be borne by Hungary. The shrewd unofficial British observer of the Hungarian scene, Blackwell, was convinced that Kossuth would not hesitate to play the part of a Hungarian Cromwell by making himself the President of a Federal Republic.[73] Other observers and members of Batthyány's cabinet also feared that, if Hungary pushed Austria too far, an appeal would be made to Russia for military aid to reconquer Hungary.[74]

Besides finance, the new Hungarian government also sought to gain control of the Hungarian regiments in the Habsburg army, of which only four were serving in Hungary, while six were in Italy and five in Austria and Bohemia. Foreign affairs were dealt with by the elderly Pál Esterházy, a former ambassador to Great Britain, but his position *vis-à-vis* the Ministry of Foreign Affairs in Vienna was never clearly defined.

But the problem which was to prove to be the undoing of the new Hungarian government was the status of the other provinces which, although part of Hungary, were not inhabited by Hungarians (Croatia and its eastern part, the Military Frontier, Slavonia and Transylvania). The Hungarian government had hoped that the new liberal institutions granted to the country by a reluctant Emperor would be as welcome to the other nationalities as they were to the Hungarians themselves, and would compensate for the Hungarians' wish that the other provinces should be incorporated into Hungary and ruled from Budapest. The other nationalities, of which the Croats were the most prominent, soon began to put their own demands to Vienna for independence, just as the Hungarians had done.

The conservative members of the government in Vienna were well aware of the dangers posed to the unity of the Empire by the granting of independence to Hungary, and soon came to realise that the Croatian problem in particular offered a good opportunity to turn the tables on the Hungarians. Under the April Laws Croatia was to be incorporated into Hungary. On 23 March the government in Vienna appointed the fiercely anti-Hungarian Baron Jelačić, a colonel in one of the military frontier regiments, as the Ban (governor) of Croatia. Jelačić was also a friend of Ljudevit Gaj, the leader of the Illyrian movement for the unity of all the Southern Slavs.[75] The following month Jelačić, who had been promoted to the rank of general, was given command of all troops in Croatia and on the Military Frontier. Shortly afterwards he instructed all Croatian officials to break off communication with the Hungarian government in Budapest. A Hungarian refusal to send more Hungarian troops to Italy[76] was followed by an Austrian decision on 7 May to replace Jelačić as commander of all troops in Croatia and on the Military Frontier. The Hungarians appeared to have gained a further victory when it was agreed by the Emperor in Innsbruck on 10 June that Jelačić should be deprived of all his offices in return for a Hungarian promise to send more troops to Italy.

The Croats were not the only nationality which was growing restive. On 10 May the Slovaks staged a rally at Liptovský Mikuláš which demanded national rights and the use of the Slovak language, a demand which was to be rejected by the government in Budapest. On 15 May a mass meeting of Rumanians at Blaj protested against the intention of the Diet of Transylvania to approve the union of the province with Hungary without adequate safeguards for the rights of its Rumanian inhabitants. On 13 May, at a congress held at Karlovac, the Serbs of Hungary, many of whom had settled in the south at the end of the eighteenth century when they fled from the Turks, proclaimed the establishment of an autonomous Serbian province, the *vojvodina*, under the leadership of a Colonel Šupljikać, an officer in the frontier force serving in Italy. In his absence, authority was vested in the newly-elected Orthodox Serbian Patriarch Rajačić and an executive committee headed by Djordje Stratimirović, a young cavalry officer. The Austrians refused to support Rajačić, who now began to look to the Croats and the Principality of Serbia in the Ottoman Empire for support. On 24 May a curious war began in which units of the Habsburg army fought each other, while maintaining their loyalty to the same ruler, the Emperor of Austria and King of Hungary. In the early stages of this war the government in Vienna took the side of the Hungarian government, but this attitude was to change later in the year as a result of events in Hungary.

As if these problems were not enough, the government in Vienna had also been faced in early March with demands from a National Committee in Prague for the usual civil rights, including the equality of the Czech and German languages. On 22 March a petition was presented to the Emperor appealing for the union of Bohemia, Moravia and Austrian Silesia, a request which the hard-pressed government conceded, subject to ratification by the Austrian parliament. However, shortly afterwards a rift was to occur between the Germans and the Czechs in Bohemia when František Palacký, the Czech historian, rejected an invitation from the *Vorparlament* in Frankfurt to represent the three provinces in their deliberations on the future of Germany. In his famous reply of 11 April Palacký justified his rejection on the grounds that he was a Czech and not a German and that it was essential for the Danubian states to unite in order to protect themselves from German and Russian domination. In words which have often been misquoted, he wrote that if the Austrian state had not already existed, it would have been a behest in the interests of Europe and humanity to create it.[77] As a result, the Germans in Bohemia seceded from the National Committee and elected their own delegates to the Frankfurt Parliament, in which the Habsburg Empire was to be under-represented because of the absence of Czech delegates (120 members out of a possible total of 190, compared with a Prussian representation of 198). At the end of May the Governor of Bohemia attempted to establish a provisional government as a rival to the Committee of Public Safety which had been established in Vienna, but this attempt did not meet with the approval of the Emperor in Innsbruck.

Meanwhile Palacký had convened a Slavonic Congress in Prague to act as a counterweight to the Frankfurt Parliament and the Hungarian Parliament, which had now moved from Bratislava to Budapest. Most of the Slavonic peoples were represented, with the exception of the Bulgarians, Montenegrins and Lusatian Serbs, but only a few non-Austrian Slavs attended. Because of the presence of Poles, the Russian authorities ensured that there was no official representation and as a result, the only two Russians present were the emigré Bakunin and one of the Old Believer priests from Bukovina.[78]

The Congress which began its work on 2 June was dominated by the Czechs and their new-found allies the Slovaks, who had been swift to make common cause with the Czechs after the rejection of their demands by the Hungarians in May. But the disputes between the various nationalities doomed to failure any attempt to draw up a practical programme for the future of the Austrian Slavs, and the final manifesto published on 12 June (Whit Monday) was little more than an emotional appeal to the nations of Europe not to forget the rights of the Slavs. For practical reasons, the delegates had been forced to use German as a common language, which provoked the comment from the Baltic German Baron Meyendorff in Berlin to the cosmopolitan Nesselrode that Panslavism was 'the most foolish of all the forms of revolution imagined in our time'.[79]

It was unfortunate for the Czechs that the closing of the congress was made the occasion for a popular demonstration by workers and students in Prague which was, in some respects, the counterpart of the disturbances which had taken place in Vienna the previous month. On this occasion, however, there was an Austrian general on hand, Prince Windischgraetz, who had returned to Prague on 20 May. He was delighted to be given the opportunity to deal with the disturbances and despite the death of his wife from a stray bullet and attempts by Palacký to mediate, he did not hesitate to act firmly. After withdrawing his troops to the heights outside the city, he began to bombard Prague on 16 June. The insurrection was soon suppressed, the National Committee dissolved and martial law proclaimed. The Governor of Bohemia was convinced that the Poles had been responsible for the disturbances.[80] It was a notable victory for the Austrian government, and gave fresh heart to the Emperor and his advisers in Innsbruck as they made their plans to restore order.

Nicholas was equally heartened by the news of Windischgraetz's success, and sent congratulations along with condolences about the death of his wife.[81] Contrary to the belief of many contemporary observers, including the Hungarian government, neither of the Tsar nor his advisers had any wish to support the idea of uniting the Slavs under the aegis of Russia. Nicholas was a great admirer of Peter the Great and viewed the ideas of the Slavophiles in Moscow with suspicion. Shortly after the Slavonic Congress was over, an approach by a group of Polish emigrés in Paris to the Third Department in Paris urging the creation of a Pan-slav state was rejected as a matter of course.[82]

Now that order had been restored in the Duchy of Posen, Nicholas' main concern continued to be the revival of the independent state of Cracow and the secession of Galicia. The Tsar's views about the undesirability of absorbing the Slavonic provinces of the Habsburg Empire were shared by Nesselrode, but he was less worried about Galicia and urged Nicholas not to act hastily. The Habsburg Empire like the Ottoman Empire, was remarkably resilient and could well recover from the present misfortunes. A Russian occupation of Galicia might provoke an alliance between France and the states of Germany, directed at Russia. The Russian army had been mobilised and Russian finances could bear the strain of the extra expenditure, if Nicholas was prudent. Accordingly, Russia should continue to observe the situation, while being ready for any emergency.[83]

Nesselrode's advice to the Tsar was sound, since Russia was faced by its own internal problems. For the second time in his reign, Nicholas had to contend with a serious cholera epidemic which spread into Russia from the east at the end of 1847. By May 1848, the disease had reached Moscow, and by the end of June Saint Petersburg was also affected. The Tsar was understandably worried about the effects on the army, especially when the epidemic moved west to Warsaw. In 1831 Nicholas had personally intervened in a cholera riot in the Haymarket in Saint Petersburg and had not forgotten the deaths from cholera of his elder brother, the Grand Duke Constantine, and General Diebitsch, the Commander-in-Chief of the Russian forces in Poland, in the same year. For the remainder of 1848 and throughout 1849, Nicholas' letters to Paskevich are full of references to the effects of the epidemic together with admonitions to his 'father commander' to take precautions.[84] Beside the cholera epidemic, 1848 was to turn out, like 1847, to be a year of poor harvests, especially in southern Russia, with consequent food shortages and the loss of revenue from Russia's grain exports from the port of Odessa which until then had been rapidly growing. A further cause for concern was a series of fires in provincial towns where the majority of the buildings were constructed of timber; the town of Orel was almost completely destroyed.[85]

The month of July brought no improvement in the settlement of the differences between the Hungarian government and the Croats and Serbs. In Budapest Hungarian attempts to exploit the differences between the Catholic Croats and Orthodox Serbs were a failure.[86] In Innsbruck, the court decided to reinstate Jelačić who, unlike the Hungarians, could ensure that the Croat regiments fighting in Italy remained loyal to the Emperor. On 11 July, in a speech to the newly-opened Hungarian parliament in Budapest, Kossuth declared that Hungary was in danger and appealed for the raising of an army of

200 000 men and a credit of 42 million forints.

Both the Croats and the Serbs believed that Russia would be sympathetic to their attempts to shake off Hungarian rule. A Croatian approach to Fonton, the Russian chargé d'affaires in Vienna, was rejected and the delegation was informed that Russia's only wish was to ensure the preservation of a united Habsburg Empire.[87] Disappointed by the Russian reaction, and still uncertain of the attitude of the Austrian government, the Croats entered into negotiations with Czartoryski's faction of the Polish emigration, in an effort to win the support of the French and Turkish governments for their national aspirations.[88]

The Serbs from Hungary were even more assiduous in their efforts to seek Russian support for their cause, and were well aware of the support the Russians had given to the Obrenović family in the Principality of Serbia before Mikhail Obrenović had been deposed in 1842. Their first approach was made to Fonton at the end of June[89] and throughout 1848 the Patriarch Rajačić made approaches either direct to the Russian Holy Synod in Saint Petersburg or to the Russian consul in Belgrade.[90] The Serbian requests fell on deaf ears, however. Unlike the Austrian government in the first half of 1848, Nicholas took the view that the Serbs from Hungary were right to take up arms against the Hungarian government in Budapest, provided they maintained their loyalty to the Emperor Ferdinand.[91] A special Russian envoy was also sent to Belgrade in May to dampen down the enthusiasm of Alexander Karadjordjević for a Serbian revolt, and to point out that Russia did not intend to support the return of the Obrenović family to the throne of the principality because its members viewed the revolt of the Hungarian Serbs with favour. It remained Nicholas' wish that the subjects of the Serbian principality should not revolt against their lawful ruler, the Sultan of Turkey.[92]

By the middle of July it seemed to Nicholas that the situation in the Habsburg Empire was becoming more serious in its implications for Russia than that in Germany, largely because there appeared to be no-one capable of preventing it from disintegrating into a collection of independent states.[93] His pessimism was increased by Windischgraetz's reply to the letter of condolence he had sent after the suppression of the revolt in Prague. Writing in strict confidence, the Austrian military leader made no secret of his lack of confidence in his own government's ability to master the situation and, like Ficquelmont, warned Nicholas that the day would come when Russian military aid would be needed to restore order in Austria.[94]

In Innsbruck Medem and Ponsonby continued to support the Empress and the Archduchess Sophie in their efforts to prevent the return of the Emperor to Vienna. Nor did they approve the proposal made by the Archduke John (who was finding it impossible to deal with the affairs of the government, as well as those of the Frankfurt Parliament) that he should be replaced in Vienna as the Emperor's *alter ego* by the Archduke Francis Charles.[95] Both ambassadors also became aware of the proposal which was gaining increasing favour as a solution to Austria's difficulties that Ferdinand should abdicate, that Francis Charles should renounce his rights to the throne and that his son, Francis Joseph, who would be eighteen in August, should succeed as Emperor.[96] However, Ferdinand was eventually unable to resist the pressures for him to return to Vienna, and, after rejecting a request that he should visit Budapest, the court left Innsbruck on 8 August, much to the annoyance of the Archduchess Sophie who wept bitterly. Nicholas' comment on receiving Medem's despatch about the decision to return to Vienna was suitably brief: '*C'est pitoyable*'.[97]

Another European monarch, however, had been successful in mastering the situation in his own country. This was King Ferdinand of the Two Sicilies. After Piedmont's declaration of war on Austria, Pope Pius IX had publicly rebuked the commander of the Papal troops, the Piedmontese General Durando, for implying that the Pope approved the use of force by Piedmont to drive the Austrians out of Italy. Because of the Pope's refusal to sanction the war, King Ferdinand ordered his troops to withdraw from northern Italy in order that he could reconquer Sicily, where he had been deposed on 13 April. On 15 May there was an insurrection in Naples, which was suppressed after heavy fighting. Both Nicholas and Nesselrode wished that King Ferdinand's success in dealing with revolution could be emulated by his fellow monarchs in Austria and Prussia.[98]

There was also satisfaction in Saint Petersburg over events in France in June. The French government's decision to close the national workshops which had been set up at the end of February to ease the lot of the poor and unemployed led to an outbreak of violence in Paris which began on 23 June. Within a few days, General Cavaignac, the Minister of War, an experienced soldier who had fought in Algeria for many years, had restored order after desperate fighting on both sides of the barricades which had been erected in the streets of Paris. Nicholas immediately ordered Nesselrode to send a congratulatory letter to the General as from one soldier to another. In due course, Cavaignac took charge of the government until elections could be held, and sent one of his trusted senior officers, General Le Flô, to Saint Petersburg with the aim of improving France's relations with Russia.[99]

But for Nicholas the best news of all was to come at the end of July, when he learnt of Radetzky's crushing defeat of the Italian force at Custozza, which followed several weeks of inconclusive negotiations with Great Britain and France about the future of Austria's Italian possessions. Radetzky had been angered by the policy of the government in Vienna that these should be given up and had sent Felix Schwarzenberg, the former Austrian Minister in Naples, to Innsbruck to persuade the Emperor to abandon the idea and to send reinforcements to his army in Italy. On 6 August the Austrian army entered Milan and after the signing of an armistice the remainder of the year was spent in a further series of negotiations with Great Britain and France which were to drag on until 1849. Radetzky's victory was a clear demonstration of the fact that a loyal army, even a multi-racial one, was the best means of restoring order. Nicholas responded to Radetzky's success by awarding him the rare distinction of the Order of Saint George (First Class), and wrote to Paskevich that the future salvation of the Habsburg monarchy lay in the Austrian government's proper use of men such as Radetzky, of whom he had formed a good opinion when he met him during his Italian visit of 1845.[100] While Radetzky in his reply did not go so far as Windischgraetz in suggesting that Austria's salvation lay in military assistance from Russia, he reminded the Tsar of the glorious days in the Napoleonic Wars when the Austrian and Russian armies had fought side by side to preserve the freedom of Europe.[101]

The Austrian victory in Italy encouraged the Emperor and his advisers to take decisive action on the problem of Hungary. After the Emperor's return to Vienna, there were further disorders in the capital from 21 to 23 August, which were soon suppressed, and the Committee of Public Safety was disbanded. On 26 August Jelačić was informed that he would be reinstated, a decision which he immediately made known to Rajačić.[102] At the same time the Hungarian government in Budapest, under the influence of the Minister of Justice, Ferenc Deák, who was to play such an important part in the Compromise negotiated with Austria in 1867, decided to grant a large measure of autonomy to Croatia. However, on 30 August the Emperor sent the Archduke Stephen, the Palatine of Hungary, a rescript which stated that the April Laws were incompatible with the existing legal basis for Hungary's status in the Empire, the Pragmatic Sanction of 1723. Hungary should now abandon its plans to incorporate Croatia and the Military Frontier and also relinquish control of its finances and defence. Earlier in the month the Austrians had also protested about the activities of the Hungarian delegates who had been sent in May to the Frankfurt Parliament where they had proposed the formation of a German–Hungarian alliance against the Serbs, Croats and Russia. On 4 September the Hungarian Parliament approved the despatch of a delegation to Vienna to discuss the Emperor's demands. While the delegation was *en route*, Kossuth, who had persuaded the Palatine to approve the issue in early August of Hungarian bank notes for one and two forints, to match Austrian one and two gulden notes issued in March, carried out an unconstitutional act by issuing a five forint note on the basis of a loan approved by the Hungarian Parliament, but not ratified either by the Palatine or the Emperor.

On 10 September on his return to Budapest Batthyány resigned as Prime Minister. The following day, Jelačić and a force of 50 000 men crossed the river Drava between Croatia and Hungary, intending to march on Budapest. The invasion was not successful and led to two defeats for the Croatian forces at Pákozd on 29 September and Ozora on 7 October. Meanwhile neither the attempts of the Palatine nor those of General Lamberg, the Commissioner of the Hungarian Forces appointed by the government in Vienna, to effect a reconciliation were successful. The Palatine resigned and the unfortunate Lamberg was murdered by an infuriated mob in Budapest on 28 September. The final outcome was a decree issued on 3 October by the Emperor dissolving the Hungarian Parliament which was rejected by that body. On 8 October the rule of Kossuth began when he was elected President of the Committee of National Defence.

In Saint Petersburg Nicholas could only hope that Jelačić, who at last appeared to have the full support of the Emperor and the Austrian government, would be as successful in dealing with the rebellious Hungarians, as Windischgraetz and Radetzky had been elsewhere.[103] While Paskevich agreed that it would be desirable for Jelačić to capture Budapest and then turn his attention to Vienna, he was less optimistic than Nicholas about his success on the battlefield, a view which was justified by events.[104] Meanwhile, Nicholas' chief anxiety still remained the expectation of trouble in Cracow which was a further justification, along with the possibility of a republic being declared in Prussia, for not reducing the strength of the Russian forces during the winter months.[105] On 18 September Nesselrode sent Medem a copy of an intelligence memorandum about Polish emigré activities in Cracow and Galicia, prepared by Paskevich's staff in Warsaw, which was to be passed to the Austrian government.[106] For Wessenberg the problem was only one of many with which the Austrian government was faced, and in his reply to Medem he stated that he would have to discuss the matter with the Minister of the Interior.[107] As Medem already knew, the latter was having difficulties in dealing with protests from the large Slav membership of the Austrian Parliament (some 190 out of a total of 400 members) about the handing-back to the authorities in Russian Poland of deserters from the Russian army who had sought refuge in Galicia. Nicholas' reaction to Medem's report on this subject had been a threat to withdraw the Russian Embassy from Vienna.[108]

The unsatisfactory Austrian reply to the Tsar's request for action could only increase his concern about the future outlook for his other ally. His prediction of further trouble in Galicia was to prove justified, and Austria was to face another revolt in the capital before it could turn its attention once more to the situation in Hungary. On that occasion, it would prove unable to subdue the Hungarians without the aid of Russia.

2 The Russian Intervention in the Danubian Principalities

As we have seen in the previous chapter, Nicholas' main preoccupation during the first months of 1848 was with the effects of the February revolution in Paris in Russia and Poland, as well as the Habsburg Empire, Prussia and Germany. However, Nicholas could not ignore the possible repercussions of the disturbances in western Europe on the Christian provinces of the Ottoman Empire, especially the Danubian principalities and Serbia. The growth of national feeling, the discontent of the peasantry with labour conditions, the desire of the intellectuals for constitutional government, the influence of Great Britain and France and, above all, the activities of the Polish emigration in these areas filled him with the same misgivings as they did in western Europe.[1]

After the Galician revolt of 1846 many Poles sought refuge in Moldavia and some were able to find posts in the local administration.[2] Both factions of the Polish emigration had sent agents to the Danubian principalities, but as usual there had been no co-operation between these agents.[3] In Moldavia Faustyn Filanowicz, the representative of the Polish democrats, achieved more than the representative of Prince Czartoryski, since he was successful in recruiting a Polish legion from Poles resident in the principality. Both the Austrian and Russian consuls in Jassy watched these activities with growing concern and protested to Michael Sturdza, the *hospodar* (local ruler), about them, demanding the expulsion of those Poles who were residing illegally in Moldavia. As a result of the reports received in Saint Petersburg from K. E. Kotzebue, the Russian consul in Jassy, the Russian government decided to send a special agent from the Third Department to the principalities to carry out a detailed investigation of Polish émigré activities. In the report which this agent submitted in early 1848, reference was made to the support given to some of the Poles by disaffected Moldavian boyars, and the unofficial links which the Polish emigration maintained with the French and Turkish governments as well as the Serbian authorities in Belgrade.[4] By the time that the disturbances in western Europe occurred in early 1848, the Russian government was in little doubt that there would be similar disturbances in the Danubian principalities and other parts of the Ottoman Empire, and that Polish emigrés would be involved in fostering them. Shortly after he had published his manifesto of 26 March 1848 about Russia's policy of non-intervention, Nicholas gave orders for appropriate action to be taken on diplomatic channels. On 28 March Nesselrode sent V. P. Titov, the Russian ambassador in Constantinople, a strongly-worded despatch which made it clear that Russia would not tolerate the spread of anarchy fostered by France and the Polish emigration to the Ottoman Empire. The Turkish government was warned to be on the alert for possible disturbances.[5] An equally strongly-worded despatch was sent to Kotzebue, who had been transferred to Bucharest from Jassy the previous year. Kotzebue was instructed to remind the *hospodars* in both Moldavia and Wallachia of Russia's special interest in the two principalities, and as much publicity as possible was to be given to the expressed wish of Nicholas not to allow revolution to spread to those parts of the Ottoman Empire which he considered to be under his protection.[6]

In view of the rivalry between Great Britain and Russia in the Near East, it was important for Russia to try to win British support for this policy. A copy of Nesselrode's despatch to Titov was therefore sent to the Russian ambassador in London for onward transmission to Palmerston. In fact, Brunnow, the ambassador, had anticipated his government's action, and had already discussed the possible effect of events in France in the Christian provinces of the Ottoman Empire with Palmerston, and with Stratford Canning, who was about to leave London on his special mission to several European capitals before finally arriving at Constantinople to resume his duties as ambassador. Both agreed with Brunnow that every effort should be made to preserve peace in the Ottoman Empire and try to isolate it from what was happening elsewhere in Europe.[7] At this stage Palmerston did no more than take note of the Russian despatch, but it is noteworthy that about this time he was to receive despatches from two British representatives abroad, warning him that Russia might decide to occupy the Danubian principalities as a precautionary measure because of the disturbances which had already taken place in the Habsburg Empire.[8]

Russian fears of disturbances in the Danubian principalities as a result of what had happened in France were to prove justified. On 20 March, a few days before Nesselrode had sent his despatches to

Bucharest and Constantinople, Nicolae Bălcescu, the leader of the radical group of Wallachian revolutionaries, who had been living in France since 1846, called a meeting of Rumanian exiles in Paris to discuss the action to be taken if a revolt were to break out in the principalities. After much debate, it was agreed that the Moldavian and Wallachian exiles should each return to their own capitals rather than travel together to Bucharest.[9]

The first disturbances occurred in Moldavia where there was already widespread discontent with the rule of Sturdza.[10] On 8 April Sturdza agreed to the holding of a meeting in the Petersburg Hotel in Jassy, which was attended by about a thousand persons, including many disaffected boyars, the Moldavian Minister of the Interior, and the Chief of Police. A committeee was elected to draw up a petition to be presented to Sturdza. The following day the committee met in the house of one of the liberal boyars and drew up the petition, which consisted of thirty-five articles. Most of its contents was drafted in moderate terms, but it included proposals for the election of a new and more representative assembly, as well as the establishment of a national guard. Sturdza refused to accept its more radical proposals and took immediate action to prevent any further disorder. He left his palace for the barracks of his militia and ordered them into action. Over 300 persons were arrested and thirteen leaders of the revolt were sent to the port of Galaţi to be exiled in other parts of the Ottoman Empire. With the aid of the British vice-consuls in Galaţi and Brăila, six of the prisoners were able to escape and make their way to Transylvania.[11]

The Russian consul in Jassy, F. A. Tumansky, had summoned Kotzebue from Bucharest, and after his visit Sturdza issued a proclamation which faithfully reflected the contents of Nesselrode's despatch, leaving the Moldavian population in no doubt of the determination of the Russian government to maintain order in the principality.[12] For the moment, Sturdza appeared to have the situation under control.

Having given warning of his intentions, Nicholas now followed his usual practice of sending a special diplomatic envoy to the principalities to ensure that his will would be carried out. For this purpose he selected General A. O. Duhamel, who had carried out a similar mission in Wallachia in 1842.[13] In the instructions he received from the Russian Ministry of Foreign Affairs before his departure, Duhamel was informed that the activities of the Polish emigration and the effects of French liberal ideas in the principalities had not diminished since he had last been there.[14] Although the main purpose of his present mission was to lend moral support to both the *hospodars*, Duhamel was authorised to make a secret offer of 'material aid', in other words, military intervention, if 'alarming complications' were to develop. However, Russia did not wish to act unilaterally, and it was hoped that any possible military intervention which might be necessary would be carried out jointly with Turkey. Duhamel was also authorised to persuade the *hospodars* to expel any foreign trouble-makers, even at the risk of causing trouble with the British and French consular representatives in Bucharest and Jassy. There seems little doubt that Nicholas was already thinking about the effects of events in Hungary on the Danubian principalities, possibly as a result of discussions with General P. D. Kiselev, who had continued to act as a consultant on the affairs of the principalities since his departure from them in 1834.[15]

Finally, as part of the general mobilisation of the reserves of the Russian army which he had already ordered, Nicholas authorised the recall of reservists from the Fifth Infantry Corps which had taken part in the fighting in the Caucasus in the early 1840s and was well below full strength.[16] For the immediate future a small intervention force was created from the Fifteenth Infantry Division of the Fifth Infantry Corps, together with support troops from the cavalry, artillery and other arms, at Leovo on the Bessarabian bank of the river Pruth which formed the frontier with Moldavia.[17] The commanding officer of the Fifteenth Infantry Division was General D. A. Gerstenzweig, the son of an officer with the former Polish army who had fought with distinction on the Russian side during the Polish revolt of 1831. Members of the former Polish army were well represented in the Fifth Infantry Corps, and the representative of the Polish democrats in Moldavia claimed to have established links with some of them.[18] Nicholas was, of course, well aware of the international repercussions of a possible military intervention and in a letter to Paskevich who, as Commander-in-Chief of the Active Army, was responsible for the Fifth Infantry Corps despite the distance separating Warsaw from Bessarabia, he emphasised, as he had also done about possible intervention in Prussian Poland, that the frontier should not be crossed without his permission.[19]

On 13 April General Duhamel left Saint Petersburg for Jassy which he reached thirteen days later. The situation was still calm, as the Moldavian exiles from Paris had been prevented from entering the principality by the closure of the frontier. After a meeting with

Sturdza and the boyars, Duhamel was able to send a reassuring report to Saint Petersburg, and on 12 May he moved on to Bucharest.[20] On arriving in Bucharest Duhamel found a different situation. The news of the disturbances in western Europe, especially France, had made a deep impression on the politically-conscious inhabitants of the capital, and the arrival of the group of Wallachian exiles from Paris had only served to increase tension. Duhamel was also disturbed to find that there was a strained relationship between Kotzebue and the *hospodar*. However, he was pleased to learn after his arrival that the Tsar had given him discretion to make use of the intervention force assembled in Leovo, if the seriousness of the situation justified such a decision.[21]

In Constantinople the Russian ambassador continued to press Turkey to join forces with Russia in maintaining order in the principalities. On 28 April, two days after Duhamel had arrived in Jassy, the pro-western Reshid Pasha was replaced as Grand Vizier by Sarim Pasha. The new Turkish government now agreed to send its own special diplomatic envoy, Talat Effendi, a former ambassador to Prussia, to the principalities, to work together with Duhamel. On 5 June Talat Effendi reached Bucharest and announced that the Turkish government intended to support the Russians in the maintenance of the system of government laid down in the Organic Statute. A few days later Talat Effendi received a memorandum with a proposal that Moldavia and Wallachia should be united and form the nucleus of an independent Rumanian state.[22]

While Duhamel and Talat Effendi were discussing the situation with Bibescu, the Wallachian revolutionaries were making secret preparations for a revolt. Bălcescu had wanted the revolt to begin as early as Easter Day, 23 April, but he was outvoted by the more moderate revolutionary leaders, who clung to hopes of support from abroad and their fellow Rumanians in Transylvania, who had issued their own declaration of Rumanian rights at the assembly held in Blaj on 15 May. The returned exiles had not forgotten Lamartine's interest in Rumanian affairs, and Czartoryski had given them added encouragement at a meeting in Germany while they were *en route* to Rumania, as he was making his way to Berlin to support the revolt in Prussian Poland. After much discussion it was decided that the revolt should begin simultaneously both in Bucharest, and outside the capital as well.

On 21 June a mass meeting was held in the small village of Islaz in Oltenia, the western province of Wallachia. The revolutionary leaders were joined by the local prefect G. Magheru, the local military commander Christian Tell, and a local priest, Father Radu Şapcă. Ion Heliade Rădulescu, one of the moderates, read out to the assembled crowd a revolutionary programme which included the familiar demands for a representative national assembly, the creation of a national guard and the granting of land to peasants against payment. The Organic Statute imposed by the Russians was to be abolished. A provisional government was set up and after the meeting had broken up, a large crowd set off for Craiova, the regional capital.[23]

In Bucharest the *hospodar* had learnt of the proposed revolt and had carried out some arrests. However, after an unsuccessful attempt was made on his life, Bibescu yielded to the demands of the revolutionaries and signed the new constitution drawn up at the meeting at Islaz. On 26 June he abdicated and left for Transylvania. The Metropolitan Neofit replaced him as head of the provisional government. The new national tricolour flag of blue, yellow and red bearing the inscription 'Justice' and 'Fraternity' was hoisted. Bucharest was now in the hands of a revolutionary government, an uneasy coalition of liberals led by Rădulescu and radicals led by Bălcescu. Both factions wanted the union of the two principalities and an end to foreign rule, but they were to prove unable to agree about a programme of social reform, especially that of the abolition of forced labour by the peasants and the distribution of land. In the face of this situation, Kotzebue, and General Duhamel, who had vainly been trying to persuade Bibescu to take decisive action,[24] were forced to leave Bucharest. Duhamel set off for Leovo to join the Russian troops assembled there, while Kotzebue crossed the border to Focşani in Moldavia. The apparent success of the Wallachian revolution had obviously increased the likelihood of Russian military intervention.

There now followed a period of great confusion in Wallachia. On the day after the abdication of Bibescu the provisional government took an oath of loyalty to the new constitution at a large rally in Filaret Field. On 1 July right-wing boyars led by two colonels, one of whom, Ioan Odobescu, was Minister of War and a Russian supporter, carried out an unsuccessful counter-coup. A few days later, on 10 July, reports that Russian troops had entered Moldavia and were advancing on Wallachia caused the provisional government to flee from Bucharest and seek refuge at Rucăr at the foot of the Carpathian mountains. On 11 July the Metropolitan Neofit issued a proclamation restoring the old regime, but within two days this counter-coup failed and the provisional government returned to Bucharest.

If there was confusion in Bucharest about who should rule in Wallachia, there was equal confusion on the part of the Russians about the desirability of carrying out military intervention. After the outbreak of revolt in Wallachia, Duhamel had become convinced that the trouble there could spread to Moldavia where he believed that an apparent air of calm concealed hidden dangers.[25] Furthermore, he considered that the Moldavian revolutionaries who had escaped to Transylvania and subsequently moved to Bukovina were plotting with the Poles to invade the principality and overthrow Sturdza.[26] Duhamel's alarm was not shared by his Turkish counterpart, Talat Effendi, who had received a reply from the Austrian military commander in Transylvania that no such invasion was likely.[27]

Duhamel's anxieties about possible external threats to Moldavia and Wallachia had also extended to Serbia where the Russians had offered to assist the Turkish government and the Serbian authorities in Belgrade in maintaining order. However, Prince Alexander Karadjordjević rejected Duhamel's offer of military assistance after discussion with the Russian consul in Belgrade.[28]

Duhamel now started to make preparations for Russian military intervention. At this stage, however, Nicholas was only prepared to agree, albeit reluctantly, to an occupation of Moldavia, if it were to be invaded, as Duhamel expected.[29] On 1 July Duhamel was able to inform Saint Petersburg that Sturdza had made a formal request for Russian military intervention, and was willing to make arrangements to supply the Russian force on its arrival in Moldavia.[30] To begin with, Duhamel proposed a limited intervention as far as Bîrlad, and the despatch of an advance party to Jassy. On the basis of the instructions he had already received from Saint Petersburg Duhamel had no difficulty in persuading Gerstenzweig to agree to his proposal. On 7 July the Russian troops crossed the Pruth on a newly-laid bridge near Leovo and made for Bîrlad. By 10 July a detachment of Russian troops was camped outside Jassy which had now been seriously affected by the cholera epidemic which was moving westwards from Russia. Business was at a standstill, shops were closed and the streets deserted.[31]

Both Duhamel and Gerstenzweig had informed their parent ministries in Saint Petersburg, the Ministry of Foreign Affairs and the Ministry of War, about the plan to occupy Moldavia. However, nearly a fortnight was to elapse before the courier bearing this news reached Saint Petersburg which was some 1250 miles distant from Leovo. At this time in early July Nicholas, whose attentions were fully engaged by events in western Europe, was reluctant to move any of his forces abroad. He did not share Duhamel's fear that the Wallachian revolt would spread to Moldavia and, in any case, he did not expect Duhamel actually to cross the frontier without his approval. He was concerned that the Turks had not yet been persuaded to send their own troops to the principalities, and he was acutely conscious that unilateral Russian military intervention would lay him open to a charge of inconsistency in his actions, after his repeated public assertions that Russia would not intervene militarily in Europe unless its own interests were directly threatened.[32] Nicholas therefore sent a courier to Gerstenzweig, countermanding Duhamel's orders, and instructing him not to occupy Moldavia but await further orders. This courier left for Bessarabia before the arrival of further messages from the two generals informing the authorities in Saint Petersburg that Russian troops had crossed the Pruth and the occupation of Moldavia had begun.[33]

By the time the courier bearing Nicholas' instructions not to cross the Pruth reached Gerstenzweig, he was already in Bîrlad and was appalled by the realisation that he had acted contrary to the wishes of the Tsar. Duhamel, who had moved from Leovo to Jassy, hurried to Bîrlad to discuss the situation with Gerstenzweig. His attempts to persuade the general not to withdraw his troops, and remain in Bîrlad until the arrival of another courier with a reply to their later messages met with no success, even although Duhamel declared himself willing to accept full responsibility for what had happened. As Gerstenzweig was senior in rank to Duhamel, the order to withdraw to Leovo was given, and when the Russian troops arrived there, they were greeted, as Duhamel had predicted, by a courier bearing the order that the occupation of Moldavia should continue. Gerstenzweig, who by now had fallen ill and was suspected of having contracted cholera, became more and more depressed and in a fit of despair, shot himself on 14 August.

Although Nicholas and Paskevich both considered that Duhamel had acted 'extremely imprudently', the Russians could hardly refuse a formal request from Sturdza for military assistance, even although he was subsequently to deny that Duhamel had consulted him about the intervention.[34] Despite this, Nicholas still hoped that the situation in Moldavia would calm down and that the Turks would restore order in Wallachia. He wished his troops to be withdrawn at the first opportunity and replaced by those of Turkey.[35]

The provisional government in Bucharest, however, remained unaware of Nicholas' reluctance to prolong the occupation of Moldavia. They therefore began a diplomatic campaign to seek support in western Europe for their cause.[36] As a first step, they had already sent their own diplomatic representative, Ion Ghica, to Constantinople to gain the support of the Turkish government and play on the Turks' anti-Russian feelings.[37] A. G. Golescu was sent to deal with the French government, D. Brătianu to Vienna and Pest, while I. Maiorescu was sent to win the support of the Frankfurt parliament. The British consul-general Robert Colquhoun agreed to forward a communication to Palmerston, and for this purpose he made use of the Russian post. Colquhoun's letter accompanying the official request for recognition from the Wallachian government was duly intercepted and read by the Russians.[38] The Russian ambassador in London was swiftly given advance warning of the Wallachian move, and immediately got in touch with Palmerston. Brunnow believed that Palmerston had an erroneous conception of the rights conferred by treaty on Russia in the affairs of the principalities and as a result, might make difficulties. In a lengthy letter dated 17 July he advanced the familiar arguments about Russia's wish to keep order and the occupation being within treaty rights. Russia could not allow 'the Lamartines of Bucharest' to carry out their activities in an area so close to its own frontier. In addition, the Russian government hoped that the British diplomatic representatives in Constantinople and Bucharest would not give any encouragement to the revolutionaries.[39]

On 21 July Palmerston, in a formal reply, expressed the hope that the Russian occupation would be temporary. Two days later Palmerston informed Brunnow that the British government did not propose to recognise an independent Wallachian government, as it considered Wallachia to be under Turkish suzerainty. However, the British government reserved the right to consider any possible request from the Turkish government for mediation in the affair.[40] Despite this reservation, Brunnow was confident that Britain would not make any difficulties for Russia.[41] In Saint Petersburg Nesselrode informed the British ambassador that the Russian occupation of Moldavia was only provisional, and that Russia did not intend to annex any further territory.[42]

While Brunnow and Nesselrode were seeking to assure their British interlocutors of the temporary nature of the Russian intervention,

The Russian Intervention in the Danubian Principalities 45

Stratford Canning, who had returned to Constantinople on 24 June, was also pondering the consequences of the occupation. He had first learnt of the disturbances in Moldavia while he was in Vienna, where the Russian ambassador had told him that Russia was prepared to occupy the principalities.[43] He realised that the change of government in Constantinople was not likely to make his task of dealing with Turkey any easier, as the new Grand Vizier was a friend of Russia.[44] Nevertheless, on his return, Canning found that, as always, the Turks were seeking his advice about the Russian action in the principalities. There was little he could offer to bolster Turkish morale. He had a private meeting with Ion Ghica which was arranged by Michał Czajkowski, the representative of Czartoryski, with whom Canning maintained a discreet contact. Ghica subsequently reported to Bucharest that no British support for Wallachia would be forthcoming.[45] At the same time Canning began to co-ordinate his policy with that of the newly-arrived French envoy, General Jacques Aupick, who was a personal friend of General Cavaignac. Although Aupick had still not presented his credentials to the Sultan, this did not prevent him from seeking to persuade the Turks not to send their troops to the principalities, as Russia wished.[46]

Brunnow had forecast to Palmerston that the French government would not be likely to protest about the Russian occupation of Moldavia, as it would be preoccupied with more pressing internal problems after the June events in Paris. There was a flurry of activity in the left-wing press and in the French National Assembly about events in Wallachia, and, as the Third Department's representative in Paris commented, it was a strange spectacle to witness this agitation when France itself was in such a state of disorder.[47] The envoy of the Wallachian government met with a cool reception in Paris, and was unsuccessful in his efforts to obtain arms from the French government.[48] Despite this, the French Minister for Foreign Affairs tried to gain British support in protecting the Turkish position in the principalities, but at this stage Palmerston gave him no encouragement.[49]

In Austria there was also an outcry in the left-wing press against the Russian occupation. However, since the Austrian government was fully engaged in Italy and elsewhere, it was content to accept the official Russian explanation for its actions. In replying to the Austrians, the Russian government pointed out that what had happened in Moldavia was bound to have effects on the Rumanians in Transylvania. The decision to help Sturdza to restore order was thus a contribution to the maintenance of order in the Habsburg Empire.[50]

The newly-formed Hungarian government had also been taking an interest in events in the Danubian principalities and Serbia from the time of its first official cabinet meeting on 12 April. At Kossuth's suggestion, the Hungarian representative in Vienna dealing with foreign affairs was invited to discuss recent events and the possibility of a Russian occupation with the British ambassador. Lacking instructions, Ponsonby referred the matter to London, and in his reply Palmerston merely expressed the hope that there would be no revolution in these parts of the Ottoman Empire.[51] A short time afterwards Esterházy again discussed the situation in the principalities with Medem in Innsbruck and Fonton in Vienna, both of whom were well aware of the difficulties the Hungarian government was facing in dealing with the nationalities. In his conversation with Esterházy, Medem made a spirited defence of his government's policy. Nesselrode was delighted, and in his reply made the same points as had been made to the Austrians about the dangers that could result for the Habsburg empire if the Rumanians were allowed to form an independent state. In a subsequent conversation with Esterházy Medem even suggested that Russia and Hungary might join forces in the preservation of order in the area.[52] Fonton was able to confirm the Hungarian government's apparent lack of concern about the occupation of Moldavia, except for the effect that the presence of Russian troops might have on the Slav peoples of the Habsburg Empire.[53] However, in his speech of 11 July to the Hungarian parliament Kossuth kept a more open mind. The Russian forces in Moldavia could move either into Transylvania or Wallachia; they could be friendly or hostile; Hungary should be prepared for either eventuality.

Although the problems of the Danubian principalities were of less interest to Prussia than Austria, the Prussian consul in Jassy, Baron Richthofen, espoused the cause of the inhabitants of Moldavia, and forwarded a memorandum to the Prussian chargé d'affaires in Constantinople about the misrule of the *hospodar*. The chargé d'affaires forwarded it to the Grand Vizier and Nesselrode had to instruct Meyendorff in Berlin to remonstrate with the Prussian government about the consul's activities, threatening to have him expelled from the principality.

In Wallachia a group of right-wing boyars led by G. Filippescu proposed to the Russians that Moldavia and Wallachia should be united into one state and ruled by a Russian prince.[54] At the same time the provisional government petitioned Nicholas for his support in their work of 'peaceful regeneration'.[55] Nicholas was not prepared to deal with either party. Although under no illusion about the *hospodars*, he did not wish to take over the principalities, and it was axiomatic that he would ignore an approach from the provisional government. For the moment, his main concern was to involve the Turks in the restoration of the system of government laid down in the Organic Statute.

General Duhamel was far from satisfied with the support he had received from Talat Effendi who, in his view, had been too sympathetic to the revolutionaries. Faced with Russian complaints, the Turkish government agreed to replace him by Suleiman Pasha, a former ambassador to France. More importantly for the Russians, the Turks also agreed to send a force of 20 000 troops to occupy Wallachia, as Nicholas had wished. Throughout his dealings with the Turkish government at this time, Titov was at pains to stress that the Russian occupation of Moldavia was due to a local initiative by General Duhamel which the government in Saint Petersburg had reluctantly supported.[56]

The Turkish force was to be commanded by Omer Pasha, later to become famous during the Crimean War. A Croat who had served in the Habsburg army's frontier force before entering Turkish service, Omer Pasha's ability and superiority to the average Turkish officer had struck a British observer during his campaign against rebels in Albania in the early forties.[57] Even General Duhamel was to concede his ability as a general and commander of troops.[58]

On 25 July Suleiman Pasha reached Ruse on the Bulgarian bank of the Danube, where he was met by an envoy from the provisional government who assured him of the loyalty of the Wallachians to the Sultan. Six days later Suleiman Pasha and part of the Turkish forces crossed the Danube and entered Giurgiu. In a proclamation issued on the same day Suleiman made it clear that he had entered Wallachia to restore the rule of the Organic Statute and the authority of the boyars.[59]

Now that Turkey had agreed to support Russia in restoring order in Wallachia, Nicholas considered that it was an appropriate moment to explain Russia's actions to the world at large. Nesselrode was instructed to draft a suitable explanatory circular which was published in the semi-official *Journal de Saint Pétersbourg* on 31 July. The circular emphasised that the Russian occupation had been carried out in consultation with Turkey and was based on existing treaty rights. It poured scorn on the idea of a unified Rumania which was in any case not in accordance with the wishes of the majority of the population, and posed a direct threat to the security of Austria, Russia and Turkey. Nevertheless, the circular assured all concerned that Russia did not intend to make the occupation permanent.[60] By any standards, the circular was an extremely wordy defence of Russia's action, a fact which caused one Russian official to comment on its lack of dignity and to describe it as one not worthy of Nicholas himself.[61]

But for Russia what mattered was that there was no sign of any practical opposition to the action it had taken. Palmerston was prepared to accept the assurance that the occupation was only temporary and indeed, wrote privately to Bloomfield that Nicholas' 'wise and judicious conduct' had 'silenced all critics and elicited the eulogies of all impartial men'.[62] The Duke of Wellington also expressed his approval of Russia's action and wrote to Brunnow that he fully appreciated Russia's reluctance to take military action.[63] Ponsonby expressed approval to the Russian ambassador in Innsbruck. As a result, Nicholas was more than satisfied by the official British reaction to what had happened.[64] But there were others in Great Britain, such as the editor of *The Times*, who were still surprised that Nicholas had not made more use of the disturbed situation in Europe to press home Russia's advantage in dealing with Turkey.[65]

However, the situation in Wallachia was not to be restored as speedily as the Russians had hoped. The Turkish government had instructed Suleiman Pasha to listen sympathetically to the grievances of the provisional government, and the British consul-general had agreed to act as intermediary between him and the Wallachians. Within a short time, a compromise was reached, when Suleiman accepted a proposal that the provisional government should be replaced by a regency consisting of six of its members. After further discussion, the number was reduced from six to three and on 9 August the setting up of the three-man regency was officially proclaimed. Its members, Heliade Rădulescu, Christian Tell and N. Golescu, were moderate liberals, and the radicals, headed by N. Bălcescu, had no alternative but to accept this compromise. It was also agreed that an official delegation should be sent to Constantinople to assure the Sultan that Wallachia did not intend to secede from the Ottoman Empire, and to seek approval for the proposed changes in the form of government for the principality.

When General Duhamel learnt of the results of these negotiations, he was far from pleased and realised that, from the Russian point of view, Suleiman Pasha was even more unsatisfactory than Talat Effendi.[66] The Wallachians were, of course, well aware of the possibility of exploiting the differences between the Russians and Turks about dealing with the situation, and had decided before Suleiman's arrival to spare no effort, financial or otherwise, to win his support for their cause.[67] It was not long before the Russians found out that Suleiman Pasha had accepted a bribe of 20 000 ducats to defend Wallachian interests.[68] Nor were the Russians pleased at the part played in the negotiations by Colquhoun, whose anti-Russian views were becoming more and more apparent. Finally, the Poles had also not been slow to take advantage of the disturbances. Besides the activities of the Polish democrats in Moldavia, Czartoryski had sent agents to the principalities, including a military adviser for the Wallachian militia. Even the Central Committee set up by the Poles in L'vov in Galicia had sent a representative to Bucharest.[69] Since the occupation of Moldavia, an increasing number of desertions by Poles serving in the Russian army had taken place, some of whom were given shelter by liberally-minded boyars on their estates.[70] In short, it became increasingly clear to the Russians that firm action was required if the situation was not to deteriorate further. The Russians therefore decided to increase their pressure on the Turkish government to disavow the actions taken by Suleiman Pasha.

On 12 August there was another change of government in Constantinople. Reshid Pasha and Ali Pasha were restored to power as Grand Vizier and Minister of Foreign Affairs. General Aupick was at last formally accredited as French ambassador to Turkey and agreed to lend every support to Stratford Canning in their joint efforts to persuade the Turks to stand up to the Russians. As a practical soldier, one of Aupick's first moves after his official recognition was to send two of his military staff who had accompanied him to Constantinople from Paris to carry out a military reconnaissance in the principalities and acquire information about the Russian occupation force in Moldavia.[71]

The Turkish government found itself in a difficult situation in resisting Russian pressure about the actions of Suleiman Pasha. After much consultation with Stratford Canning, they agreed to appoint a *caimacan* as the Sultan's deputy in Wallachia and to abolish the three-man regency. All the reforms carried out by the provisional government were to be declared null and void. But they refused to disown Suleiman Pasha completely, and decided to send one of their most experienced diplomats, Fuad Effendi, to carry out these changes. As a further concession to the Russians, neither the Sultan nor the Grand Vizier received the Wallachian official delegation which eventually left Constantinople for Bucharest on 16 September. On 1 September Fuad Effendi left Constantinople by steamer for Varna to join the Turkish forces. He was under no illusion about his task. The Russians wished him to be the Wallachian government's executioner, while the Wallachians wanted him to bear the brunt of Russian displeasure for their actions.[72]

In Bucharest there was dismay at the unfavourable turn of events and increasing restiveness. On 18 September a mob burnt a copy of the Organic Statute and the ever-obliging Metropolitan Neofit solemnly anathematised the ashes. Attempts to organise armed resistance in the city to the threat of military occupation met with little success, and it was left to Magheru in the province of Oltenia to form a small force at Trajan's Field in Rîureni. By 7 September Fuad Effendi had reached Galaţi, where he was joined by Duhamel. After the obligatory period of quarantine the two men travelled to Giurgiu which they reached on 23 September. Some further inconclusive negotiations with the Wallachian government followed and finally, on Fuad Effendi's orders, Omer Pasha and the Turkish forces occupied Bucharest on 25 September after a clash with a detachment of Wallachian firemen on Spirei Hill. The last act of the provisional government before its members fled was to issue a formal note of protest about the Turkish occupation.[73] Fuad Effendi announced the end of the rule of the regency and the appointment of Constantine Cantacuzimo as *caimacan*, rather than G. Filippescu who had been the Russian choice. Colquhoun, realising that further resistance was futile, sent a member of his staff, Effingham Grant, who was related by marriage to one of the revolutionaries, to Trajan's Field to advise Magheru to give up the unequal struggle and disband his force. On 10 October Magheru's force dispersed. Thus it seemed that Fuad Effendi and the Turks had been successful in restoring order in Wallachia.

However, unknown to Fuad Effendi, Nicholas had grown increasingly impatient with Turkish dilatoriness in dealing with the problems of the principalities. He considered Sturdza to be venal and unprincipled, while Bibescu was imbued with French ideas. The Moldavians and Wallachians were barely civilised and little better than barbarians. They were not fit to have any other form of government than that laid down in the Organic Statute and must be made to see the error of their ways. In any case, it was one of his maxims that a ruler should not yield to popular clamour.[74] Winter was approaching, the Russian army was now fully mobilised, and there were good military reasons why Russia's left flank should be made secure. The strategic importance of the principalities in the event of further disturbances in the Habsburg Empire was obvious. General A. N. Lüders, the commander of the Fifth Infantry Corps, had now returned from leave and had been immediately sent south to take over the command of the Russian occupation force after the death of General Gerstenzweig.[75] Since the Turks seemed incapable of taking decisive action, the Russians would act for them by occupying Wallachia jointly in order to depose the revolutionaries and restore the status quo.

On 16 September Nicholas sent a letter to the Sultan giving notice of his intentions. The object of the joint occupation was to restore the legitimate authority of the sovereign of a province which formed an integral part of the Ottoman Empire. Suleiman Pasha had still not been dismissed, and it seemed unlikely that Fuad Effendi would fare any better in his attempts to deal decisively with the Wallachian rebels. Russia must be protected from a revolt in a territory so close to its own borders.[76]

Russia's growing impatience with Turkey was to cause Lord Palmerston concern as well. In a debate in the House of Commons on 4 September he had assured Lord Dudley Stuart, the champion of the Poles, that Russia's occupation of Moldavia which had been made at the request of the *hospodar*, was within treaty rights and would not be permanent.[77] A few days later he was sufficiently concerned about the worsening situation in the principalities and Russia's threatening behaviour to write to Brunnow that the Russian ambassador in Constantinople should moderate the demands he was making on the Turkish government. Brunnow, who was enjoying the pleasures of Brighton, sent a lengthy reply. Russia had every right to defend its position in the principalities. The Sultan had been misguided enough to allow himself to be dictated to by a revolutionary party of which the true instigators were the leaders of the Polish emigration. The Wallachian government had bribed Suleiman Pasha. Russia had been a patient observer of events in Wallachia since the beginning of July, hoping that the Turkish government would take some decisive action to restore the situation. Russia now had no choice but to do the Sultan's work for him. Britain should not complain. Russia was behaving no differently than Britain had done earlier in the year in April when it had taken action to deal with the Chartists.[78] General Lüders communicated Nicholas' decision to occupy Wallachia to Fuad Effendi on the day that the Turkish troops entered Bucharest.[79] Earlier in the month a regrouping of the Russian forces in Bessarabia and Wallachia had taken place and on 28 September Russian troops crossed the Moldavian/Wallachian border. The estimated strength of the Russian troops in the principalities had now risen to 34 000.[80] Lüders' official proclamation stated that the Russians were entering Wallachia in concert with the Turks to restore the rightful government. He hoped that the population would cooperate with the occupation forces.[81] Lüders had now been joined by Duhamel and Kotzebue; the Russians were thus well placed to become the dominant partner in the joint occupation force.

Fuad Effendi, who had received no warning of the Russian action from his own government, immediately protested that the Russian action was not necessary. In his view, the best guarantee for the restoration of order was to show mercy to the rebels and to improve the material conditions of the population of Wallachia. Duhamel, by contrast, compared Wallachia to a volcano which had temporarily died down, but could erupt again. In accordance with Nicholas' usual practice, the revolt must be crushed completely, the ringleaders arrested and punished, while mercy could be shown to those that had been led astray. This difference in outlook between the representatives of the occupying powers was to become all too apparent during the weeks that followed.[82]

On 14 October the first Russian troops entered Bucharest, and on the following day a solemn *Te Deum* was celebrated in the local cathedral to give thanks for their arrival without any bloodshed. Nicholas was satisfied, but he realised that some time would elapse before there was a stable situation again. One advantage of the occupation of the principalities was that it would act as a deterrent to further thoughts of revolt in the other Christian provinces of the Ottoman Empire such as Bulgaria.[83] Although the Wallachians did not offer any armed resistance, there was a final burst of activity from the Polish legion which had been raised by the Polish democrats. There were three clashes of which the most serious centred round a monastery at Vintilă-Vodă near the Moldavian frontier, where a number of Polish deserters from the Russian army had taken refuge. Colonel Yu. Ya. Skaryatin and a detachment of Cossacks were despatched to put an end to this resistance. Eight Poles were killed, twenty wounded and the remainder taken prisoner. The deserters from the Russian army were shot, while the members of the Polish legion were taken to Russia for subsequent interrogation, trial and imprisonment.[84] The Russians now began their task of gaining the upper hand in the new administration. One of their most pressing problems was the cost of the occupation. On 22 October Kotzebue informed the *caimacan* of Nicholas' decision to share the costs between the two principalities; meanwhile Russia would grant Wallachia a loan of 300 000 silver roubles (£50 000) to cover immediate expenditure.[85] Despite this Russian action it was not long before complaints were being made about non-payment by the Russians for supplies, and the arbitrary requisitioning of property belonging to foreign nationals for use as billets by the Russian troops. By contrast, the Turks had decided not to levy occupation costs and behaved in a way which did not arouse the hostility of the foreign consuls.

In Wallachia General Duhamel sent Cantacuzino his proposals for setting up a commission of enquiry to investigate the activities of those who had taken part in the revolt. He also proposed to Fuad Effendi that Bucharest should be divided into two zones of occupation, a plan which Fuad Effendi reluctantly accepted. Omer Pasha received a proposal that police duties should be carried out by the Russian and Turkish forces on alternate days. On 8 December the Russians carried out their duties for the first time and made twenty-eight arrests. Steps were taken to enforce a stricter censorship of foreign books and newspapers imported into the principalities, and to impose restrictions on travel and the issue of passports. The Wallachian militia was to be made to swear a new oath of loyalty to the *caimacan* and to the laws sanctioned by Russia and Turkey. At a formal ceremony held at the beginning of December to carry out this proposal, Duhamel and Omer Pasha made speeches calling on the local population to respect law and order, and urging them not to rely on foreign troops for this purpose.[86]

In Moldavia, Sturdza set up his own commission to investigate Polish activities, especially among the liberal boyars. Two members of the Cantacuzino family were shown to have assisted the Poles, and there was even a suggestion that the Russian consul-general Kotzebue had been implicated. The Third Department was also carrying out its own investigation; its report exonerated Kotzebue, but went into great detail about the activities of the Polish emigrés. In November 1848 Nesselrode and Orlov recommended to Nicholas that action should be taken against the members of the Cantacuzino family who had assisted the Poles. The investigation dragged on into early 1849 and in the end, the two Cantacuzinos were declared to be innocent.[87]

It was not long before the foreign consuls in Bucharest were complaining about Russian behaviour towards their nationals. One of the more important cases concerned a British subject from the Ionian Islands named Dimitrios Asprea. After his arrest by Russian soldiers on a charge of having written an anti-Russian pamphlet, he was imprisoned in a monastery. The Turkish authorities were unable to secure his release, and eventually Colquhoun's reports on the case were brought to the attention of Palmerston, who directed that a formal protest should be made to the Russian government. In Saint Petersburg the matter was ultimately referred to Nicholas and at the end of 1848, Brunnow was able to inform Palmerston that the Tsar had decreed that Asprea should be set free.[88] The whole affair had been a simple 'local police matter', the implication being that the Russians found it difficult to understand why the British government was so concerned about Asprea's rights. Just over one year later the Russian government was to learn from the Don Pacifico case that Palmerston when roused would not hesitate to take drastic action to defend the rights of a British subject. Kotzebue summed up Russian policy when he spoke to the French consul in Bucharest of 'salutary measures containing a certain element of terror which would not last long'[89] while Nesselrode wrote more diplomatically of a complete reorganisation of the local administration which would necessitate a continuing Russian presence in the principalities.[90] To Bibescu, who was still resentful that he had not been asked to resume the office of *hospodar*, Nesselrode pointed out that Russia had to investigate what had gone wrong.[91]

The Russian army did not make a good impression on the foreign consuls in Bucharest and Jassy. There was a reward of two ducats for any deserter handed back to the authorities.[92] Many of the Russian soldiers had fallen ill, and arrangements had to be made to open military hospitals in Wallachia. According to the British consul in Odessa, the Russian troops had been prevented from sending private letters back to Russia about their experiences during the occupation.[93] A Turkish officer who killed a Russian officer in a duel took refuge in the house of Omer Pasha, and General Duhamel had to be prevented from entering the house by force in order to arrest him.[94] However, despite the strained relationship between the Turks and the

Russians, life in Bucharest slowly returned to normal. In November General Duhamel was joined by his wife, and the round of balls and parties which formed part of the social life of the winter months in the capital was resumed. The British consul-general did what he could to help those who had taken part in the revolt and granted British passports whenever possible.[95] Kotzebue kept Nesselrode informed of these anti-Russian activities. In Constantinople Stratford Canning was brooding about the apparent ease with which the Russians had persuaded the Turks to agree to a joint occupation of the principalities, and wrote to Palmerston about the need to bolster Turkish morale.[96] One of his first thoughts was that part of the British and French fleets stationed in the Mediterranean should be sent to Turkish waters to show the flag. It seemed possible to him that the Russians might be tempted to do more than remain in Moldavia and Wallachia. The memories of the Serbian crisis of 1843 were still in his mind, but he was confident that Palmerston would adopt a more robust attitude than that displayed by Sir Robert Peel and Lord Aberdeen on that occasion, which the Turks had not forgotten.[97]

In Saint Petersburg Buchanan, the British chargé d'affaires, made repeated protests to Nesselrode about the Russian failure to withdraw from the principalities. Nesselrode was swift to reply that Russia was dealing with the principalities in the same way that Great Britain had dealt with disturbances in the Ionian Islands in September. Furthermore, if Great Britain wished to ensure that the stay of the Russian troops was of short duration, Palmerston would do well to restrain the activities of his representative in Bucharest, who had lost no opportunity of displaying his dislike of Russia for the last ten years. Great Britain would do well to remember that the Russian occupation was a contribution to the general maintenance of order in Europe as it ensured the stability of the Ottoman Empire.[98]

In Paris Bastide continued to express his concern to the British government about the long-term dangers of the Russian occupation and the steady erosion of Turkey's position in the principalities. At the end of October Palmerston finally agreed that the British and French representatives in Saint Petersburg should co-ordinate their protests about the Russian failure to withdraw.[99] The French government's letter of instructions to General Le Flô was sent through the open post and was thus intercepted and read. Nesselrode immediately informed Brunnow of the proposed Anglo-French initiative and authorised him to protest strongly about the 'perfidious counsel' which was being given to Turkey by the British and French governments.[100] Buchanan discussed the timing of a protest with Le Flô, but since the latter was engaged in a dispute with the Russian government about his official status, it was hardly surprising that he judged the moment to be inauspicious for making a protest about an important political matter.[101] Le Flô was to leave Saint Petersburg at the end of the year after Louis Napoleon was elected President, and there the matter was to remain until the beginning of 1849.

Thus, as 1848 drew to a close, the Russian assurance that their occupation of the principalities would not be permanent was proving to be false. For the Rumanians, the revolutions in Moldavia and Wallachia had been a failure. The hoped-for help from abroad had not been forthcoming, nor had the liberals and radicals been able to agree on a programme of internal reform in the face of opposition from the boyars about land reform. It was to require the upheaval of the Crimean War to carry the struggle for the creation of an independent Rumania a stage further. In Constantinople the Russian ambassador made it clear to the Turkish government, as their representatives in Bucharest were learning at first hand, that there would be no Russian withdrawal from Moldavia and Wallachia until the last vestiges of revolt had been rooted out.[102] Across the border Austrian difficulties with the Hungarians were increasing and were causing the Russians concern. In mid-December General Lüders ordered his troops to occupy all the passes leading from Wallachia to Transylvania, and the Turks were quick to follow suit.[103]

It seemed more and more likely that Russia would be asked to offer some kind of assistance to the hard-pressed Austrian forces in Transylvania. From the military point of view, it would be foolish to abandon the advantage afforded by the principalities as a base for any future operations against Transylvania. It was also equally clear that Russia would have to negotiate a new agreement with Turkey to justify the continuance of its occupation.

As a former Secretary of State for War, Palmerston had a keen appreciation of the military reasons which lay behind the Russian reluctance to withdraw, and did his best to persuade Canning that this was the real motive for Russia's actions which did not therefore herald the beginning of a further march on Constantinople. Nevertheless, he was willing to agree that Turkey should not relax its efforts to persuade Russia to evacuate the principalities.[104] The French consul in Jassy took a similar view, and reminded his government that if the Russians assisted the Austrians over Hungary, this would make it easier for Austria to resolve its remaining problems in Italy.[105]

At the end of December 1848 the Russians made their first move to negotiate a new agreement about the principalities with the Turkish government.[106] These negotiations were to continue throughout the first few months of 1849 until, as we shall see, the Russian decision to intervene in Hungary made it essential to bring them to a speedy conclusion.

3 The October Revolution in Vienna and its Aftermath

The occupation of the Danubian principalities had put Russia in a favourable position to give military assistance to Austria in its struggle with Hungary, if it were needed. However, when Nicholas left Saint Petersburg at the beginning of October to take part in three days of manoeuvres, he still hoped, as he had done at the end of September, that Jelačić would be able to crush the Hungarian revolt, occupy Budapest and then march on Vienna.[1]

The events which took place in the Austrian capital on 6 October were to show that Nicholas was unduly optimistic. On that day yet another revolt took place in Vienna. Its immediate cause was the reluctance of a German-speaking grenadier battalion to obey the orders issued by Count Latour, the Minister of War and an enthusiastic supporter of Jelačić, to take part in the suppression of the revolt in Hungary. Workers and students clashed with cavalry which had been sent to ensure Latour's orders were carried out. The fighting which ensued became so serious that Count Auersperg, the commander of the Vienna garrison, was forced to withdraw his troops to the suburbs. The mob then stormed the Ministry of War where the Austrian cabinet was in session. Most of the ministers including Wessenberg and Doblhoff were able to escape, but Latour was murdered and his body hanged on a lamp-post outside the building. The day ended with an assault on the city's main arsenal and the capture of some 30 000 rifles stored in it. Once again Vienna was in the hands of the radicals, who on this occasion were in complete control of the National Guard, commanded by the radical journalist Wenzel Messenhauer. On 14 October he was to be joined by one of the heroes of the Polish revolt of 1830, General Bem, who arrived in Vienna from Cracow.[2]

The following day the Emperor and the court left Vienna with an armed escort and moved to Olomouc in Moravia. The Czech members of the Austrian parliament, all of whom were loyal to the dynasty, had walked out in disgust at the behaviour of the mob the previous day. The diplomatic corps decided to remain in Vienna, unless public order broke down completely. However, the Russian ambassador, realising that he would be instructed to stay with the Emperor, reluctantly set out on his travels on 9 October, leaving Fonton as chargé d'affaires as had happened in May.[3]

On 10 October Jelačić's army, which had turned north-west after its defeat at Pákozd the previous month, crossed the river Leitha into Austria and joined forces with the Vienna garrison which was camped on the outskirts of the city. The pursuing Hungarian army under General Móga did not cross the frontier, as Kossuth wished to receive a formal invitation from the authorities in Vienna to do so. Móga himself was, in any case, far from certain whether his soldiers, many of whom were untrained and armed only with scythes and pitchforks, would be a match for the regular Austrian forces with which he would be faced.

While Ferenc Pulszky, Esterházy's deputy for foreign affairs, made strenuous efforts in Vienna to obtain the formal invitation sought by Kossuth, the court in Olomouc took stock of the situation. Since July Prince Windischgraetz had been making contigency plans and had succeeded in assembling a force of 60 000 men (mainly Croats, Bohemians and Moravians) who were loyal to the dynasty.[4] By a happy coincidence Radetzky had sent Schwarzenberg, whom he had appointed Governor of Milan after its surrender, to Vienna to persuade Wessenberg to adopt a more robust attitude in the negotiations with Piedmont following the armistice signed in August. On 8 October Windischgraetz received a letter from Schwarzenberg urging him to put an end to the anarchy prevailing in Vienna.[5] The Court summoned both men to Olomouc where they arrived in mid-October. On 16 October a decree was issued appointing Windischgraetz a Field Marshal and Commander-in-Chief of all the Austrian forces outside Italy with sweeping counter-revolutionary powers. At the same time Schwarzenberg was giving the task of forming a new government, although for the time being Wessenberg was to remain nominally in charge and sign documents which would, in fact, be drafted by Schwarzenberg and his secretary, the young diplomat Hübner.

After Windischgraetz had left for Vienna, a more conciliatory decree was issued on 19 October which informed the peoples of the monarchy that the Emperor was a constitutional monarch and that all the reforms carried out since March would remain in force, including the emancipation of the peasantry. The parliament in Vienna was not to be dissolved, as Windischgraetz had wished, but would reassemble on 15 November in the town of Kroměříž, not far from Olomouc, where it would continue the task of drafting a new constitution. The issuing of the decree of 19 October was a clear reflection of the differences between Windischgraetz, who now regarded himself as the saviour of the dynasty, and Schwarzenberg about the way in which Austria was to be ruled in future. These differences were to become more apparent in the weeks to come.

Meanwhile Jelačić and his army were waiting impatiently on the outskirts of Vienna for the arrival of Windischgraetz so that an attack could be launched on the city. Schwarzenberg was now able to report to Radetzky that order would soon be restored. In his reply Radetzky wrote that the fate of the monarchy was in the hands of a brave man,[6] words which echoed those of the Tsar who had written to Paskevich a few days earlier that what happened in Vienna would determine the future existence of the Austrian Empire.[7]

By 24 October Windischgraetz had set up his headquarters at Hietzing near the palace of Schönbrunn and encircled the city. The diplomatic corps had joined him there after moving out of the inner city. On 28 October Jelačić launched a massive attack and within a short time an armistice was arranged. It was promptly broken when the rebels learnt that the Hungarian army had crossed the frontier and would, after all, be coming to their aid. On 30 October a battle took place at Schwechat on the eastern outskirts of the city near the modern airport. The Austrian regular forces routed the ill-trained and ill-disciplined Hungarian army which streamed back across the frontier. Shortly afterwards General Móga resigned his command. The Austrian forces were now able to turn their attention to the final subjugation of Vienna.

The following day Windischgraetz began to bombard the inner city which was stormed amid scenes of fierce fighting and surrendered on 1 November. Martial law was proclaimed, the National Guard disbanded, its commander Messenhauer shot and press censorship reimposed. In a gesture of defiance to the Frankfurt Parliament, the Saxon Robert Blum, one of the four radical members who had come to Vienna to support the insurgents, was court-martialled and shot for his participation in the revolt. A break in diplomatic relations with Saxony was narrowly averted. General Bem was able to escape to Bratislava and shortly afterwards met Kossuth, who offered him the command of the Hungarian forces in Transylvania where a struggle with the Austrians had begun.

While Vienna was surrendering to Windischgraetz on 1 November,

The October Revolution in Vienna and its Aftermath 61

there was an outbreak of trouble in L'vov in Eastern Galicia. General Hammerstein, the military commandant, had been expecting trouble and soon bombarded the city into submission, as had happened in Cracow in April. Martial law was imposed and the province relapsed into a state of sullen discontent.

Although the formation of the new Austrian government was not to be announced until 27 November, Schwarzenberg had already set about his task of selecting a new cabinet which was to be composed of able administrators who would assist him in his task of restoring the authority of the government. He did not hesitate to include persons such as the liberally-minded Count Stadion, the lawyer Alexander Bach who had sided with the revolutionaries in March, and the Rhinelander Baron Bruck, who dreamt of the economic benefits to be derived from a Central Europe united under Austro-German leadership.

Unlike Windischgraetz, in whose regiment he had served as a young cavalry officer, Schwarzenberg was a realist, who appreciated the impossibility of the monarchy returning to the form of government which had existed before March. However, the reforms which he considered necessary would be carried out on his terms. Although prepared to go on paying lip-service to the parliament which he had personally closed in October before he left for Olomouc,[8] he was determined to restore the monarchy as a centralised rather than a federal state. In addition, he intended to be his own Foreign Minister and use his diplomatic skills to restore Austria's prestige in the German Confederation and in Europe. No longer would there be any discussion with Palmerston about the possibility of Austria surrendering its possessions in Northern Italy. Schwarzenberg had served in the Austrian Embassy in Saint Petersburg at the time of the Decembrist revolt in 1825. He was known to the Tsar who appears to have decided that suspicions of Schwarzenberg's complicity in the revolt were unjustified. As a former soldier, Schwarzenberg appreciated the importance of Austria's alliance with Russia from the military point of view, but he was determined to exploit the alliance for Austria's benefit. The most pressing problem he faced was the suppression of the revolt in Hungary, and it was obvious that Russia could help Austria in this task. It was agreed that Windischgraetz should make his forces ready for a winter campaign against Hungary. As Windischgraetz was later to realise, his departure from the centre of affairs was to weaken still further his ability to influence decisions about the future of the monarchy, and made it

easier for Schwarzenberg to ensure that his views prevailed in the
Council of Ministers and with the new Emperor. A request by
Windischgraetz that he should be made directly subordinate to the
Emperor was rejected, but he retained the right to correspond direct
with him, and to be kept informed of the major decisions of the new
government.

Nicholas was swift to react to the news of the suppression of the
revolt in Vienna. He had been in little doubt that Windischgraetz
would succeed, and his only fear had been that the rebels would be
allowed to surrender without a fight. He was especially anxious that
his old enemy Bem should be taught a lesson.[9] He decided to send
a special envoy, Baron Lieven, to Vienna with awards for the two
Austrian commanders. Jelačić received the Order of Saint Vladimir
(First Class) and a picture of a saint from the Tsarina, while
Windischgraetz received Russia's highest distinction, the Order of
Saint Andrew in diamonds. In a characteristically impulsive gesture,
Nicholas tore off the star of the order from his own unform, telling
Lieven that he should inform Windischgraetz that he had worn it for
six years.[10] A letter to the Emperor Ferdinand congratulated him on
the good example he had set his fellow monarchs in suppressing the
revolt.[11]

It was natural that Nicholas' thoughts should turn to Berlin where
he was hoping that the King of Prussia would take decisive action.
While his wife had written to her brother the Crown Prince William
and the Russian ambassador of her shame at what was happening in
Prussia, and her wish that a Jelačić would appear to restore order,
the Tsar was writing once again to General Dohna in Kaliningrad
urging him to be the Jelačić of Prussia, and as usual reminding him
that he could treat the Russian army as a reserve.[12]

The situation in Berlin came to a head in October, as it had done
in Vienna. In the middle of the month the resignation of General
Pfuel as Prime Minister in protest against a proposal made by the
Prussian parliament that the nobility should be abolished was followed
by a proposal made at the meeting of a Democratic Congress in
Berlin that the Prussian parliament should support the revolt in
Vienna. Emboldened by the news of Windischgraetz's victory, the
King instructed his new Prime Minister General Brandenburg to take
appropriate action. On 9 November it was announced that the
Prussian parliament would be transferred to Brandenburg, and the
following day General Wrangel occupied Berlin. Although parliament
had voted against the decision to transfer it from the capital, there

was no bloodshed. As in Vienna, martial law was proclaimed, the Guard disbanded and press censorship reimposed. On 5 December new parliamentary elections were announced and a new constitution proclaimed against the wishes of the Prussian conservatives who, like Windischgraetz, wished to revert to the pre-March system of government. Although Nicholas was glad that order had at last been restored in Berlin, he regretted that there had been no assault on the city and nothing to compare with the shooting of Blum. What was needed now in both Vienna and Berlin was the 'extirpation of evil', a frank recognition of past mistakes and no half-measures in restoring the old order. The Tsar believed that Schwarzenberg and Windischgraetz would probably prove to be more effective than his brother-in-law, who did not inspire him with confidence.[13]

But the first reports about Austrian affairs to reach Saint Petersburg from Vienna and Olomouc after the suppression of the revolts in Vienna and L'vov revealed all too clearly the differences of opinion between Windischgraetz and Schwarzenberg about the future system of government which should be imposed on Austria. While Schwarzenberg spoke to Medem of the necessity of reconciling the authority of the Emperor with the rights laid down in the constitution,[14] Windischgraetz talked to Fonton of the difficulties he was facing in gaining acceptance of his view that parliament should be dissolved, if it would not carry out the wishes of the monarch and the government.[15] Like Nicholas, Windischgraetz completely failed to understand the workings of a constitutional monarchy, and was to earn a rebuke from Palmerston about a message he had sent to Queen Victoria at the time of the revolt in Vienna seeking her support.[16]

However, both Schwarzenberg and Windischgraetz did not underrate the military difficulties that lay ahead of Austria. After the suppression of the revolt in L'vov Schwarzenberg informed Medem that the local authorities in Galicia had been given to understand that Russian troops on the other side of the border would always be available to come to their assistance if necessary. Indeed, the Austrian authorities would have liked to let it be known in the province that Russian intervention was possible in the event of further disorder. However, Schwarzenberg was careful to add that he hoped he would not have to avail himself of the 'obliging support' of Paskevich's forces.[17] When Paskevich read his copy of Medem's despatches, which had been sent to Warsaw under flying seal, he at once realised the possible international complications that might ensue from a

Russian intervention and requested guidance from Nesselrode. He assumed that the provisions of the agreement reached with Austria and Prussia at Mnichovo Hradiště in 1833 still applied, despite the changes in government in both countries. More specifically, he wished to know what level of Austrian authority would be empowered to request Russian military assistance. Since he could not afford to wait fifteen days for a reply from Saint Petersburg if he were asked to assist, for example, in the suppression of another revolt in Cracow, he hoped that Nesselrode's instructions on the subject would be 'categoric' and 'without reservations'.[18]

However, the Tsar was not to be rushed into making a quick decision about offering military aid to the new government in Austria. While he had great faith in Windischgraetz and had been moved by the latter's firm conviction that the 'noble heart' of the Tsar would respond to an appeal to save the Habsburg monarchy,[19] if the Austrian army was not able to do so, he was still doubtful about the wisdom of assisting a government which apparently intended to turn Austria into a constitutional monarchy. As he commented on a despatch from Medem, such a course of action would condemn the monarchy to a perpetual struggle between the sovereign's power and the so-called delegates of the nation.[20] He had already made his views known to Lieven before his departure for Austria, and had entrusted him with a number of messages which he preferred not to put in writing.[21] Fonton had been instructed to assure Windischgraetz that he could count on Russian military assistance if it were needed.[22] Nicholas had even agreed that Austrian troops could seek asylum in Moldavia and Wallachia if they were forced to retreat across the border now that fighting had broken out in Transylvania.[23] He would finally make up his mind about Austria when Lieven returned from his visit. At the back of his mind there were further worries about next year's budget: it was possible that Russia would have to seek another loan abroad.[24] Accordingly, Medem was instructed to give no more than a general assurance to Schwarzenberg about Russian military assistance. The last thing that the Tsar wished to do was to assist Austria in the establishment of a form of government of which he disapproved in a place so close to Russian Poland. Medem must find out as much as possible about Austria's future system of government which, in the Tsar's view, needed to be autocratic and centralised with a strong and loyal army.[25]

While Nicholas refused to give a definite undertaking, the Austrian military commanders in Cracow, L'vov and Transylvania continued to have doubts about their ability to deal with the troubles in their territories without reinforcements from elsewhere, preferably from the Russian troops which were near at hand. In his replies Windischgraetz assured them that Russian assistance would be forthcoming, but authority to seek it must be sought through him.[26] At the same time Windischgraetz did his best to impress upon Schwarzenberg the importance of the use of Russian forces as a means of easing the pressure on his hard-pressed commanders in the different parts of the monarchy.[27]

The Tsar also persisted in his refusal to become more deeply involved in Italian affairs. He declined a request from Schwarzenberg to sell to Austria a number of Russian naval steamships in order that Austria could wage a more effective war at sea against the Republic of Venice which still continued to hold out.[28] Nor would he agree to support Austria by taking part in a general European peace conference to settle the differences between Austria and Piedmont.[29] Likewise an appeal for assistance from the Pope, who had been forced to flee from Rome after a revolution in November, elicited no more than a polite expression of moral support. Russia's geographical position precluded the possibility of anything more positive. However, the Russian ambassador to the Papal States, who had dutifully followed the Pope from Rome to Gaeta in the Kingdom of Naples, was enjoined to remain with him, even if the Pope decided to return to Rome; under no circumstances, however, was he to go to France if the Pope accepted a French offer of asylum.[30]

Although the Tsar had welcomed General Cavaignac's friend Le Flô on his arrival in Saint Petersburg in September, he was in no hurry to recognise the French republic until he knew the outcome of the presidential election which was to be held in France in December. His preference was for Cavaignac, and there would be an advantage for Russia in a friendly relationship with a France which could act as a counterweight to a united Germany, if unification were to take place.[31] Nicholas always enjoyed dealing with a diplomat who was a professional soldier by training, but Nesselrode confided to his son-in-law in Naples that Le Flô did not understand politics. The French general therefore spent a frustrating three months in the Russian capital where he was shunned by society and his fellow diplomats with the exception of his British colleague who, as we have seen in the previous chapter, vainly tried to enlist his support in protesting to the Russians about their occupation of the Danubian principalities.[32] Even after Le Flô had returned to France, when Louis Napoleon had been elected President, Nicholas remained suspicious of the French government's intentions, and was unconvinced that Louis Napoleon would remain in power. It is not surprising, therefore, that the Third Department representative in Paris sought no support from his superiors in Saint Petersburg for a proposal put to him by one of his journalist contacts that Russia should give Louis Napoleon financial support during his electoral campaign.[33] The Russian decision to accord full recognition to the new French government was therefore deferred until the pressure of events and the decision to intervene in Hungary in April 1849 made it a necessity to do so.

About this time the Spanish government sent an envoy to Saint Petersburg in an attempt to restore diplomatic relations which had been broken off in 1835 shortly after the outbreak of the Carlist War. The Tsar saw no reason to alter his view that Queen Isabella had wrongfully deprived her uncle Don Carlos of the Spanish throne after her father's death in 1833. In 1842 Russia had restored diplomatic relations with Portugal (which had been broken off at the same time as with Spain), but Nicholas had no wish to become more deeply involved at this juncture in the complicated affairs of the Iberian peninsula which had been a subject of dispute between Great Britain and France in 1846. Only after his death was the situation to change and diplomatic relations were resumed in 1856.[34]

By 5 December Baron Lieven had returned to Saint Petersburg and was able to report personally to the Tsar about his visits to Olomouc, Vienna and Warsaw. There is little on record about this visit, apart from a brief letter from Lieven written while he was in Vienna. It appears that Lieven's visit only confirmed Nicholas in his view that the new Austrian government had taken on an impossible task. Even if it succeeded in defeating the Hungarians on the battlefield, much would still have to be done afterwards to rebuild an empire which had been shattered to its foundations.[35] Lieven confirmed Fonton's message that Windischgraetz could count on Russian military support and could make use of the troops stationed in Russian Poland and the western provinces.[36] After Lieven had left, Fonton was able to forward to Saint Petersburg details of Austria's plans for the forthcoming campaign, and also to give the Tsar some idea of the thinking in Vienna about Hungary's future place in the monarchy once the campaign was over.[37]

However, there is no indication that Lieven was informed during his visit about the decision taken in early November that Ferdinand should abdicate in favour of Francis Joseph.[38] Consequently the arrival in Saint Petersburg of the Austrian court's special envoy, the Archduke William, took Nicholas by surprise.[39] The Archduke brought with him letters from the Emperor, Francis Joseph and the Archduchess Sophie, all of which begged the Tsar to give the new ruler of the Habsburg Empire the same support as he had given his predecessors. Sophie did not conceal from the Tsar the anguish she had felt during the past months about events in Austria and hoped that he would be spared the same ordeal. Her words struck a sympathetic chord with Nicholas' wife.[40]

The Austrians had also been distressed that two Hungarian regiments bearing Nicholas' name had gone over to the rebels. By way of recompense, Francis Joseph offered Nicholas the rank of Field Marshal in the Austrian army, an honour which the Tsar declined to accept on the grounds that he did not have the rank of Field Marshal in his own army.[41]

The Archduke's visit provided confirmation of the view expressed by Medem (who continued to remain in Olomouc, unlike the remainder of the diplomatic corps) that the new Austrian government wished to have an *entente cordiale* with Russia.[42] Two of his entourage openly stated that the parliament in Kroměříž would be dissolved and a constitution, drawn up in Vienna, imposed on the monarchy, as soon as the forthcoming campaign in Hungary was over.[43] Nesselrode expressed his satisfaction about Austria's foreign policy in his reply to Medem, adding that the Russian government completely approved of the robust line of conduct it was adopting towards Palmerston who continued to press Austria to relinquish its Italian possessions.[44]

For his part, Nicholas was pleased at the prospect of being able to take under his wing the new Austrian emperor, to whom he had given a lesson in arms-drill at their first meeting in Vienna when Francis Joseph was only five years old.[45] He was reasonably optimistic that Windischgraetz would defeat the Hungarians, who in his view were no longer engaged in a national war, but were being supported by 'a gang of revolutionaries', reinforced by Polish emigrés.[46] His second son Constantine was despatched to Vienna with appropriate replies to the letters sent to the Tsar, but was enjoined simply to listen and not become involved in political discussions.[47] At the conclusion of the visit Francis Joseph wrote yet again to the Tsar, expressing the hope that the armies of Austria and Russia would work together, as they had done in the past, to defend the principles of order and justice in Europe.[48] The young Emperor set great store by the military virtues of obedience to orders and discipline, and at this early stage in his reign he was to be much influenced by his chamberlain, General Grünne, who had left the service of the Archduke Stephen in Hungary earlier in the year because he disapproved of the Palatine's attitude towards the Hungarian independence movement.

While the alliance between the two empires was being consolidated at the highest political level, Schwarzenberg took immediate action to fill the post of the ambassadorship to Russia which still remained vacant as a result of the confused political situation of the past months. He saw no reason to reject Metternich's original choice for the post, Count Karl von Buol-Schauenstein, who was related by marriage to the Russian ambassador in Berlin. Buol was a career diplomat who had been reluctant to take up his new appointment until Austria had a government which was likely to remain in power for some time to come. He left Olomouc for Warsaw and Saint Petersburg on 18 December and arrived there on 26 December. The very next day he saw Nesselrode and had his first audience with the Tsar two days later.

In the instructions he received shortly after his arrival, Schwarzenberg made it clear that Buol's main task was the restoration of the Austrian alliance with Russia 'not exactly on the old footing, but in a form conforming to the interests and dignity of Austria'.[49] Every effort was to be made to make use of the Tsar's evident goodwill towards the young Francis Joseph and his wish to see the Habsburg monarchy remain intact and maintain its preponderant position in the German Confederation.

However, on assuming office, Schwarzenberg found himself faced with exactly the same problem as that which had faced Metternich at the beginning of 1848. This was the weakness of Austria's financial situation, which had been made even worse by Kossuth's decision to issue Hungary's own currency. If a solution was not found to Austria's financial difficulties, there was a grave risk that the government would collapse. Accordingly, Buol was told that his first task was to seek a loan from Russia to assist Austria while the army continued its task of restoring order throughout the monarchy. If he succeeded in this, he would have rendered his country the greatest possible service.[50] The timing of the Austrian request could not have been more unfortunate, since the Tsar's decision not to reduce the size of the Russian forces during the winter months had only served to increase the strain on Russia's already over-stretched resources.

Out of a total deficit in 1848 of 30 million silver roubles (£5 million) two-thirds had been caused by extra defence expenditure. Fortunately gold production in Siberia continued to be satisfactory, but the State Bank had been forced to issue 3 million silver roubles to provide extra cover for the increase in paper money. Despite this, Nicholas was in no doubt that the financial strain was worth it if Russia was thereby protected from revolution.[51]

It was therefore hardly surprising that neither Nesselrode nor the Tsar showed any willingness to discuss the question of a loan at Buol's first meetings with them. Nesselrode told Buol privately that Russia had its own financial problems and it was agreed that the matter would be raised again at a later meeting. The question of a loan was to haunt Buol for the next few weeks: the negotiations were to drag on until June when they were overtaken by the more pressing matter of Russian military intervention. Russia declined to advance Austria any ready money, and an offer of a loan in French bonds was unacceptable.[52] At one stage in the negotiations Nicholas told Buol quite bluntly that Austria could not have any money from him because he needed it all for himself.[53]

Instead of a discussion about the terms of a loan, the Tsar was much more interested at his first audience with Buol in learning more from him about Schwarzenberg's plans for the future organisation of the monarchy. He made it clear that he was opposed to the granting of a constitution, and hoped that Francis Joseph would not follow the example of the King of Prussia. It was essential that Austria should continue to play an important part in the German Confederation. Buol, who was doubtless well aware of Schwarzenberg's plan to impose his own constitution on the monarchy, avoided further discussion of this topic, and reminded the Tsar that the future of the Habsburg monarchy depended on the successful outcome of the offensive against Hungary which had begun on 15 December. The audience ended with a proposal from the Tsar that he should meet Francis Joseph in Warsaw in the spring.[54]

While all these changes had been taking place in Vienna and Olomouc, much had also been happening in Hungary since Kossuth had been appointed Head of the Committee of National Defence under the authority of the Hungarian parliament. After the defeat of the Hungarian army at Schwechat there was little optimism about the future among the moderates, who still hoped that some kind of reconciliation could be reached with the government in Vienna. Since the resignation of Batthyány and other ministers in September the Hungarian cabinet had ceased to exist. Kossuth's efforts to form another cabinet met with no success, partly because the moderates felt he was closely allied with the radicals, especially László Madarász, who was to become Minister of the Interior in 1849. As for the higher aristocracy, they would, in the words of the British ambassador in Vienna, have been only too glad to send Kossuth to the gallows.[55] It was at this time that the so-called 'Peace Party' came into being whose efforts to effect a reconciliation with the government in Vienna were to continue for the rest of the year and into 1849.

Kossuth continued the efforts which Batthyány had begun to gain recognition for Hungary's independence abroad, but his efforts were to be no more successful than those of the Wallachian government during its brief period of independence. The two Hungarian delegates sent to the Frankfurt Parliament in May were withdrawn in September since their credentials had expired. One of them, László Szalay, was then sent to Britain where he made a vain effort in December to persuade Palmerston to recognise the independence of Hungary. The reply from Palmerston's Under-Secretary at the Foreign Office stated tersely that the British government had no knowledge of Hungary 'except as one of the component parts of the Austrian Empire'.[56] Nor did László Teleki fare any better in Paris, where Batthyány had sent him at the end of August. Neither Cavaignac nor his Foreign Minister Bastide were interested in a French proposal made earlier in the year that there should be an exchange of diplomatic envoys. Szalay left London, but was eventually replaced by Ferenc Pulszky, who had left Hungary in December at the time of the Austrian invasion. Both Teleki and Pulszky worked hard in journalistic circles in Paris and London to win support for Hungary and achieved a measure of success. Indeed, at the suggestion of Metternich (who was living in London) the Austrians were to mount a counter-offensive in the British press towards the end of 1849, but neither of the Hungarians were able to persuade the British and French governments to alter their attitude about the recognition of Hungarian independence.

At the end of November Kossuth made an attempt to reach a negotiated settlement with Austria by making use of the good offices of William Stiles, the diplomatic representative of the United States of America in Vienna. Kossuth's letter was brought to Stiles by a female courier in a clandestine fashion, and as a result, the approach was immediately reported to the Austrian authorities by the locally-employed US consul, who was a police informer. Stiles, however, had no intention of concealing the approach, and discussed it at once with Schwarzenberg and Windischgraetz. The Austrian reply was uncompromising; the Hungarians must surrender unconditionally.[57] Shortly afterwards the Hungarians learnt of the abdication of the Emperor Ferdinand and the accession of Francis Joseph. After a debate in parliament Kossuth persuaded the deputies on 7 December to agree to the issue of a proclamation stating that this was an unconstitutional act. According to the Hungarian constitution, the Emperor Ferdinand was still the lawful ruler of Hungary, while Francis Joseph was a usurper. The proclamation was of little interest to the government in Vienna, who were determined to bring the Hungarians into line with the other nationalities in the monarchy, and were not interested in legal arguments about the Hungarian constitution.

By far the most pressing task facing Kossuth and the Committee of National Defence was to ensure that the Hungarian national army would be capable of defeating the Austrians after its crushing defeat at Schwechat. The political and military reorganisation which the Austrians had been compelled to carry out after the defeat of the revolt in Vienna gave the Hungarians a valuable six weeks' respite from fighting which was turned to good account by the officer whom Kossuth appointed on 1 November to replace General Móga. This was Artúr Görgey, who was to become as great a rival of Kossuth as Széchenyi had been in the years before 1848. Born in 1818, Görgey's father was a member of the Hungarian minor nobility, while his mother was of German origin. As a result of financial difficulties in his family, Görgey, who had originally wished to become a Lutheran pastor, decided to join the Habsburg army as an engineering cadet. After obtaining his commission he became a cavalry officer and served under Windischgraetz in Bohemia. In 1845, despite Windischgraetz's attempt to prevent him from doing so, he resigned his commission, partly because he found it impossible to live on his pay, and partly because he was bored by the tedium of life as a soldier in peacetime. He then went to study chemistry at Prague University and was offered a post at L'vov University after graduation. By this time he had married a young French governess as poor as himself.

The events of March and April 1848 made him decide to volunteer for the Hungarian national army, the *honvéd*, which was created by the Batthyány government, and in June 1848 he was commissioned as a captain. His first tasks were the study of the manufacture of percussion caps, and the acquisition of information to help Hungary establish its own munitions factory. Other assignments followed, and by September Görgey was a major in command of a National Guard unit in the area between the rivers Danube and Tisza. It was at this time that he acquired notoriety by ordering the court-martial and hanging of a Hungarian magnate, Count Ödön Zichy, a member of one of Hungary's most prominent families. The charge against Zichy was one of treason and collaboration with General Jelačić. The hanging took place on 30 September, and was a clear demonstration of Görgey's commitment to the Hungarian national cause. Half-scholar and half-soldier, Görgey, who on his own admission thought in German, had decided that he was prepared to defend the rights of Hungary which were enshrined in the constitution.[58] Görgey was also able to demonstrate his skill as a soldier by helping to defeat the Croatian force commanded by General Roth at Ozora on 7 October. Even although Görgey had already demonstrated an unfortunate tendency to disobey the orders of his superiors if he disagreed with them, it was clear to Kossuth that a young officer of his ability and commitment to the Hungarian cause was the type he was seeking to restore the morale of the Hungarian army after its defeat at Schwechat.

The Hungarian army which existed at the beginning of November 1848 was a mixed force consisting of regular Habsburg units, National Guard formations (which were usually poorly equipped and lacked training), and a number of *honvéd* battalions which were to increase rapidly as a result of the introduction of conscription in September. There was a serious shortage of senior officers, which made it impossible to organise the army on the traditional basis of the infantry regiment. Thus the battalion became the basic fighting unit to which cavalry and artillery formations were added to form the larger brigades and divisions which made up each army corps. It was not until the beginning of 1849 that any attempt was made to form a traditional command structure, but even after this had been done, there was a lack of co-ordination at the top, and each corps commander tended to operate independently.

In theory, the corps commanders were subordinate to the Minister of Defence, General Mészáros, who had been transferred from a regimental command in Italy to his post in Batthyány's cabinet in April 1848. In practice, Mészáros was little more than an administrative channel for the flood of orders issued by Kossuth as the civilian commander-in-chief, and he resigned his post after the deposition of the Habsburgs in April 1849. In fact, Kossuth never succeeded in imposing his will on his corps commanders, who were all professional soldiers except for the radical politician, General Perczel. Most of the professional officers in the army were loyal to the Emperor as King of Hungary and to the constitution, rather than to the revolution, and were consequently regarded with some suspicion by Kossuth and the more radical politicians.

Unlike Kossuth who was first and foremost a politician who found himself having to deal with military affairs by virtue of the office he held, Görgey was a professional soldier of a distinctly practical nature. Soldiers needed discipline, boots, bullets and pay, rather than high-flown oratory about the defence of freedom and their native land. Nor did he believe in the virtues of partisan warfare waged by irregular troops of which Kossuth was an enthusiastic exponent, possibly under the influence of General Bem.[59] In this respect, Görgey was being somewhat unfair to Kossuth who was making desperate efforts at this time to obtain supplies and equipment for the Hungarian forces.[60] It was inevitable, therefore, that a clash would occur before long between the two men about the proper response to Windischgraetz's invasion.

When Görgey was given his command, his task was to defend western Hungary from the Austrians. Windischgraetz's main force moved along the right bank of the Danube making for Budapest with Görgey conducting an orderly withdrawal in the face of an enemy who were superior in numbers (52 000 men compared with Görgey's 30 000). In order to preserve the mobility of his own force, Görgey left a garrison in the fortress of Komárno on the Danube and decided not to make a stand at Győr as had been originally planned, but to continue his withdrawal in the general direction of Budapest. He was certain that the main aim of the Austrian army would be the capture of Budapest in the expectation that this would lead to the collapse of Hungarian resistance. He further reasoned that Windischgraetz would not be anxious to cross the river Tisza into eastern Hungary so long as the virtually impregnable fortress of Komárno on the Danube, which had already refused an Austrian request to surrender, posed a threat to the Austrian lines of communication. The longer he could keep his army intact by avoiding a major battle with the enemy, the better. This reasoning (which was to prove to be entirely accurate) did not meet with the approval of Kossuth who constantly urged Görgey to make a stand and engage the enemy.

On 30 December the Hungarian situation was made worse when a force commanded by General Perczel was heavily defeated by the Austrians at Mór some fifty miles west of Budapest. The following day there was a stormy debate in the Hungarian parliament about future policy. Eventually it was decided that the Committee of National Defence and parliament should evacuate the capital and move to Debrecen in eastern Hungary. At the same time it was agreed that a delegation headed by Batthyány, the former Prime Minister, and the ever-hopeful Deák should travel to Windischgraetz's headquarters to offer an armistice in exchange for Austrian recognition of the April Laws. The evacuation from Budapest began on New Year's Eve by train on the newly-built railway as far as Szolnok[61] and then by road to Debrecen. The crown of Saint Stephen and the banknote printing press were safely evacuated, but the precious metal reserve of gold and silver worth 2 million Austrian gulden (£200 000), which Kossuth had carefully built up, was left behind and subsequently fell into Austrian hands. There are good grounds for believing that this was a deliberate act by Ferenc Duschek, the Habsburg official who worked as Under-Secretary in the Hungarian Ministry of Finance.[62]

The peace delegation reached Windischgraetz's headquarters at Bicske on 3 January and met with the same reception as that accorded to Stiles in Vienna. The Hungarian terms were rejected with scorn and in a famous phrase, Windischgraetz, who refused to admit Batthyány to his presence, informed the delegation that he did not negotiate with rebels. Its members were allowed to notify the parliament of the failure of their mission, but were not permitted to return to Hungarian-occupied territory. Batthyány was arrested in Pest a few days after it was occupied by the Austrians and remained in prison until he was executed on 6 October.

On 4 January the Hungarians suffered a further defeat at the hands of the Austrians when General Schlick's forces which had crossed into northeast Hungary from Galicia defeated a small force led by Mészáros near Kosiče. Two days earlier a Hungarian council of war chaired in Kossuth's absence by László Csányi, a government commissioner, adopted a plan put forward by another former professional officer, Colonel Klapka. Budapest was to be abandoned and central Hungary between the Danube and Tisza evacuated. General Perczel was to defend the southern part of Hungary while Görgey's forces were to move north to attack a small Austrian force led by General Simunich which had entered northwest Hungary. After defeating Simunich Görgey was then to turn north-east and move through northern Hungary (the territory of modern Slovakia) to secure the mining towns before reaching Košice. On 4 January

Görgey's forces crossed the Danube from Buda to Pest over the newly-constructed Chain Bridge and moved north to Vác. For the next few weeks Görgey would be out of touch with Kossuth and the parliament in Debrecen, which now lay open to an attack by the Austrian forces of both Windischgraetz and Schlick. About midday on 5 January Windischgraetz and his staff entered Budapest in triumph. The capture of the Hungarian capital had taken only three weeks and there was a widespread feeling in Vienna that the war would soon be over. On the same day Görgey, who had been struggling to keep his army in being in the face of large-scale defections as a result of recent Hungarian set-backs, decided to issue a manifesto about the political aims of his army. The Vác manifesto, as the document came to be known, made it clear that Görgey's Army of the Upper Danube would remain loyal to the constitution sanctioned by the Emperor as King of Hungary and would take its orders from a Minister of War appointed by the King. The latter statement was a clear challenge to the authority of Kossuth and the Committee of National Defence. The army was also prepared to come to an arrangement with the government in Vienna subject to certain safeguards. As the first public expression of the differences between Görgey and Kossuth, the manifesto only served to widen the breach between the two men. At the same time it served a definite military purpose by stemming the flow of defections.

Kossuth drew the erroneous conclusion from the publication of the manifesto that Görgey was about to make a separate peace with the Austrians, but his assumption was wrong. Görgey had no intention of giving up the struggle, as he made clear at the end of January to an emissary from Windischgraetz who promised him immunity, if his army surrendered unconditionally. The emissary was sent away with a copy of the Vác manifesto.

In Olomouc, the young Francis Joseph could feel glad that Windischgraetz's campaign had started well. On Christmas Eve his parents had given him as a present the portraits of the three saviours of the monarchy, Windischgraetz, Jelačić and Radetzky.[63] The occupation of Bratislava on 18 December was followed by the capture of Győr ten days later and the arrival of a special courier, Count Móric Pálffy, with a box containing the keys of the town.[64]

In Saint Petersburg the Tsar was also feeling guardedly optimistic. Although he had decided to keep the Russian forces at full strength despite the strain on Russia's finances, he doubted whether they would be needed in Hungary where the war appeared to be over.

He hoped the rebels would not be able to escape punishment by escaping to Turkey. However, he was still uncertain about future events in Europe in the coming year, but saw no reason for Russia to do more than watch and wait. Meanwhile he hoped Paskevich would be spared many further years of life to continue as the guardian of the wall he had built to protect Russia from the tide of revolution.[65]

But Windischgraetz was not to follow up his initial military success, and would soon be in difficulties with the government in Vienna about the way in which he was attempting to administer occupied Hungary. Nor would he be able to prevent the Hungarians from recovering from their earlier defeats. The first Hungarian success was to come in Transylvania where General Bem was to cause the Tsar to revise his opinion about Windischgraetz's military ability, and where events were to lead to the first Russian intervention in the Habsburg Empire.

4 The Russian Intervention in Transylvania and its Consequences

One of the consequences of the Austrian government's decision to reject the April Laws was the ending of the union between Hungary and Transylvania which the Emperor had ratified in June. The Austrian change in attitude towards Hungary only served to increase the confusion in a province where the diversity of races, languages and religions was one of the greatest in the Habsburg empire. Out of a population of about two million, more than half were Rumanians, the majority of whom were peasants under an obligation to work on the estates of their Hungarian landlords and who had no political rights. The Hungarians, who were the second largest group, were closely identified with their fellow Hungarian speakers, the Széklers, who were, however, of a different racial origin. The third largest group were the German-speaking Saxons whose settlements dated back to the fourteenth century. The Rumanians were Greek Orthodox or Uniate, but their church did not receive the same official recognition as the churches of the Catholic Hungarians, Lutheran Saxons and Calvinist or Unitarian Széklers. It was therefore hardly surprising that the Rumanians had bitterly opposed the union with Hungary and had made every effort to persuade the Emperor Ferdinand to grant them a measure of political freedom.

At the end of September a second National Assembly was held at Blaj, at which the Rumanians reaffirmed their rejection of the union with Hungary and their loyalty to the Emperor. With Austrian approval, a Rumanian Pacification Committee (later to be called a National Committee) was established, and authority was given for the creation of a National Guard and a national army consisting of fifteen Rumanian legions which would be armed by the Austrians. A belated attempt made by the Hungarian special commissioner Baron Miklós Vay to offer concessions to the Rumanians was rejected.[1] Two Rumanian Frontier Guard regiments announced that they would no longer take orders from the Hungarian Ministry of War.

After their meeting at Blaj the leaders of the Rumanian National Committee travelled to Sibiu for talks with General Anton Puchner, the sixty-nine-year-old Hungarian-speaking commander of the Austrian forces in Transylvania, who had fought with distinction in the Napoleonic Wars. An agreement on future cooperation was reached, but Puchner was careful to avoid giving any commitment to the Rumanians about their future status in the monarchy. On 18 October Puchner announced that he was taking over the civil administration of Transylvania, now that the Palatine of Hungary was no longer in office. He declared that the activities of the Hungarian Committee of National Defence and its emissaries were illegal, and exhorted all the peoples of the province to fight for the Emperor in the forthcoming struggle with the Hungarians. Bishop Şaguna, the Rumanian Orthodox Bishop, and the Rumanian National Committee immediately issued their own proclamations calling on all Rumanians to rise up against Hungarian rule. The Uniate Bishop, János Leményi, declined to follow their example and remained loyal to the Hungarians. The Saxons decided to throw in their lot with the Rumanians and Puchner sought assistance from their spiritual leader, the Lutheran pastor Stephan Roth who had attended the first National Assembly held at Blaj in May.[2] At the same time the Széklers proclaimed their loyalty to the Hungarians at an assembly held at Lutiţa, and two Székler Frontier Guard regiments announced that they would no longer take orders from the Austrian military authorities. It was not long before fighting broke out between the various nationalities and the province was plunged into a vicious civil war.

On 1 November Puchner wrote a long report to Windischgraetz about the problems with which he was faced. His chief anxiety was the shortage of troops with which to defend the province, and the poor communications both with Vienna and the units stationed in the north. He was doubtful whether the Rumanians and Saxons would be of much practical use, and he was anticipating difficulties in defeating the Széklers who were renowned for their fighting qualities. If it was impossible to receive reinforcements from Galicia, he hoped he might be allowed to make use of the Russian troops stationed in the Danubian principalities.[3] As we have mentioned in the previous chapter, Puchner was not the only Austrian military commander to raise the question of Russian military aid with Windischgraetz at this time, and like the others, he was informed that the government in Vienna would have to approve any such request.

At the beginning of November Puchner's forces in the province went into action with the dual aim of restoring imperial authority and attacking the main Hungarian forces in the rear. The task did not prove to be as difficult as Puchner had expected. On 17 November the administrative capital of Cluj was occupied and by the end of the month Austrian units had reached Ciucea near the Hungarian border. Only in the extreme south-east, in the county of Trei Scaune, was there any serious resistance which came, as Puchner had expected, from the Széklers. The possibility that the town of Braşov would be captured caused the local Austrian commander, Colonel Stutterheim, to get in touch with General Engelhardt, the commander of the Russian troops sent up to the Wallachian frontier in November by General Lüders. In a letter written to Stutterheim on 11 December, Engelhardt, while expressing sympathy and hoping that the Austrians would defeat the Széklers, made it clear that he had no authority to allow his troops to cross the frontier.[4]

While these events were taking place, Kossuth had decided to offer the command of the Hungarian forces in Transylvania to General Bem, who, it will be recalled, had succeeded in escaping to Bratislava after the collapse of the revolt in Vienna. Bem, who was opposed to the creation of special Polish units in the Hungarian army, was not deterred by the prospect of taking over an army composed of soldiers who were strangers to him. He confidently predicted that he would defeat the Austrians and re-occupy Cluj by New Year's Day 1849.[5] The appointment was announced officially on 1 December and within a few days Bem had arrived in south-east Hungary to take over command of the Hungarian army. On 17 December he held his first parade and addressed his officers in German, which he spoke with a strong Polish accent. He warned them that he intended to impose strict discipline and would shoot those who disobeyed his orders. On the other hand, those who fought well would be rewarded. His methods were to prove to be successful and he became very popular, especially with the Széklers.[6]

After a short delay to allow for the arrival of reinforcements, Bem went into action on 20 December, and by 26 December he had carried out his promise to Kossuth and re-occupied Cluj. In a proclamation Bem stated that he had come with the Hungarian army to free Transylvania from the yoke of reaction and military despotism. He then set off in a north-west direction to drive the Austrian forces out of northern Transylvania and on 2 January 1849 his forces occupied the towns of Năsăud and Bistriţa. The commander of the Austrian forces, Colonel Urban, was forced to retreat into Bukovina and on 5 January

1849 an engagement took place at Vatra Dornei inside the province.
With the occupation of Cluj, Bistriţa and the two mountain passes leading into Bukovina, the whole of northern Transylvania was now in Hungarian hands. In just over a fortnight Bem had transformed the situation and fully justified the hopes which Kossuth had placed in him. The Hungarian leader was not slow to make the most of Bem's success, which did little to endear the Pole to Görgey and the other Hungarian generals, as they continued their slow withdrawal into northern and eastern Hungary. In a burst of enthusiasm Petőfi, who was to be killed later in the year while fighting with Bem's army, wrote of the invincible power of the union which had now been created between the Hungarian and Polish nations.[7] But Kossuth's decision to employ the services of General Bem and another prominent Polish emigré, General Dembiński, only made it easier for the government in Vienna to remind others, including the Tsar, that the Hungarian revolt had ceased to be a purely national one.

The entry of Bem's forces into Bukovina on 5 January, the same day on which Windischgraetz's army had made its triumphant entry into Budapest, caused consternation in Vienna and Saint Petersburg because of the threat it posed to Galicia, Russian Poland and Russia's western provinces. In eastern Galicia, General Hammerstein, fearful of another rising, imposed a state of siege. Like General Puchner, he had discussed the question of the use of Russian troops with Windischgraetz in November and received the same reply that the government in Vienna must give their approval to any such request. He now wrote directly to Schwarzenberg urging him to seek Russian military assistance.[8] At the same time he made an unofficial appeal through the Russian consul in Brody to General Cheodaev, the commander of the Russian Fourth Corps stationed in the western provinces, for assistance in dealing with Bem's invasion, pointing out that he believed Bem intended to attack Chernovtsy, the provincial capital. Cheodaev's Chief of Staff, Colonel Veselitsky, replied that the Russian troops had no authority to cross the frontier.

When Paskevich learnt of the approach, he ordered the formation of two special detachments to deal with the threatened incursion. At the same time he informed the Tsar and added that he had sent two officers to discuss the matter further with Hammerstein and Cheodaev. Secret orders were issued to Cheodaev authorising him to cross the border and to deal with the threat of attack and then return to Russia. The Tsar was content with Paskevich's action, but stressed that any Russian forces which crossed the frontier must return immediately, once they had defeated Bem's forces.[9] At the same time an order was issued about taking stricter security measures on the frontier with Galicia.[10] However, Bem did not penetrate any further into Bukovina as the Austrians had expected. Instead, he left a small force in northern Transylvania and turned south to join the Széklers.

In Sibiu and Braşov the leaders of the Rumanian and Saxon communities were becoming increasingly concerned about the activities of the Széklers (or Mongols, as Bishop Şaguna preferred to call them). Puchner had already asked General Lüders to take his pay chest and archives into safe keeping. This request was followed by the visit to Bucharest of a deputation of Saxons from Braşov and a joint Rumanian and Saxon deputation from Sibiu requesting Russian military aid on humanitarian grounds to protect the population. Lüders refused the request of both delegations, pointing out that he had received instructions from the Tsar in November not to cross the frontier into Transylvania. Nevertheless, he agreed to take all possible steps to protect any refugees who might cross the frontier and to seek further guidance from Saint Petersburg.[11] An approach to Fuad Effendi for the use of Turkish troops was equally unsuccessful but, like Lüders, Fuad Effendi agreed to seek instructions from his government. The leader of the delegation from Sibiu was Bishop Şaguna, who was planning to travel to Olomouc to plead the rights of the Rumanians with Francis Joseph. It was therefore natural that he should approach the Austrian consul-general in Bucharest for support from Vienna for his proposal that Russian troops should assist the Austrians.[12] Shortly after these visits, to which Puchner had given his reluctant agreement, General Pfersmann from Sibiu met Lüders' Chief of Staff, Colonel Nepokoychitsky, at the frontier to plead for the despatch of a small number of Russian troops, but was told that nothing could be done until an answer had been received from Saint Petersburg.[13]

In Budapest Windischgraetz was as concerned as his army commanders about the Hungarian successes in Transylvania. Fully aware of the views of Schwarzenberg and other ministers, he made a tentative appeal to Francis Joseph that the question of Russian military aid should be re-examined.[14] But Schwarzenberg remained adamant that Austria should fight its own battles, and after a meeting of the Council of Ministers on 12 January,[15] both Hammerstein and Windischgraetz were informed of the undesirability of calling in the Russians.[16] The same view was repeated to the Russian ambassador,[17] nor did the

Tsar's approval of Paskevich's actions in support of Hammerstein make Schwarzenberg change his mind.[18]

Despite Schwarzenberg's reaction, Windischgraetz continued to plead even more urgently for Russian assistance after he had received Puchner's reports about the deteriorating situation in the south-east of Transylvania. Realising that the entry of Russian troops would have international repercussions, he suggested that Puchner should take the initiative, and that the appropriate diplomatic action to regularise the intervention could be taken *post facto*.[19] In Saint Petersburg the Tsar was equally sympathetic to the plight of the Austrian military and the Saxon inhabitants of Sibiu and Braşov. Instructions were therefore sent to Lüders authorising him to make a limited intervention if there was a direct request received from the local Austrian military commander, a course of action with which Buol had perforce agreed, since he lacked any instructions from Vienna.[20] In Nicholas' view, Russia should continue to take action only when there was a direct threat to Russian territory. Even Hammerstein's withdrawal of his request for aid in the face of Schwarzenberg's unwillingness to approve it appeared to the Tsar to be a further example of the Austrian government's hypocritical attitude to the realities facing military commanders. Apart from this, the Tsar feared that Austria was faced with the prospect of a long-drawn-out war with Hungary which would only undermine the position of the Habsburg monarchy in the German Confederation and in the struggle to prevent Prussia assuming the leadership of a united Germany.[21]

In fact, Schwarzenberg realised as well as the Tsar that military realities would probably make it necessary for Puchner to seek assistance from the Russians. But he was determined that he would not be forced to make an official appeal to the Russians, and he therefore wrote to both Windischgraetz and Buol that Austria ought to be able to restore order without foreign aid.[22] However, his instructions to General Puchner were worded in a much more ambiguous manner, and were despatched by the hand of a special courier who was to provide verbal amplification of the written instructions. The official line of the Austrian government remained unchanged, and Puchner was to await the arrival of reinforcements which would probably be delayed because of the distance and the winter weather. However, if Puchner found himself compelled to seek Russian help because of the exigencies of the local situation, he was to send a full report to Vienna justifying his action and to explain to Lüders that he had acted on his own initiative, without the approval of his government.²³ Unfortunately for Schwarzenberg, his carefully-worded letter did not reach Puchner until 5 February, by which time it had been overtaken by events.

On 16 January General Bem, continuing his advance south, had defeated Puchner at Găneşti and forced him to retreat to Sibiu. On the evening of 20 January, the day on which Schwarzenberg wrote his letter, Puchner called a meeting of his military council in Sibiu to discuss the question of seeking Russian military aid. In the face of a report that Braşov was about to be captured by the Széklers, the council finally decided to seek Russian assistance. Puchner sent one of his officers to Bucharest to arrange the despatch of Russian troops, while he left Sibiu to take command of the Austrian forces which were about to commence fighting with Bem.²⁴ Puchner's envoy reached Bucharest the following evening at the same time as a Russian courier arrived from Saint Petersburg with the Tsar's instructions to Lüders that he was authorised to make a positive response to a definite request from the local Austrian military commander. Besides this visit, Lüders also received requests for aid from two other Austrian generals, General Pfersmann in Sibiu and General Schurtter in Braşov. As a result of these requests, he decided to assemble two small columns which could relieve the Austrians in both towns, and wrote to Puchner that he was prepared to do so, provided he received a definite request to send aid in order that he could justify his action to the Tsar.²⁵ Two letters confirming the necessity for Russian aid arrived shortly afterwards from General Pfersmann, who had now assumed command in Sibiu in Puchner's absence, and General Schurtter. The two relief columns which Lüders had assembled each consisted of infantry, a small number of guns, and a large detachment of Cossacks. The column commanded by Major-General Engelhardt was expected to reach the frontier by 1 February and would then move on Braşov. If the town had already been captured, it was to halt at the frontier and await further orders. The same arrangements were to apply to the second column commanded by Colonel Skaryatin, which was destined to relieve Sibiu.²⁶

Both General Lüders and General Duhamel realised that the operations on which they were about to embark would be most unwelcome to the Turks, since the Russian army was using part of the territory of the Ottoman Empire as a base for military operations against another power, even although Russia was responding to an invitation from one of its allies. Besides this, they had already been instructed to adopt a firm attitude towards any members of the Hungarian forces who sought refuge in the Danubian principalities. The Tsar wished any Hungarians to be disarmed and handed back to the Austrian authorities, whereas the Turks were prepared to adopt a more humane attitude. Lüders and Duhamel were therefore not surprised to receive protests from Fuad Effendi about Russian policy, which was regarded as an infringement of Turkish neutrality.[27] Fuad Effendi also ensured that the British consul-general in Bucharest was kept fully informed of his exchanges with the Russians and complained bitterly to Colquhoun about the high-handed behaviour of the Russian generals.[28]

In Constantinople, Stratford Canning and his French colleague were as disturbed as Fuad Effendi at the course of events. They were well aware that the Russians, who were seeking a new legal basis for their continuing occupation of the Danubian principalities, were meeting with the normal delaying tactics used by the Turks on such occasions. Nevertheless, Canning felt that the Turks deserved some moral support, and as always, his thoughts turned to the possible deployment of a British and French naval squadron in the eastern Mediterranean to act as a deterrent to the Russians if they had 'great schemes in view'.[29] However, Canning was to receive no support for this proposal from Palmerston, who adhered to the view he had already expressed that the Russian occupation of the Danubian principalities had been carried out for limited purposes and that Russia did not intend to attack Turkey.[30]

On 4 February Skaryatin's relief column helped General Puchner to defeat Bem's forces at an engagement to the north of Sibiu. Three days earlier Engelhardt's column had made its way in extremely difficult wintry conditions through the mountain pass to the south of Braşov and occupied the town, which was threatened by an attack from the Széklers. The Austrians were delighted that they had at last received some assistance from the Russians, and continued their efforts to defeat the Hungarians elsewhere in the province, secure in the knowledge that the Russian troops were protecting their rear and lines of communication with southern Hungary. However, by mid-February Bem had succeeded in driving Puchner back to Sibiu, and an attempt by Urban in northern Transylvania to join forces with Puchner and cut Bem's lines of communication with Debrecen in northern Hungary was unsuccessful. Thus by the end of February the final outcome of the Austrian attempt to defeat the Hungarians in Transylvania was still uncertain.[31]

In Olomouc, Schwarzenberg was far from pleased by events in Transylvania, and requested the Russian ambassador to inform Lüders that he wished the Russian occupation of Sibiu and Braşov to last as short a time as possible.[32] At the same time he instructed Buol in Saint Petersburg to thank the Russians for their prompt action in saving the two Saxon towns from devastation by the Hungarians and Széklers.[33] Puchner, however, was requested to give an explanation for his failure to obey the orders he had received not to seek assistance from the Russians.[34] As an old and experienced officer, he had anticipated receiving such a letter, and had already taken the precaution of sending an interim reply, pointing out to Schwarzenberg that his original letter had taken a fortnight to arrive and had actually been received while fighting was in progress. The Russians had been summoned to the relief of Sibiu and Braşov by representatives of the local population, and not as a result of an official Austrian request. The same points were made at greater length in a formal reply to Schwarzenberg's letter, which Puchner was not able to send until the following month.[35]

The Tsar was not unduly concerned about what had happened. There had been an epidemic of measles in his family and he had been ill, possibly with shingles. The winter had been as severe as in 1848, but it had helped to reduce the number of cholera victims. As always, he was preoccupied with the situation in Germany, and the fear that war might break out again between Denmark and Prussia over Schleswig-Holstein. Nor was Nesselrode unduly perturbed, as he considered that Russia's response was a clear demonstration to the European powers of the strength of Russia's alliance with Austria, despite all that had happened in the previous year.[36] Nevertheless, a circular was sent to Russian missions abroad on 21 February outlining the reasons for the Russian action. The intervention had been carried out for humanitarian reasons and would only be temporary. Austria was sufficiently strong to be able to suppress the revolt in Transylvania without any further assistance from Russia.[37] As we have seen, Canning had been unable to persuade Palmerston to take any decisive action and as usual, the Duke of Wellington expressed his approval to Baron Brunnow in London of the Russian government's action. Nor was the new French government particularly interested. In Constantinople the Austrian ambassador did not hesitate to blame Windischgraetz for what had happened, and was careful to point out that the Austrian government had not made an official request.[38]

In Debrecen, Kossuth decided that the arrival of Russian troops in Transylvania offered Hungary an opportunity to present its case for an independent existence to another foreign government. Bem's political commissioner, László Csányi, who had been sent to Transylvania at the end of January, was therefore instructed to establish diplomatic relations with the commander of the Russian troops in the frontier area. Besides pleading Hungary's cause, the Hungarian envoy was to mention the possibility of the Hungarian crown being offered to the Duke of Leuchtenberg, one of the Tsar's son-in-laws. Kossuth's belief that the Tsar would be sympathetic to the Hungarian cause only demonstrated his complete inability to grasp the realities of foreign affairs. There is no evidence that Csányi made any attempt to carry out Kossuth's instructions which were, ironically enough, sent to the person who had originally reported in February that the Russian troops were Rumanian peasants dressed up by the Saxons to look like Russians. It need hardly be said that Kossuth preferred to reply on more trustworthy information, such as newspaper reports and those of General Bem whose experience of the Russian army was considerable.[39]

Meanwhile, General Lüders did his best to carry out the request he had received from Vienna and Saint Petersburg and enquired from Puchner when the two relief columns could be withdrawn now that they had served their original purpose. Puchner declined to let them go, as he needed them to protect his rear while he mounted an attack against Bem at Mediaş to the north of Sibiu.[40] The Tsar saw no reason to disagree with this decision, even although he was reluctant to allow his troops to remain in Transylvania any longer than was necessary.[41] On 2 March Puchner defeated Bem at Mediaş, but failed to follow up his success. Bem succeeded in eluding Puchner's forces which had turned east towards Sighişoara, and made straight for Sibiu, which he was able to occupy without much difficulty on 11 March. Colonel Skaryatin, realising that he could not hope to defend the town against a force which greatly outnumbered his own, withdrew to the Wallachian frontier. After further fighting, he was able to re-enter Wallachia through the Turnu Roşu mountain pass. By the time Puchner's forces reached the outskirts of Sibiu after several days marching from Sighişoara, it had already been occupied by Bem's forces. At this stage Puchner had to hand over command of the Austrian forces to General Kalliány because of illness.

In Braşov General Engelhardt was anxiously awaiting the arrival of the Austrian forces in order to be able to defend the town. When Kalliány's tired and hungry troops reached Braşov after beating off

The Russian Intervention in Transylvania and its Consequences 87

a Hungarian attack on the way, he realised, like Skaryatin, that the situation was hopeless. On 20 March he evacuated the town and retreated in good order into Wallachia, closely followed by a demoralised and exhausted Austrian force of some 8000 men, many of whom had to walk barefoot in the snow.[42] With the exception of the fortress of Alba Julia, which was to remain in Austrian hands throughout the war, Bem had reconquered the whole of Transylvania in the short space of three months.

For Bem, the capture of Sibiu was an important victory. He now began his efforts to reconcile the nationalities, which led to disputes with Csańyi and Kossuth who were unrelenting in their view that the Rumanians and Saxons had betrayed the interests of Hungary. According to one Hungarian participant in the campaign, many of the Russian prisoners Bem had captured were organised into a special Polish unit which afterwards fought alongside the Hungarians.[43]

Bem also met Effingham Grant from the British consulate-general in Bucharest, whom Colquhoun had sent to Transylvania with the agreement of Canning and Palmerston to obtain a first-hand report on Russian participation in the fighting. Grant appears to have given Bem the impression that Britain was opposed to the Russian action, and Bem optimistically informed the commander of the Hungarian forces in Bistriţa that he believed Britain would take steps to prevent a second Russian attempt to come to the aid of the Austrians. Grant also agreed to forward letters from Bem to the French consul-general in Bucharest, one of which was addressed to the French Vice-President whom Bem knew personally.[44] After Grant's departure, Bem suggested to the British and French representatives in Bucharest that their countries should send agents to his headquarters, a request which the Foreign Office refused.[45] Bem also took the opportunity to write to Fuad Effendi about the problems of the refugees who had fled from Transylvania to Wallachia. A proposal that Wallachia should establish diplomatic relations with Hungary was ignored by the *caimacan*.[46] This flurry of quasi-diplomatic activity was duly noted by the Russians and Austrians who were able to intercept Bem's letter to Bistriţa, and, as we shall see, they were to use it to good effect at a later date.

Both Duhamel and Lüders were extremely disconcerted by the Austrian debacle in Transylvania and the effects this could have elsewhere. While Lüders' thoughts turned to Galicia and Russian Poland,[47] Duhamel even suggested that Puchner's dislike of his Saxon allies had led him to take bribes from the Hungarians.[48] Austrian and Russian military co-operation in dealing with the Hungarian revolt had begun badly, and Colquhoun forecast that the bad feeling existing between the two armies would almost certainly grow worse. The Russians in Bucharest were especially worried about the likely reaction of the Tsar to the news of their enforced retreat.[49] In fact, Nicholas did not blame his commanders for what had happened and reserved his censure, as did Paskevich, for the Austrians. Nevertheless, in Nicholas' mind, the Poles were now the dominating force in the Hungarian army in Transylvania, and he believed they would seek to turn the province into a fortress. It was clear that the suppression of the Hungarian revolt was going to be a long-drawn-out affair.[50] Nicholas' views were shared by Nesselrode who, although relieved at the absence of a serious protest from Britain and France, felt that what had happened was 'a sad ending to our first involvement in the great social struggle taking place in the West'.[51]

General Puchner's failure to reimpose imperial authority in Transylvania was to be matched by Windischgraetz's failure to follow up his initial success in Hungary. At the beginning of February Görgey's forces ended their long march through Slovakia and broke through the Austrian positions in the Pass of Brezovica to the north west of Prešov. By 10 February they had reached Košice and were able to link up with Klapka's forces. General Schlick was forced to abandon north-east Hungary and moved west to join the main body of the Austrian army in the area of Budapest. Görgey's army was still intact, and the Austrian delay in moving on Debrecen had allowed Kossuth valuable time to reorganise and to establish a new base in Oradea, to the south-east of Debrecen, from which the Hungarian forces could be supplied.

While Görgey's forces had been out of contact with Debrecen, Kossuth had also decided to reorganise the *honvéd* by appointing a Commander-in-Chief and dividing it into eight army corps, of which Görgey's army was to be one. The person chosen to be the Commander-in-Chief was the Polish emigré general, Henryk Dembiński, who had been recruited in Paris at the end of 1848 by Kossuth's diplomatic representative, László Teleki. The fifty-seven year old general had been born in Galicia and trained as a military engineer. He had been personally decorated by Napoleon on the battlefield at Smolensk during the French invasion of Russia in 1812, and had fought against the Russians in 1831. During his years in emigration he had helped the Egyptians in their struggle against the Turks. Kossuth's choice of another Pole to command the Hungarian forces was an unpopular move, which was regarded by many Hungarian officers as a further proof of his lack of confidence in the man who had issued the Declaration of Vác. In addition, as we have already mentioned, it was a further indication to the Tsar that his old enemies the Poles were playing an increasingly important part in the Hungarian revolt. The appointment was accepted with bad grace by Görgey, and it was inevitable that the two men would clash about the future conduct of military operations, especially as Dembiński was not in the habit of discussing his plans with his subordinates.[52]

Besides appointing two Poles to senior posts in the Hungarian forces, Kossuth also agreed to the organisation of a Polish legion, although both Bem and Dembiński were opposed to the idea. Four companies were formed under the command of two participants in the 1830 revolt against the Russians, Józef Wysocki and Jerzy Bułharyn. Many of the Poles who enlisted in the legion had come to Hungary from Galicia. The total strength of the legion was about 3000, and although the Poles fought bravely, their endless squabbles both among themselves and with the Hungarians caused Kossuth much trouble and marred their fighting record.[53]

It was some time before Dembiński made a move against Windischgraetz. On 26 February a battle took place at Kápolna, some sixty miles north-east of Budapest. The fighting continued for a further two days and resulted in a Hungarian retreat to the east of the Tisza. There was a difference of opinion between Dembiński and Görgey in the way in which the retreat across the Tisza should be carried out. This led to a demand being made by many Hungarian officers to Bertalan Szemere, Kossuth's representative with the army, that Dembiński should be removed from his command. Kossuth was compelled to intervene personally and had no choice but to remove Dembiński. His successor was the *honvéd*'s Chief of Staff, General Antal Vetter, who was given command of all the Hungarian forces outside Transylvania. In early March Vetter became ill and as a result, Kossuth had to replace him by Görgey. However, he was only prepared to appoint Görgey as deputy Commander-in-Chief with control over the Tisza army. Although Kossuth claimed the right to act as the supreme commander of all Hungarian forces in the field, in practice the two main Hungarian armies were to be controlled by Görgey and Bem.

As a result of his apparent victory at Kápolna, Windischgraetz became more confident that the war against Hungary would soon be over. Although he was completely opposed to the granting of any kind of constitution, he was in no position to prevent Schwarzenberg and his colleagues deciding that the time had now come to pre-empt the publication of the draft constitution being prepared by the Austrian Parliament in Kroměříž. On 4 March the parliament was dissolved and the so-called 'bestowed constitution' drafted by Count Stadion was promulgated. The constitution provided for a unified and centralised state with an elected parliament and a responsible government under a Prime Minister. Hungary was divided into provinces according to nationality, which were to be treated as administrative areas. In fact, the constitution was never put into effect because of the emergency situation which still existed in the Habsburg empire. Nevertheless, its provisions enraged Hungarians of all shades of opinion, and was to cause Kossuth to respond to it by proclaiming Hungary's complete independence the following month.

Schwarzenberg was well aware that the granting of any kind of constitution would not be received favourably by the Tsar. He therefore took good care to ensure that its true nature was fully explained to the Russian diplomats in Austria, as well as Buol in Saint Petersburg. Both Medem and Fonton reported favourably[54] but Buol did not succeed in convincing the Tsar. Nicholas told him that the dilution of power which was inherent in a representative system of government could only lead to mutual deception.[55] Accordingly Nesselrode was only able to send Medem qualified approval of the Austrian proposal, although the Russians realised that there was nothing they could do to persuade the Austrian government to alter its decision.[56]

Schwarzenberg's faith that the Austrian army would help him in his task of restoring Austria's prestige abroad was to prove justified by Radetzky's victory over the Piedmontese army at Novara on 23 March. Twelve days earlier Piedmont had denounced the armstice signed in August the previous year and like Kossuth, the King had appointed a Polish emigré, General Wojciech Chrzanowski, as Chief of Staff of his army. Radetzky had expected the armistice to be broken and was well-prepared for a fresh outbreak of hostilities. After his defeat, King Charles Albert abdicated and his successor, Victor Emmanuel II, sued for an armistice. On 6 August a peace treaty signed at Milan brought the war between Austria and Piedmont to a conclusion. The Tsar was overjoyed by Radetzky's success and immediately announced his intention of appointing Radetzky a Field Marshal in the Russian army.

Nor did the discomfiture of another Polish emigré pass unnoticed.⁵⁷

Besides this good news from Italy, Schwarzenberg was also heartened to learn that on 3 April the King of Prussia had decided not to accept the offer of the imperial crown of Germany which the Frankfurt Parliament had made to him. For the remainder of the year, Austria and Prussia were to continue their struggle to occupy the central position in the German Confederation, but the final confrontation between them on this issue was not to take place until the end of 1850.

For the time being, the most important issue facing Austria was the resolution of the conflict with Hungary. Unfortunately, Windischgraetz's attempts to re-impose Austrian administration in the country had run into serious difficulties, especially in the financial field. Since the break with Austria in September, Kossuth had continued to print paper money for use in Hungary, with the result that it was in circulation everywhere when Windischgraetz and his army entered Budapest in January. Besides printing notes of larger denomination, the Hungarian government had also issued small denomination notes to replace the coins used for small change which had vanished from circulation. In the absence of any clear instructions from the Austrian Ministry of Finance, Windischgraetz had no alternative but to allow his troops and other officials to be paid in this money. The situation was also made worse by the issue of a decree on 3 March during Windischgraetz's absence from Budapest stating that the Austrian government did not propose to ban or confiscate the Kossuth notes. On his return to the capital Windischgraetz had hastily to rescind the decree and announce details of the exchange of the one and two forint notes issued on a legal basis and the banning of the other higher denomination notes.⁵⁸

As a result of Windischgraetz's failure to deal satisfactorily with this and other administrative matters in Hungary, the Austrian government decided to send a senior official with many years of financial and administrative experience to Windischgraetz's headquarters to make his own appraisal of the situation. The person chosen for this unrewarding mission was Kübeck von Kübau, who had retired in March 1848 because of illness, but had been recalled to service in December by the new government. He set off for Budapest on 17 March, having noted gloomily in his diary four days previously that Austrian finances were heading for a catastrophe.⁵⁹

On 23 March the Austrian Council of Ministers met to consider the military situation in Hungary in the light of the news which had just been received of the capture of Sibiu by Bem and his forces. There was much criticism of Windischgraetz's conduct of the campaign. However, after hearing a report from an official of the Ministry of War about the poor state of the Austrian army reserves, the council finally decided that Galicia was the only province from which it would be prudent to withdraw troops to assist the hard-pressed Austrian forces in Transylvania. At the same time it was agreed that Russia should be asked to deploy more troops along the frontier with Galicia.[60]

Although Schwarzenberg was still reluctant to allow Russian troops to cross the frontier into Galicia, he had realised for some time that the Austrian army was unlikely to be able to fight effectively in so many different places at once. Prussia's terms for aid were unacceptable, since they required Austria to abandon its position in the German Confederation. Accordingly, Schwarzenberg had no alternative but to turn to Russia, and it was obvious that Hungary was the place where the Tsar would be able to assist, provided that Austria could convince him that the Hungarian revolt was as serious a threat to Russia as it was to the Habsburg monarchy.[61]

Schwarzenberg therefore decided to accompany his official request for the deployment of Russian troops along the Galician frontier with a private letter to Buol in Saint Petersburg, which raised for the first time the possibility of Russia coming to Austria's assistance in Hungary, if the Austrians were unable to suppress the revolt themselves. Using words he had read only a few days earlier in a letter from Windischgraetz, Schwarzenberg stressed the fact that Hungary had now become the centre of activity for all those who were promoting the cause of revolution.[62] Despite the victory of Radetzky at Novara on 23 March, the same arguments were repeated to Buol even more forcefully only three days later, with great emphasis on the role of the Poles.[63] Nor did Schwarzenberg neglect the opportunity to discuss the matter with Medem in Olomouc, who wrote to Warsaw and Saint Petersburg that in his view the Austrian army was not strong enough to subdue the Hungarians without outside assistance. Medem also emphasised the role of the Poles and pointed out that Russia's interests were now converging with those of Austria, since assistance to Austria to suppress the revolt in Hungary would be equivalent to assisting in the suppression of a revolt which might spread to Russian Poland and elsewhere. In addition, Medem wrote for the first time of the dissatisfaction which was increasingly being felt in Austrian government circles with

The Russian Intervention in Transylvania and its Consequences 93

Windischgraetz's conduct of military and civil affairs in Hungary.⁶⁴ Despite these approaches to the Russian government, Schwarzenberg cautioned General Hammerstein in Galicia against following the example of General Puchner in Transylvania in seeking Russian military assistance. On the same day that Schwarzenberg wrote to Hammerstein, the latter was expressing the opinion that the withdrawal of troops from Galicia would be a dangerous action. The only solution to the problem was to allow the Russians to occupy the province.⁶⁵ Hammerstein's view was not shared by the civilian governor of Galicia, Count Goluchowski, who saw no necessity for a Russian occupation once the Austrian troops had left. It was finally decided that the troops should be moved, but Hammerstein was careful to reply to Schwarzenberg that he considered he had authority to seek Russian aid, but would only resort to this painful necessity if he had no other alternative.⁶⁶

Kübeck's arrival in Budapest on 18 March was a clear indication to Windischgraetz that there was disquiet in Olomouc and Vienna about his handling of affairs in Hungary. He told Kübeck that he had been unable to advance on Debrecen because of the threat that the fortress of Komárno posed to his lines of communication. He proposed to attack it at once and hoped to capture it within a few days. Success would mean the automatic release of a further 8000 troops for offensive operations. If he failed, he saw no alternative to seeking Russian assistance to protect himself in the north and east. He proposed that 40 000 Russians should enter northern Hungary, while 10 000 should advance into northern Transylvania from Bukovina. With this assistance he could then bring the war to a successful conclusion. He pointed out to Schwarzenberg that it would be better to seek Russian aid before he had been defeated, which would make the request less painful; an argument which must have struck Schwarzenberg as odd after the effect produced on the Russians by Bem's successes in Transylvania.⁶⁷

While Kübeck was content to let others who were better qualified pass judgement on Windischgraetz's conduct of military operations, he did feel competent to make his own appraisal of the state of the administration in Hungary. It was clear to him that Windischgraetz was attempting to do too much and had put his trust in subordinates who were not fit to carry out the tasks with which they had been entrusted. In addition, Windischgraetz was at odds with the government in Vienna and was reluctant to hand over the administration to anyone else. In short, drastic measures would have to be taken to remedy the situation.[68] On 29 March the Austrian Council of Ministers rejected Windischgraetz's proposal to seek Russian military assistance. Nor were they able to approve a plan put forward by Jelačić to launch an attack against Debrecen from south Hungary, since it required the use of a reserve of fifteen battalions which did not exist and was unlikely to be formed in the foreseeable future. At the suggestion of the Minister of War, General Welden, the military governor of Vienna, was invited to give his views. Welden had already prepared a written appreciation of the military situation which was unsparing in its criticism of Windischgraetz, who was accused of having attempted to do too many things at once. Although he had rendered great services to the monarchy, he would have to be replaced. However, it appears from the record of the meeting of the Council of Ministers that Welden confined his remarks to expressing his opposition to seeking Russian assistance which would be 'a complete moral defeat' and 'a confession of weakness before all Europe'. He would be taking part in the attack on Komárno, and on his return, he intended to put forward a plan for an attack in northern Hungary. The meeting concluded with the announcement that Windischgraetz had been summoned to Olomouc to discuss the situation with Francis Joseph personally.[69]

Both Schwarzenberg and Kübeck were only too conscious of the criticism which was being voiced about Windischgraetz. They knew that several of the officers on the Field Marshal's staff had not hesitated to write to General Grünne about their dissatisfaction with the conduct of the war in Hungary. It must be assumed that Grünne discussed these letters with Francis Joseph, if he did not actually show them to him.[70] Schwarzenberg was especially anxious to protect Windischgraetz, since he was related to him by marriage. But his warnings to his brother-in-law fell on deaf ears, as Windischgraetz vigorously defended his actions and his choice of staff. Realising that he was also losing influence with the Emperor, he even went as far as to complain to Schwarzenberg that the Emperor appeared to be irked by the man who had done so much to save the monarchy.[71] Finally, on Palm Sunday (1 April), as a result of the deteriorating military situation in Hungary, Windischgraetz decided that he would stay with the army and not travel to Olomouc. At the same time he continued to insist on the need for Russian aid in Transylvania.[72] Kübeck could only sympathise with Windischgraetz, who was surrounded by intrigue on all sides. There was a serious lack of intelligence about the Hungarian army and many of those in the Hungarian administration were secret sympathisers of Kossuth.[73] Two further meetings of the Austrian Council of Ministers took place on 31 March and 3 April. At Schwarzenberg's suggestion, it was agreed that the Emperor should make a personal visit to Hungary to inspire loyalty to the dynasty. After much discussion about the situation in Transylvania, with Schwarzenberg emphasising the international character of the revolt, the council decided to rely on the plans put forward by General Welden rather than appeal to the Russians for assistance. However, Schwarzenberg informed the council that he proposed to ensure that the Russians would give him assistance in Transylvania without a formal request being made.[74]

After the meeting of the Council of Ministers on 3 April Schwarzenberg immediately got in touch with Medem. He spoke of the threat which Transylvania now posed to its neighbouring territories, including the Danubian principalities. As proof of the seriousness of the threat and the role played by the Poles, Schwarzenberg showed Medem the account of Bem's conversation with Effingham Grant contained in the letter from Bem which the Austrians had intercepted. In addition, Schwarzenberg informed Medem that Kossuth was believed to have signed an agreement to co-operate with the Polish emigrés. He proposed that Russia should occupy Transylvania with a force of 25 000 to 30 000 men which would leave Austria free to subdue the revolt in Hungary. Medem agreed to forward the request to Saint Petersburg if it was sent in identical terms in Austrian diplomatic channels.[75]

Schwarzenberg's request, accompanied by documentary evidence, was duly forwarded to Buol. The arguments used with Medem were repeated even more forcefully in the expectation that Buol would be preaching to the converted and that the Russians would be only too glad to assist the Austrians.[76] A few days later Medem, who by now was paying visits to Vienna from Olomouc, forwarded to Saint Petersburg, Warsaw and Bucharest the detailed Austrian plan prepared by General Welden for the Russian entry into Transylvania. In addition, the Austrians provided details of the staff officers they proposed to send to Bucharest, Galicia and Bukovina to act as liaison officers between the Russian forces and the Austrian military and civilian authorities.[77]

In Saint Petersburg, the Tsar had decided not to cancel a visit to Moscow over Easter because of the death of his brother-in-law King William II of Holland. The purpose of the visit was the dedication of the reconstructed Great Palace in the Kremlin, originally built by Catherine the Great and burnt down during the French retreat in 1812. His main concern continued to be the future of the German Confederation, in which he wished Austria still to play an important part. For this reason, he hoped that the Austrians would be able to restore order in Hungary despite what happened in Transylvania. At least the new French government did not appear to wish to provoke a European war by taking the side of Piedmont.[78] However, Great Britain's encouragement of the Turks to procrastinate about a new agreement on the Danubian principalities was a source of irritation.

Nicholas was also still uneasy about the internal situation in Russia and personally interviewed Yuriy Samarin, the author of *Letters from Riga*, to remonstrate with him about the critical remarks he had made concerning the Baltic Germans and their failure to integrate with Russia. In Nicholas' view, such remarks were enough to cause the outbreak of another Decembrist revolt.[79] Nor was the Tsar pleased by the remarks made by the young law official Ivan Aksakov whose arrest he had ordered. Like the other Slavophiles, Aksakov believed that Russia should encourage all the Slavs to unite under Russian protection. This was tantamount to incitement to revolt against lawful authority and the spread of such ideas must be prevented.[80] However, both men were released with a warning to exercise more care in future about what they wrote.

Since it was almost certain that the Danubian principalities would again be used as a base for operations against Transylvania, the Tsar decided to bring matters to a head in Russia's negotiations with Turkey by sending a special envoy to Constantinople. For this mission he chose General Grabbe, a veteran of the Russian wars against Napoleon, Turkey and Poland who had met the Sultan during a visit he had paid to Moldavia in 1846.[81] Grabbe was accompanied by a staff of four, which included two of Nicholas' trusted aides-de-camp who were to report on the Turkish army and navy. The Tsar briefed the two young officers personally on 2 March in his study in the Winter Palace.[82] The object of the mission was to prevent any complication developing in Russia's relations with the Ottoman Empire at a time when it seemed likely that Russia might be fully engaged in western Europe.[83] The party left Odessa on board the steamer *Vladimir* in the early hours of 15 April (which was Easter Sunday by the Russian calendar) and arrived in Constantinople the following day.

The extent of Polish involvement in the rebellion against Austria

The Russian Intervention in Transylvania and its Consequences 97

in Hungary had been brought home to Kübeck during his visit to Budapest.[84] It had also struck Nesselrode, who commented to Meyendorff that the involvement of the Poles in so many different places brought Austria and Russia closer together in their attempts to prevent the re-establishment of an independent Poland. But it was still difficult for Russia to decide on the best method of helping Austria.[85] The Tsar, for his part, was quite prepared to use the Third and Fourth Infantry Corps to occupy eastern Galicia and Bukovina, but he was not prepared to operate with small detachments, as had happened in Transylvania. Russian troops were already assembled in large numbers along the frontier with Galicia, so there was no need to reinforce them as the Austrians had requested. In addition he was insistent that the Russian troops should operate quite independently of the Austrians, and should not be placed under Windischgraetz's command. Nesselrode also reminded Buol that a Russian occupation of eastern Galicia and Bukovina might cause France to abandon its policy of non-intervention in Italy, and he hoped that the Austrians had given due consideration to this possibility.[86]

On 6 April the Tsar, accompanied by the Grand Dukes Alexander and Constantine, set off by sleigh (with wheels in reserve) on muddy roads which thawed during the day and froze over at night. Nesselrode and Chernyshev, who was now President of the Council of State as well as Minister of War, were left in Saint Petersburg to deal with any further requests from the Austrians for aid and to supervise the negotiations with Turkey about the Danubian principalities. Nicholas intended to spend most of the month in Moscow, and on his return, to carry out an inspection of the Russian army in Poland in May in conjunction with Paskevich, whose annual visit to Saint Petersburg had been cancelled because of the uncertainties of the international situation.[87]

However, the pressure of events in April was to cause a revision of the plans of both the Tsar and Schwarzenberg for putting an end to the revolt in Hungary. At the beginning of the month Görgey went over to the offensive and advanced rapidly on Budapest. On 6 April, which was Good Friday in western Europe, he defeated Jelačić at Isaszeg and occupied Gödöllő the following day. Windischgraetz fell back on the capital, expecting that the Hungarians would wish to attack it. Although Görgey persuaded Kossuth at a meeting in Gödöllő that raising the siege of Komárno was more important, he was unable to persuade Kossuth not to make a final break with Austria by deposing the Habsburgs as a counter-move to the constitution of 4 March. Görgey then ordered the main body of his forces under Klapka and Damjanich to move north towards Vác where the river Danube changes direction from north to west. By a skilful deception operation, he made it appear to Windischgraetz that he might still launch an attack on Budapest, and defeated the Austrians at Vác on 10 April. In the south Kossuth had ordered the forces of General Perczel to attack the joint Austrian and Serbian forces in the Bácska, while Bem was instructed to move towards the Bánát so that he could link up with Perczel's forces.

On 11 April a worried Kübeck (who had already moved from his exposed position in Pest to the safety of the fortress of Buda) left for Vienna to report to Schwarzenberg on a situation which was growing rapidly worse.

5 The Russian Decision to Intervene in Hungary

When Kübeck reported to Schwarzenberg in Vienna on the morning of 13 April, he was greeted with the news that on the previous day at a meeting in Olomouc the Council of Ministers had approved the decision taken by the Emperor to dismiss Windischgraetz and replace him by Welden. A proposal to order the Field Marshal to remove three of his senior officers from their posts, in the expectation that the order would not be obeyed, thus making it easier to dismiss Windischgraetz himself, had been rejected by Francis Joseph. Using words he had read a few days earlier in a letter sent to General Grünne by Colonel Schobeln, Windischgraetz's chief adjutant, the Emperor informed his ministers that half-measures were of no use in the crisis facing Austria. Too much was at stake for Windischgraetz to be allowed to remain in charge in Hungary any longer. General Welden would assume command of the army as soon as possible, and would be assisted in running the civilian administration of Hungary by Baron Samu Jósika, the last civilian administrator of Transylvania before the union with Hungary. On his return from Budapest Windischgraetz would be sent on indefinite leave, and it was hoped to find him another post in due course.[1]

Later in the day Kübeck delivered his own report about the situation in Hungary to the Council of Ministers. He repeated much of what it had already heard during the past few days about the deteriorating situation and the difficulties with which Austria was faced in fighting what was no longer 'a war of armies' but 'a people's war'. If Austria's own forces were judged to be inadequate and foreign aid was considered necessary, a decision should be taken quickly. Kübeck concluded his report by outlining the reasons for the present state of affairs, beginning with Windischgraetz's failure to follow up his initial success in capturing Budapest, and ending with the unfortunate episode about the authorisation of the use of Kossuth notes which he had been compelled to countermand. Schwarzenberg confirmed the correctness of Kübeck's appreciation of the situation but, despite this, the Council of Ministers decided to defer taking a definite decision about seeking Russian aid until Welden had submitted his first report after he had assumed command.[2]

Schwarzenberg was well aware that the taking of a decision about Russian aid could not be postponed indefinitely. Immediately after the meeting he informed Medem that the Austrian government was content to accept the conditions which the Tsar had laid down for the operational use of Russian troops. He pointed out that the Austrian officers who had been sent to liaise with the Russian forces had only been instructed to provide any local assistance and information which the Russians might require. Nevertheless, he asked that the number of troops to be sent to Transylvania should be increased from 30 000 to 40 000. He also drew attention to the possibility of further disturbances occurring in Cracow where Polish emigrés were especially active. In a letter to Buol, written after he had spoken to Medem, Schwarzenberg expressed the hope that the Russians would have already entered Transylvania in accordance with his earlier request.[3] Medem passed on the Austrian acceptance of the Tsar's conditions to Saint Petersburg, as well as giving an account of the replacement of Windischgraetz by Welden. In addition, he sent further details of the Austrian plan for the deployment of Russian troops along the Galician frontier and in Transylvania as an auxiliary force for their own operations.[4] As a final precaution, Schwarzenberg informed Hammerstein that, if there were further troubles in Galicia which could not be suppressed without assistance, a request for aid from the Russians could be made direct to Paskevich in Warsaw without prior approval from Vienna.[5]

It was unfortunate for Schwarzenberg that the letter he had sent to Buol on 6 April asking the Tsar to send 30 000 troops to Transylvania did not reach Saint Petersburg until 16 April. Nesselrode had no choice but to refer the Austrian request to the Tsar, who was already hard at work in Moscow. Paskevich, however, had been able to read Medem's letters and had sent his comments on them to the Tsar. He was totally opposed to the idea of sending any Russian troops from the Danubian principalities into Transylvania which was, from the Russian point of view, 'a side issue'. Instead, he proposed that part of the Russian army in Poland and the western provinces should occupy Galicia and Bukovina, as well as the approaches to all the Carpathian mountain passes leading into Transylvania.[6] The Tsar's own reaction to Schwarzenberg's request was identical. He was particularly annoyed that the Austrian Prime Minister was attempting to dictate to him about the best method of deploying the Russian army which, in his view, was about to be used to pull Austria's chestnuts out of the fire as a result of the incompetence of its own generals. Russia had other interests besides its alliance with the Habsburg monarchy. It was still possible that France would intervene in Italy, and the German situation was as uncertain as ever. However, the Tsar was prepared to accept Paskevich's recommendation that the Third and Fourth Infantry Corps should move into Galicia and Bukovina. He proposed to send one of his senior staff officers, General Berg, to Warsaw and Olomouc to discuss the necessary arrangements with Paskevich and the Austrians.[7] In order to ensure that there was no repetitition of the ill-fated partial intervention in Transylvania, Lüders received strict instructions to ignore any local Austrian requests for aid, and await further orders from the Minister of War about the future deployment of the troops in the Danubian principalities. There was no harm in his retaining one or two of the Austrian liaison officers sent to Bucharest on his staff, but the remainder should be requested to leave.[8]

While the Tsar was in Moscow, Count Orlov brought him up to date with the results of an investigation which had been going on since early 1848 into the activities of a discussion group formed by M. V. Butashevich-Petrashevsky, an official in the Ministry of Foreign Affairs. The group was accused of disseminating socialist and communist ideas, especially those of the French philosopher Charles Fourier, whose works the Russian authorities had been trying to ban. It was decided to delay the arrest of the members of the group (which included the young Dostoevsky) until the Tsar had returned to Saint Petersburg. Nicholas was also displeased by what he saw of the behaviour of the Slavophiles in Moscow and instructed the Minister of the Interior to issue a decree forbidding Russian noblemen to wear beards and traditional Russian costume instead of western attire.[9]

On 15 April (Easter Sunday in the Russian calendar) the Great Palace in the Kremlin was opened after a solemn service of dedication. One of its rooms was the Tsar's study, which looked out on to the river Moskva and was adorned with paintings of the battles which had taken place during Napoleon's invasion of Russia in 1812. It was in this room that Nicholas finally decided to intervene in Hungary. It appears that a decision in principle was taken on the evening of 19 April when a grand masked ball for 16 000 guests was held in the palace,[10] but the final decision to allow Russian forces to move into Galicia and Bukovina was not taken until 25 April, after the Tsar had received from Paskevich a plan for sending two columns of Russian troops into northern Hungary as a follow-up to the occupation of the two provinces.[11]

There has been much debate among historians about the reasons for Nicholas' decision to intervene in Hungary. It is clear that the decision was taken with reluctance, since the Tsar from the outset was under no illusion that he would receive any thanks from Austria for his action. Despite all the promises he had made over the years to his fellow monarchs in Austria and Prussia about coming to their aid in the event of revolution, there can be little doubt that he was finally persuaded to act as a result of the Polish involvement in the Hungarian revolt. The prospect of the disturbances in Hungary spreading through Galicia and Bukovina into Russian Poland and the western provinces transformed a threat to the stability of the Habsburg monarchy into a threat to Russia itself, which had to be countered by a massive intervention using all the available resources of the Russian army.[12] Subsequent events were to show that the number of Poles who actually fought with the Hungarians had been much exaggerated, but Schwarzenberg was well aware that it was convincing proof of the Polish involvement which would tip the balance in persuading the Tsar to intervene.[13]

While the Tsar and Paskevich were considering how to respond to Austria's request for aid, the Hungarians continued their successful campaign. On 19 April an Austrian force commanded by General Wohlgemuth, who had just arrived in Hungary from Italy, was defeated at Kolta to the north east of Budapest. A few days later the Hungarians were able to raise the siege of Komárno after they had laid a pontoon bridge across the Danube to replace the normal bridge which the Austrians had destroyed. Now that the Hungarian forces could cross the Danube from Komárno, Welden was faced with a serious threat to his lines of communication. He therefore ordered the evacuation of Budapest, but left a garrison behind in the fortress in Buda under the command of General Hentzi. On 23 April the Hungarian army entered the city in triumph. Welden withdrew the main body of the Austrian forces westwards across the river Rába towards Vienna, while Jelačić's corps withdrew south to join the hard-pressed Austrian forces there. In a despairing letter to Schwarzenberg, Welden wrote that only the Russian occupation of Galicia could save the monarchy.[14]

In southern Hungary the Austrians had fared no better than in the north, as Perczel's army proved more than a match for the joint Austro-Serbian force commanded by the Croatian-born General Todorović. On 27 March Perczel had been able to relieve the Hungarian garrison in the fortress of Petrovaradin. A week later his forces sacked and burnt Srbobran, where many Serbs were massacred in retaliation for earlier Serbian atrocities. By 19 April almost all the Bácska was in Hungarian hands. Further east, Kossuth had persuaded Bem after his successful reconquest of Transylvania to move into the eastern Bánát in an attempt to capture the Austrian-held forts of Arad and Timişoara and to link up with Perczel's forces before moving further west towards the Danube. By 19 April Bem had defeated General Leiningen and occupied Caranşebes and Lugoj. Both Perczel and Bem were to continue their successful operations for the remainder of April and the first half of May. By that time Perczel had moved as far south as Pančevo just outside Belgrade while Bem had driven General Malkovsky's forces back into Wallachia and was in touch with the Turks in Orşova on the Wallachian frontier.

In Transylvania the only remaining resistance to the Hungarians was centred in the town of Abrud in the Apuşeni mountains, where the Wallachian guerrilla leader Avram Iancu was to wage a successful war throughout the month of May and early June. Kossuth's attempt to negotiate a settlement with him failed when his special envoy Ioan Dragoş was killed after an armistice was broken by a local Hungarian commander. Iancu's forces were to be a thorn in the flesh to Bem when he returned to Transylvania in June, and were to be of assistance to Lüders' army when it moved into Transylvania at the end of June.[15]

As the Russians had been prepared to come to the aid of the Saxons in Transylvania, the Serbian Patriarch Rajačić believed that they would be equally willing to come to the aid of his fellow countrymen. However, he received no support for this idea from the Austrian and Russian consul-generals in Belgrade, and therefore decided to act on his own initiative by sending two delegates to Bucharest to appeal directly to General Lüders. On 14 April both Lüders and Duhamel informed the Serbian delegates that they had no authority to allow Russian troops to join the Austrian Serbs in their struggle against the Hungarians. However, Lüders agreed to refer their request to General Puchner. The delegates met with the same response from Fuad Effendi.[16] In due course, the Tsar announced his approval of Lüders' decision. He had no wish to be accused of fostering the ambitions of the Austrian Serbs to form a union with their compatriots in the Principality of Serbia. Even although he had donated 3 000 muskets to the Serbs in Belgrade, he wished Serbia to resist the blandishments of the Polish emigration and to make every effort to preserve peace among the Christian subjects of the Sultan, especially in Bosnia and Bulgaria. Later in the summer the Russians were to try unsuccessfully to persuade Prince Alexander to expel the representatives of the Polish emigration who were resident in Belgrade, several of whom had French passports.[17]

The successes gained by the Hungarian armies had persuaded Kossuth that the time was now ripe for him to respond to the Austrian constitution of 4 March. Undeterred by the opposition of Görgey and the members of the peace party, he first discussed his proposed response in parliament. On 14 April at a public meeting of the parliament, which was held in the Protestant church in Debrecen, Kossuth made his historic declaration of the independence of Hungary and the dethronement of the Habsburgs. The Committee of National Defence was dissolved, and Kossuth was elected Governor of Hungary with the right to rule the country until a new form of government had been established. Kossuth also announced his intention of seeking better relations with the other nationalities in Hungary and stated his belief, which had no foundation in reality, that the nations of Europe would rally to the cause of Hungarian independence. As we have seen, neither Great Britain nor France was interested in establishing diplomatic relations with an independent Hungary. Nor was Turkey to be persuaded to move from her policy of neutrality, despite the despatch of Count Gyula Andrássy, the future Foreign Minister of Hungary after 1867, to Constantinople in May. A treaty was signed with the Republic of Venice on 3 June 1849, which was of no significance whatsoever, and indeed Kossuth only learned of its successful conclusion when he was in exile.

It is also important to note that the Declaration of Independence had no influence either on the Austrian decision to seek Russian aid, or on the Tsar's decision to intervene in Hungary. The news of what had happened in Debrecen on 14 April did not reach Vienna until 2 May and was made public the following day. Only then did the Russian embassy in Vienna inform Saint Petersburg, but the Tsar does not appear to have attached any great significance to the event.

In Vienna the Austrian Council of Ministers met on 21 April to consider the implications of Welden's despairing report of 20 April. There was much discussion about the measures to be taken to prevent a further outbreak of trouble in Vienna. Although it was agreed that Jelačić should be allowed to move south in accordance with the orders he had already received from Welden, it was hoped that his corps would not become completely detached from the main body of the Austrian army. But the most important item on the agenda was the question of Russian aid. Schwarzenberg pointed out that the decision to make an official request for military aid from Russia would have unfortunate effects on Austria's international standing in Europe. After a lengthy debate, it was finally agreed that Welden should be asked to submit 'a well-considered and categorical declaration' about the necessity for Russian aid. At the same time Schwarzenberg would write to Warsaw about the need to have Russian troops available for use in an emergency.[18]

After the meeting was over Schwarzenberg immediately requested Medem to ask Paskevich to order the Russian troops concentrated on the Galician frontier to move into the province with a view to their eventual use in Hungary. Medem wasted no time in forwarding the Austrian request to Warsaw, emphasising yet again the prominent role which the Poles were playing in the Hungarian revolt. In a letter to Buol, Schwarzenberg also drew attention to the threat to Vienna where, as he put it, the cinders which were still smouldering after the suppression of the revolt in October, could burst into flame again, if the Hungarians were able to mount an attack on the capital.[19]

But Paskevich, like the Tsar, had no intention of allowing Schwarzenberg to dictate to him about the deployment of the troops he commanded. He was still awaiting the arrival of General Berg from Saint Petersburg, as well as the Tsar's reaction to the plan he had sent to Moscow on 19 April. On 24 April he replied that he had no authority from the Tsar to allow Russian troops to move into Austrian territory. In any case, he would like to discuss the arrangements for supplying his troops with food and ammunition with an Austrian officer in Warsaw.[20] At the same time Paskevich took the precaution of informing Hammerstein in Galicia, who had been in direct touch with him, that General Cheodaev, the commander of the Fourth Infantry Corps in the western provinces, had no authority to move his troops into eastern Galicia without Paskevich's permission.[21] On 26 April Medem informed Schwarzenberg of the Tsar's refusal to send Russian troops into Transylvania and of his agreement in principle to the occupation of Galicia and Bukovina.[22] The following day Schwarzenberg arranged for Colonel Schobeln to be sent to Warsaw to discuss the arrangements for the occupation with Paskevich, in accordance with his request.[23]

On 23 April Welden submitted his formal justification for seeking Russian aid, in accordance with Schwarzenberg's instructions,[24] which was approved by the Council of Ministers the following day.[25] Faced with the refusal of Paskevich and local Russian commanders to move their troops without the Tsar's authority, Schwarzenberg realised that his attempt to persuade the Russians to intervene without a formal request had failed. He therefore had no choice but to arrange with considerable reluctance for a formal letter from Francis Joseph to Nicholas to be drafted, in which the Tsar was requested to come to Austria's aid in suppressing the Hungarian revolt. Because of the international revolutionary character it had assumed, the revolt seemed about to develop into a European war. The letter was signed on 1 May and was taken to Saint Petersburg (via Warsaw) by Prince Lobkowitz, a senior adjutant of the Emperor.[26] On the same day, an official announcement about the Austrian request for military aid and Russia's willingness to grant it appeared in the *Wiener Zeitung*.

On 27 April General Berg arrived in Warsaw, and after a rapid discussion with Paskevich and Hilfferding, the Head of his Political Chancery, set off for Olomouc and Vienna.[27] At midday on 30 April Paskevich received the Tsar's letter of 25 April sent from Moscow, authorising him to move Russian troops across the frontier. The Tsar also approved the despatch of a reinforced Third Infantry Corps through the Dukla Pass from Galicia into northern Hungary, but was opposed to the despatch of a second column down the valley of the river Váh toward Bratislava.

That evening Colonel Schobeln arrived in Warsaw and gave Paskevich a gloomy report on the situation facing the Austrian government. Not only were there fears of disturbances in Bratislava, Prague and Vienna, but it was believed that the Hungarians might invade Moravia. Paskevich duly informed the Tsar, adding that he was worried about the lack of supplies and forage in northern Hungary, and enquiring whether he should take command of the invading force. He assured Nicholas that morale in the Russian army was high, a view which was not shared by other observers, such as the British consul-general in Warsaw.[28] After talking to Schobeln, Paskevich wrote to Berg, informing him of the Tsar's decision to allow Russian troops to cross the frontier, and sending him full details of the movements of Russian troops which would now be taking place.[29]

While these events had been occurring in Austria and Warsaw, the Tsar had set off on his return journey from Moscow to Saint Petersburg somewhat later than he had planned because of flooding of the river Volga. On 29 April he met outside Novgorod a courier carrying Paskevich's letter of 24 April. He was relieved to learn that

Paskevich had not yielded to Schwarzenberg's pressure to send Russian troops across the frontier, and reiterated his view that the scale of the Russian intervention should be sufficiently large to ensure that there could be no doubt about the outcome. The Tsar saw no point in going anywhere near Vienna; Galicia should be the first priority, especially as there were rumours that Bem was about to invade the province from Transylvania.[30] In fact, the Tsar's fears about a threatened Hungarian/Polish invasion of Galicia were unfounded. As early as December 1848, Kossuth had been persuaded by a senior officer in the Polish legion to consider the idea, but had prudently decided to seek the views of others, including Bem. The latter took the view that the Ukrainian peasants in the province would almost certainly regard him and his army as an ally of the Polish landlords, rather than a liberating force, and that such an invasion might well lead to a repetition of the massacres of 1846. Bem was not alone in holding this view, and as a result on 6 May the Hungarian government finally abandoned the idea.[31]

On 5 May the Tsar received Paskevich's account of his meeting with Colonel Schobeln. After reading it, he realised that the situation in Austria was far worse than he had imagined, and that any Russian intervention could no longer be in the nature of a diversionary operation but would have to be on a massive scale despite the extra strain that this would impose on Russia's finances. Paskevich would have to command the army and would have to be replaced temporarily as Viceroy of Poland during his absence in the field. It also seemed to him that the Austrians were unlikely to be of much assistance, and in his own mind the Tsar was already preparing himself for the capture of Vienna by the Hungarians. The Tsar remained concerned about exposing his troops to subversive ideas while they were outside the country, and Paskevich was instructed to ensure that bookshops in Galicia were sealed until the authorities had had time to remove any subversive literature. He even suggested that there should be a ban on the printing of books in Russian-occupied territory.[32]

However, Paskevich was to find it difficult to ignore Austrian pressure for assistance in dealing with the threat of a Hungarian attack on Vienna. On 1 May Schwarzenberg decided to send a senior Austrian general, Count Caboga, to Warsaw to lend added weight to the discussions which Schobeln had begun with Paskevich about the Russian occupation of Galicia. The choice of Caboga was deliberate, as he had been a member of the Austrian group of observers attached to Paskevich's headquarters during the Russo-Turkish war of 1829.[33]

At the same time Schwarzenberg began the process of seeking permission from the Prussian government to allow Russian troops to be transported by rail through Prussian Silesia while in transit from Russian Poland to Moravia. By 5 May the Prussian government had given its agreement to the Austrian request.[34] On 1 May the Austrians evacuated Győr in north-west Hungary, and Welden began to fall back on Bratislava where he proposed to make a stand against the Hungarians. By this time General Berg had received details of Paskevich's plan approved by the Tsar for an intervention in northern Hungary. On 3 May he travelled from Vienna to Bratislava by steamer with Schwarzenberg and Cordon, the Minister of War, for a meeting with Welden to discuss the situation. At Welden's request the meeting was held on board the Austrian steamer in order that Berg could not have the opportunity of observing at first hand the sorry state of the Austrian forces.

Berg's report to Paskevich and the Tsar after the meeting was far from reassuring. Welden's forces, which amounted to barely 35 000 combat troops, situated on both banks of the Danube, were facing an enemy force estimated at 80 000 (60 000 Hungarians and 20 000 Poles). There was a serious risk that the Austrians would not be able to defend Vienna against a Hungarian attack. A covering letter from Schwarzenberg confirmed the gravity of the situation and stated quite bluntly that the only hope of saving the Austrian capital lay in the prompt despatch of a Russian force to operate against the right flank of the Hungarian army.[35]

After Welden had returned to his headquarters at Rusovce just south of Bratislava, he informed Schwarzenberg that as he had no reserves he would probably have to go on retreating. He also pointed out that a Russian intervention in northern Hungary through the Dukla pass would not help to save Vienna. In addition, Welden found that he was under fire from the Minister of Finance about the increase in military expenditure he had requested.[36] Schwarzenberg could not but sympathise with Welden. Austria's financial problems were always at the back of his mind, and he was especially perturbed about the fate of the precious metal reserve stored in the Central Bank which could not be moved elsewhere and must not be allowed to fall into Hungarian hands.[37] He therefore decided that the time had come to implement his plan for the despatch of a Russian force by rail from Poland through Prussia to Moravia. On 4 May he sent a letter to Caboga urging him to do all in his power to persuade Paskevich to send a force of 25 000 by rail to Uherské Hradiště or

The Russian Decision to Intervene in Hungary 109

Hodonin in Moravia as a means of helping the Austrians to defend Vienna. Schwarzenberg informed Paskevich that Berg supported the request. He also added that, in his view, the Tsar would not object to a change in the original Russian intervention plan, given the seriousness of the threat to Vienna, of which he had been unaware when he had approved it.[38] On 5 May Medem reinforced Schwarzenberg's plea and pointed out that Radetzky had informed the Austrian Minister of War that he was unable to release any troops from Italy to reinforce the Austrian army fighting in Hungary.[39]

On 6 May Caboga sent a positive reply to Schwarzenberg's request, which had been written in Paskevich's study after an emotional meeting. He had fallen on his knees and, with tears in his eyes, had begged Paskevich to help Austria to prevent Vienna falling into Hungarian hands by sending a small intervention force there by rail. Well aware that he would probably incur the Tsar's displeasure, Paskevich decided to act on his own initiative and agreed to send a composite division of infantry units from the Third Infantry Corps supported by artillery. The force, which was to consist of 13 000 men and 48 guns, would be commanded by Lieutenant-General Panyutin. It was to be used only for the defence of Vienna; if this proved not to be necessary, it was to be kept in reserve and not combined with other Austrian forces for operations elsewhere.[40]

Paskevich informed the Tsar by telegram of his action and followed this up with two longer reports on 7 May. He explained that he had felt unable to refuse a request to save the Austrian capital, given that the Tsar was willing to intervene. Furthermore, there had been renewed disturbances in Germany and he was certain that the appearance of a Russian division in Moravia could not but have a profound moral effect in Austria, Hungary and Germany.[41] The Tsar, however, was far from pleased about Paskevich's action which he regarded as yet another departure from the traditional Russian military practice of operating in the mass. In any case, he saw no reason why Austria should not survive the temporary loss of its capital, as it had done during the Napoleonic Wars, and as Russia had, when it abandoned Moscow to Napoleon's army in 1812. However, Nicholas was mindful that he had served under Paskevich as a young brigade commander, and as he had no wish to quarrel with the 'hero of Warsaw,' he was content to abide by Paskevich's decision which he was sure had been taken for sound military reasons.[42] In fact, the Tsar did not forget the matter, and two years later, when it was discussed at a meeting between him and Francis

Joseph, at which Paskevich was also present, he said quite frankly to Paskevich that he would have paid dearly for his action, if Panyutin's division had perished.[43] The arrangements for moving Panyutin's division by rail from Cracow through Prussia to Moravia went smoothly. All ranks were issued with rations for four days and a stock of ready money, in case the Austrians proved unable to supply the Russians on their arrival. The troops sat in combat order in open wagons and received a warm welcome from the Prussians at the stations through which they passed. The advance party left Cracow on 9 May and within two days 31 trains had transported 14 512 men, 1933 horses and 36 guns a distance of 185 miles to Uherské Hradiště. During the following three days the division received all its heavy baggage. The normal marching time would have been fifteen days, and instead of an estimated fall-out rate of 850 to 1000 men and 150 horses, there were no losses during the journey.[44] By 15 May the threat to Vienna had passed, as the Hungarian army had not continued its expected advance on the capital from Komárno.

In fact, the Hungarians had been compelled to call a halt to their advance after raising the siege of Komárno, as Görgey's army had run out of ammunition and other supplies. Nor was there any plan in existence about what should be done next. Kossuth, who was still mistrustful of Görgey, had decided to appoint him Minister of War, a post which Görgey was willing to accept, since it would give him the opportunity to reorganise the Hungarian army in accordance with his own ideas. However, his officers made it clear that they would be reluctant to let him go and as a result, Görgey decided to send one of his senior officers to represent him in Debrecen. His first choice was Damjanich, who broke a leg in a carriage accident and had to be replaced by Klapka. There was much discussion about the next move to be made by the Hungarian army, and eventually Görgey decided to attempt the capture of the fortress of Buda before continuing his westward advance. It was a fateful decision which was to mark a turning-point in Hungarian fortunes.

Although Nicholas' decision to intervene in Hungary on a grand scale made him impatient for news of the situation in Austria, he still remained uneasy about the internal situation in Russia. On 3 May Orlov had sent him a further report about the Petrashevsky case, and Nicholas had authorised the final round-up of all the participants. In a revealing comment on Orlov's report, he wrote that even if the affair was only a lot of nonsense, it was still criminal and inadmissible.

During the night of 4/5 May thirty-four arrests took place after responsibility for the case had formally been transferred from the Ministry of the Interior to the Third Department.[45] On 6 May the Austrian ambassador dined with the Tsar and his family. Before dinner Nicholas spoke to Buol about the security situation in Galicia and the need to take suitable measures to remove the Poles living there who had been expelled from Russian Poland after the 1830 revolt.[46] On the evening of 7 May Prince Lobkowitz arrived in Saint Petersburg and was received in audience by the Tsar the following morning. Nicholas announced that he would be using 120 000 troops to intervene in Hungary and was willing to allow Paskevich to divide the Russian intervention force by sending a column down the valley of the river Váh in addition to the despatch of the main column through the Dukla pass. However, Lobkowitz was unable to provide much information about Austrian military plans, and like Buol, was given the Tsar's views about the need to tighten up security in Galicia.[47] Shortly afterwards the Tsar sent a suitable reply to Francis Joseph's letter of 1 May brought by Lobkowitz. In it he expressed the hope that the Almighty would bless the armies of Austria and Russia who were once again united in a common struggle against the 'genius of revolution', an enemy no less formidable than Napoleon had been in earlier times.[48]

At the same time Nicholas wrote to the King of Prussia, drawing his attention to the harmful consequences for Germany which could result from a Hungarian victory over Austria. He urged Frederick William to settle the Schleswig-Holstein question and put an end to the war with Denmark. Still fearful about the state of Prussia, he sent Rauch, the Prussian military representative, to Warsaw with a letter instructing Paskevich to arrange for direct contact between the Prussian military commanders in East Prussia and their opposite numbers in Russia. The Prussian ambassador had also agreed to try to persuade the King of Prussia to allow the units of General Dohna and Brüneck to operate jointly with the Russians, in the event of further trouble.[49]

After his meeting with Lobkowitz the Tsar sent for Baron Korff and instructed him to prepare the final version of a manifesto he had drafted about the forthcoming intervention in Hungary. By the late evening Korff had completed his task, and on the following day the manifesto, which was composed in the usual grandiloquent style favoured by the Tsar, was published.[50] After mentioning his earlier manifesto of 26 March 1848, and the continuing troubles in western

Europe, the Tsar referred to the successful Russian and Turkish joint intervention in the Danubian principalities. Unfortunately, Austria, because of the war in Italy, had been unable to suppress the revolt in Hungary and Transylvania, where the rebels had been aided by other nationalities, especially the Poles, many of whom were exiles from Russian Poland. As a result, the Emperor of Austria had asked the Tsar to help him in the struggle against a common foe. The manifesto ended with an invocation to the 'God of armies who alone disposes of victory' to come to the aid of those who were about to crush the revolt and annihilate the miscreants who dared to disturb the repose of Russia. The Tsar was certain that his faithful subjects would support him in carrying out this divinely-appointed task.[51]

As usual, Nesselrode issued a separate commentary on the Tsar's manifesto which was published in the *Journal de Saint Pétersbourg* on 11 May 1849. Russia was intervening in Hungary for two reasons. The first was because of the long-standing alliance between the two countries, and the second was the threat posed by the Hungarian revolt to Russia's own interests. It had become 'half Polish' and was aiming to restore the ancient Kingdom of Poland. More than 20 000 Poles were now fighting alongside the Hungarians, and there was a serious risk that the revolt would spread through Galicia into Russian Poland. It was unfortunate that Russia could no longer remain a passive spectator of events in Europe, but by defending Russia's own interests, the Tsar was also defending the cause of law and order.[52]

The official Russian press dutifully restated the words of the manifesto. In a poem entitled 'The Word of the Times', the author thanked God that Russia had been chosen to protect its own interests and those of Europe at the same time.[53] However, there was less enthusiasm in official circles for the intervention. Orlov's deputy in the Third Department, General Dubel't, with memories of the Decembrist revolt in mind, believed that there was a grave danger of the Russian army being affected by subversive ideas while it was serving abroad. On its return it would be sure to disseminate them and thus cause the authorities further trouble.[54] In the western provinces the Governor-General of Kiev, General Bibikov, expressed concerned about the impending departure of the Fourth Infantry Corps from an area which was especially vulnerable to the activities of Polish emigré agents.[55] Even the Russian army officers in Warsaw referred to the intervention as 'a mere act of quixotic chivalry', a phrase which would gain wide currency in Russia during the Crimean War as a result of Austria's refusal to abandon its neutrality.[56] An official in Saint Petersburg wrote in his diary that the lack of sympathy in Russian society for the intervention was a mixture of discontent about the extra military expenditure, a dislike of Austria and a fear of the spread of subversive ideas from the west.[57] More succinctly, the British chargé d'affaires simply wrote of the 'general disgust' felt by all classes for the war.[58]

In taking his decision to intervene in Hungary, the Tsar had given careful thought to the likely reaction of France and Great Britain. As we have seen, after General Cavaignac had restored order in June 1848, Nicholas had gradually abandoned his hostility to France, but had continued to be wary of the future intentions of Louis Napoleon. After the Austrians had defeated the Piedmontese at Novara in March 1849, Louis Napoleon decided that he could steal a march on Austria and could win much support among French Catholics if he intervened in the Papal States in order to restore the temporal power of the Pope. On 24 April an expedition led by General Oudinot landed at Cività Vecchia, and after an initial defeat by Garibaldi and an abortive series of negotiations with the representatives of the Roman republic, the French succeeded in restoring the Pope's authority by the end of June.

On 5 May Nesselrode expressed Russian approval of the French action to their representative in Saint Petersburg.[59] Three days later the Tsar decided to recognise the French republic and restore full diplomatic relations. As France had intervened in Rome to restore the Pope, the Russians calculated that the French government would find it difficult to protest about the Tsar's decision to help Austria to suppress the Hungarian revolt. It was for that reason that this moment had been chosen to recognise the French republic.[60] The Russian calculation proved to be correct. In the course of a debate in the French National Assembly, the Prime Minister, Odilon Barrot, was able to silence those who were protesting about the forthcoming Russian intervention in Hungary by reminding them that Russia now recognised the French republic.[61] Both the British diplomatic representatives in Vienna and Saint Petersburg reported that their French colleagues had received no instructions from Paris to protest about the intervention.[62] Nor was Kossuth's representative in Paris, László Teleki, able to influence the French government in any way.

At the end of May Alexis de Tocqueville became the new French Minister of Foreign Affairs, but there was still no change in the French attitude.[63] Towards the end of July Tocqueville appointed General Lamoricière, a veteran of the French campaign in Algeria, as the new French ambassador to Russia. Shortly before his departure Tocqueville informed him that as there was nothing practical that France could do to influence events in Hungary, there was no point in indulging in 'sterile agitation' and in displaying 'impotent goodwill'. Accordingly, Lamoricière was to be a passive observer of the situation and nothing more.[64]

As for Great Britain, Nesselrode had advised the Tsar that Palmerston was unlikely to do more than protest about the Russian intervention in Hungary.[65] Once again the Russian forecast about the likely reaction of the British government proved to be correct. Ever since Russian troops had occupied the Danubian principalities, Palmerston had adhered to the view that they would remain there until the Hungarian revolt had been suppressed. Consequently there was no point in trying to persuade the Tsar to withdraw his troops until that had happened.[66] As the weeks went by and Austria proved unable to regain control in Hungary, Palmerston realised that it was inevitable that Austria would appeal to Russia, rather than her other ally Prussia, for assistance, and that there was nothing a British government could do to prevent this happening. As he wrote to the Prime Minister at the beginning of April 1849, 'we cannot outbid Russia in these matters; no fair words of ours can outweigh the fine divisions of an autocrat'. However, Palmerston was also convinced that Austria would be unable to tolerate a strong Russian military presence in the Danubian principalities and that, in the long run, this would cause difficulties in the relationship between the two countries.[67] As a result, the British chargé d'affaires in Saint Petersburg and the consul-general in Warsaw were instructed not to make any formal expression of opinion on the matter, while the chargé d'affaires in Vienna did not receive anything apart from a copy of the despatch to Saint Petersburg and a copy of the Russian circular on the intervention.[68]

It was a realistic assessment of the situation from the British point of view, although a considerable disappointment to Kossuth, who mistakenly believed that Great Britain and France would be prepared to recognise an independent Hungary or at least mediate with Austria. Indeed, Kossuth had sent an envoy, Samu Vass, through Constantinople to Paris and London at the end of April with the object of persuading Britain and France to persuade Austria to grant Hungary reasonable peace terms.[69] Palmerston was prepared to meet Kossuth's envoy in London, Ferenc Pulszky, privately, but there was no question of reversing his official policy which was fully endorsed by the Prime Minister, Lord John Russell.[70] Nevertheless, there was a good deal of popular support for the Hungarian cause, and on 21 July in a debate in the House of Commons shortly before the summer recess Palmerston made a vigorous defence of the government's policy of non-intervention. While making it clear that he regarded the Habsburg Empire as an essential element in the European balance of power, he also expressed the hope that Austria would settle its differences with Hungary when the fighting was over. Palmerston was a firm believer in constitutional forms of government and because he was reluctant to involve Britain in a war over Hungary, this did not mean, as certain historians have claimed,[71] that he was a secret supporter of the Tsar's counter-revolutionary policies.

The Russian ambassador in London, Baron Brunnow, was delighted that there would be no opposition from the British government, and hastened to report to Nesselrode his conversations with Palmerston on the subject. The first of these took place on 9 May when Brunnow gave Palmerston details of General Berg's mission to Warsaw and Vienna. It was on that occasion that Palmerston stated that he hoped the Russians would be able to make it a short campaign. Nine days later, after a conversation with the Prime Minister, Brunnow was able to confirm that the British government would make no difficulties for Russia.[72] As usual, the Duke of Wellington had approved of the forthcoming intervention and had emphasised to Brunnow that the Tsar should intervene on a grand scale. The Tsar, who always paid great attention to the Duke's views on military matters, underlined his words when he read Brunnow's despatch.[73] Lord Aberdeen, the former Tory Foreign Secretary, was equally approving and wrote to his old friend Princess Lieven that he regarded the Tsar as 'our anchor of safety in the West'.[74]

There was considerable satisfaction in Saint Petersburg that Great Britain and France would make no difficulties about the Russian intervention. In addition, the Tsar was pleased to learn during May that order was slowly being restored in Italy in the aftermath of Radetzky's victory at Novara. Besides the French intervention in Rome, the King of Naples had finally recaptured Palermo in Sicily, and the Austrians had been able to restore the Grand Duke of Tuscany to his throne in Florence. An attempt by Piedmont to restore diplomatic relations with Russia was made about this time, but was rejected until Piedmont was able to prove that it had dismissed all the Poles who had been serving in the Piedmontese army.[75]

However, it was important for the Tsar to know the outcome of

General Grabbe's mission to Constantinople before he could consider that all his diplomatic preparations for the forthcoming intervention were complete. On 11 May the Tsar received the news that Grabbe's mission had been successful. On 1 May the Turkish government had ratified the Act of Balta Liman which established a new relationship with Russia on the Danubian principalities. By the terms of this agreement, the *hospodars* were no longer to be appointed for life, but for seven years only; they were to be nominated by the Porte, but had to be approved by Russia. The assemblies of boyars were to be abolished and replaced by appointed councils composed of members of the higher nobility and clergy. Russia and Turkey were each to appoint commissioners in Moldavia and Wallachia, and were to maintain occupation forces in each principality until order had been restored. The strength of the occupation forces was to be reduced to 10 000 when order had been restored and then both countries could evacuate the principalities. The whole agreement was to last for seven years.[76] In due course, Barbu Ştirbei and Grigore Ghica were appointed *hospodars* in Wallachia and Moldavia.

The Turkish government had been reluctant to conclude a new agreement with the Russians, and throughout the negotiations with Grabbe had hoped that the British and French governments would support them in their efforts to resist Russian pressure.[77] Since neither government was prepared to take any decisive action, there was little that either Stratford Canning or General Aupick could do, apart from insisting that the Turks should not sign a new full-scale convention. General Grabbe, who was well aware of Canning's opposition, believed that the Turks were frightened.[78] They had just suppressed a minor revolt in Bulgaria which the Poles claimed (quite unjustifiably) had been organised by the Russians.[79] Grabbe was content to abandon the idea of a convention and in its place, to sign an act (*senet* in Turkish). As he recorded in his diary, using the words of a line from Boileau, '*Un sonnet parfait vaut seul un long poème*'.[80]

Once again Canning was depressed by the ease with which the Russians had succeeded in imposing their will on Turkey. In his despatch to Palmerston, he too reported that the Turks were frightened and had been disappointed at the lack of support from Britain and France, words which were sidelined by Palmerston.[81] The latter was annoyed by what had happened and instructed Buchanan to protest in Saint Petersburg.[82] But in a letter to Canning, he did no more than praise him for having done his best with limited diplomatic means, while adding that 'many circumstances and various consider-

The Russian Decision to Intervene in Hungary 117

ations' had prevented the British government from doing more to assist the Turks to resist Grabbe's demands.[83]

On 8 May General Grabbe and his staff left Constantinople for Odessa. After spending a fortnight in quarantine, they set off for Warsaw to report on the results of their mission. On 13 May the Tsar sent an effusive letter of thanks to the Sultan, in which he referred to the 'principles of perfect understanding and solidarity' that existed between their two countries, now that a new agreement had been negotiated.[84] But there were others in Russia and Austria who, like Palmerston, were less certain about the long-term future of Russia's relationship with Turkey. Among these were Duhamel and Buol, both of whom felt that the uneasy situation existing in Moldavia and Wallachia since the events of 1848 and the continuing decline of the Ottoman Empire could only lead to further trouble between Austria and Russia in the future.[85] For the moment, however, the Tsar had every reason to be satisfied, since the success of Grabbe's mission had freed him and Paskevich from their anxieties about the use of the Danubian principalities and Lüders' Fifth Infantry Corps in the plans they were making for the intervention in Hungary. The way was now clear for a second intervention in Transylvania on a large scale, which would produce a different result from the small-scale intervention which had taken place earlier in the year.

Part II
The Intervention

6 Russian Preparations for War

For the remainder of the month of May and the first half of June, the Russians were fully occupied with their preparations for the intervention in Hungary. Having issued his manifesto about the intervention, renegotiated the occupation of the Danubian principalities with Turkey, restored diplomatic relations with France, and received assurances that the British government would not oppose his action, Nicholas was now free to turn his attention to the detailed military planning which he most enjoyed. He set to work issuing orders about troop movements and the build-up of the reserves which would ensure that Russia was not left bare of troops while the major part of the army was deployed outside the country.[1]

The first phase of the intervention was the move of the Second, Third and Fourth Infantry Corps from Poland and western Russia into Galicia and Bukovina. In their place the First Infantry Corps and the Grenadier Corps supported by reserve cavalry divisions would move into Russian Poland, while the Sixth Infantry Corps, which was composed of reservists, would occupy western Russia.[2] In order to maintain order in Lithuania, where some Poles had tried to seize the arsenal in Vilnius,[3] Nicholas issued orders that the Guards should be moved there from Saint Petersburg for the duration of the campaign.

Nicholas himself decided to move to Warsaw in order to be near the centre of military operations. Warsaw would also be a convenient place for the meeting with Francis Joseph which he had been trying to arrange since the beginning of the year. Besides discussing the details of the intervention, it would be possible to consider what should be done about the confused political situation in Germany which was causing concern to both Austria and Russia. During Nicholas' absence in Warsaw, and his eldest son's absence with the guards in Lithuania, the day-to-day administration of Russia was entrusted to a secret committee chaired by Prince P. M. Volkonsky, the Minister of the Imperial Court. Count Chernyshev, the Minister for War, was given full responsibility for military matters; in the event of any disturbances in Saint Petersburg, he was authorised to assume command of the troops in the capital.[5]

On 14 May Nicholas, accompanied by Nesselrode and the Prussian Ambassador, left Saint Petersburg for Warsaw which they reached two days later. On his arrival Nicholas immediately plunged into detailed discussions with Paskevich, whom he had already appointed to be commander of the Russian intervention force.[6] Paskevich welcomed the arrival of Nicholas since the Tsar's presence in Warsaw would free him from the necessity of having to take any further difficult decisions such as the despatch of Panyutin's division to Vienna.[7]

A week later, on 21 May, Francis Joseph, accompanied by Schwarzenberg and General Grünne, arrived in Warsaw by train from Cracow. A few days earlier it had been considered safe for the Austrian emperor to travel from Olomouc to Vienna where he had carried out an inspection of the Austrian army as it regrouped in the area of Bratislava. Nicholas met him at the railway station and escorted him to his own apartments in the Łazienki Palace in its spacious park on the outskirts of Warsaw. Francis Joseph could not help contrasting the calm atmosphere in Warsaw with the tense situation which still prevailed in Vienna.[8] During the round of official ceremonies and entertainments which were to follow, Nicholas was to spare no effort to establish a close personal relationship with the young monarch. At the same time there was much discussion between the two emperors and their officials about matters of common interest.

The decision of the King of Prussia to reject the offer of the crown of a united Germany made by the Frankfurt Parliament had led to a final outbreak of trouble in southern Germany. At the beginning of May there were disturbances in the Bavarian Palatinate in the Rhineland, as well as revolts in Baden and Saxony where Prussian troops assisted the local authorities in suppressing them. The revolt in Saxony, in which the Russian emigré Mikhail Bakunin played a prominent part, was soon crushed, but the fighting in Baden, in which Polish emigrés were involved, was to last until 20 July.

In Prussia, Frederick William IV's liberally-minded adviser, Radowitz, had persuaded the King to accept a plan according to which a German empire, headed by Prussia, would form part of a larger federation which would include the whole Habsburg empire. During the discussions on this subject in Warsaw, Schwarzenberg reiterated to Rochow and General Rauch, the Prussian military representative in Saint Petersburg, the views he had already expressed since he had become Prime Minister that such a plan was unacceptable to Austria. Schwarzenberg enjoyed the full support of the Tsar, who continued to be disturbed at the prospect of Russia having as a neighbour a liberal German empire united under the leadership of his vacillating brother-in-law. Beside this, Nicholas wished to settle the question of Schleswig-Holstein where fighting had again broken out in March 1849 after the expiry of the armistice signed at Malmö between Denmark and Prussia in August the previous year. Nicholas' support for Denmark remained unwavering, and he warned Prussia that an attack on any ships of the Russian naval units which he proposed to send into the Baltic to assist the Danes, as he had done the previous year, would be treated as a *casus belli*.[9] In the face of this unyielding attitude, Frederick William IV became more conciliatory, much to the Tsar's delight,[10] and a few weeks later, as a result of further mediation by Great Britain, an armistice was signed between Denmark and Prussia on 10 July.

In contrast with his firm stance on Schleswig-Holstein, Nicholas reminded the Austrians that he expected them to solve their remaining problems in Italy, especially the suppression of the Republic of Venice, without any Russian military assistance. However, because of the preoccupations of Austria and Prussia in dealing with the disturbances in Hungary, Italy and southern Germany, it became apparent that any attempt to resolve the problem of the future of Germany would have to be deferred until later in the year. A suggestion that Schwarzenberg should visit Berlin after the conclusion of the talks in Warsaw was therefore dropped, and the Austrians and Russians were thus able to devote the remainder of the visit to a discussion of the intervention in Hungary.

After his death Nicholas was to be accused of having been quixotic in agreeing to offer military assistance to Austria without any compensation for the effort involved. The Tsar was content not to seek any expansion of Russia's territory, although it appears that there was discussion with some of his advisers about the annexation of Galicia. However, after consideration of the advantages and disadvantages of such a course of action, it was decided that the extra money and manpower required to maintain order in the province would impose too great a burden on Russia's resources.[11] Nicholas' only stipulation was that Austria should refund to Russia the cost of the supplies, transport and medical care which the intervention army would require. He did not even insist on the repayment of the extra money which was normally paid to Russian troops when they were sent abroad on active service. A joint commission of Austrian and Russian officials headed by General Caboga and General Rönne, a member of Paskevich's staff, was set up to work out detailed arrangements and draw up a convention. In the ensuing discussions, which went on until early June, Austria also agreed to assist with the setting-up of supply depots, military hospitals, the organisation of a military postal service, and the provision of further ammunition, when the stocks the Russians brought with them became exhausted. Almost as an afterthought the final article of the convention dealt with the extradition of Austrian and Russian subjects taken prisoner during the fighting with the Hungarians. The convention was finally signed in Warsaw on 10 June and ratified in Vienna by Schwarzenberg on behalf of Francis Joseph on 21 June, four days after the Russian intervention had begun.[12]

One of the most important problems to be resolved by the two emperors during their meeting was that of the supreme command of the Austrian and Russian forces. Paskevich knew from his experiences during the Napoleonic Wars of the difficulties Alexander I had faced in dealing with the Austrians during the Fourth Coalition in 1813 and 1814. Although Nicholas lacked this practical experience, he was under no illusions about the difficulties of conducting a coalition war and rightly did not see himself cast in the role of a conciliator of conflicting interests.[13] Nevertheless, now that Windischgraetz was no longer in command of the Austrian army, he proposed to Francis Joseph that Paskevich, by virtue of his age and experience, should be the supreme commander of the intervention armies: but was doubtless not surprised by the Austrian Emperor's refusal to consider such a suggestion when the Austrian army was fighting against his own subjects.[14] In fact, Paskevich was far from enthusiastic about Nicholas' decision to intervene in Hungary, and hoped that it might be possible to achieve a reconciliation between the Austrian government and the Hungarians which would leave the Russian army intact for the war about the future of Germany which he was convinced would have to be fought before long.[15] Nicholas, on the other hand, considered that the Hungarians could have been defeated without much difficulty, if the Austrians had made their formal request for Russian assistance much earlier. Because of the delay, the situation had continued to deteriorate with the result that there was now no alternative to intervention on a massive scale. Having reached this conclusion, Nicholas had no intention of being deflected from his purpose.[16]

Despite the obvious military disadvantages of separate commands, it was finally agreed that although the Austrian and Russian armies would operate independently, each commander would keep the other informed of his plans through their liaison officers.[17] General Berg, who earlier in the year had been rejected by Paskevich as a field commander, but was highly regarded by Nicholas, was to remain with the Austrian army, and have the unenviable task of liaising with the Austrian commander throughout the campaign. He was to incur the hostility of Paskevich who constantly accused him of failing to defend Russia's interests sufficiently vigorously in the face of Austrian criticism of Paskevich's conduct of operations. General Caboga, however, was more fortunate and was withdrawn after concluding his negotiations on supplies. His replacement was General Parrot who was to find himself ignored by Paskevich most of the time.

It was also agreed that Panyutin's division should take its orders from the Austrian commander rather than Paskevich. In return, General Hammerstein's forces in Galicia were placed under Paskevich's command. Since Nesselrode was to remain in Warsaw with Nicholas for the duration of the campaign, it was decided that the Austrian ambassador should be invited to take up residence there, in order to facilitate diplomatic communication with the Austrian government.[18]

The next important military matter for discussion was the Russian operational plan. When General Welden had made his original request for assistance, he had proposed that five separate Russian columns should cross the Carpathians into Hungary.[19] Both Nicholas and Paskevich were opposed to any such proposal, since it ran counter to the traditional Russian principle of not splitting an army into small groups. Nevertheless, in drafting his first plan, Paskevich did make provision for a column commanded by General Rüdiger of the Third Infantry Corps to be sent down to the valley of the river Váh in a south-westerly direction to relieve the Austrian forces in the area of the fortress of Komárno, which still remained in Hungarian hands. However, the main Russian column was to enter Hungary by the Dukla pass and move in the direction of Budapest, after occupying Bardejov and Prešov in northern Hungary. It was considered that a thrust south from the Dukla pass would split the Hungarian forces and thus assist the Austrians. Because of the time required to collect supplies for his large army, Paskevich did not expect to be able to move into Hungary until 17 June, and the Austrians were therefore requested not to launch their own offensive until that date. With considerable reluctance, the Austrians accepted the Russian plan and the delay in launching the intervention.[20]

Besides discussing operations in Hungary, the Austrians and Russians also considered how best to restore the situation in Transylvania in the aftermath of the defeat of General Puchner's forces and the unsuccessful Russian intervention earlier in the year. The satisfactory outcome of the Russian negotiations with Turkey on the Danubian principalities meant that General Lüders' Fifth Infantry Corps was available for operations elsewhere. General Jelačić, commanding the Austrian forces in southern Hungary, proposed that this corps should join forces with his troops in the Bánát. It was suggested that Lüders could move west to Osijek via Orşova, crossing the Principality of Serbia, or could advance north along the left banks of the Danube and Tisza to Szeged where it might be possible for him to link up with the main Russian army, if it had succeeded in advancing so far south.[21]

Chernyshev sent Lüders details of the two options on 14 May, the day on which Nicholas set off for Warsaw. One of the advantages of an advance to Osijek was the prospect of the co-operation of the Serbs who, it was believed, would be only too willing to help their fellow Slavs and co-religionists in the struggle against the Hungarians. However, the road to Osijek was long and involved several river crossings; furthermore, there was doubt about the availability of supplies being available in the Bánát. The Tsar's preference was for an advance north to Szeged. He was even prepared to allow Lüders to move off before the arrival of units from Russia to replace the Fifth Infantry Corps in the Danubian principalities, and to allow Omer Pasha, the local Turkish commander, to assume charge on a temporary basis of the Russian troops left behind until General Dannenberg arrived in Bucharest from Odessa as Lüder's replacement.

The day after the Tsar's departure, Chernyshev wrote again to Lüders informing him that Nicholas had agreed, albeit reluctantly, to independent operations by his force. Accordingly Lüders could, if he wished, attempt the reconquest of Transylvania, but if he had any doubts about the security situation in the Danubian principalities, he was not to move.[22] However, after his discussions with Paskevich in Warsaw, Nicholas changed his mind about allowing Lüders to operate independently of the main Russian force. For the time being, Lüders was to continue making preparations for an offensive and was to inform Nicholas personally of his choice of the options with which he had been presented.[23]

On 23 May the Austrian Emperor and his party left Warsaw.

Francis Joseph had made a good impression on Nicholas, who wrote to his wife that Austria was fortunate to have as its ruler a man who was so imbued with 'the right ideas'.[24] Paskevich was equally impressed and commented to Chernyshev about the touching farewell which had taken place at the railway station between the two rulers.[25] A British diplomat, who had also witnessed the scene, even went so far as to suggest to Palmerston that Nicholas had succeeded in transforming Francis Joseph into a youthful ally and imperial protegé.[26] The official letters exchanged after the visit appeared to set the seal on the cordial relationship which had been established, but subsequent events were to show that the young Francis Joseph, under the guidance of his advisers, had no intention of becoming the obedient protegé of his elder Russian ally.[27]

Schwarzenberg had been warned that the Austrians would have to handle Paskevich carefully. His counsellor on this matter, the wily Prokesch-Osten, Austrian ambassador in Berlin, drew attention to Paskevich's unwillingness to listen to the advice of others and his susceptibility to flattery. The award of a high Austrian decoration would not come amiss.[28] Schwarzenberg followed this advice and the messenger from Vienna bearing Francis Joseph's letter of thanks to Nicholas also carried the Grand Cross of Saint Stephen in diamonds for Paskevich.[29] However, it would need more than the award of a medal to solve the problems that were to arise as a result of the absence of a united command of the Austrian and Russian armies. Within a few weeks Schwarzenberg would feel impelled to make another journey to Warsaw to ask Nicholas to remove Paskevich from the command of the Russian army.

Paskevich's refusal to commence operations before 17 June did not please the Austrians. Through General Berg they warned Paskevich that from the beginning of July the Russian army would suffer severely from the effects of the hot Hungarian summer climate, especially when operating in the marshy area of the Tisza. There would be much illness.[30] Nicholas, for his part, was determined to resist Austrian pressure to move before Paskevich had completed his preparations. In a letter to Berg he made it clear that he would not tolerate any Austrian deviation from the operational plan agreed in Warsaw without Paskevich's prior approval.[31] Nesselrode seconded the Tsar's view by advising Schwarzenberg that Nicholas wished to see the text of any Austrian orders issued to General Hammerstein in Galicia.[32]

Austrian impatience at the delay in starting operations was

increased by the news of the capture of Buda by the Hungarians, an event which had occurred on the day on which Francis Joseph had arrived in Warsaw. The siege of Buda had taken the Hungarians longer than expected, because Görgey's forces lacked the necessary heavy artillery which had to be transported from the fortress of Komárno. Furthermore, the Hungarians had confidently expected that General Hentzi, the Hungarian-born commander of the Austrian garrison left behind in Buda by Welden, would surrender to them. Hentzi's refusal to do so led to heavy fighting between the Croat troops in the garrison and the attacking Hungarian army. In the end, during the final assault, the defection of the garrison's Italian troops to the Hungarians helped to turn the tide and Hentzi himself was killed.[33] An Austrian attempt to blow up the Chain Bridge across the Danube was frustrated, although planks were removed from the roadway to make it impassable for troops. The Hungarian government was delighted with the news of the capture of Buda, but the delight was to be short-lived. There can be no doubt that the Hungarian decision to capture Buda rather than continue the pursuit of the retreating Austrian army across the border was a blunder of the first order, which gave both the Austrians and Russians valuable time to regroup their forces and concert their preparations for their joint intervention.

On 25 May, the day after he had left Warsaw, Schwarzenberg attended a meeting held in Bratislava to review the military situation. The meeting was also attended by General Berg, the Austrian Minister of War, General Welden, and the officer recently arrived from Italy who had been selected to replace him. This was the notorious General Haynau, who had already gained a reputation during the occupation of Brescia in Italy for his cruelty and ruthlessness in dealing with those he had defeated. In the face of Berg's insistence that Panyutin's division should be treated as a reserve unit of the Austrian army, the Austrians withdrew a proposal to make immediate use of the division in the Váh valley.[34]

Nevertheless, after he had returned to Vienna, Schwarzenberg made an appeal to Paskevich to occupy the Carpathian passes, since a token demonstration of force by the Russians at this stage would at least serve to deter the Hungarians from moving westwards and attacking Moravia, Lower Austria or Styria.[35] Three days later Schwarzenberg renewed his appeal, and, as if to lend force to his request, enclosed a copy with translations into Hungarian and Slovak of a proclamation approved by the Austrian Council of Ministers which was to be issued to the local population by the Russian army. The proclamation stated that the Russian army was not entering Hungary as an enemy, but as a friend and ally in response to an appeal made by Francis Joseph as King of Hungary to the Emperor of Russia for assistance in restoring his legal rights in the country.[36] At the same time Schwarzenberg took the opportunity to complain to Nesselrode about a breach of protocol by Paskevich who had written directly to General Welden, contrary to the agreement made in Warsaw that correspondence between the two commanders was to be sent on liaison channels.[37] Nesselrode hastened to apologise for Paskevich's *faux pas* and by way of soothing Schwarzenberg's ruffled feelings, informed him that Nicholas had been pleased to award him the Order of Alexander Nevsky.[38]

At the end of May the Austrians informed the Russians officially of the replacement of Welden by Haynau. A protegé of Radetzky, Haynau maintained a close link with his old commander, and always sent his operational plans to Radetzky's Chief of Staff for comment. His efforts to persuade the Hungarian-born General Benedek to become his own Chief of Staff were unsuccessful, since Benedek preferred to fight as a regimental officer.[39] General Berg who paid a brief visit to Warsaw at the beginning of June had been favourably impressed by Haynau's energy and decisiveness and was able to deliver a reassuring report about him to Nicholas.[40] Paskevich, however, was more cautious in welcoming the change and continued to have reservations about the prospect of conducting a campaign in which there would be no commander-in-chief of all the forces involved.[41] In the event, it was not long once the campaign had started before both Haynau and Paskevich became engaged in an acrimonious correspondence with each other, while simultaneously making complaints to their respective superiors about the impossibility of working together.

While all these official discussions had been taking place between the Austrian and Russian governments, the Second, Third and Fourth Infantry Corps of the Russian army had begun assembling in Bukovina and Galicia preparatory to crossing the Hungarian frontier. On 5 May the main body of the Fourth Infantry Corps, commanded by General Cheodaev, set off from its quarters in Volhynia in western Russia and crossed the Austrian frontier eight days later. In his order of the day Cheodaev exhorted his troops to be disciplined and well-behaved in the task to which they had been called by the Tsar of helping the Austrian government to maintain order in Galicia.[42]

Enthusiastic crowds turned out to greet the Russian columns of soldiers as they marched along the roads through the towns and villages. On their arrival in L'vov there was an official reception given by General Hammerstein, who sent a favourable report to Schwarzenberg about the fine military qualities of the Russian troops.[43] By contrast, the gendarmerie officers attached to the Russian army noted with concern that the bookshops in L'vov were full of anti-Russian propaganda. It was reported in Berlin that the Russians wasted no time in establishing close contact with the Austrian police and postal authorities, and were already behaving as if they were in occupied enemy territory.[44]

While the Fourth Infantry Corps was occupying eastern Galicia, the Third Infantry Corps, closely followed by the Second Infantry Corps commanded by General Kupriyanov, moved into western Galicia. General F. V. Rüdiger,[45] the commander of the Third Infantry Corps, and his staff set up their headquarters in Cracow where they arrived by train from Warsaw on 20 May.

At first the Russian officers were favourably impressed by Galicia, but, as the days passed, they became aware of the deep-seated racial tensions that lurked beneath the surface in the aftermath of the 1846 uprising. While the Ukrainian peasants made no secret of their dislike of the Polish landlords and proclaimed their loyalty to the Habsburgs, the Polish landlords spoke bitterly of the excesses committed by the peasants in 1846 and Austrian official connivance at what had occurred. Relations with the Austrian army were generally friendly and the Russians were able to see at first-hand how the Austrians made use of soldiers from the non-Slavonic speaking provinces of their empire to garrison a province such as Galicia, inhabited by Slavs.

Since the local Austrian authorities appeared to be ill-informed about the Hungarian forces in northern Hungary, both the Third and Fourth Infantry Corps sent patrols south to the frontier area to collect as much tactical information as possible. A small force of infantry and cavalry with supporting artillery was formed from units of the Third Infantry Corps and placed under the command of Lieutenant-General Sass. It occupied the area south of Cracow near Jordanów, and on 16 May one of its patrols had the first Russian encounter with the Hungarian forces.[46] The Cossack units in the Russian army played a major part in this reconnaissance activity and proved adept at exploring the minor roads and crossing points in this area of the Carpathians. The local population welcomed the soldiers of an army who spoke a language little different from their own, and told the Russian patrols that many of the men from the villages had gone into hiding in the woods in order to avoid being drafted into the Hungarian army.[47]

In Cracow General Rüdiger began his efforts to persuade the Austrian authorities to improve the security situation in Galicia about which the Tsar had already expressed his concern to General Lobkowitz when he had visited Saint Petersburg at the beginning of May. Shortly after his arrival Rüdiger requested General Legeditsch, the town commandant of Cracow, to arrange the deportation of the sister of General Bem and the son of General Dembiński. In both cases Legeditsch could only give orders for a stricter surveillance of their activities, as he had no powers to carry out deportations. This example of Austrian inability to satisfy the Tsar's demands was immediately reported to Warsaw and, as we shall see, was to cause Nicholas considerable concern.[48]

However, if General Legeditsch was unable to satisfy the Russians in this matter, he was able to perform a major service by giving them the opportunity to obtain up-to-date information about Görgey and the Hungarian forces from a first-hand source, a paternal uncle of the general. Johann Görgey was an elderly retired hussar officer who, anxious not to lose his pension, wished to travel to Vienna to reaffirm his loyalty to the Emperor. When he called on the Austrian authorities in Cracow for this purpose, Legeditsch arranged for him to be interviewed by the Russians.

The information obtained at this interview was to give the Russians their first insight into the disagreements in the Hungarian leadership. Görgey's uncle described his nephew's disapproval of Kossuth's decision to proclaim the Declaration of Independence in Debrecen, as well as his dislike of the Poles in the Hungarian army, especially General Dembiński. General Rüdiger asked outright whether it would be possible to bribe Görgey to surrender, and was told that he was not interested in money. If the Hungarian revolt had not taken place in 1848 Görgey would almost certainly have gone on working as a chemist and not resumed his abandoned military career.

Besides this glimpse into the rift between Görgey and Kossuth, the Russians were able to compile a detailed order of battle of the Hungarian army, which included an account of the strengths and weaknesses of the various corps and their commanders. The final section of the report dealt with the general state of the country, the attitude of the population towards the latest political developments, and the likely development of the military situation.[49]

On 2 June a courier took the report to Warsaw where it earned a special word of praise from the Tsar. In Vienna, General Berg, doubtless influenced by the Austrians, believed that the report exaggerated the strength of the Hungarian force and still held to his belief that the massive intervention being prepared was not necessary.[50]

While Rüdiger's staff-officers busied themselves with preparations for the campaign, the ordinary Russian officers whiled away their time in Cracow waiting for action. They went sightseeing and visiting the famous salt mines at Wieliczka nearby. Their was much carousing in local hotels at dinner parties, where young Austrian and Russian officers drank toasts to success in the battles to come. But, despite the generally friendly relationship between the two armies, there were signs of the future hostility that was to develop between them. For example, in Cracow the friendship that developed between some Russian and Hungarian cavalry officers who had remained loyal to the Emperor, but were still viewed with suspicion by the Austrians, led to an official complaint being made to the Russian authorities.[51]

In Warsaw Paskevich was as concerned as his corps commanders about the shortage of accurate information about Hungary. In April the previous year he had already taken steps to improve the acquisition of military intelligence by persuading Nesselrode and the Tsar to agree that Russian missions abroad should be given the task of undertaking the systematic collection of military and topographical information.[52] Detailed instructions were drawn up for the gendarmerie officers who were to accompany the Russian army about the acquisition of information from deserters from the Hungarian army.[53] But despite these efforts, there were to be repeated complaints throughout the campaign about the difficulty of obtaining information from the local population about the Hungarian forces and their movements.

As a result of his experiences in previous campaigns outside Russia, Paskevich was aware of the advantage to be derived from the use of dissident national groups. During the Turkish campaign of 1828–9, the Russians derived great benefit from Bulgarians who offered their services to the Russian army. In his own operations in Asiatic Turkey Paskevich made skilful use of the Kurds.[54] It was not surprising, therefore, that Paskevich and his staff were alert to the possibilities of exploiting the racial antagonisms which existed in the Habsburg empire, although they realised that the Tsar would be most reluctant to offer any encouragement to the political aspirations of any nationality which wished to overthrow its lawful ruler. The first approach of this kind was made by two officers of the former Slovak militia to the troops of General Sass' advance guard operating along the Galician–Hungarian frontier. The two Slovaks proposed that they should be allowed to reorganise the militia and fight alongside the Russians, after they had renewed their assurances of loyalty to the Austrian Emperor. In his memorandum to Paskevich about this approach, Rüdiger included the suggestion that many members of the Hungarian army would be willing to desert if the Austrian government were to grant an amnesty. Both Paskevich and Nicholas agreed with Rüdiger's proposal, but insisted that anyone who received an amnesty must agree to take up arms against his former comrades. With the addition of this proviso, Rüdiger's proposal for recreating the Slovak militia was forwarded to Vienna on both military and diplomatic channels because of the political implications of the proposal to grant an amnesty.[55]

Schwarzenberg's reply to both the Russian proposals was unequivocal. The Austrians had already tried to make use of local militia units and had met with little success. Their members were often motivated by reasons other than a wish to defend the Habsburg Empire. The chance to loot and settle old scores were often prime attractions. Nor should it be forgotten that the Hungarians had been successful in planting their agents in these units. For these reasons the Austrians had abandoned the idea and were not in favour of an attempt being made to revive the disbanded Slovak militia.[56] On the wider issue of the possible granting of an amnesty, Schwarzenberg considered that such a measure would be interpreted as a sign of weakness on the part of the Austrians, and would be opposed by the majority of Habsburg officers of all nationalities who had remained loyal to the Emperor. In any case, military success must be the prerequisite of any such action; in that event, the granting of an amnesty would be interpreted as a sign of generosity rather than weakness.[57] A few days later the arrest of two officials in the Austrian Ministry of Foreign Affairs, one Hungarian and one Pole, on charges of espionage provided Schwarzenberg with a further opportunity of demonstrating to the Russians the dangers incurred in dealing with the Hungarians.[58] It is ironic that while Schwarzenberg was advising the Russians to exercise caution, the local Hungarian authorities in northern Hungary were already concerned about the impact of the impending Russian invasion on the Slovak and Ukrainian inhabitants of the area and were warning Kossuth of possible adverse effects.[59]

However, Paskevich and Rüdiger were not to be deterred by Schwarzenberg's advice, and both continued to pursue the matter. Each wrote to General Legeditsch in Cracow asking the Austrian army to supply them with weapons for 500 volunteers. On 13 June the Austrian Council of Ministers approved this request, but despite a lengthy exchange of correspondence on Austrian military channels about the availability of the weapons, the request still remained unfulfilled by the end of July, when it had long been overtaken by other events.[60]

Important as these matters were, Paskevich was much more preoccupied with the problem of ensuring that there would be adequate supplies and transport available for the huge number of troops the Tsar had decided to send into Hungary. As a young divisional commander in 1814, he had learnt the importance of ensuring that his troops had enough food, rather than allowing them to fend for themselves and live off the land. In his view, it was neither possible nor desirable to prevent half-starved soldiers from looting, and the best deterrent against this kind of behaviour was an efficient and well-organised supply system.[61] As he had grown older, Paskevich saw no reason to change his views, and even his enemies in the Russian army conceded that he excelled in ensuring that the troops under his command were properly fed.

When the disturbances in western Europe had begun in 1848, Paskevich had immediately started to build up reserves of supplies in Russian Poland against the threat of an invasion from the west.[62] With the move of the Russian army into Galicia and Bukovina, Paskevich wished to establish a further chain of supply depots for use by the troops while they were on the march and during their occupation of the Austrian provinces. In addition, he planned to build up stockpiles of supplies in depots to be established along the slopes of the Northern Carpathians which could be used by the Russian army after it had entered northern Hungary, where no supplies were expected to be available. As we have seen, Paskevich's estimate that he would need five weeks to amass the reserves he required had influenced the starting date of the intervention. His own private belief was that the Austrians would not be able to assist him, despite their optimistic assurances that all would be well.[63]

Nevertheless, Paskevich dutifully sent one of his staff-officers, Colonel Sattler, to L'vov to discuss the supply problem with General Hammerstein. Sattler's first reports were reassuring, but by the end of May both he and Hammerstein made it clear that the Austrians could not supply even one-tenth of the Russian requirements for the reserves they wished to establish in depots near Jordanów and the Dukla pass. The Russians would simply have to rely on their own resources.[64] From Cracow General Rüdiger reported in equally gloomy terms that Imre Péchy, the Austrian official sent to liaise with him about supplies, had frankly admitted that he had neither the money nor the means to carry out the Russian requests.[65] Shortly afterwards Péchy wrote from Warsaw to his own authorities in Vienna that the main reason he could not satisfy the Russians' demands was a shortage of money. As he put it in a letter sent personally to Schwarzenberg, with nothing it was only possible to achieve nothing.[66] An alarmed Paskevich wrote to Chernyshev about the difficulties he was experiencing, and hinted that he might have to delay the start of the Russian offensive.[67]

In fact, Paskevich was being somewhat pessimistic. His decision to go ahead with his own arrangements for the transport of supplies from the reserves in Poland by road and by the Warsaw–Cracow railway, rather than wait for Austrian assistance, had ensured that his army would have enough supplies with which to start the offensive on 17 June. As a prudent commander, he had begun early to prepare sufficient stocks of dried biscuit, the Russian soldier's basic food. In early May the flour mills in Warsaw were already at work grinding corn for this purpose.[68] The Austrians had promised to assist the Russians with the provision of field bakeries, but when the Russians arrived in Cracow, they found that nothing had been done. General Rüdiger therefore put his engineers to work building brick ovens and within three days thirty-six ovens were available for the Russian army bakers, who worked day and night in shifts preparing the required reserve of biscuit.[69]

Nor did it prove too difficult to raise the extra transport needed to carry the supplies from the railhead in Cracow and the towns in eastern Galicia to the forward area. Paskevich raised mobile units, equipped with vehicles bought from the Polish postal authorities. Oxen were also purchased to haul the carts on the steep roads crossing the Carpathians. Afterwards they were to be slaughtered to supplement the normal meat ration for the army.[70] Large numbers of scythes were acquired to cut grass which would replace the usual supplies of forage for the horses of the cavalry and artillery units. An order was issued that horses were not to be ridden across the Carpathians, but led by the bridle.

Besides ensuring that his army would have adequate supplies, Paskevich made appropriate preparations for dealing with the sick and wounded. It was estimated that there would be 18 000 hospital cases and 30 000 casualities. According to the plan drawn up by Paskevich's staff, the main headquarters of the army and each infantry corps was to be equipped with a mobile hospital. These hospitals were raised in Kiev, but in the event only two mobile hospitals reached their destination, the Fourth and Fifth Infantry Corps, before the end of the campaign. The mobile hospital for the main headquarters succeeded in reaching its destination, but as the transport allocated to it proved to be quite unsuitable for use in the Carpathians, it was of limited value.[71]

Finally, because of the chaotic financial situation in Hungary and the determination of the Austrian government to put an end to the circulation of the Hungarian paper money issued by Kossuth, arrangements were made to keep the Russian army well supplied with ready money for payment of the supplies they expected to buy in Hungary. The sum of 16 million silver roubles was sent from Saint Petersburg to Warsaw for this purpose.[72]

As a result of all his efforts, Paskevich had accumulated by 13 June supplies in Cracow sufficient to feed 120 000 men for one month and in Dukla for 160 000 men for fifteen days. There were rations immediately available to last for twenty days and an order was issued to all unit commanders to have a ten days' supply of spirit available for immediate use with transport to carry it.[73]

The Austrians, meanwhile, had appointed a civil commissioner for Hungary, whose task was the restoration of Habsburg authority in the areas to be occupied by the Russian army. He was Count Ferenc Zichy, a Hungarian magnate, who had already worked with Windischgraetz earlier in the year. Both Nicholas and Paskevich welcomed the appointment and as a mark of his approval, the Tsar invited Zichy to dine with him on 10 June during a visit to Warsaw.[74]

In Bucharest, Lüders was making his own preparations while awaiting the Tsar's approval of his plan to attempt the reconquest of Transylvania. He was as thorough as Paskevich, and equally sceptical about Austrian ability to supply his troops after they had entered the province. It is of interest that the medical supplies issued to the Fifth Infantry Corps included chloroform, which had first been used in Great Britain two years earlier.[75]

Despite reservations which Paskevich had expressed about independent operations by the Fifth Infantry Corps, Nicholas accepted

Lüder's operational plan without any hesitation, especially as the Austrians were unable to provide the Russians with any information about Jelačić's plans for operations in southern Hungary. The Austrians had also yielded to Nicholas' request that the ageing and unsuccessful General Puchner should be replaced by a younger officer and had appointed Clam-Gallas in his stead.[76] On 2 June Nicholas' formal agreement was sent to Lüders. The starting-date for his operations was to be co-ordinated with that of Paskevich to whom he was to report on operational matters, while sending a copy of all his reports to the Tsar in Warsaw for information.[77]

Nicholas' decision to allow Lüders to attempt the re-conquest of Transylvania was one of three factors which caused Paskevich to modify the operational plan discussed with Francis Joseph and Schwarzenberg in Warsaw. The other two were the fall of Buda and the retreat of the Austrian army to the Bratislava area. The Austrian forces now amounted to 80 000 men including Panyutin's division and the reinforcements which the Austrians had been able to transfer from Galicia as a result of the Russian occupation of the province. Because of the lack of information about Jelačić's 50 000-strong army in the south, Paskevich was obliged to take no account of its likely movements in revising his plan.

Paskevich's original operational plan had been influenced by the following considerations. The area in which his army was about to operate was a large treeless plain intersected by the rivers Danube and Tisza. Its northern and eastern extremities were protected by the Carpathian mountains which, it was feared, would afford protection to Hungarian partisans. The area around the Tisza was marshy with an unhealthy climate and had few good roads. The Hungarian forces were divided into four main groups. The most important group was the Upper Danube Army of 52 000 men, commanded by Görgey, which was concentrated in the area of the fortress of Komárno on the Danube and still posed a threat to Vienna. On the southern side of the Carpathians the invading Russian army would be faced by the Upper Tisza army of 50 000 men, commanded by General Dembiński, who was soon to resign. In the south an army of 36 000 men commanded by General Perczel occupied the northern Bánát, while a small force laid siege to the Austrian-held fortresses of Arad and Timişoara. The southern Bánát and Transylvania were held by a force of 37 000 men commanded by General Bem, part of which was besieging the Austrian-held fortress of Alba Julia. The total strength of the Hungarian forces, including its reserves, was estimated to be 162 000 men. As a result of the fall of Buda to the Hungarians, Paskevich reasoned that the Austrian army concentrated near Bratislava would be unable to launch a serious offensive because of the constant threat of an attack on Vienna. He calculated that a general should have at his disposal one and a half, or preferably twice as many troops as his enemy, in order to be certain of victory. Nor did he consider that his original intention of sending General Rüdiger's column down the valley of the river Váh would tip the balance in favour of the Austrians, since the Hungarian army would be easily able to move its troops from one side of the river Danube to the other. He therefore decided to use Rüdiger's column for his own purposes. It would enter northern Hungary to the west of his own column at Nowy Targ and link up further south with the main Russian column after it had crossed the Dukla pass, possibly at Košice. The distance from Dukla to Košice was 75 miles, and according to Paskevich's calculations his troops would arrive there by 27 June. From Košice he proposed to make a massive thrust towards Pest in the expectation that this would drive the Hungarians towards the main Austrian army advancing east from Bratislava. However, if the Hungarians decided to make for Debrecen and crossed the river Tisza, Paskevich intended to cross the river near Tokaj and defeat them in battle, possibly with the assistance of Lüders' force advancing north through Transylvania.[78]

Because of the possible threat from Hungarian partisans to his lines of communications, running back from Hungary through Galicia and Bukovina to Poland and Russia, Paskevich intended to leave troops in each of the towns he occupied to guard them against possible attack. Despite the resulting reduction in strength of his own force, he still estimated that together with Rüdiger's column he would enjoy the overwhelming superiority in strength which he regarded as essential to be certain of victory.[79] In order to protect his rear in western Galicia, a small force of units of the Second Infantry Corps based in Cracow commanded by General Grabbe would enter Hungary and move down the Árva valley to Dolný Kubin. Similarly, central and eastern Galicia would be protected by a small force commanded by General Osten-Sacken based in Stryj to the south of L'vov.

Since General Lüder's force was under his command, Paskevich also issued orders for its deployment. Lüders' main task was to be the re-conquest of Transylvania, together with the disarming of the Széklers, and, if possible, the raising of the siege of Alba Julia.

General Grotenhjelm's force in Bukovina could be used by Lüders to assist him in these operations, together with the Austrian troops in these areas, but Paskevich reserved the right to use Grotenhjelm's forces for his own purposes, especially if the Hungarians mounted an incursion into Bukovina or eastern Galicia. In addition, Lüders, who was aware from intercepted correspondence of the last-minute attempts of the Hungarians and Rumanians to reconcile their differences, was given full authority to offer financial support and material aid to the Rumanian irregular forces commanded by Avram Iancu which were operating in the Apuşeni mountains in Transylvania after the collapse of the negotiations with the Hungarians at the beginning of May.[80]

Paskevich calculated that three months would be required to defeat the Hungarians. He was anxious to make the war short, as he still clung to the view he had expressed earlier that the intervention in Hungary was of less importance than the war the Russian army would shortly have to fight to decide the future of Germany.[81] The total strength of the Russian forces under his command amounted to nearly 190 000 men and 600 guns. His revised operational plan fully demonstrated the traditional Russian preference for operating in the mass.[82] It was evident that it could only be a question of time before the Hungarians succumbed to the overwhelming strength of the combined Austrian and Russian armies.

But although the Russian army was ready to move by mid-June, as promised to the Austrians, Nicholas was still determined to show the Austrians that his aid could not be taken for granted. The bone of contention was the security situation in Galicia and Austrian laxness in dealing with it.

The rise to prominence of Generals Bem and Dembiński and the formation of a Polish Legion to fight alongside the Hungarians had only served to increase Nicholas' and Paskevich's doubts about officers of Polish origin serving in the Russian army. From time to time Paskevich had issued secret orders to corps commanders about the need to keep a watchful eye on the activities of officers of Polish origin.[83] In May 1849 General Lüders found it necessary to execute one of his officers for carrying on a treasonable correspondence with Bem, and as a result these precautions were increased.[84] A Russian hussar regiment was left in Wallachia rather than being used in Transylvania because many of its officers and men were of Polish origin.[85] In Galicia General Hammerstein was requested to issue an order to the local population in Austria about rewards for handing over Russian deserters.[86] In Austria, General Panyutin also issued an order to his regimental commanders about surveillance of officers of Polish origin.[87]

Nicholas had discussed the problem with Francis Joseph and Schwarzenberg during their visit to Warsaw in the hope that the Austrians would take steps to improve security in Galicia. Because of the Austrian failure to do so, Nicholas decided to raise the question again with the Austrian ambassador when he arrived in Warsaw on 9 June to take up residence. At this audience Nicholas pointed out that the security situation in Galicia directly affected the efficiency of the Russian army. Most of the persons in whom the Russians were interested were Russian subjects. Nicholas did not wish to play the part of an executioner, but he could not understand why the Austrians were unable to deport Dembiński's son and Bem's sister. He also reverted to the case of Count Józef Załuski, a former Russian officer who had led Russian troops into an ambush during the Russo–Turkish war of 1828; after fighting against the Russians during the Polish revolt of 1830, Załuski had gone to live in Galicia.[88]

Shortly after his interview with Buol, Nicholas expressed his views even more forcefully to General Berg in Vienna. Although the Russian army was ready to move on 17 June as promised, it would not advance 'a single step' if the Austrians failed to carry out his request to improve security. There was little point in moving into the rebellious province of Hungary if the Austrians were unable to restore order in Galicia.[89] It was typical of Nicholas that in this instance his blunt language was more of a threat than a serious intention not to carry out his promise of assistance.[90]

However, in the face of such stern language, Schwarzenberg had no option but to comply with Nicholas' requests for action. He immediately sent instructions to General Hammerstein about the rounding-up of suspect Russians and Poles in Galicia, who were to be kept in safe custody for the duration of the crisis. Those who could legally be extradited were to be handed over to the Russians. If the local authorities did not have sufficient resources to do what was necessary, they could call on the Russians for assistance.[91] In a further letter to Buol, Schwarzenberg added that any Poles found travelling without proper documents would be drafted into the Austrian army.[92] A study of the original drafts of this correspondence shows that Schwarzenberg intended to grant Nicholas' request for the extradition of Count Załuski, but was prevented from doing so by the legal complications connected with the extradition of a person who had been granted Austrian citizenship.[93]

While the Austrians were responding to the Tsar's threat not to move his forces into Hungary, Nicholas made his preparations for a visit to the frontier area for a final inspection of the Russian army. His advisers, fearing an attempt at assassination, tried to dissuade him, but Nicholas' mind was made up. On the evening of 13 June a special train left Warsaw for Cracow carrying Nicholas, Paskevich, Orlov, Adlerberg and the Grand Duke Constantine, who was to undergo his baptism of fire during the campaign.[94]

On his arrival in Cracow Nicholas inspected the Russian troops stationed there and then moved on south to Żmigród, a small town to the north-east of Dukla where Paskevich's column was assembled. While he was there, he was visited by the Archduke William of Austria who bore a letter from Francis Joseph expressing the hope that Providence would bless the Austrian and Russian cause.[95] At the same time, Nicholas learned of the action taken by the Austrians to improve security in Galicia, but he was determined that Załuski should not escape. He therefore raised the matter with Count Zichy who was accompanying the Russian army.[96] Two days later General Hammerstein received a formal request from Paskevich for the arrest of Załuski. In the light of Schwarzenberg's general directive, Hammerstein had no hesitation in satisfying the Russian request. On 19 June Załuski was arrested, handed over to the Russians and taken to the fortress of Zamość in Russian Poland to await trial.[97] The civil governor of Galicia was far from pleased by Hammerstein's action, and there followed a lengthy legal battle between the Austrian and Russian governments about the fate of an Austrian citizen who had been handed over to the Russians illegally. This dispute about the ultimate fate of Załuski was to continue throughout the Hungarian campaign until it was finally settled by the handing-back of Załuski to the Austrians at the end of August, after trial by court-martial and commutation of the death-sentence.[98]

On the day of the Tsar's arrival in Żmigród, Colonel Khrulev, a cavalry officer who was to distinguish himself later in the campaign, returned from the frontier area with forty prisoners captured in an attack on a Hungarian outpost. They were paraded in the square of the town in front of the house occupied by Nicholas.[99] On 15 June General Rüdiger's column crossed the Hungarian frontier to carry out its role of protecting the flank and rear of the main column of the Russian army in the event of a Hungarian attack. By 17 June it had reached Stará L'ubovňa, twenty-five miles distant from the right flank of the main column. On 16 June General Berg informed General Haynau that Paskevich had no objection to the start of the Austrian offensive.[100]

On Sunday 17 June a church service was held, after which Nicholas' Order of the Day of 13 June, issued in Warsaw, was read out to the troops. The Russian army was going to the aid of an ally faced with the task of suppressing a revolt in Hungary which was a recurrence of the rebellion in Poland crushed by the Russians eighteen years earlier. The Tsar was confident that Paskevich would be as successful as he had been on that occasion.[101]

On the same day the main body of the Russian army, consisting of the Second and Fourth Infantry Corps, crossed into Hungary. It was divided into four columns and moved off from four points along a start line covering nearly forty miles from Grybów through Gorlice and Żmigród to Dukla. Nicholas remained with Paskevich's staff and entered Hungary with them. The sight of the endless columns marching across the Carpathians on a hot summer's day must have gladdened his heart. In one village a Uniate priest rushed forward with a cross which the Tsar solemnly kissed, while the inhabitants fell on their knees at the sight of the Russian emperor and shouted: 'Our Tsar! Our Tsar!'[102]

The following day Nicholas made his way back to Cracow. After inspecting some of the Russian forces in Poland at Kalisz, he arrived back in Warsaw in the early morning of 21 June.

7 The First Half of the Campaign

Contrary to his expectations, Paskevich did not encounter any serious resistance from the Hungarians as the Russian army advanced south from the Dukla pass into northern Hungary. On 18 June, the day on which the Russian advance guard occupied Bardejov, Dembiński, rather than occupy a position subordinate to Görgey, handed over command of the Upper Tisza Army to his fellow Pole, Wysocki, the commander of the Ninth Corps of the Hungarian army. From captured prisoners Rüdiger soon learnt that Wysocki's forces amounted to far less than the original Russian estimate of 50 000 to 60 000 men.[1]

On 23 June Paskevich and his staff, followed by the main Russian column, made a triumphal entry into Prešov, where they were joined by General Rüdiger and units of the Third Infantry Corps which had made their way south from the frontier with some difficulty along side-roads made of brushwood. While older ladies waved their handkerchiefs from the balconies, young girls in white dresses threw flowers at the Russians as they marched up the main street to the cathedral square.[2] Paskevich wrote to the Tsar that he was finding it difficult to catch up with an enemy who did nothing but retreat.[3] On 25 June the Russians made an equally triumphant entry into Košice, while the Cossacks and Caucasian irregular troops attached to Paskevich's headquarters gave chase to the retreating Hungarians.[4] At this stage Paskevich decided to divide his forces. The Second and Third Infantry Corps were sent in a south-west direction towards Budapest and occupied Miskolc on 30 June. The Fourth Infantry Corps was sent in a south-east direction towards Debrecen and occupied Tokaj on 28 June in order to secure a base for crossing the river Tisza. At the same time Paskevich carried out his plan of transforming the towns he had occupied into strongpoints, in order to protect his lines of communication with Russian Poland.

Further west the small force of General Grabbe, whose task was the protection of western Galicia, had moved south down the valley of the river Árva as far as its junction with the valley of the river Váh without encountering any opposition from the Hungarians. By 30 June Grabbe's troops had occupied the towns of Ružomberok and Liptovský Mikuláš.[5]

In fourteen days the main body of the Russian army had advanced 125 miles through mountainous country and had sustained few casualties. However, the uninterrupted progress was beginning to present Paskevich with various problems, and he therefore decided to call a temporary halt to the advance on Budapest after the Second and Third Infantry Corps had occupied Miskolc. By far the most important problem facing him was the lack of supplies in northern Hungary for his huge army. As he had insisted that his baggage and supply train should use the same road as the main column, it was taking a long time in catching up because of its size (over 4000 vehicles). By the time the leading carts had reached their stopping place for the night, the rear carts were just setting off from the starting point.[6] In the occupied towns there was no flour for the baking of bread and biscuit, and arrangements had to be made to purchase hand-grinding mills.[7] Nor was there any fodder for the horses which had to make do with grass cut by scythe in the fields where they were tethered. Attempts to requisition supplies locally proved unsuccessful, as Count Zichy and the Austrian liaison officers tried to find new officials to take the place of those appointed by Kossuth who had fled at the approach of the Russians.[8] In an effort to ease the supply situation, Paskevich ordered Cheodaev to move from Tokaj to Debrecen which Kossuth and the Hungarian government had vacated in early June. Apart from the killing and maiming of a group of Austrian prisoners by the Hungarians, this brief incursion proved to be successful. After a three-day occupation lasting from 3 to 6 July the Fourth Corps left to rejoin the main army, crossing the Tisza again at Tokaj. With them they brought a huge consignment of supplies sufficient to last 30 000 men for twenty-one days, which was transported in more than 300 locally-requisitioned carts.[9]

In addition to the shortage of supplies, Paskevich found that the local inhabitants were unwilling to accept the currency notes issued by the Austrians as a temporary substitute for the Kossuth notes which had to be surrendered and were then burnt. However, there was no hesitation about accepting Russian gold and silver coins in payment for purchases made by the Russian army. Because there was a serious shortage of small change, the Russian soldiers became accustomed to receiving the torn-off half or quarter of an Austrian one or two gulden note instead of the usual copper coins of smaller denominations.[10] So serious did Paskevich consider this problem that he asked Nesselrode to enquire from the Austrian government whether it would be possible to send a consignment of Austrian coins and paper money to Russian-occupied territory.[11]

However, the problems connected with the shortage of supplies and money were soon to be overtaken by those of disease. Towards the end of June the cholera epidemic which had reached European Russia from the East the previous year flared up again throughout the Russian army. Its worst effects were felt in the Fourth Infantry Corps where the sickness began on 24 June. By the end of the month nearly 5000 men had fallen ill.[12] The troops, who were worn out after marching during the day, often in great heat, usually had to bivouac in the open on ground which soon turned into a quagmire after heavy rain.[13] During their halts on the march the soldiers quenched their thirst by drinking water from dirty streams and pools and by eating unripe fruit and grapes from the orchards and vineyards through which they passed. There was no clear understanding of the cause of the disease, as it was not until 1883 that the germ causing cholera, the comma bacillus, was discovered. The first symptons felt by the victims were usually diarrhoea and vomiting. Troops who collapsed on the march were left by the roadside to be picked up by the units following behind. Those that had not already died were loaded on to carts and transported back to Košice where the Austrians had opened a temporary military hospital for 2500 patients, which was soon filled to overflowing. Private residences and other public buildings were hastily requisitioned in a desperate attempt to find accommodation for the sick and the dying. Because of the delay in the arrival of the Russian field hospitals, there was a serious shortage of doctors and medical supplies. To make matters worse, several days of heavy rainfalls during the period after the occupation of Košice lowered the resistance of the troops and increased the risk of infection. On one occasion a convoy was sent back from Košice to Miskolc where the sick men had to spend a night lying in an open field in pouring rain without any shelter.[14] By the middle of July the worst of the epidemic was over, but it is estimated that during the three months from 1 June to 30 September more than 20 000 soldiers fell ill, of whom 7414 died.[15] The true figures were probably much higher.

While Paskevich and the main Russian army had been occupying northern Hungary, General Grotenhjelm and General Lüders, aided by small Austrian units, had begun the reconquest of Transylvania. They faced the army of General Bem which, although slightly larger in number, had many new recruits. Its strength lay in its artillery to which Bem, as a former artillery officer, had paid particular attention.

After issuing a stirring order of the day to his troops on 13 June in which he exhorted them to remember Suvorov's maxim – 'The bullet is a fool, but the bayonet is a fine fellow' – Lüders and the main column of his army began their advance from Wallachia into Transylvania through the Predeal pass towards Braşov.[16] Although every effort had been made to reduce the size of the baggage and supply train, it still tailed back behind the army for twelve miles. After a brief battle the Russians occupied the town on 21 June and the Hungarians retreated north. The Austrian liaison officer, Colonel Dorsner, set about restoring Habsburg rule, while the Russians sought to find out more about the movements of their retreating enemy, a task which proved to be far from easy, as both their Rumanian and Saxon allies proved to have no aptitude for the collection of tactical intelligence.[17]

In the north the small force of General Grotenhjelm which was supported by an Austrian unit under Colonel Urban crossed into Transylvania from Bukovina on 18 June and headed for Bistriţa. After successfully beating off an attack by Bem on 27 June in the area of Rusul-Bîrgaului, Grotenhjelm decided to call a halt to his advance, while he and Lüders both waited to see what Bem would do next. The two forces were about 150 miles apart, but because of the mountainous terrain and the uncertainties of the situation, were only able to communicate with each other by using a circuitous route through Moldavia and Wallachia.

Although the Tsar was only too well aware of the effects of the cholera epidemic, he was delighted with the news of the successful beginning of the campaign and wrote to Paskevich that he was glad there had been so few casualties. He regretted that he could not be in the field with his army and pressed Paskevich to keep him fully informed by using as couriers young aides-de-camp who could be entrusted with verbal messages which it was considered undesirable to put in writing. Meanwhile he busied himself with the deployment of the Russian reserves in Poland and western Russia, in case they should be needed. Two divisions of dragoons under the command of General Shabel'sky were sent to Galicia, while further reinforcements were sent to General Grabbe.[18]

In Budapest, to which the Hungarian government and parliament had returned at the beginning of June, Kossuth continued his efforts to persuade a reluctant Bem to replace Görgey as Commander-in-Chief. Despite a personal meeting with Bem in Oradea on 18 June,

1. Emperor Nicholas I of Russia (*Anonymous painting, 1856*).

2. Emperor Francis Joseph of Austria (*Bildarchiv d'Österreich*).

3. Prince Alfred Windischgraetz (*School of Slavonic and East European Studies, University of London*).

4. (*above*) Count Karl von Buol-Schauenstein (*SSEES, University of London*).

5. (*right*) Prince Felix Schwarzenberg (*Bildarchiv d'Österreich*).

6. General Julius Haynau (*SSEES, University of London*).

7. Lajos Kossuth (*The Mansell Collection*).

8. General Artúr Görgey (*SSEES, University of London*).

9. (*above*) General György Klapka (*SSEES, University of London*).

10. (*right*) General József Bem (*SSEES, University of London*).

11. General Henryk Dembiński (*Hulton-Deutsch Collection*).

12. (*above*) Count Karl V. Nesselrode (*SSEES, University of London*).

13. (*right*) Field Marshal Ivan F. Paskevich (*Hulton-Deutsch Collection*)

14. (*right*) Count Pavel I. Medem.

15. General Aleksandr O. Duhamel (*SSEES, University of London*).

16. General Aleksandr N. Lüders (*SSEES, University of London*).

17. General Fyodor V. Rüdiger (*SSEES, University of London*).

Kossuth failed to induce him to leave the army in Transylvania to which he had returned after the successful conclusion of his operations in the Bánát. Kossuth's mistrust of Görgey had been increased by Görgey's visit to Debrecen at the end of May for inconclusive talks with the Peace Party about the withdrawal of the Declaration of Independence, an event which, in Görgey's view, was bound to lead to Russian intervention and the consequent defeat of Hungary. At this time Görgey still clung to his belief that if he were able to inflict a crushing defeat on the Austrian army, the Austrian government would be prepared to agree to a negotiated settlement with Hungary, rather than appeal to Russia for military assistance. Görgey could not know that the Austrians had reluctantly decided to seek Russian aid before the Declaration of Independence was proclaimed, but it is curious that he still did not realise that Schwarzenberg would be unlikely to negotiate with those whom he regarded as rebels. On 5 June, the day on which Kossuth entered Budapest, Haynau gave further proof of the Austrian attitude by ordering the execution of two captured Hungarian officers who had been sentenced to death earlier in the year for treason and rebellion, but had been granted a stay of execution by Windischgraetz and Welden. The news of the executions was to make it chillingly clear to former Habsburg officers serving with the Hungarian army that they could expect little mercy from the Austrians in the event of defeat.

It was mid-May before the news of the official announcement of the Austrian request for Russian aid reached Debrecen. On 18 May Kossuth issued the first of a series of proclamations about the impending Russian intervention, which were designed to appeal to European public opinion as much as to the population of Hungary. These eloquent appeals for a holy war against the Russian invaders and a scorched-earth policy were to have little effect on the majority of the population. Nor did the invading Russian army turn out to be as savage and cruel as Kossuth had portrayed it. With the exception of looting (carried out chiefly by the Cossacks and the small number of Caucasian irregular troops attached to Paskevich's headquarters) the strictly-disciplined Russian army and its officers made a good impression on the ordinary inhabitants, especially on their fellow Slavs. As one contemporary Slovak observer wrote at the end of the campaign, the Russians returned to their own country blessed by the Slovaks, respected by the Hungarians and filled with hatred for the Germans.[19] For his part, the ordinary Russian soldier discovered to his surprise that the Habsburg empire did not consist merely of

Germans, but was inhabited by many different nationalities.[20]

The return of the government to Budapest had brought with it further administrative problems for Kossuth. One of the most serious was the delay in reassembling the cumbersome and heavy machinery required to print the Kossuth notes. It did not start work again until early June, and it is from this date that a serious shortage of money began, making it difficult to make regular payments to the army.[21] Besides this, there was growing concern about a lack of gunpowder and saltpetre to supply the main Hungarian munitions factory in Oradea, as well as worries about a shortage of weapons, uniforms and footwear.[22] In the weeks that followed, Kossuth, while wrestling with the problems caused by the lack of unity among his generals, did his best to make good these deficiencies. It was no easy task, and as he wrote to Bem on one occasion, he was not the Almighty and could not create something out of nothing.[23]

Convinced more than ever that the government in Budapest did not understand military matters, Görgey returned on 19 June to the army in western Hungary. During his absences he had arranged for its affairs to be managed by a headquarters staff based in Tata which was directed by his Chief of Staff, Colonel Bayer. Haynau had now begun to regroup the Austrian forces which were spread out in a wide arc 100 miles in length in front of his headquarters in Bratislava on both sides of the Danube. He had decided to transfer all the Austrian forces except for the Second Corps to the right bank of the Danube in order that he could capture Győr and then make a drive on Budapest. Like Paskevich he hoped that the war would be over by the middle of August.

On 16 June, while Görgey was absent in Budapest, the Austrians defeated the Hungarians at Žihárec (Zsigárd in Hungarian), largely because of the inexperience of the Hungarian corps commanders. On 20 June fighting was resumed between the Austrians and the Hungarians slightly further north in the area of the village of Tešedikovo (Pered in Hungarian). Late in the afternoon Haynau decided to make use of Panyutin's division which had been kept in reserve at Pezinok near Bratislava and was, like the rest of the Russian army, suffering from cholera. The following day when fighting was resumed, it fought alongside the Austrian Fourth Corps under General Wohlgemuth and helped to turn the tide in favour of the Austrians. The Hungarians proved unable to make a stand against the Russian infantry as they advanced in close columns with fixed bayonets, drums beating and banners flying, as if they were on parade.[24] By the evening, the 'Kossuths', as the Russians called the Hungarians, had retreated across the river Váh south towards Komárno. Three days later Haynau moved his headquarters forward from Bratislava to Magyaróvár and Francis Joseph became the Supreme Commander of all the Austrian armies.

The Austrians were filled with admiration for the bearing of the Russian troops under fire. Haynau informed Berg and Colonel Benckendorff, one of the Tsar's aides-de-camp who was visiting Panyutin's division, that he could not have won the battle without its assistance.[25] General Wohlgemuth was equally complimentary about his new-found allies.[26] However, one Russian officer noticed that one of Wohlgemuth's divisional commanders, the Hungarian-born General Herzinger, in the course of a visit to the Russian wounded, did not hesitate to trample on a prostrate wounded soldier who turned out to be a fellow-Hungarian.[27] On 27 June the division was inspected in Magyaróvár by Francis Joseph who praised the conduct of the troops and greeted them with the traditional Russian words of thanks.[28] The successful cooperation between the two armies on the battlefield appeared to augur well for the future.

After witnessing the Russians in action, Görgey returned to Budapest on 23 June where he was given full details about the scale of the Russian intervention in northern Hungary and Transylvania. On 26 June he attended a meeting of ministers and senior military officers called by Kossuth to discuss the situation. While Dembiński, who was now a member of the general staff of the *honvéd*, proposed that the Hungarian forces should retreat south and regroup in an area at the junction of the Tisza and Maros, Görgey persuaded those present to agree to his plan that all the Hungarian forces should be concentrated in the area around the fortress of Komárno to which the government should move from Budapest. Although he was now aware of the full extent of the Russian intervention, he still adhered to his view that Hungary should make one last effort to defeat the Austrians, Hungary's real enemies, before they could join forces with the Russians to inflict the *coup de grâce* on Hungary.[29] The following day Görgey again had to return to the front to deal with the Austrian assault on Győr, which was captured on 28 June in an operation in which Francis Joseph personally took part, until he was persuaded by Schwarzenberg and others to withdraw. The Tsar who so impressed after reading an account of the Emperor's bravery under fire that he awarded him the Saint George medal (Fourth Class), a decoration which Francis Joseph was to wear on his uniform for the rest of his life.³⁰ At the same time Colonel Benckendorff was to report on his return to Warsaw after the battle that Haynau had no compunction in shooting 'foreign dilettanti' among the Hungarian prisoners *'sans autre forme de procès'*.³¹

On 27 June Kossuth issued yet another proclamation calling on the population to rise up against the Russians, while Dembiński, in the absence of Görgey, had no difficulty in persuading the government, especially after the capture of Győr, that they would do well to agree to his original plan to regroup the Hungarian forces in the south. On 29 June the government and parliament decided to move to Szeged, as they had been advised that the Austrians would soon reach Budapest.³² The evacuation of the capital began on 8 July. Once again the banknote printing press had to be dismantled and reassembled in a new location, with the result that no money was printed for a fortnight. Part of the railway track to Cegléd was torn up, but a proposal by Dembiński that the Chain Bridge should be blown up was dropped after the Minister of Justice had obtained an assurance from the engineers that it could be made unuseable by removing the planks from the roadway.³³

Meanwhile a fresh dispute had broken out between Görgey and Kossuth about the implementation of an order to burn down the village of Ács, east of Győr, before the Austrians could occupy it. Görgey flew into a rage and wrote to Kossuth that he was fighting for the Hungarian people rather than the government and would not hesitate to lay down his arms, if it was in the people's interest to do so. On receiving this letter on 1 July an equally enraged Kossuth decided to dismiss Görgey as Commander in Chief and replace him by Mészáros with Dembiński as his Chief of Staff. At the same time Görgey had assured a visiting delegation sent by Kossuth to his headquarters that he would accept the government's decision to move south, but was insistent that he would not be able to move his forces until 3 July. At this point fate intervened to prevent the implementation of Kossuth's decision to dismiss Görgey.

On 2 July Haynau decided to attack Görgey's forces gathered round Komárno before moving on Budapest. Once again Panyutin's division saved the day for the Austrians when it was brought into action in the early evening to assist the hard-pressed troops of General Schlick, the commander of the Austrian First Corps. More seriously for the Hungarians, Görgey received a severe head wound in the course of the battle which was to put him out of action for several days. In addition, his replacement Mészáros, who had arrived outside

The First Half of the Campaign

Komárno by steamer from Budapest, abandoned his attempt to land when he heard gunfire and returned to the capital. That evening, while the Hungarian forces were recovering from the shock of the news about Görgey's wound, they learnt to their dismay that Kossuth had intended to dismiss their commander. Faced with the refusal of the officers to accept the decision, Klapka and Nagy Sándor travelled to Budapest to inform Kossuth that he must reinstate Görgey. This Kossuth agreed to do, and after Görgey had given a further assurance that he would move south he resigned as Minister of War, in which post he was replaced later in July by Lajos Aulich. At the same time Kossuth had instructed Klapka to remain in Komárno with 18 000 men (the Second and Eighth Corps), while the remaining 20 000 of Görgey's army (the First, Third and Seventh Corps) were to leave Komárno by either the left or right banks in order to move south. On 11 July there was a further battle between the Hungarians and Austrians in the area of Komárno in which the Russian artillery in Panyutin's division tipped the scales in favour of the Austrians. The performance of the troops under his command in both the battles of Komárno was to earn Panyutin a special word of praise from Francis Joseph and did not pass unnoticed by the Tsar.[34]

On 12 July Görgey, who, because of his wound, had been forced to remain a spectator during the previous day's battle, set out from Komárno with three of the Hungarian corps along the left bank of the Danube, which was free of Austrian troops, on the long march south to join the Hungarian forces and government in Szeged. It was his hope that he would be able to reach Vác on the Danube and Gödöllő to the east of Budapest before the Russians. Klapka, who had originally decided to leave with Görgey, changed his mind and remained with two corps in the fortress, secure in the knowledge that he had sufficient stocks of food, supplies and ammunition to be able to withstand a lengthy siege by the Austrians.

While he was attacking the Hungarians near Komárno, Haynau had not lost sight of his aim of advancing on Budapest, and in the late afternoon of 11 July a cavalry unit of the Third Corps commanded by General Ramberg entered Buda. After making the roadway of the Chain Bridge useable, they crossed into Pest and linked up on 12 July with a party of Cossacks commanded by Captain Adlerberg which Paskevich had sent on ahead of his main force.

In southern Hungary Jelačić's army was initially successful in driving the Hungarians out of the Bácska, while the fortress of Timişoara continued to hold out against the Hungarians. However, on 1 July the fortress of Arad was compelled to surrender to the Hungarians, who were to benefit from the large quantity of supplies left behind by the departing Austrian garrison, as it marched off to Styria after an honourable capitulation and agreement not to fight the Hungarians for another six months. On 14 July the Hungarians also inflicted a severe defeat on Jelačić's forces at Mali Idos (Hegyes in Hungarian) and had to retreat across the Danube to the right bank in order to regroup. The lack of progress made by the Austrian forces in southern Hungary was to influence Haynau's decisions about his future movements to a considerable extent.

Although the Austrians and Panyutin's division had fought well together, this cooperation in the field was unfortunately not matched at a higher level by the commanders of the two armies. The first bone of contention was Paskevich's reluctance to disclose his plans to his Austrian allies, and his refusal to allow Grabbe's force to be diverted from its task of protecting western Galicia, instead of continuing its advance down the valley of the river Váh to link up with the Austrian Second Corps commanded by General Csorich, which still remained on the left bank of the Danube. Haynau had been planning to use Grabbe's force to complete the encirclement of the fortress of Komárno on its northern side and found the Russian refusal to allow it to move south all the more incomprehensible in the light of the provision made in Paskevich's original operational plan for the despatch of a second Russian column down the Váh valley.

The matter was first raised by Schwarzenberg on 19 June direct with Paskevich, as well as through the two liaison officers, Berg and Parrot. A week later Schwarzenberg wrote to Buol in Warsaw instructing him to complain to Nesselrode in the hope that the latter could bring his influence to bear on the Tsar.[35] At the same time General Berg was persuaded to enter the fray and was tactless enough to refer to the Austrian failure to understand the actions of their 'auxiliary army' in a letter he addressed personally to the Tsar. On a more practical note, he foolishly sent a letter to Count Adlerberg about the necessity of sending some bakers to Panyutin's division. The Tsar, who had seized on the Austrian complaint about the movements of Grabbe's forces as soon as it had been raised, was swift to defend Paskevich, whose judgement he trusted. He therefore instructed Adlerberg to administer a stern rebuke to Berg for daring to take the side of the Austrians and for making the extraordinary suggestion that the Russian army should depart from its normal custom of expecting its rank and file to bake its own bread. Simultaneously the Tsar informed Paskevich of his displeasure with Berg and urged him to restrain his anger when he replied to Berg and the Austrians.[36] Buol also pointed out to Schwarzenberg that no-one in Warsaw, not even the Tsar, was prepared to give orders to Paskevich about the conduct of the campaign, and this included the movements of Grabbe's force.[37] Berg quickly made amends for what he described as his excess of zeal in pressing the Austrian request and wrote a suitably abject reply to the Tsar, while requesting Adlerberg to do his best to make the Tsar appreciate the difficulty of his liaison task. Paskevich, however, who disliked Berg, was not to forgive 'Monsieur Berg', as he called him, and referred to him as 'our Austrian general, who is not even a good one, and knows nothing about the Russian army'.[38]

Schwarzenberg's next move was to send Colonel Benckendorff back to Warsaw after the capture of Győr with a personal letter from Francis Joseph requesting the Tsar to order Grabbe's force to advance south to Banská Bystrica.[39] The Tsar still declined to yield to Austrian pressure, but advised Paskevich that he personally saw no reason why Grabbe should not be allowed to move south, once he had received his reinforcements.[40] Meanwhile Grabbe, who had no high opinion of Paskevich's military ability, was fending off requests from General Csorich and one of his divisional commanders, General Pott, to join forces with them. After careful consideration, Grabbe decided not to await the arrival of reinforcements but to move south. By 8 July his troops had occupied Banská Bystrica and had moved as far south as Banská Stiavnica, but were still some distance from the river Váh and the Austrian Second Corps.

The disagreement between the Austrians and Russians about the role of Grabbe's forces was to run like a red thread throughout the correspondence exchanged between Haynau and Paskevich, which became increasingly bitter as the campaign went on. It was soon followed by another dispute which was to lead to further recriminations between the two commanders.

After his occupation of Miskolc at the end of June, Paskevich had informed Berg and Haynau by separate means that he had been forced to call a temporary halt to his advance on Budapest until he could ensure that he had enough supplies to last his forces for the next twenty-five days. Haynau's response was to urge Paskevich to continue his advance on Pest, while his own forces advanced on Buda. It was in any case desirable that the two armies should join forces, and Paskevich would find that his supply problems would disappear once he had left the mountainous area of northern Hungary and moved into the plain.[41] At the same time Haynau also informed Paskevich that he was expecting Görgey to break out of Komárno and make for Vác along the left bank of the Danube. If Paskevich sent troops to occupy Vác, Görgey would be trapped between the two armies.[42]

While this exchange of letters had been taking place, Paskevich had collected enough supplies during his stay in Miskolc to be able to continue his advance. However, he was still worried about the threat of Hungarian guerrilla attacks on his lines of communication with Poland, and obtained the Tsar's agreement to allow General Osten-Sacken's force in eastern Galicia to move south to reinforce the units commanded by General Sel'van which were already carrying out guard duties in Russian-occupied territory.[43] The Tsar's agreement was the more readily given because the Austrians themselves had asked the Russians in Warsaw and General Grabbe direct for assistance in dealing with the threat of Hungarian guerrilla attacks being made from northern Hungary into Galicia.[44]

On 8 July Paskevich set off from Miskolc with the Second and Third Infantry Corps down the main road to Budapest. The advance was painfully slow (about twelve miles a day), because Paskevich had no knowledge of the exact whereabouts of the Hungarian forces and was still encumbered by his huge baggage and supply train. By 13 July the Third Infantry Corps had reached Hatvan, closely followed by the Second Infantry Corps in Gyöngyös, while the Fourth Infantry Corps was kept further back in Mezőkövesd. On 14 July Paskevich received Haynau's letter of 10 July about the possible breakout of Görgey's forces from Komárno towards Vác and on the following day part of his Caucasian cavalry commanded by Prince Bebutov was able to confirm this when they clashed with the Hungarians to the north of Vác. General Rüdiger, the commander of the Third Infantry Corps, then ordered the cavalry of General Sass to go to the aid of Bebutov. In his enthusiasm Sass, who had distinguished himself in the Caucasus, allowed himself to be drawn on to the plain on the outskirts of Vác, where his cavalry were severely mauled by the Hungarian artillery positioned on the surrounding high ground. He was eventually rescued by the arrival of more Russian cavalry and troops from the Third Infantry Corps under the personal command of General Rüdiger.

The news about the possible breakout of Görgey's forces from

Komárno caused Paskevich to become even more anxious about the threat to his lines of communication. He promptly ordered the Fourth Infantry Corps to stop the advance from Mezőkövesd and then turn back to Miskolc, an order which was equally promptly countermanded when he learnt of Sass' clash with the Hungarians near Vác. The remainder of 15 July and the first half of 16 July were spent in ensuring that the Russian army would be ready for a full-scale battle with Görgey's army in the area to the south of Vác. While Paskevich urged on his troops from the saddle and a carriage for eighteen hours, the infantry marched between twenty-five and thirty miles over marshy ground. The result was that everyone became exhausted and despite the insistence of Rüdiger and Paskevich's Chief of Staff that the attack ought not to be delayed, Paskevich eventually retired to bed, having decided that the attack would take place the following morning.[45]

Görgey, who realised that Paskevich had now succeeded in blocking his route south, decided to move north through the mountains of northern Hungary by a circuitous route in the hope that he would be able to cross the Tisza and then move south before the Russians could catch up with him. On the evening of 16 July he ordered his troops to begin evacuating Vác and to move north towards Balassagyarmat and Lučenec. There was only one bridge across the Danube and the approach to it in the town became jammed with troops and civilian refugees fleeing from the advancing Austrian and Russian armies. The following morning the Russians engaged the Hungarian rearguard as it was covering the withdrawal, but by the evening Görgey's forces had successfully withdrawn and were making their way north-east, pursued by Rüdiger's Third Infantry Corps. Görgey himself narrowly escaped capture by a party of Russian Cossacks.[46] One of the casualties in the battle was Colonel Langenau, the Austrian liaison officer attached to Rüdiger, who lost a leg. He had not enjoyed working with the Russians, and only the day before the battle had written a letter to Schwarzenberg complaining about his position and the Russian refusal to disclose their plans to him.[47] Paskevich's decision to delay his attack had cost him the opportunity to gain a decisive victory and he was to be much criticised for this action in the ensuing weeks.

While Görgey's forces set off on their long detour through the mountains, Paskevich had to deal with an attack from the Hungarian forces in the south led by General Perczel. On 20 July there was a battle at Tura to the east of Budapest in which Russian cavalry units commanded by Lieutenant-General Tolstoy successfully drove back the Hungarians. Perczel retreated to Szolnok from where he was ordered south to defend the lower reaches of the Tisza against an attack by the advancing Austrian forces.

Paskevich now decided that he would move his army east to secure a crossing-point on the river Tisza before Görgey could do so. As he was to write later, he had decided that the war could be won only by manoeuvres and not by battles with an enemy who declined to fight.[48] However, his ever-present concern for the protection of his lines of communication led him to order the garrison in Košice to withdraw to Prešov, not least to prevent a Russian convoy carrying 300 000 roubles in gold coins from falling into the hands of the Hungarians.[49] In the event, the withdrawal proved to be unnecessary and the town was re-occupied by Osten-Sacken's forces from Galicia on 29 July. Despite Rüdiger's pleas to be allowed to continue his pursuit of a totally demoralised enemy, the Third Infantry Corps was ordered to disengage and move east in parallel with the Second Infantry Corps to cross the Tisza. While the Fourth Infantry Corps was left in Mezőkövesd and warned to be ready to move on Miskolc, Grabbe's force was ordered to assist in the defeat of Görgey rather than assist the Austrians with the siege of Komárno. Paskevich also proposed that Haynau should be asked to send part of his army to Szolnok to protect his rear.

In order to make his intentions fully clear to Haynau, who had entered Budapest on 19 July, Paskevich sent General Freytag to the capital to discuss his plan with the Austrian commander. At this time he was feeling far from pleased with Haynau because he had refused to release supplies in Budapest to Count Zichy and General Sattler on the grounds that he needed them for the Austrian army.[50] He therefore instructed Freytag to threaten Haynau with the withdrawal of Panyutin's division from his army if he refused to send Austrian troops to Szolnok. Freytag, with the assistance of Berg, persuaded Haynau to agree to Paskevich's request and wisely decided not to refer to the threat to withdraw Panyutin's division.[51]

However, the reluctance of Haynau and Paskevich to meet to discuss the next phase of the campaign was to lead to a further round of mutual recriminations, as Haynau now decided to change his mind about crossing the Danube as a result of the outcome of the battle at Komárno on 11 July. Because of the Russian reluctance to allow him to use Grabbe's troops and his fear that Görgey might seek to avoid a pitched battle with the Russians and turn west again, Haynau

The First Half of the Campaign 157

decided to leave Schlick's First Corps behind to assist Csorich in the Komárno area and, after occupying Budapest, to move south to assist Jelačić as a result of his defeat on 14 July. Haynau's concern that Görgey might turn west and threaten Moravia was reflected in an Austrian approach to Prussia to strengthen defences in Silesia, and a renewed appeal made to Paskevich, Berg and Grabbe personally that Russian troops should be moved to the Komárno area.[52] Despite his promise to Freytag to send Austrian troops to Szolnok, Haynau also suggested to Paskevich that he should move one of his three infantry corps there which could then continue its advance south to Oradea and link up with the Russian and Austrian forces operating in Transylvania.[53]

Paskevich's anger with Haynau's change of plan was made clear in a letter he wrote to Berg expressing astonishment at the decision to move south to assist Jelačić.[54] Officially he informed Haynau of his plans to move east and protect his lines of communication, adding that he intended to use Grabbe's forces for his own purposes,[55] a decision which Grabbe confirmed both to Haynau and the local Austrian commanders in the Komárno area.[56] Paskevich was not to forgive Haynau for this change of plan, and after the war was over, he was to incorporate it in the official Russian history of the campaign and use it as the main justification for the failure to defeat Görgey at Vác.[57] While there were sound military reasons for Haynau's decision to move south, it seems highly probable that he had no wish to put himself in a situation where he would have been compelled to defer to the wishes of an officer who was far senior to him in age and rank. In any case, Paskevich flatly refused to divide his forces and preferred to operate in the mass, a procedure which the Austrians found incomprehensible. The mutual recriminations were to continue for the rest of the campaign, with both commanders protesting vigorously to their superiors in Saint Petersburg and Vienna about the impossibility of cooperating with each other. All that Berg could do was to try to persuade Haynau to moderate his language as, for example, when he waxed sarcastic about Paskevich's concern about a possible Hungarian attack on Košice.[58]

In the midst of his preoccupations with Görgey and Haynau, Paskevich was still endeavouring to exercise control over the operations of the Russian forces in Transylvania. His orders to Grotenhjelm and Lüders still rested on the assumption that, after defeating General Bem, they would be able to link up with either the main Russian army as it advanced south or with Jelačić's army in southern Hungary.[59] In fact, both the Russian generals were operating independently of each other and were communicating more easily with the Tsar in Warsaw.

In southern Transylvania, Lüders followed up his initial success in occupying Braşov by moving west and occupying Făgăraş on 12 July. The small Austrian force of Clam-Gallas, which was seriously affected by cholera, followed behind and occupied Braşov on 13 July in order that the Széklers could be kept in check. Other Russian units defeated the Hungarians to the north of the town at Ozun (Uzon in Hungarian) and Sfîntul Gheorghe on 2 and 5 July. Finally, on 21 July Lüders entered Sibiu much to the relief of its Saxon inhabitants who welcomed the arrival of the Russian forces, as they had done earlier in the year.[60] As the Austrians were unable to supply bread and fodder locally Lüders was compelled to obtain his supplies from Wallachia and received assistance from the Turkish forces, especially with the supply of biscuit.[61] The successful capture of Sibiu completed Lüders' occupation of the southern strip of Transylvania and ensured that he was now free to move north from a well-protected base area with safe lines of communication into Wallachia.

Grotenhjelm, however, was unable to do more than ensure that Bem did not break through into Bukovina. Nevertheless, he was able to defeat Bem's forces near Bistriţa on 10 July and then turned southeast to occupy Reghin on 23 July. By this time Bem had decided to turn his attention to the defeat of the Russian and Austrian forces in the south.

On 14 July Kossuth had signed an agreement in Szeged with Nicolae Bălcescu and Cezar Bolliac from Wallachia, whereby the Hungarian government agreed to recognise the Rumanians as a separate nationality with the right to use their own language. In return, the Rumanians agreed to raise a Rumanian legion to fight alongside the Hungarians. Bem, who had rejected yet another invitation from Kossuth to become Commander-in-Chief, decided to launch an invasion of Moldavia in an effort to cut the lines of communication of the Russian army. After skirmishing with Clam-Gallas' forces near Sfîntul Gheorghe, he entered Moldavia on 23 July through the Oituz pass. His forces were able to advance as far as Ocna, but contrary to Bem's hopes, the Moldavians had no wish to rise up against the Russians. Nor were the Turks anxious to be drawn into the fighting between the Austrians, Russians and Hungarians.[62] Fearing that Clam-Gallas would cut off his retreat into Transylvania, Bem began to withdraw his forces on 26 July. The operation had failed in its purpose and only caused Lüders a slight delay as he prepared to advance north from Sibiu into the centre of Transylvania.[63]

The news that the Fourth Infantry Corps had occupied Debrecen without bloodshed reached the Tsar in Warsaw on 9 July. It seemed to him that Paskevich should have no difficulty in capturing Budapest, an event which he expected to take place by 23 July at the latest. Although Nicholas was not the man to shirk his duty, he decided that on this occasion he could afford to leave Warsaw for a few days in order to make a flying visit to Peterhof to see his wife and family. On 13 July the Tsarina was due to celebrate her fifty-first birthday, but, more importantly, she, like the Tsar, was still mourning the death on 28 June at the age of seven of Alexandra, the eldest child of the Tsarevich.[64] On 10 July the Tsar left Warsaw and arrived in Peterhof on the evening of 12 July, accompanied only by his *valet de chambre* in a two-wheeled carriage of the kind used by Russian couriers, as his own coach had caught fire near Luga, some 125 miles from Saint Petersburg.[65]

After comforting his wife and family the Tsar then had a meeting with Prince Volkonsky who had been left in charge during his absence in Warsaw. As always, one of the most important matters was the strain on Russia's finances caused by the war in Hungary and the continuing struggle in the Caucasus. The Tsar decided to break off the negotiations with Baring Brothers in London for a foreign loan which had been in progress since early June, and to authorise the Ministry of Finance to issue a new series of credit notes which would produce the sum of 21 million silver roubles (= £3½ million).[66]

More immediately, there were reports that Bem might be planning to invade Galicia through Bukovina; if this were to happen, the Tsar doubted whether Grotenhjelm's relatively small force would be able to prevent this. Accordingly, Osten-Sacken and Shabel'sky were ordered to be on the alert but, as we have seen, Bem had decided to invade Moldavia rather than Galicia and as a result, Osten-Sacken's force was able to occupy northern Hungary, as had been originally intended.[67] On 21 July the Tsar left his private residence at Aleksandriya near Saint Petersburg to return to Warsaw which he reached on the evening of 24 July.

During his return journey Nicholas received a number of reports about the progress of the war from couriers he met as they were *en route* from Warsaw to Saint Petersburg. The most important of these dealt with Paskevich's failure to defeat Görgey at Vác, which was a considerable disappointment. At first, the Tsar was prepared to accept Haynau's change of plan as a contributory factor in Görgey's escape, but after he had read a report from Vienna about Jelačić's defeat at Mali Idos, he revised his opinion. On his return to Warsaw Nicholas informed Paskevich that he did not wish the whole Russian army to advance any further south than Oradea and considered that two infantry corps were more than enough to defeat Görgey, even if his army was not as demoralised as Rüdiger believed. The Tsar was already beginning to think about Austria's problems in Hungary once the war was over, and was contemplating sending his eldest son to Vienna to discuss this matter with Francis Joseph. Nor had he forgotten about the unresolved question of the leadership in Germany and the rivalry between Austria and Prussia.[68] As a result, he began to make his wishes known about the gradual withdrawal of the Russian army from Hungary, including Panyutin's division which he wished to revert to Paskevich's control. The bright spot in the reports was the success of Lüders' operations, which was why he was confident that the Russian forces in Moldavia would have little difficulty in forcing Bem to withdraw into Transylvania.[69]

However, as July drew to a close the Tsar became increasingly aware that there was growing criticism of Paskevich and his handling of the campaign among his senior advisers. As Buol wrote to Schwarzenberg, Paskevich had many enemies and few friends, apart from the Tsar.[70] While Nicholas was prepared to make allowances for the strain placed on the sixty-seven-year-old Paskevich by the Hungarian climate and the physical exertions of the campaign, he was finding it more and more difficult to understand why Görgey remained undefeated. Rumours soon began to circulate in Warsaw that Paskevich would be replaced if he failed to prevent Görgey linking up with the Hungarian forces in the south.[71] But luck was on Paskevich's side and he was soon to be given the chance to bring the war to a conclusion by other means than a victory on the battlefield.

At about three o'clock in the afternoon of 20 July a small Russian detachment about 700 strong, forming part of General Sass' cavalry unit, commanded by Colonel Khrulev, had caught up near Lučenec with the Hungarian First Corps, commanded by Nagy Sándor, which formed the rearguard of Görgey's army. In order to avoid defeat or capture, Khrulev began to parley with the Hungarians and was eventually able to persuade them to allow two of his officers, Captain Kotlyarov and Junior Lieutenant Rüdiger, a nephew of the commander of the Third Infantry Corps, to be escorted to Görgey's headquarters at Rimavská Sobota. Meanwhile, an unsuccessful attempt was made to declare a one-day armistice and Khrulev, after sending back part of his detachment, attempted to deceive the Hungarians about the numbers of his troops by causing a large number of camp fires to be lit.

On arriving at the Hungarian headquarters in the early hours of 21 July, the two officers attempted to persuade Görgey, who was still recovering from the effects of his head wound, that he would do well to surrender to Paskevich, as he was surrounded by Russian forces on all sides. Görgey, suspecting that an attempt was being made to delay his advance south, asked for a written document about surrender terms. This was prepared on the spot by Lieutenant Rüdiger who spoke and wrote German. Meanwhile Görgey informed the French-speaking Kotlyarov that the Hungarians would prefer to be ruled by the Russians rather than by the Austrians, and appears to have made a reference to the crown of Hungary being offered to a Russian prince. The Russians were then allowed to return bearing a reply which stated that Görgey had no authority to negotiate a surrender, as he was not the head of the government. A further reply would follow in forty-eight hours after due consideration had been given to the Russian proposal.[72] After consultation with his three corps commanders, Görgey sent two of his officers with a reply addressed to Paskevich. It stated that the Hungarian army would only be willing to lay down its arms if Russia agreed to guarantee the constitution of 1848. On 22 July Görgey found that he was able to enter Miskolc unopposed, as Russian troops had withdrawn from it. On 25 and 26 July there were skirmishes to the south of Miskolc between Poeltenberg's corps and the advance guard of the Russian Fourth Infantry Corps, but the Russians were unable to prevent Görgey's moving east across the river Sajó.

While Colonel Khrulev had been making his attempt to enter into negotiations with Görgey, General Rüdiger had also decided to take a similar initiative without Paskevich's prior authority. On 19 July he had occupied accommodation in Balassagyarmat which had been just vacated by Görgey, and learnt that the latter did not believe that Hungary could defeat the Russian intervention force.[73] Remembering his conversation in Cracow with Görgey's uncle about the disagreements between Görgey and Kossuth, he decided to send the Hungarian general a letter by the hand of a Hungarian widow, Baroness Bory, who by chance was visiting his headquarters to seek compensation for looting by some Cossacks, and claimed to be related to Görgey.[74] In his letter Rüdiger appealed to Görgey to avoid further bloodshed in his hopeless situation and to propose conditions for surrender.[75] On 24 July Baroness Bory was able to deliver the letter to Görgey at his headquarters at Alsózsolca near Miskolc. Görgey, believing that Rüdiger was acting on behalf of Paskevich, discussed the matter with some of his senior officers. He decided to accept Rüdiger's proposal in principle and asked for further details of Paskevich's surrender terms. However, he requested Baroness Bory to return to Rüdiger via Nagy Sándor's headquarters at Szikszó with his reply which was sealed. While she spent the night there, Nagy Sándor arranged for the reply to be clandestinely removed, opened and resealed, a fact which did not escape the baroness's notice. Nagy Sándor, who was as mistrustful as Kossuth of Görgey's intentions, believed that Görgey was attempting to negotiate a surrender without Kossuth's knowledge, whereas Görgey had been careful to report the Russian approaches to the Hungarian government.[76] The episode of the sealed letter made it inevitable that Görgey's exchanges with the Russians became the subject of the wildest speculation in the army. The atmosphere of suspicion was further increased when his two emissaries to the Russians returned with a gift of pistols from General Sass and Colonel Khrulev. This had been made in response to some small presents given by two of Görgey's aides-de-camp to Captain Kotlyarov and Lieutenant Rüdiger, which Sass and Khrulev mistakenly assumed had come from Görgey personally.[77]

Görgey, not wishing to be outdone by the Russians, decided to reciprocate the gift and sent two officers to Miskolc to deliver his own pair of pistols. On their arrival they found the Fourth Infantry Corps in occupation and were introduced to General Cheodaev, the corps commander, General Kuznetsov, the Ataman of the Cossacks and General Simonich, the Provost Marshal. After handing over the pistols, the envoys informed the astonished Russians that Görgey and Kossuth had authorised them to offer the Hungarian crown to the Tsar's son-in-law, the Duke of Leuchtenberg, provided he agreed to guarantee the constitution of 1848.[78] In addition, the envoys spoke of the Hungarian wish to surrender to the Russians rather than the Austrians, while Simonich admitted that the Russians had no love for their Austrian allies. The Russians agreed to inform Paskevich of the Hungarian proposals, but warned the envoys that the Tsar was most unlikely to agree to them.[79]

General Rüdiger duly informed Paskevich of his action, but did not reply formally to the letter brought back by Baroness Bory. As Paskevich subsequently informed the Tsar, Rüdiger had acted entirely on his own initiative and he would have no hesitation in disowning his corps commander, if there were unfortunate consequences.[80] Nevertheless, it was becoming obvious that Görgey appeared to be willing to surrender to the Russians, and Paskevich therefore instructed Berg to seek Haynau's views about surrender terms. The text of Paskevich's letter to Berg has not been published, but it is clear from Berg's reply that Paskevich referred only to the Khrulev episode and mentioned the possibility of offering Görgey money and the Hungarians an amnesty. In his reply, which he cleared with Haynau before despatch, Berg stated that there was no objection to giving Görgey money. However, the words 'amnesty' and 'capitulation' should not be used in any agreement that might be made between Russia and Hungary, as the Austrians intended that the case of each individual Hungarian officer should be examined before a specially convened tribunal.[81]

On 24 July Paskevich wrote to the Tsar about the two attempts which had been made to open negotiations with Görgey. The complete text of this letter has not been published, but it is possible to reconstruct most of it from the parts which appear in the works of three Russian historians who had access to official papers.[82] Like the Tsar, Paskevich was concerned about the long-term future of the Habsburg empire and Hungary's place in it, when the war was over. He was also afraid that he would not be able to finish the campaign by mid-August as he had hoped, and made no secret of his own poor health. It appeared that the Hungarians wished to surrender to the Russians rather than the Austrians and it seemed foolish not to take advantage of disagreements which existed between Görgey and Kossuth. There seems little doubt that Paskevich suggested offering Görgey money or a pension, and he certainly mentioned the offer of the Hungarian crown to a member of the Tsar's family, possibly the Grand Duke Constantine whose presence in the Russian army was known to the Hungarians.

In the printed version of the Tsar's reply to Paskevich there is no reference to the suggestion that money should be offered to Görgey.[83] However, it appears reasonably certain that the proposal was made and rejected, since another printed Russian source dealing with a later episode in the war, the fall of Komárno in October, refers to the Tsar's dislike of bribery as a means of ending a conflict, instead of accepting the risk of further bloodshed.[84] There is also evidence that the Tsar, by nature, had little taste for deception and preferred a straight fight on the battlefield.[85] The Tsar was 'amused' by Colonel

Khrulev's resourcefulness in extricating himself from the tight corner in which he had found himself, but he was adamant that he would not allow the Grand Duke Constantine, nor any other member of his family, to rule Hungary as king in the way that he had ruled Poland before the revolt of 1830. There the matter rested for the time being, but it was not to be long before the negotiations with the Russians were resumed, as Hungary's position continued to deteriorate and Haynau advanced steadily south towards Szeged.

8 The Second Half of the Campaign

Paskevich began his preparations for crossing the Tisza by sending a detachment commanded by Prince Gorchakov, his Chief of Staff, to secure a bridgehead on the left bank at Tiszafüred. After a twenty-mile march from Kerecsend in the scorching heat, the detachment reached the right bank of the river about five o'clock in the afternoon. Although the ground near the river was very marshy, it had dried out in places as a result of the heat. When darkness fell, the Russian and Austrian engineers began to lay a pontoon bridge under cover of artillery fire. During the night the Hungarians set fire to the bridge across the river which was soon destroyed. However, by the following morning the pontoon bridge had been successfully laid and Tiszafüred occupied.[1] There the Russians found the wounded survivors from a detachment of the Voznesensk Uhlan Regiment of the Fourth Infantry Corps, whose young Polish commander, Cornet K. Rulikowski, had deliberately allowed his troops to be ambushed by the Hungarians while they were out foraging near Poroszló on 23 July.[2]

Paskevich then sent his son to Warsaw to inform the Tsar that he intended to concentrate his forces at Tiszafüred and then move on Debrecen.[3] However, as he still had no definite information about Görgey's movements, Paskevich was hesitant about following up Gorchakov's success, in case Görgey decided not to cross the Tisza. Consequently, there followed a period of great confusion for the Russian army, as Paskevich issued orders which were often countermanded almost immediately.

On 27 July General Grabbe's force reached Miskolc, the same day on which General Osten-Sacken's detachment reached Prešov further north. Paskevich intended that both these detachments should move east towards Tokaj in order to assist him in defeating Görgey, should he move in that direction. To his surprise Grabbe learnt from General Cheodaev that his Fourth Infantry Corps was being withdrawn from Miskolc in order to assist Paskevich, if he were attacked by the Hungarians. Having failed to persuade Cheodaev to ignore Paskevich's order and combine their forces, Grabbe took a conscious decision to continue the advance towards Tokaj with his small detachment, in the full knowledge that he might be defeated by

Görgey's army which was superior in numbers. On 28 July his detachment came across the Hungarian army at Gesztely, east of Miskolc and was drawn into an artillery duel which Grabbe was forced to break off after four hours because of a shortage of ammunition. At this juncture he received an order from Paskevich sent earlier in the day, instructing him not to advance to Tokaj, but to move to Vatta, south of Miskolc. Learning that the inhabitants of Miskolc might be preparing to create disturbances, Grabbe prudently decided to retreat north-west and eventually reached Putnok. He sent a full account of the confused orders he had received from Paskevich not only to the Tsar, but also to other senior members of his staff in Warsaw, in order that they should be left in no doubt about Paskevich's incompetence.[4]

One of Paskevich's other worries at this time was the possibility that Osten-Sacken's detachment might be defeated by Görgey, thus posing a threat to his lines of communication and supply bases in northern Hungary.[5] In order to lessen the chances of this happening, Paskevich decided that he must be able to operate on both sides of the Tisza. Accordingly, on 29 July he ordered the engineers to dismantle the pontoon bridge at Tiszafüred and move it twelve miles upstream to Tiszacsege, to which the Second and Third Infantry Corps were also ordered to move, while the Fourth Infantry Corps remained on the right bank at Mezőkövesd. Thus the main body of Paskevich's army was now divided into two groups some twenty miles apart, ready for an attack by Görgey from any direction.

However, Görgey, who had been summoned by Kossuth to a meeting at Karcag, south-west of Debrecen, had no intention of allowing his army to be drawn into a pitched battle with the Russians. When he learnt of the advance south from Prešov of Osten-Sacken's detachment and the successful establishment of the Russian bridgehead at Tiszafüred, he cancelled the meeting with Kossuth at Karcag and immediately ordered his army to cross the Tisza at Tokaj, an operation which was completed without mishap on 29 July. From there he moved on Nyiregyháza and gave further orders for a wide sweep to be made to the east of Debrecen through Vámospércs and Kismarja en route for Oradea. In order to protect the main body of his army from a possible Russian attack, Nagy Sándor's corps was to continue acting as a rearguard on the right flank, but was ordered to avoid a battle and to withdraw towards Berettyóújfalu.[6]

Meanwhile, Paskevich, who was still completely in the dark about Görgey's movements, continued manoeuvring his army, despite the attempts made by his staff to persuade him that his fears of an attack by Görgey were exaggerated.[7] On 30 July he decided to move the Second Infantry Corps which, together with the Third Corps, had advanced up the left bank to link up with the Fourth Corps at Mezőkövesd. The confusion on the bridge at Tiszacsege was considerable, as many of the heavier guns and vehicles became stuck in the muddy approaches to the bridge on the left bank. On 1 August Paskevich learnt that Osten-Sacken's detachment had successfully occupied Tokaj and that Görgey had crossed the Tisza after all. He quickly moved the Second Infantry Corps back to the left bank of the Tisza to join the Third Corps which had been left there in order that both corps could advance on Debrecen. According to one source, Paskevich did not keep the Tsar informed of all his actions at this time, but, despite this, the Tsar was to learn about them from the letters of the Grand Duke Constantine, who had personally witnessed the scene on the bridge at Tiszacsege and had vainly tried to persuade Paskevich to make more use of his cavalry to find out Görgey's whereabouts.[8]

On 2 August Paskevich ordered Grabbe's detachment to return to its original task of protecting western Galicia. In his diary, Grabbe recorded his relief at being withdrawn from 'this chaos of contradictory, illogical and unsuccessful movements of a large army'.[9] In Warsaw, the Tsar was becoming more and more perplexed by Paskevich's continuing inability to inflict a decisive defeat on Görgey. After he received on 3 August an account of the action at Gesztely from Grabbe's courier, the aide-de-camp Isakov, who had taken part in the action, he sent a letter to Paskevich (from whom he had heard nothing for over a week) in which he asked his 'father-commander' a number of searching questions about the reasons for Görgey's success.[10]

Meanwhile, the Second and Third Infantry Corps, followed by their enormous baggage trains, set off across the treeless expanse of plain from Tiszacsege to Debrecen. A violent thunderstorm with hail which rapidly transformed the ground into a quagmire interrupted their march in the blazing heat, but by the evening of 1 August they had reached Balmazújváros, some fifteen miles to the north of Debrecen. In order to find out more about the movements of Görgey's forces, Paskevich sent out on reconnaissance a detachment of Caucasian irregular cavalry commanded by Prince Bebutov. In the early morning of 2 August Bebutov sent back no less than five reports about the strength and position of the Hungarian forces facing the

Russians. It was evident from captured prisoners that the troops opposing the Russians were those of Nagy Sándor's First Corps, while the Hungarian Third and Seventh Corps were by-passing Debrecen and making for Oradea.[11] Despite these reports, the ever-cautious Paskevich ordered further reconnaissance operations to be carried out by Generals Gorchakov and Freytag, who reported in similar terms.[12]

Still under the illusion that he would have to fight a major battle, Paskevich began lining up his troops in battle formation. At first the open plain presented no obstacle to their advance, but when the Russian troops encountered fields of maize which were so high that the tops of the lances of the cavalry were barely visible, they had to be reformed into columns in order to be able to continue their forward movement. Indeed, the Second Light Cavalry division which was being kept in reserve by Paskevich, received strict instructions not to move from its hiding place in the fields of maize without further orders, and as a result remained completely inactive throughout the fighting, much to the amazement of the rest of the army.[13]

While the main body of the Russian army was carrying out its complicated redeployment into columns, the Russian advance guard soon found itself engaged in an artillery duel with the Hungarians. The light guns of the Russian horse artillery were no match for the well-concealed heavier weapons of their Hungarian opponents, but Paskevich refused to allow heavier Russian guns to be brought into action until the redeployment manoeuvres had been completed, a procedure which occupied most of the early hours of the afternoon. At this stage of the battle the Commander of the Second Infantry Corps, Lieutenant General Kupriyanov, was wounded and lost his right leg, while the Grand Duke Constantine was nearly killed by a cannon ball.[14]

Nagy Sándor, who had been fêted by the inhabitants when he arrived in Debrecen the previous day, was attending a banquet being given in his honour when the artillery duel began about one o'clock in the afternoon. As his corps had been reinforced by the Hungarian detachment which had tried to prevent the establishment of the Russian bridgehead at Tiszafüred, he decided, despite the entreaties of his staff, to disregard Görgey's orders to avoid a battle and make a stand against the Russians. It was a fatal decision. With the eventual arrival on the battlefield of heavier Russian artillery, it was not long before his troops were compelled to withdraw, hotly pursued by Bebutov's Caucasian irregulars, shouting 'Allah, Allah' as they galloped through the streets of Debrecen, ruthlessly cutting down the startled Hungarian soldiers who fell on their knees, seeking to surrender.[15] The Caucasian cavalry pursued the Hungarians for some distance outside the town but were eventually recalled and later began to loot and pillage the town, terrifying the inhabitants with their wild behaviour, before order was restored.[16] At eight o'clock in the evening, as the sun began to set, Paskevich entered the town, while the remnants of Nagy Sándor's forces rapidly made their way south to rejoin the main body of Görgey's army which entered Oradea on 5 August.

Despite the apparent Russian victory, Görgey had once again succeeded in preventing Paskevich from inflicting a decisive defeat on the main part of his army. Although the Tsar was pleased by the victory and the part played in it by the Caucasian irregular cavalry, to whom he awarded banners of St George, he had no hesitation in expressing his displeasure to Paskevich about Görgey's escape and requested a full explanation of the reasons for Paskevich's failure to prevent it.[17] In his official report Paskevich made his by now familiar excuse about the need for great caution when fighting an opponent such as Görgey, and also pointed out that his troops had almost run out of drinking water after their long march across the Hungarian plain in the heat without any halts.[18]

After occupying Debrecen, Paskevich found that his army had supplies available for only two days, and that, despite Austrian assurances to the contrary, there was little prospect of obtaining further supplies locally. There were also local financial difficulties since, besides the complete absence of copper coinage for small change, the Austrian government was unable to provide Count Zichy with any substitute for the Kossuth notes in use by the local population. Despite the plea of a special delegation that an extension should be granted until alternative means of payment became available, the notes were immediately called in and destroyed.[19] Paskevich at once issued a series of orders about the despatch of food and money from his bases in northern Hungary and Galicia which would ensure that his forces did not lack the supplies they needed for the remainder of the campaign.[20]

On 6 August a service was held in the Reform church in Debrecen during which the Superintendent of the Calvinist church, acting on Paskevich's orders, preached a sermon about the restoration of the authority of Francis Joseph who had been wrongfully deposed on 14 April. When the service was over, Paskevich wrote to Schwarzenberg about 'this act of correction', which had been intended to demonstrate to the local population that the armies of Russia and Austria were fighting with the same purpose in mind. At the same time Paskevich pointed out to Schwarzenberg that Austria's failure to provide his army with the necessary supplies was the cause of his delay in continuing his pursuit of the enemy, which he much regretted.[21] In a letter written on the same day to Haynau Paskevich stated that he expected to have to remain in Debrecen for at least eight days until supplies arrived.[22]

In due course Osten-Sacken's detachment marched into Debrecen in immaculate order, as if it were taking part in a parade in Saint Petersburg. The warm welcome it received from Paskevich was in marked contrast to the cool reception accorded to General Cheodaev and the Fourth Infantry Corps, decimated by cholera, which finally reached Debrecen from the right bank of the Tisza on 11 August.[23] In order to ensure that he did not lose contact with Görgey, Paskevich despatched General Rüdiger and the Third Infantry Corps from Debrecen on 7 August. By 10 August they had reached Oradea hard on the heels of Görgey, who had now been ordered to move further south to Arad. In Oradea Rüdiger found ample supplies of food for the Russian army; not only were there large stores of rye, oats and flour, but the town fortress contained four large ovens which could be used to bake bread and dried biscuit.[24]

While Paskevich had been unsuccessfully pursuing Görgey's army, General Lüders had been making preparations to inflict a crushing defeat on Bem's forces in Transylvania. He divided his army into three columns which were to move north on Sighişoara. The left-hand column, under his own command, was to advance from Sibiu, where a small garrison under General Hasford was left behind to protect the Russian supply line through the Turnu Roşu pass into Wallachia. The centre column, commanded by General Dyck was to advance from Făgăraş, towards Odorheiul Săcuiesc; while the right-hand column commanded by the Austrian general Clam-Gallas was to move from Braşov north to Miercurea-Ciuc. At the same time General Grotenhjelm's detachment in northern Transylvania was ordered to advance south of Sighişoara, and General Dannenberg in Moldavia was ordered to send a detachment through the Oituz pass into Transylvania. Thus Bem's forces would be attacked from five different directions.[25]

All went according to plan and on 29 July Lüders' column entered Sighişoara without meeting any resistance, while the columns of Dyck and Clam-Gallas also reached their destinations with only minor skirmishes. On learning that Lüders was advancing north, Colonel Stein's detachment outside the fortress of Alba Julia broke off the siege, but was heavily defeated on 1 August at Mercurea by General Hasford who had made a rapid sortie from Sibiu for that purpose. On 3 August he returned to his task of protecting the Russian lines of communication into Wallachia.

Bem's response to the five-pronged Russian attack was characteristically bold. He would advance with his force of 7000 men on Sighişoara from Odorheiul Săcuiesc in the hope that he would be able to defeat Lüders and then recapture Sibiu and the Turnu Roşu pass. The battle of Sighişoara began at nine o'clock on the morning of 31 July and after nine hours' fierce fighting ended in a complete victory for the Russians. The Hungarians suffered heavy casualties (1200 men killed and over 500 taken prisoner), whereas Russian losses amounted to barely 250 men killed and wounded.[26] Bem, who was wounded in the leg, narrowly escaped capture and lost his carriage with all his official papers, which were subsequently read by the Russians and Austrians with considerable interest. One of the Hungarian casualties was the poet Sándor Petőfi, who was serving as one of Bem's adjutants. The Russians mourned the loss of Lüders' Chief of Staff, Major-General Skaryatin, for whom a memorial was later erected on the battlefield.[27] The Tsar, although saddened by the death of Skaryatin, issued a special order on 10 August praising the Russian troops for their courage, while the Tsarevich sent Lüders his own epaulettes and aiguillettes as a special token of gratitude.[28]

Undeterred by his defeat at Sighişoara, Bem decided not to give up his planned attack on General Hasford's garrison in Sibiu. He collected the remnants of Colonel Stein's detachment and reinforcements of 4000 men which arrived from Cluj, and set off for Mediaş to the west of Sighişoara. Meanwhile Lüders, believing that Bem would move east after his defeat, had set off for Tîrgu Mureş where he joined forces with General Grotenhjelm. When he received news that Bem was moving south to attack Sibiu, he sent three Cossacks, each with a copy of identical orders, to Hasford urging him to hold on and informing him that his forces hoped to reach Sibiu by 6 August.

On 3 August Lüders' infantry loaded their packs on to the carts of the baggage train and set off on a series of forced marches to Sibiu. In three days they covered a distance of ninety-five miles and reached the town on the morning of 6 August, as Lüders had hoped. The previous day General Hasford had fought Bem's forces for ten hours before evacuating the town and withdrawing south towards the Turnu Roşu pass. Bem was taken by surprise by the arrival of Lüders' troops, which he had confidently believed were still some distance away. After further heavy fighting on 6 August the Hungarians had lost over 1 000 men killed and over 1 000 prisoners, while Russian casualties were slightly less than fifty. Once again Bem narrowly escaped capture, as he fled from the battlefield in a cart because of the leg wound he had received at Sighişoara. While the defeated Hungarian forces retreated north-west to Mercurea, Lüders granted his exhausted troops a rest of four days after their exertions.[29] In due course he was to receive the Order of Saint George (Second Class) from an overjoyed Tsar, while all the troops who had taken part in the forced marches each received a silver rouble.[30] With his victory at Sibiu, Lüders had achieved his aim of inflicting a decisive defeat on Bem's forces in Transylvania. It was an achievement which stood out in marked contrast to the failure of Paskevich to inflict a similar defeat on Görgey.

Lüders' success in defeating Bem was shortly to be matched by Haynau. After his occupation of Budapest, Haynau lost no time in making his plans for moving south to Szeged. He divided his forces into three columns, placing the Fourth Corps under its new commander Prince Liechtenstein[31] on the left, Panyutin's division with the artillery reserve in the middle, and the Third Corps on the right. He also ordered Schlick's First Corps to withdraw from the siege of Komárno and join the Fourth Corps.

The Hungarian forces commanded by Perczel and Vetter did nothing to impede the Austrian advance south, since it was planned to make a stand in Szeged where fortification work was being carried out. By 26 July the Austrians had occupied Cegléd and Kecskemét, and by 30 July Ramberg's Fourth Corps had occupied Subotica to the south west of Szeged.

In Szeged the Hungarian government and the remnants of the parliament busied themselves with matters which were remote from the realities of the military situation. On 28 July the parliament belatedly passed a nationalities law guaranteeing equal rights to the minorities, as well as a law granting Jews the same rights as Hungarian citizens. A request by the Minister of Finance for a new loan of 60 million forints was passed without any hesitation. The Prime Minister Szemere then announced that the parliament would have to be dissolved because of the Austrian advance on Szeged. On 29 July

The Second Half of the Campaign 173

the Council of Ministers discussed the appointment of a commander-in-chief and in the absence of Bem in Transylvania and the continuing mistrust of Görgey, the appointment of Dembiński was announced on 30 July. Kossuth and the government then moved to the fortress of Arad, some sixty miles east of Szeged.

After a disagreement between Dembiński and Vetter about the defence of Szeged which ended with Vetter's removal from his command, Dembiński finally decided that Szeged could not be defended and withdrew on 2 August to Szőreg to the south east. On the same day the Austrians were able to occupy the west bank of the Tisza at Szeged. After some fierce fighting and the laying of a pontoon bridge across the river to replace the bridge destroyed by the Hungarians, the Austrians and the Russians crossed the river and established a bridgehead on the east bank on 4 August.[32] The Austrian casualties although light included three generals, one of whom was the commander of the Fourth Corps.[33]

After crossing the Tisza, Haynau now had to dislodge Dembiński from the position he occupied at Szőreg. By this time Dembiński had decided not to obey Kossuth's order to move to Arad where it was intended that he should join forces with Görgey. Instead, he decided to leave Szőreg on the evening of 5 August and move further south to Timişoara where the Austrian garrison was still under siege. However, Haynau was able to launch an attack late in the afternoon of 5 August before preparations for withdrawal had been completed. By the onset of darkness, the Austrians had routed the Hungarians who suffered heavy casualties (400 dead and wounded and 400 taken prisoner). With this victory, Haynau had relieved the pressure on Jelačić and could now move into the Bánát and complete the destruction of the southern group of Hungarian forces. When Kossuth learnt that Dembiński had decided to disobey the government's orders to move to Arad, he dismissed him as Commander-in-Chief and ordered Bem, despite his defeat at Sighişoara, to take up the appointment.

Although Haynau's swift advance south had been so successful, his decision to withdraw Schlick's First Corps from the force besieging Komárno gave Klapka the opportunity to threaten the Austrian lines of communication. On 27 July in an attack on Tata one of his divisions captured a valuable consignment of Austrian mail which included a letter from Berg to the Tsar. In his letter, Berg wrote of Austrian and Russian anxieties that the war might drag on until the autumn and winter, instead of being over by mid-August as both Haynau and Paskevich had hoped. In addition, Görgey had written to Klapka after defeating Grabbe at Gesztely, reminding him that the fortress of Komárno still had a part to play in the campaign.[34] As a result, Klapka decided to make a sortie on 3 August from the fortress and on 5 August he recaptured Győr, cutting Austrian communications between Vienna and Budapest. Haynau was unperturbed by the news, and after ensuring that Csorich's Second Corps was reinforced by Austrian reserves and detaching one of his own brigades to protect his lines of communication, he continued with his plans to raise the siege of Timişoara.

On 4 August General Vécsey's Fifth Corps, which was besieging Timişoara, made a final attempt to capture the fortress. It met with no success and the commander of the Austrian garrison also rejected the terms for an honourable surrender. After this failure Vécsey withdrew his siege artillary to Arad. Meanwhile Dembiński began assembling into one army the remainder of the Fifth Corps, together with the Fourth, Ninth and Tenth Corps, as well as General Kmety's division which had arrived in the area from north-west Hungary. Altogether he disposed of 45 000 troops, as well as 10 000 peasants auxiliaries. Although Haynau could only muster 28 000 men, he enjoyed a considerable advantage in artillery (192 guns against 100 Hungarian). On 9 August Bem arrived from Transylvania to take over command of the army from Dembiński. Rejecting Dembiński's advice to avoid a decisive battle with Haynau and continue the withdrawal, he decided to make one final attempt to defeat the Austrians. As he wrote to Czartoryski's representative in Constantinople, 'either Timişoara will be the grave of Hungarian freedom, or the Hungarians will once again arise'.[35]

On the same day as Bem took over from Dembiński, Görgey had reached Arad where, contrary to his expectations, he found no army, but only Kossuth and some members of the government. (The other members had already moved to Lugoj, east of Timişoara.) Realising that the failure to join forces with Dembiński would make it difficult to inflict the decisive defeat on the Austrians for which he had hoped, he nevertheless decided to send Nagy Sándor's First Corps to Timişoara in the hope that it would arrive in time to provide Dembiński with reinforcements. However, on 10 August the Hungarian First Corps encountered General Schlick's First Corps which Haynau had sent towards Arad and after a short artillery duel, was compelled to withdraw to Arad.

In the early morning of 9 August the battle for Timişoara began.

The Second Half of the Campaign

After the usual artillery duel which went in favour of the Austrians who easily outgunned the Hungarians,[36] Bem launched an attack which at first brought him success. But at the critical moment the intervention of the forces of Colonel Baumgarten from Panyutin's division rallied the Austrians[37] and the subsequent arrival later in the afternoon of the Austrian Fourth Corps under Prince Liechtenstein soon decided the outcome. Bem, realising that he could not withdraw north to Arad as he had hoped, had no choice but to withdraw east to Lugoj, still hoping that the remnants of his army would be able to join up with Görgey's army. As darkness was falling Haynau and the Austrian forces entered the fortress by the west gate and ended a siege which had lasted 107 days. They had arrived in the nick of time since the Austrian garrison could only have held out for a further ten days.[38] The overjoyed Austrian garrison gave an enthusiastic welcome to the Austrian and Russian troops who continued to be amazed by the number of different nationalities to be found among the Hungarian prisoners.[39] The exact number of Hungarian casualties is not on record, but at least 6000 prisoners were taken, while many of the Hungarians threw away their weapons and fled from the battlefield. In so doing Bem fell from his horse and broke his collar bone. The battle was the last decisive engagement of the campaign and put an end to any lingering hopes that the two Hungarian armies would be able to join forces and make a final stand in Arad.

While Haynau had been steadily advancing south, he had continued to complain bitterly to his old commander Radetzky and to Schwarzenberg about the impossibility of cooperating with Paskevich and the Russian army.[40] Since it appeared from Buol's reports that Paskevich's conduct of the campaign was the subject of considerable criticism in Warsaw, Schwarzenberg had little difficulty in persuading Francis Joseph to agree to a visit being made to Warsaw in order to propose the dismissal of Paskevich, just as Francis Joseph had dismissed Windischgraetz earlier in the year. Accordingly, Schwarzenberg set off for Warsaw bearing with him a carefully-worded letter from the Emperor to the Tsar which although full of the usual expressions of mutual esteem, made it clear that the Austrians were not satisfied with the results of the campaign which they were anxious to conclude before the onset of bad weather in the autumn.[41]

On arriving in Warsaw on 7 August Nesselrode informed an astonished Schwarzenberg that the Russians believed that the Hungarians were on the brink of collapse and that Görgey was willing to surrender.[42] Accordingly, when he saw the Tsar, Schwarzenberg had to modify his plan of action. Besides discussing the misunderstandings between Paskevich and Haynau, whom Schwarzenberg admitted was a difficult person, there was considerable debate about Hungary's future after the war was over, in the course of which Nicholas refused an Austrian request to go on occupying Galicia.[43] In his official reply to Francis Joseph, Nicholas readily agreed that it was unfortunate that the campaign had not yet been brought to a successful conclusion, but as the Emperor would learn from Schwarzenberg, the Tsar was confident that Paskevich would be successful in defeating Görgey.[44]

On the same day that Nicholas sent his reply to Francis Joseph, Paskevich wrote a long letter in which he sought to justify his actions and put much of the blame for all that had happened on Haynau and the unfortunate Berg.[45] Privately, he believed that the person responsible for the campaign to remove him from office was not Schwarzenberg, but Nesselrode.[46] In an effort to repay Schwarzenberg's frankness about Haynau, the Tsar instructed Nesselrode to send a copy of this letter to Vienna in order that the Austrians should be aware of the strength of Paskevich's own feelings on the subject.[47]

In fact, Austrian and Russian worries that the campaign would be prolonged into the autumn were to prove groundless, as Paskevich was to present the Tsar with his hoped-for victory much sooner than anticipated. As a result of a discussion held on 30 July about Görgey's negotiations with the Russians, the Hungarian government sent the Prime Minister, Bertalan Szemere, and the Foreign Minister, Kázmér Batthyány, to Görgey's headquarters to decide on further action. On 2 August at Vámospércs after much discussion, during which Görgey learnt that Kossuth was prepared to offer the Hungarian crown to a member of the Tsar's family,[48] Szemere decided to send a formal letter from the Hungarian government to Paskevich. On the evening of 4 August there arrived at Görgey's headquarters, which had now moved to Bihar, Lieutenant Miloradovich, the personal adjutant of General Sass. He had been sent by Paskevich with money for the maintenance of some Russian officers who were prisoners of the Hungarians, and also to return Görgey's present of pistols to Sass and Khrulev. Görgey declined to accept the pistols and eventually Miloradovich was persuaded to return to his headquarters with them. In addition he took a letter from Görgey addressed to General Cheodaev, enclosing copies of Görgey's correspondence with Rüdiger and the letter drafted by Szemere, which was accompanied by a long memorandum on Hungary's grievances against Austria prepared by Batthyány.[49]

When Görgey read Szemere's letter and Batthyány's accompanying memorandum, he did not hesitate to let the ministers know that he considered both documents to be unsatisfactory. In his view, they would almost certainly produce no reply from the Russians, just as Görgey's own reply to Rüdiger's letter seeking to enter into negotiations had remained unanswered. As a result of this exchange of views, Szemere drafted a second letter to Paskevich which it was eventually agreed should be taken to the Russians by a suitably high-ranking person authorised to act as a plenipotentiary of the government. The choice fell on General Poeltenberg, the Commander of the Seventh Corps, who spoke French. On 7 July Poeltenberg, accompanied by two officers, set off for Oradea with Szemere's letter, the text of which was not shown to Görgey before departure.[50]

On 8 August Poeltenberg's party reached the Russian outposts outside Oradea and were escorted to Rüdiger's headquarters at Ártánd. Rüdiger immediately sent Szemere's second letter by a courier to Paskevich in Debrecen who, only a few hours earlier, had received Szemere's first letter brought back by Lieutenant Miloradovich. While Rüdiger awaited further instructions from Paskevich, he invited the Hungarians to dinner. In conversation after the meal, General Frolov, Rüdiger's Chief of Staff, did his best to persuade the Hungarians that further resistance was hopeless. He also reminded them that the decision of the Hungarian government to ally themselves with the Poles had made Russian intervention inevitable.[51] Early in the morning of 9 August Poeltenberg was given the official Russian reply to the Hungarian government's offer to negotiate. Drafted by Rüdiger on Paskevich's instructions, it was brief and to the point. The Russian army had come to Hungary to fight and not to negotiate. If the Hungarians wished to surrender, they should address themselves to General Haynau.[52] Poeltenberg and his party were then escorted back to Arad. In a deliberate effort to mislead their Russian escort about Görgey's exact whereabouts they spent most of the day travelling along side roads before their Russian escorts left them to return to Oradea. As a result Poeltenberg did not reach Arad until 11 August.

As soon as the Hungarians had set off on their return journey, Paskevich informed Schwarzenberg and Haynau about his refusal to accept the Hungarian government's offer to negotiate a surrender. Nor were Count Zichy and General Parrot slow to follow his example.[53] The Tsar did not receive the news until 13 August and was perfectly satisfied. Paskevich had acted 'purely, clearly and nobly'; the Austrians could have no cause for complaint.[54] However, the Russians did not yet realise that the Austrians had no intention of negotiating a surrender with the Hungarians, despite a suggestion that had been put forward earlier in August by Captain Graebe, the liaison officer attached to Osten-Sacken's detachment, that Görgey would be willing to negotiate.[55] The Austrian attitude at this time is clearly revealed in the conversations of General Kempen, the future head of the gendarmerie, with Francis Joseph and Schwarzenberg when he was being transferred from Bratislava to Budapest towards the end of July. There was to be no mercy for those that had rebelled. While Francis Joseph deplored the guilt of those in high places, who ought to have known better, Schwarzenberg spoke ominously of the heads which would have to fall 'like the poppies in the field at harvest time'.[56]

On 10 August Kossuth called a meeting of the Hungarian War Council to discuss the situation. News of the result of the battle at Timişoara the previous day had not yet reached Arad, nor was anything known about Klapka's successful sortie from Komárno. Although Görgey's army had reached Arad without having suffered major losses, the continual forced marches had reduced it to a pitiful condition. It was short of ammution, money and boots, as Szemere had seen with his own eyes when he visited Görgey's headquarters to discuss the negotiations with the Russians.[57] At the meeting of the War Council Görgey stated that he was not prepared to fight under Bem as Commander-in-Chief, nor did he see any merit in seeking to continue the war in Transylvania since he was sceptical that the Rumanians could be persuaded to rebel against the Russians. Depending on the outcome of the engagement at Timişoara, he would be prepared to continue his efforts to defeat the Austrians. However, if Bem were defeated, the only sensible course of action left to the Hungarians was to surrender to the Russians. The meeting ended without a decision being taken and was resumed in private between Görgey and Kossuth. At this meeting Görgey adhered to his view that he would surrender to the Russians if Bem were defeated, whereas Kossuth (who later denied it) stated that he would shoot himself, if that were to happen.

During the night a letter from General Guyon, the commander of the Fourth Corps, with news of the defeat at Timişoara reached Arad. On 11 August Kossuth was persuaded to abdicate and transfer power to Görgey. However, he refused to hand over to him the Crown of Saint Stephen and the Hungarian regalia. After signing the abdication decree on 11 August, Kossuth left Arad in disguise and travelled to Bem's headquarters at Lugoj. At a final meeting of the parliament the twelve members present officially declared that the war had been lost.

On the same day Görgey issued his own manifesto in which he informed the nation that he would use any means he considered necessary to bring the war to an end. At a meeting of the War Council he read out the text of the Russian letter of 9 August which had been brought back by Poeltenberg. Despite its contents Görgey intended to continue with his surrender plans as there was no practical alternative.[58] Accordingly, Görgey wrote to Rüdiger explaining to him that Kossuth had abdicated and handed over power to him. In order to avoid further bloodshed, he was willing to surrender unconditionally, confident that the Tsar would ensure that those Hungarian officers who had previously served with the Habsburg army would be treated fairly. It was his hope that the commanders of the other Hungarian units would follow his example. Emphasising that he wished to surrender to the Russians and not to the Austrians, he informed Rüdiger as a sign of his good faith that his army would be in Şiria (Világos in Hungarian) on 12 August and Ineu on 13 August.[59] A copy of this letter was also sent to General Damjanich, the commander of the Arad garrison, who was asked to let Görgey know whether he wished to surrender the fortress to the Russians.[60]

On the evening of 11 August a party of three officers led by Colonel Bethlen took Görgey's letter to Rüdiger's headquarters at Chişineu Criş. According to one Russian account, the Hungarians were so overcome with emotion when they handed over the letter that they could hardly speak. Rüdiger, who was doubtless not surprised by what had happened, assured the Hungarians that the Tsar would be magnanimous, as he usually was to those who expressed regret for their actions.[61] After giving the Hungarians a meal, the Russians then escorted the party back to Şiria where Görgey had set up his headquarters in the house of one of the local landowners, Baron János Bohus.

Two hours after their arrival, at midday on 12 August, General Frolov and a party of Russian officers arrived at Görgey's headquarters to discuss the details of the surrender. After establishing the genuineness of Görgey's offer, Frolov informed him that the Russians would seal off the area in which the surrender was to take place in order to prevent the Austrians becoming involved. He then despatched one of his party to Rüdiger with a full report. In the early afternoon Görgey entertained the Russians to a lunch which appeared to one of those present to be a somewhat melancholy occasion, rather like a funeral feast. Frolov then left while Görgey began advising the Poles to leave and reassuring his army that they had nothing to fear from his decision to surrender to the Russians.[62] Shortly after midnight one of Rüdiger's adjutants returned to confirm the exact time and place of the surrender which was due to take place on the plain between Zărand and Seleuş, to the north of Şiria.[63]

Later in the day Görgey ordered the Minister of Finance to transfer the Hungarian financial reserves to Şiria from Arad in order that he could pay the troops the arrears they were owed. In addition, Görgey consulted his senior officers about the demands he proposed to put to the Russians in a letter which he would hand over during the surrender. These included a request that the Hungarians (including the civilians who had attached themselves to the army) should not be handed over to the Austrians as criminals, and that the Tsar should intervene with the Emperor of Austria about the future fate of Hungary.[64]

On receiving the news from Rüdiger that Görgey was willing to surrender unconditionally, Paskevich immediately informed the Tsar, in words which were identical with those he had used at the time of the capture of Warsaw on 8 September 1831. Hungary was at the Tsar's feet. Paskevich had authorised Rüdiger to accept Görgey's offer and after disarming the Hungarian army, to send Görgey to Russian headquarters where he would remain until the Tsar's wishes about his future fate were known. Detailed arrangements about the transfer of the Hungarian prisoners into Austrian custody would be discussed with Haynau in due course.[65] In a separate letter, Paskevich asked Haynau to cease operations against Görgey and emphasised the likelihood of Görgey being able to persuade the other leaders of the Hungarian forces to follow his example.[66] The letter was taken to Haynau by the hand of General Buturlin who was empowered to explain the background to the surrender to Berg verbally. As Paskevich pointed out to Berg, it was essential that Austria did not interfere with the surrender arrangements.[67] At the same time Paskevich informed Rüdiger that he and the main body of the army would be moving from Debrecen to Oradea which they expected to reach on 13 August. A special detachment under General Karlovich was sent from Debrecen to north-east Hungary where the Hungarians were still holding out in the fortress of Mukachevo.[68]

By nine o'clock on the morning of Monday 13 August Rüdiger

had drawn up his troops on the plain between Zărand and Seleuş in a square with the south side open to await the arrival of Görgey's army. It was a hot, sultry day with a cloudless blue sky. The Russian artillery, drawn up alongside the infantry and cavalry, had its linstocks smouldering and was ready to open fire, if the surrender did not go smoothly.[69] Shortly after noon, a cloud of dust on the horizon heralded the arrival of the Hungarian army. Half an hour later Görgey and his suite rode forward to meet the Russians. After confirming to one of Rüdiger's staff-officers that he was still willing to surrender, Görgey was directed to the area set aside for his meeting with Rüdiger which was to take place in full view of both armies. The Russian general then rode towards Görgey who had ordered his suite to fall behind. Görgey who was wearing a white hat with a feather, saluted and offered Rüdiger his sword which was refused. After shaking hands, Görgey handed over a report about the number of troops surrendering, together with the letter he had written outlining his demands. According to his report, the total strength of the army amounted to 30 889 men (including 11 generals and 1 426 senior officers) as well as 9 839 horses, 144 guns, 29 banners and 31 standards.[70] The Russians had also requested Görgey's official papers, but accepted his explanation that they had been lost during the long march south. In fact, they had been buried on Görgey's instructions and were to be retrieved after the war was over.[71]

Both Görgey and Rüdiger were anxious that the surrender should be completed before darkness fell. Although Nagy Sándor's First Corps was taking longer than anticipated to reach the place of surrender, it was decided to begin the surrender before the whole army was assembled. After Rüdiger had carried out an inspection, Görgey ordered his troops to begin laying down their arms. He then bade farewell to his troops amid scenes of great emotion and left with his suite, escorted by General Frolov, for Rüdiger's headquarters at Chişineu Criş which he reached early the next morning. The Hungarian infantry now began to pile their arms, while the cavalry dismounted from their horses and left their weapons hanging on the pommels of their saddles. By eight o'clock, as darkness was falling, most of the army had surrendered and the Russians began the task of escorting the long columns of prisoners to Zărand. In accordance with Görgey's request, the generals and officers were allowed to retain their sidearms. A Hungarian hussar officer remarked to a Russian cavalry officer as he surveyed the scene: *'Consummatum est'* and then added, in Slovak, the words: 'An evil time has come, brother'.[72]

That evening Paskevich once again sent his son to Warsaw to convey the news of the surrender to the Tsar. In his letter of congratulation, Paskevich recommended that Görgey should be allowed to reside in Russia as their Tsar's 'trophy', since his decision to surrender to the Russians had been so much influenced by the trust he was prepared to put in the Tsar's magnanimity. The unspoken message in this letter was clear. In return for an unofficial promise from Paskevich of an amnesty which it was hoped that the Tsar would be able to persuade the Austrians to grant, Görgey had decided, in order to spare Hungary further suffering, to put an end to the fighting and surrender to the Russians.[73] At the same time Paskevich congratulated Rüdiger on having brought the surrender negotiations to a successful conclusion. Although he would have preferred a different outcome to the war, he was more than satisfied with the result, especially as he had initially been sceptical about the outcome of the negotiations.[74] Rüdiger duly informed Haynau of the day's events and also warned the Austrian commander that two envoys from the garrison at Arad had let it be known that they wished to surrender the fortress to the Russians rather than the Austrians. Rüdiger then went on to express regret that the Austrian and Russian armies had still not been able to join forces, and requested the return to Russian control of Panyutin's division.[75]

In fact, Haynau was well aware of what had happened. Although the Austrian liaison officer attached to the Russian army had been kept at a distance while the surrender was taking place,[76] one of Schlick's officers, Captain Soltyk, who had been sent on ahead of Haynau's army to contact Rüdiger's corps, had joined a Russian column moving south to Şiria and had witnessed the surrender. After receiving the news, Haynau sent Soltyk to Vienna which he reached on 17 April. At first it was believed that Görgey had surrendered to the Austrians, but the following day the true version of events became known. Francis Joseph received the news by telegram in Bad Ischl where he was celebrating his nineteenth birthday with his parents, and at once made preparations to return to Vienna.[77]

Haynau was also aware that the fortress of Arad did not wish to surrender to the Austrians, as Damjanich had made clear in his response to two Austrian envoys sent to him by Schlick on 12 August.[78] He had no intention of allowing Arad to surrender to the Russians, as he wished to lay his hands on the stores and valuables held in the fortress, which he mistakenly believed included the

Hungarian crown.[79] He therefore began to make preparations to arrange for its surrender to the forces of General Schlick, including Panyutin's division.[80] At the same time Rüdiger continued with his own preparations to obtain the surrender of the garrison, especially as Damjanich's envoys had threatened to blow up the virtually impregnable fortress rather than surrender it to the Austrians.[81] Making use of a letter written by Görgey on 14 August in which he appealed to Damjanich to avoid further bloodshed and trust the Russians,[82] Rüdiger sent General Buturlin to Arad to negotiate a surrender and then to Timişoara to inform Haynau of the results of his mission. After some discussion Buturlin succeeded in persuading Damjanich to allow the garrison to surrender unconditionally to the Russians at three o'clock in the afternoon of 17 August, while all the property and weapons stored in the fortress would be handed over to the Austrians.[83] These conditions were accepted by Schlick and also by Haynau who, however, changed his mind not long after Buturlin had left Timişoara to return to Arad on the evening of 15 August and ordered Schlick to oppose the Russians by force, if necessary, since the Austrian forces surrounding the fortress far outnumbered the small Russian detachment stationed there.[84]

The next day Schlick received the surrender of Ferenc Duschek, the Hungarian Minister of Finance, together with his staff who brought with them the Hungarian gold and silver reserves and the printing press for the Kossuth notes. In conversation with his Austrian captors, Duschek emphasised the importance and value of the property stored in the fortress.[85] While Schlick was digesting this information, he was horrified to receive Haynau's order about opposing the surrender of the fortress to the Russians and wisely decided to ignore it, informing Buturlin that he was prepared to face a court-martial rather than be responsible for causing an incident which might provoke a European conflict. In Timişoara, an equally alarmed Berg eventually persuaded Haynau to rescind the order about the surrender of the garrison (but not the property) to the Russians. A Russian officer was hastily despatched to Arad to inform Schlick and Buturlin that wiser counsels had prevailed.[86]

At five o'clock in the afternoon Buturlin and the Russian cavalry of Colonel Khrulev received the surrender of the fortress and its garrison of 3768 men and 143 guns from Damjanich who, accompanied by his young wife, was walking on crutches because of a leg wound. After the garrison had been marched off by the Russians into captivity, the fortress and its contents were turned over to the

Austrians.⁸⁷ As a result of Hungarian treachery, Haynau was able to lay his hands on the copies of Görgey's correspondence with the Russians about his surrender, which he promptly sent to Francis Joseph and Berg for their information.⁸⁸

Although the surrender of Arad took place without any serious incident, the friction that had occurred during the negotiations did nothing to improve the relationship between the Austrian and Russian armies, as Count Zichy frankly wrote to Schwarzenberg.⁸⁹ It also led to a heated exchange of correspondence between Berg and Rüdiger, who rejected Berg's contention that the Hungarian garrison should have been handed over to the Austrians after the surrender.⁹⁰ Paskevich was quite certain he had acted correctly and informed the Tsar that he had been anxious to prevent the garrison carrying out sorties in the surrounding countryside.⁹¹

The relationship between the two armies was to deteriorate still further in the days that followed the surrender of Görgey and the fortress of Arad. At a dinner given to Görgey and the Hungarian generals by Rüdiger at his headquarters on 14 August, a toast was drunk to the happy resolution of the conflict, an incident which Haynau at once reported to Francis Joseph.⁹² The Austrians were shocked to observe the fraternisation between the Russians and the Hungarians whom they continued to regard as rebels. Count Zichy found it particularly distasteful to have to sit at the same table as the person who had executed one of his relatives.⁹³ Although Haynau wrote a letter to Panyutin thanking him for the services his division had rendered during the campaign,⁹⁴ the relationship was again made worse by the victory bulletin he issued on 18 August which stated that the Austrian army had played a decisive role in defeating Görgey and capturing the fortress of Arad. The Russian army was not to forget this bulletin, which was regarded as a distortion of the facts and was to lead to a formal complaint from Berg which Haynau chose to ignore.⁹⁵

9 After the Surrender

The arrival of Paskevich's son in Warsaw on the morning of 16 August so soon after his previous visit was a sure sign to the Tsar's staff that some important event had occurred.[1] Nicholas had just received the news of Lüders' defeat of Bem at Sibiu on 6 August and when he learnt of Görgey's surrender he fell on his knees in front of the icon on the wall of his study in the Łazienki Palace and thanked the Almighty for his favours to Russia. He was particularly glad that Russian blood would no longer have to be sacrificed for a cause which was not directly the cause of Russia.[2] As a sign of his especial favour, he issued an order that in future Paskevich was to receive the same honours as himself from the Russian army, while Rüdiger was awarded the Order of Saint Andrew. Thinking of the future, the Tsar also informed Paskevich that he would shortly send him detailed plans for the immediate withdrawal of the Russian army from Hungary and Transylvania to their winter quarters in Poland and the Danubian principalities. Any Russian Poles among the prisoners were to be rounded up and sent to Zamość, while those from Galicia should be handed back to the Austrians.[3]

The Tsarevich, who had been preparing for a visit to Vienna, was ordered to leave the same evening to discuss with Francis Joseph the future of Görgey and the possibility of granting a general amnesty to those Hungarians who had surrendered. In his two letters to the Austrian Emperor, the Tsar explained that he was sending his eldest son because there were certain matters which could best be dealt with orally rather than in writing. If the Emperor found it inconvenient to allow Görgey to reside in his empire, the Tsar would be prepared to grant him asylum in Russia with a guarantee that he would be given no opportunity to create any further disturbance in Hungary. At the same time the Tsar suggested that Francis Joseph should exercise a combination of clemency and firmness in dealing with the affairs of Hungary. He himself had always favoured a policy of punishing only the ringleaders in any revolt and pardoning those who had been led astray. It was his hope that Francis Joseph could be persuaded to adopt a similar policy.[4] At dinner on the evening of 16 August the Tsar repeated the same view to the Austrian ambassador.[5]

The Tsar's ideas about an amnesty were entirely in keeping with those of Paskevich who was to write in similar terms to the Russian ambassador in Vienna asking him to pass on letters on the subject to the Emperor and Schwarzenberg. In all three of his letters Paskevich stressed that the surrender had been unconditional, and that the Austrians now had an opportunity of demonstrating their magnanimity. It was important that the war should not be prolonged and advantage taken of Görgey's willingness to send letters to the other Hungarian leaders advising them to follow his example.[6] In a separate letter to Haynau, Paskevich drew attention to the need to counter the influence of Bem, who had now been appointed Commander-in-Chief. Well aware that he could not hope for an amnesty, Bem would undoubtedly seek to prolong the revolt. As a final point, Paskevich reminded Haynau of the importance of obtaining the surrender of the fortresses still held by the Hungarians, especially Komárno.[7]

In addition to writing these letters to the Austrians, Paskevich also informed the Tsar about his reaction to the demands contained in Görgey's letter which had been handed over to Rüdiger during the surrender ceremony. All Görgey's demands except the request to retain moveable property had been rejected. In any case, several of them were matters which should be decided by the Austrians rather than the Russians. What concerned Paskevich most of all was the granting of a general amnesty, and he hoped that the Tsar would support him in pressing the Austrians to do so. After all, the Emperor Francis had not hesitated to send Colonel Caboga to Warsaw for this purpose after the suppression of the Polish revolt in September 1831. Indeed, Paskevich also considered that the Hungarians should have their former constitution restored to them, in order that the Habsburg empire, whose existence was so important to Russia, should continue in being without the threat of a war of revenge being waged by the Hungarians. So strongly did Paskevich feel about this that he and the Grand Duke Constantine had persuaded Count Zichy to draw up a memorandum about the future of Hungary and submit it to Schwarzenberg.[8]

Paskevich's views on the granting of an amnesty were shared just as strongly by Rüdiger, who was concerned as a result of his conversation with Schlick after the surrender of Arad that the Austrians would show no mercy to the Hungarians. In a letter to Paskevich he expressed the view that the surrender of Görgey's army had been a unique case not covered by the arrangements about prisoners contained in the convention signed in Warsaw in June. However, Rüdiger would obey the orders he had received to hand over the Hungarian prisoners to the Austrians. In his reply, Paskevich assured Rüdiger that everything possible was being done both by the Tsar and himself to obtain an amnesty.[9]

Neither Paskevich nor Rüdiger need have worried that the Tsar would not support them on the question of granting an amnesty. In general, the Tsar shared their view that Austria should attempt to be conciliatory towards the Hungarians. However, neither Görgey nor any other Hungarian could be allowed to enter Russian service, even if it was eventually decided that Görgey should settle in Russia. It should not be forgotten that the Russian army had been dealing with rebel subjects who had revolted against their lawful ruler and the Tsar did not want his soldiers to be contaminated by such ideas. As part of his share of the victory, the Tsar wanted Görgey's sword for his collection of military trophies housed in the Arsenal in Tsarskoe Selo, and gave orders for the captured standards and banners of the Hungarian army to be sent to Warsaw.[10] After those belonging to the Austrian army had been returned to the Emperor by Paskevich's son,[11] the Tsar gave orders for the remainder to be transferred to Russia, where they were paraded through the streets of Saint Petersburg on 11 September.

Like Paskevich, the Tsar fully realised the importance of obtaining the surrender of the fortresses still held by the Hungarians. On 16 August he decided to send his aide-de-camp Isakov (now promoted to the rank of lieutenant-colonel), who had brought the news of Grabbe's defeat at Gesztely, back to Hungary in order to negotiate the surrender of Komárno, in concert with the Austrians. Armed with a copy of Görgey's letter to Rüdiger of 11 August, he was to try to persuade Klapka to lay down his arms in order to avoid further bloodshed, and was authorised to inform Grabbe that he could accept the surrender, if Klapka was unwilling to surrender to the Austrians. At midnight on 16 August Isakov left Warsaw for Vienna by train in the company of the Tsarevich and his party.[12] On the same day as the Tsar personally briefed Isakov about his mission, Paskevich sent one of his own staff-officers, Colonel Anichkov, on a similar mission, armed in this instance with a letter written by Görgey to Klapka personally, as well as a letter to Schwarzenberg seeking his approval for Anichkov's mission.[13] At the same time Haynau was determined that Komárno should surrender to the Austrians rather than the Russians, and on 16 August he wrote a letter to Paskevich asking him to release Görgey from captivity so that he could travel to Komárno to persuade Klapka to surrender.[14]

On the morning of 18 August the Tsarevich and his party arrived in Vienna to be greeted with the news that Francis Joseph was in Bad Ischl. After a short meeting with Schwarzenberg, the Tsarevich set off in the afternoon by coach for Ischl while Isakov left for the Austrian army headquarters at Győr. The following afternoon Francis Joseph and the Tsarevich returned to the Palace of Schönbrunn after meeting each other in Strengberg on the road from Ischl to Vienna.

The Austrian Council of Ministers had first begun to discuss the punishment of those who had rebelled in Hungary in early May. Various proposals had been put forward, including the possibility of deportation outside Europe, the confiscation of property and the imposition of heavy fines. Schwarzenberg had even considered whether a special penal colony for Hungarians, run by the Austrian army, could be established in Russia. While the war was in progress, no definite decision was taken, although Haynau was ordered not to execute former Habsburg officers after capture, in order not to provoke reprisals and a prolonged resistance.[15] On 16 August the matter was again discussed in the Council of Ministers in the light of Paskevich's letter to 9 August about the Poeltenberg mission. The possibility of a surrender led to a willingness to be less harsh in dealing with the Hungarians, although Schwarzenberg informed Paskevich that Austria could not negotiate with Hungary on a government to government basis.[16] With the arrival of the news of Görgey's surrender and the return to Vienna of Francis Joseph accompanied by the Tsarevich, the matter had now become urgent. On 20 August at a meeting of the Council of Ministers chaired by the Emperor it was agreed that Görgey could be pardoned, but would be sent into exile at Klagenfurt in Carinthia. However, there could be no question of granting a general amnesty along the lines proposed by the Tsar and Paskevich. Although junior officers (from captain downwards) and the rank and file (from sergeant downwards) could be granted an amnesty, there were to be no exceptions for senior officers in the Hungarian army, nor for any former Habsburg officers. All such persons, together with civilian members of the Hungarian administration and members of parliament, were to be tried by a military court. Foreign nationals were to be handed over to Austria's allies or punished, as appropriate.[17]

The decision taken by the Council of Ministers not to grant a general amnesty and to punish former Habsburg officers was welcome news to Haynau, who had issued a decree of a similar nature two days earlier. Haynau was thirsting for revenge and had no doubt in his own mind that the only way to restore order in Hungary was by hanging and shooting a few hundred revolutionaries.[18] His instructions to Prince Liechtenstein about the handing-over of the Hungarian prisoners made it clear that no mercy would be shown to those officers who had broken their oath of loyalty to the Emperor. Like most officers in the Austrian army, Haynau was appalled by the friendly welcome given to Görgey and the other generals by Rüdiger and his staff, and instructed Liechtenstein to ask Paskevich to hand over Görgey, once he had written his letters to the commanders of the other Hungarian units which had not surrendered. The request was rejected by Paskevich who described it to the Tsar as 'ignoble'.[19]

Despite the decision not to grant a general amnesty, Francis Joseph and Schwarzenberg could not completely ignore the representations made by the Tsarevich, nor those of the British and French governments who were both urging the Austrian government to think of the future in its dealings with Hungary. Furthermore, negotiations with Venice about a surrender were still in progress; Komárno was still in Hungarian hands; and an apparently Magyarophile Russian army was still in Hungary. As a result, it was decided not to grant Haynau unrestricted judicial powers and on 25 August General Grünne, the Emperor's personal adjutant, arrived in Arad with orders that no executions were to be carried out until the death sentences had been confirmed in Vienna. A furious Haynau had no choice but to obey.[20] He was under no illusion that the Russians had exerted considerable pressure on the Austrian government to pardon Görgey and grant a general amnesty, and was well aware of the disapproval of Austrian policy expressed by the British government. He wrote in scathing terms to his old comrades-in-arms about the Austrian government's reluctance to allow him a free hand and the duplicity and anti-Austrian behaviour of Paskevich and Rüdiger. As it happened, the Hungarian prisoners in Russian custody were handed over to Haynau on 25 August, and in a letter to Radetzky, he remarked that if Grünne had arrived in Arad two days later, he would have found the generals hanging on the gallows.[21] However, on 28 August, three days after the news of the surrender of Venice had reached Vienna, the Austrian Council of Ministers decided to revert to its original policy towards the captured Hungarian senior officers and Haynau was given discretionary powers about executions, provided that he notified Vienna that they were taking place.[22] On the morning of 23 August the Tsarevich arrived back in Warsaw from Vienna and informed his father of the results of his conversations with Francis Joseph.

While his son had been absent in Vienna, the Tsar had held a special victory parade in Warsaw at which the troops were commanded by the Grand Duke Michael. During the service which preceded the parade Nicholas fell on his knees and, in the words of the British Consul General, 'seemed unfeignedly and deeply absorbed by the religious feeling of the hour', unlike the remainder of his senior staff.[23] In conversation with the newly arrived French ambassador, General Lamoricière, the Tsar spoke of the fight against anarchy and demagogy which had just come to an end. It was no different to the revolt which General Cavaignac had suppressed in June 1848, and the Tsar was sure that the French government fully understood the similarity.[24] The day after the parade in Warsaw a special service of thanksgiving was held in Saint Petersburg, during which a salvo of 101 guns was fired from the guns in the fortress of Saint Peter and Saint Paul. In reply to a question from one of the imprisoned members of the Petrashevsky group about the reason for the salvo, the commandant of the fortress replied, somewhat grandiosely, that the Tsar had conquered Europe.[25] The same sentiment was echoed in a special victory poem which referred to the Russian sword having restored calm and justice to Europe after the defeat of the Hungarians.[26] In his victory manifesto of 29 August and his special order of the day to the Russian army of 3 September the Tsar also wrote of Divine Providence which had enabled Russia to fulfil its holy vocation, and he was grateful to his army for the zeal with which it had executed his orders.[27] On a less exalted note Nesselrode issued a circular on 31 August informing Russian missions abroad that now that the threat to Russia's security had been removed and the integrity of the Habsburg empire was restored, there was no longer any need for the Russian army to remain abroad. The Tsar had ordered it to return to Russia and had no intention of seeking any territorial compensation.[28]

The Tsar was not displeased by the results of the Tsarevich's mission to Vienna. He had been quite certain that Görgey would be pardoned and he was content to accept Francis Joseph's assurance that the Austrians would deal leniently with former Habsburg officers, provided that they were not guilty of other crimes. The ultimate fate of the Hungarian civilians and members of parliament who had surrendered to the Russians did not greatly interest him. All that now remained was to bring back the Russian army. Paskevich was therefore ordered to release Görgey and the other Hungarian prisoners in accordance with the Emperor's wishes.[29]

At the same time the two Emperors carried out the customary

award of decorations to the commanders of the armies which had succeeded in defeating the Hungarians. The Tsar was especially lavish and awarded Haynau the Order of Saint Andrew in diamonds despite all the difficulties which had occurred between him and Paskevich. Francis Joseph made the Tsar the honorary commanding officer of the Fifth Cuirassier Regiment and also awarded Paskevich the Grand Cross of the Order of Maria Theresa.[30] Numerous other awards were made to the officers in both armies and the Tsar gave orders for a special campaign medal to be struck which bore the inscription 'For the pacification of Hungary and Transylvania' on its obverse side.[31]

On 27 August an Austrian officer from Haynau's headquarters arrived in Oradea with the Emperor's pardon and instructions for Görgey to prepare for his journey to Klagenfurt.[32] The next day Paskevich received letters from the Emperor and Schwarzenberg with which there was enclosed the Order of Maria Theresa. In his letter Francis Joseph made it clear that it was not possible simply to draw a veil over what had happened in Hungary. He had to think of the other peoples in the Habsburg empire and for this reason he had been unable to grant a general amnesty.[33] Reluctantly Paskevich gave orders for Görgey to be allowed to leave for Klagenfurt escorted by an Austrian officer, rather than travel to Vienna with a Russian officer, as the Tsar had wished. Paskevich had formed a high opinion of Görgey during his short stay in his headquarters, as had the Grand Duke Constantine and many of the other Russian officers, who had found him willing to talk about the campaign and his problems in dealing with Kossuth.[34] When Paskevich found out that Görgey had no money for the expenses of his journey which he was required to pay out of his own pocket, he gave him a loan of 5000 gold roubles to assist him. Görgey's decision to accept the money, part of which he distributed to other members of his staff, was to give rise in later years to the unfounded belief that Paskevich had paid him handsomely for surrendering to the Russians.[35] On 29 August Görgey, accompanied by his wife, doctor and Austrian escort, set off for Klagenfurt and his long years in exile. The following day Paskevich and his headquarters staff left Oradea for Warsaw.

Since their surrender the Hungarian prisoners had been held in a makeshift camp which had been set up at Sarkad to the north of Arad under the supervision of General Anrep, the commander of the Second Cavalry Division. It was not long before cholera broke out because of the insanitary conditions which were not improved by two days of continuous rain. Many of the Hungarian prisoners escaped while they were in the hands of the Russians and some who originally came from Galicia persuaded their captors to allow them to enlist in the Russian army as batmen.[36] In an effort to alleviate the sufferings of the prisoners, Paskevich authorised the transfer of many of the officers to the estate of Count Wenckheim at Gyula, not far from Sarkad. On 23 August General Anrep formally handed over the Hungarian prisoners to General Montenuovo and General Reischach of the Austrian army, who immediately ordered the Hungarian officers to hand over their swords.[37] On 28 August Haynau wrote to Radetzky that he now regarded 'the drama of this great revolution' as ended. In a few days he would be leaving for Budapest and Vienna to thank the Emperor for the award of the Grand Cross of the Order of Saint Stephen.[38] On 31 August one of the Tsar's aides-de-camp arrived in Budapest with the Order of Saint Andrew, an event which reconciled Haynau with the Russians for one day at least, as one Austrian observer cynically recorded in his diary.[39]

On 23 August the Tsar was shocked to learn that his younger brother the Grand Duke Michael had suffered a stroke while inspecting troops. On 9 September he died without having regained consciousness. The following day the Tsar and Tsarevich left Warsaw for Saint Petersburg where the funeral took place on 30 September.[40] The death of his younger brother and the realisation that he was now the sole survivor of the four sons of the Emperor Paul had a profound effect on the Tsar, who looked pale and tired and gave one observer the impression that he was brooding about the number of years left to him to live.[41]

Nesselrode, like the Tsar, also suffered a personal misfortune at this time. His wife, who had been taking the cure at Bad Gastein in Austria, died quite suddenly of apoplexy on 18 August. After he had received the news of her death, Nesselrode withdrew from public life for the next ten days and on 10 September he followed the Tsar back to Saint Petersburg. The next day the Austrian and Prussian ambassadors also left Warsaw to pay brief visits to Vienna and Berlin, while the newly-arrived French ambassador set off for Saint Petersburg. Paskevich could now resume his duties as Viceroy of Poland and supervise the return of the Russian army from Hungary to its winter quarters.

After their defeat at Timişoara, the Hungarian forces remaining in the field were so demoralised that most of them decided to follow Görgey's example and surrender to the Russians. Despite Bem's efforts to persuade the Hungarians to continue the struggle, Kossuth realised that the situation was hopeless and laid down unrealistic conditions for reassuming the leadership with which Bem found it impossible to comply.[42] After burying the Hungarian crown and regalia near Orşova and issuing a farewell proclamation, he crossed the Danube on 7 August with the assistance of the Polish emigrés in the Serbian principality[43] and was eventually interned in the fortress of Vidin, along with Dembiński and many of the other Hungarian military and civilian leaders. In due course, the Hungarian refugees in Turkey were joined by about 2000 members of the Polish and Italian legions who had also retreated south. On 20 August Wysocki, the commander of the Polish legion, issued a farewell proclamation to the Hungarian nation in which he expressed the hope that the Hungarians would one day be able to be reconciled with the Rumanians and the Slavs.[44] By 25 August Austrian forces commanded by General Wallmoden had reached the Turkish frontier and occupied Orşova.

Further north, Austrian troops occupied Lugoj on 15 August after a short battle with Hungarian forces commanded by Bem and Guyon, which retreated from the town and then moved off in different directions. On 19 August a unit of about 1700 men surrendered at Deva to an Austrian advance guard commanded by Prince Liechtenstein, while the brigades commanded by Colonel Lázár and General Dessewffy (about 4000 men) surrendered on the same day to Austrian cavalry commanded by General Simbschen at Caransebeş. Two days later the remnants of General Vécsey's Fifth Corps (about 7940 men) who had declined to follow Bem into Transylvania and turned north, were persuaded to surrender to Rüdiger at Ineu as a result of a letter from Görgey advising Vécsey to lay down his arms.

In Transylvania General Lüders was regrouping the Russian forces after his victory at Sibiu on 6 August in order to move west and link up with the main Russian army under Paskevich. His first aim was to attack General Stein and raise the siege of Alba Iulia, while General Grotenhjelm's forces in the northern part of the province were ordered to move on Cluj from Tîrgu-Mureş. A special unit commanded by General Dyck was set up in Mediaş in order to act as a link between the two groups of Russian forces.

On the morning of 12 August Lüders' forces encountered units of Stein's force at Sebeş, to the south of Alba Iulia. The Hungarians put up little resistance and as a result of repeated attacks by a unit of Russian horse artillery commanded by Captain Dekonsky, their retreat soon became a rout. On this occasion the Russians took more than 1700 prisoners, while their own casualities were minimal (five killed and thirty-four wounded). The following day Lüders was able to raise the siege of Alba Iulia which had lasted 136 days.

Continuing his advance along the valley of the river Maros, Lüders reached Orăștie on 13 August. The following day Iancu and a group of Rumanian partisans arrived in the town, seeking assistance from the Russians after the collapse of their negotiations with the Hungarians. In accordance with his directive from Paskevich, Lüders gave them money and munitions. At the same time he urged the Russian authorities in Warsaw to persuade the Austrian government to do more to support the Rumanians in their struggle against the Hungarians.[45] After the campaign was over Lüders was to pay a generous tribute to the support he had received from Iancu and his partisans, who had helped the Russians by pinning down part of the Hungarian forces.[46] Between 16 and 24 August the force commanded by Colonel Inczédy (about 1200 men), which had been trying to prevent a break-out by Iancu's partisans from their mountain stronghold, was disbanded and surrendered to a Russian unit commanded by General Löwenhagen which had been sent to the area.

By 17 August Lüders had occupied Simeria to the west of Orăștie where he learnt of the surrender at Șiria from returning Rumanian and Saxon members of Görgey's army who had been allowed to return home. The area was still occupied by the main part of Bem's army which had been compelled to evacuate the nearby town of Deva because of a serious explosion on 13 August in the powder factory which had been set up in the castle. In order to shorten the war, Lüders decided to try to persuade Bem to follow Görgey's example and sent one of his officers to negotiate a surrender. The offer was angrily rejected by Bem[47] and after a vain attempt to persuade the Hungarians to fight, he handed over the command to Colonel Beke on 18 August and set off for Turkey which he reached five days later. The same afternoon the major part of the army (315 officers and 7660 other ranks, with seventy-four guns and thirteen standards) surrendered to Lüders on the same terms as Görgey, while the next day a smaller unit commanded by Colonel Frummer (about 1900 men) surrendered to General Hasford at Hațeg.[48] On 19 August General Ramberg's Third Corps arriving in Deva and linked up with Lüders' forces, thus bringing an end to the fighting in southern Transylvania.

With the arrival of Austrian troops, arrangements were made for the captured Hungarian officers to be sent to Sibiu, while the other

After the Surrender

ranks, along with the guns and baggage, were removed to the fortress at Alba Iulia. However, the Russians retained the captured standards which were sent first to Paskevich in Oradea and from there to the Tsar in Warsaw.[49] Although Lüders' troops were unable to fraternise with their Hungarian captives in the same way as had happened after the surrender of Görgey, Lüders arranged for the officers to be given money with which to buy food for the journey to Sibiu, while the ordinary Russian soldiers shared their rations with the Hungarian rank-and-file.[50]

Now that the campaign was over Lüders agreed with Ramberg that he would withdraw his forces to the area between Sibiu and Făgăraş. The detachment commanded by General Dyck was withdrawn from Mediaş and it was replaced by the Austrian unit commanded by General Clam-Gallas. When Lüders arrived in Sibiu on 25 August he was given a triumphal welcome by the local population who were glad that the fighting had at last been brought to an end as a result of the Russian intervention. Three days later General Wohlgemuth arrived in the town to take up his duties as Governor of Transylvania. Shortly afterwards the Austrian Council of Ministers gave Wohlgemuth the same instructions about the trials and executions of the Hungarian prisoners as had been sent to Haynau.[51] On 31 August Lüders held a special service of thanksgiving and victory parade for his troops. On 2 September an Austrian courier arrived with a flattering letter for Lüders from Francis Joseph, and the award of the Order of Maria Theresa. On 7 September Lüders left Sibiu to return to Bucharest where he issued a special Order of the Day to his troops on 9 September in which he expressed his warmest thanks to all ranks in his corps for the splendid efforts they had made in the course of the campaign.[52]

In the northern part of Transylvania General Grotenhjelm was as successful as Lüders in putting an end to hostilities. After occupying Cluj on 15 August, part of his forces drove the Hungarian detachment of Colonel Gál back to Ciucea where it rejected a surrender proposal from a Russian detachment under Colonel Mel'nikov which was advancing eastwards from Hungary. At the same time Grotenhjelm had begun surrender negotiations with the isolated detachment of Colonel Kazinczy in north-east Hungary which, after moving into Transylvania, had occupied Dej on 15 August and was being pursued by the Austrian troops of Colonel Urban. On 25 August the combined forces of Gál and Kazinczy (about 4000 men and fifty-six guns) surrendered unconditionally to Grotenhjelm at Jibou, to the north of Dej.⁵³ According to one Russian observer, Grotenhjelm was forced to rebuke Urban for his impolite behaviour to the elderly Kazinczy after he had surrendered and several of the Hungarians are alleged to have warned the Russians that they would live to regret having helped Austria to suppress the revolt in Hungary.⁵⁴ After handing over the Hungarian prisoners to the Austrians, Grotenhjelm withdrew his forces east to Bistriţa to await further orders.

In north-east Hungary the detachment of General Karlovich which had set off from Debrecen met with little resistance and soon reached the fortress of Mukachevo. After his arrival, Karlovich entered into surrender negotiations with the garrison. Two envoys were sent to Oradea to talk to Görgey and on their return, the garrison (thirty-two officers, 329 other ranks and twenty-one guns) surrendered unconditionally on 26 August. In due course, the keys were returned to the Austrians from Warsaw.⁵⁵ After the surrender, the Russians entertained the Hungarian garrison to dinner and a young Russian officer, who was present, was to remember with sadness the arrival of gendarme officers to arrest the commandant, Colonel Mezösy, and hand him over to the Austrians.⁵⁶ As had happened elsewhere in Hungary, there were financial problems arising from the destruction of the Kossuth notes, but the local population were impressed by the religious fervour of the Russian army, their sympathy for the cause of Hungary and their disparaging remarks about the Austrians.⁵⁷

In southern Hungary, the Austrians informed the garrison of the fortress of Petrovaradin of Görgey's surrender. After a delegation had returned from a visit to Haynau's headquarters at Arad, the garrison (about 8000 men) surrendered to the forces of Jelačić on 7 September.

On 25 August the Tsar, who was already saddened by the illness of his brother Michael, received the news that the remnants of Bem's army had surrendered to Lüders. Although pleased that this part of the Hungarian forces had surrendered to Russia rather than Austria, he was becoming increasingly anxious that the army should be withdrawn from Hungary and Transylvania as soon as possible since he was concerned about the possibility of trouble between Austria and Prussia.⁵⁸ After discussion with the Austrians, it was agreed that small Russian detachments would remain in Transylvania and north-east Hungary until Austrian units could replace them. In addition, Grabbe's detachment was permitted to remain with the Austrians near Komárno until the surrender negotiations had been concluded.⁵⁹

At the end of August the withdrawal of the Russian army began.

By mid-October the Second Infantry Corps had returned to Russian Poland, while the Fourth Infantry Corps was back in the western provinces of Russia (Volhynia and Podolia). Some units of the Third Infantry Corps remained throughout September and October in northern Hungary, where Rüdiger set up a temporary headquarters in Prešov, but by the beginning of November the whole corps had returned to Poland. In Transylvania, the major part of the Fifth Infantry Corps began to return to Moldavia and Wallachia at the beginning of September and by the end of November the remaining Russian troops of the Fifteenth Infantry Division were also back in their winter quarters. The Guards were brought back to Saint Petersburg from Lithuania where their place was taken by the grenadier corps.[60] It was typical of the Tsar that one of his last acts before leaving Warsaw for Saint Petersburg was to draw up detailed instructions for Paskevich about the inspections which he wished to be carried out after the troops had returned to their winter quarters. Among other things, the Tsar gave orders that no training was to take place for a whole month afterwards.[61]

Although the Austrian army admired the fighting qualities of the Russian soldiers, most of its members had few regrets about the departure of their allies, whose openly-expressed sympathies for the Hungarian cause and obvious rapport with the Slavonic-speaking Slovaks and Ukrainians had become an increasing source of irritation. Nor was the Russian army sorry that the campaign had come to an end. The army had done its duty in accordance with the Tsar's orders but found, somewhat to its surprise, that it had little hatred for the Hungarians and had almost nothing in common with the Germanic officers in the Habsburg army. Accusations by some of the more arrogant Austrian officers in cafes and restaurants that the Russians were little better than mercenaries were bitterly resented and led to duels, which in at least one case led to the death of an Austrian officer.[62]

For their part, the Russian authorities were worried by the degree of fraternisation with the Hungarians, as some members of the army had taken the opportunity of their service abroad to defect and join the Hungarian army.[63] Indeed, the Austrian Ministry of the Interior had warned its own authorities in Galicia as early as June 1849 to be on the alert for appeals to Russian soldiers to defect which were being sent by post from Brussels via Leipzig inside the uncut pages of French novels.[64] Those Russians who were captured after the campaign was over were court-martialled and, in most cases, executed or severely punished. The Russian field postal service which had been established for the duration of the campaign did not function efficiently, and when an officer from Panyutin's division went to collect his mail from the post office at the Russian headquarters in Oradea at the end of the campaign he found a huge pile of unsorted mail.[65] There is also evidence that the authorities discouraged the army from writing letters to Russia about their experiences abroad and deliberately destroyed mail when it arrived in Warsaw or Odessa *en route* to Russia.[66]

On the whole, the withdrawal proceeded without incident, although there was some reluctance on the part of Austrian officials to take back unused stores from the Russian supply depots in northern Hungary. With the aid of Count Zichy, the problems were resolved and the Austrians even agreed to send the unused stores from the Cracow depot back to Poland by rail at their own expense.[67] Zichy was also to be involved in an official Austrian complaint to the Russian government that some of the Russian officers left behind in Hungary to recover from illness had been expressing subversive political views. As the Petrashevsky investigation was well under way, the Tsar, always fearful about the loyalty of the army, informed Paskevich that he was sending a senior officer from his staff to Galicia and Hungary to investigate the Austrian allegations. In due course Paskevich, who carried out his own investigation, was able to reassure the Tsar that the Austrian accusations were unfounded and resulted to a considerable extent from the hostility which had developed between the two armies.[68] However, it was to be some time before the last Russian convalescents left Hungary. As late as April 1850, there were still Russian soldiers in the hospital in Debrecen where the last one died on 23 July 1850.[69]

According to official figures, Russian casualties in the eight-week campaign were remarkably light. Out of a total of 190 000 men barely 2 per cent were killed or wounded in the fighting (708 killed, 2320 wounded, of whom 278 died of wounds, and 127 were shell-shocked). However, the casualties caused by sickness, especially cholera, were incomparably greater. Out of a total number of 85 387 cases of sickness there were 10 885 deaths, of which deaths from cholera amounted to 7788. Thus out of a total number of deaths of 11 871 only one in twelve was killed by enemy action.[70] Generally speaking, there were proportionately more casualties caused by enemy action in the fighting in Transylvania, where the Fifth Infantry Corps were less seriously affected by cholera.[71] By the end of June 1850 a further

23 000 men serving in the three Infantry Corps stationed in Russian Poland had been declared unfit for further service and had been replaced. Thus the total number of casualties in the army (excluding the Fourth and Fifty Infantry Corps) amounted to nearly 35 000.[72] It is difficult to compare these figures with those of the Austrian and Hungarian armies, since neither force appears to have kept proper medical records.

Another matter which had to be dealt with after the campaign was the settlement of accounts with Austria. A special committee chaired by his Chief of Staff was set up by Paskevich to draw up the Russian accounts for the campaign, while Count Zichy was put in charge of the group of Austrian officials. Paskevich estimated that the war had cost Russia 10 million roubles.[73] He had not forgotten the length of time that Austria had taken to settle its accounts with Russia after the Napoleonic Wars (they were not settled until 1821) and he hoped that Austria would keep its side of the agreement signed in June. It soon became apparent that Austria was finding difficulty in agreeing to an immediate settlement and after much discussion between Paskevich and Zichy, the Tsar finally decided that Austria would repay Russia the sum of $4\frac{1}{2}$ million roubles, of which half a million was the estimated cost of the operations in Transylvania.[74] In the event, the amount of the account submitted to the Austrian government in February 1850 for the Russian operations in Hungary and Galicia was 3 483 236 roubles $96\frac{1}{2}$ kopecks. The Austrian Minister of Finance was delighted with the Tsar's generosity, but still wished to delay payment because of Austria's own financial problems. He therefore suggested combining the new debt with the debt still outstanding from the assistance given by the Russians in suppressing the revolt in Cracow in 1846. Eventually Zichy persuaded the Emperor and Schwarzenberg to intervene and take a final decision about immediate payment.[75] As a result, an agreement was signed in Warsaw on 2 April 1850 as a supplement to the convention of 10 June 1849. By its terms Austria agreed to pay 3 million roubles in cash in three annual instalments with interest. The amount was to be paid in salt from the mines at Bochnia and Wieliczka in Galicia. Thus the debt was not finally settled until 31 July 1853, shortly before the outbreak of the Crimean War.[76]

Zichy had good reason to be pleased with the results of his negotiations and in due course travelled to Saint Petersburg to express his gratitude to the Tsar in person on behalf of Francis Joseph. Nicholas' generosity in deciding to charge Austria only 4 million roubles for the costs of the campaign in Hungary, was, in the words of the British representative in Warsaw, 'all the more deserving of notice, as it is well known that the Russian available funds are anything but abundant'.[77] By the end of 1849 it was apparent that there could be a large budget deficit, since the increase in total military expenditure alone was 38½ million roubles more than the original estimate. Accordingly, the Tsar decided to revive the negotiations with Baring Brothers abandoned in July by requesting a loan of £5½ million (31 million silver roubles) for the completion of the railway from Saint Petersburg to Moscow, the construction of which had begun in 1842. The official Russian decree about the loan was signed on 21 December 1849. A few days later, on 9 January 1850, Baring Brothers received their first notification of the Tsar's decision when a bank official from Saint Petersburg visited them in London and handed over a letter and copy of the decree. In the face of a threat that the Russian government would go elsewhere in the City, if the loan were not granted, Baring Brothers, after consultation with their partners in Amsterdam, acceded to the request.[78] It was generally believed in liberal circles in Great Britain that the true purpose of the Russian loan was to finance the costs of the intervention in Hungary, especially as the Russian government never published details of its budget. There is strong evidence to support this belief from material in Russian archives which indicates that the Tsar approved the insertion of a false figure for Russian military expenditure (60½ million as opposed to 99 million roubles) in the 1850 budget estimate submitted for approval to the Council of State at the end of December 1849. One of the reasons for this decision was a desire to prevent the true size of the 1849 deficit becoming widely known and affecting the loan negotiations with Baring Brothers.[79] Nevertheless the British ambassador in Saint Petersburg was assured that the loan had been requested because of an increase in the cost of building the railway compared with the original estimate, and in 1851 the Saint Petersburg to Moscow railway was completed and opened to the public.[80]

Throughout the month of September the remaining preoccupation of the Austrian army was the raising of the siege of Komárno. After his successful sortie and the capture of Győr in early August, Klapka hoped he would be able to continue harassing the Austrians further afield. A raiding column from the fortress, commanded by Colonel Mednyánszky, received reinforcements of 3000 men from an irregular unit under the government commissar Noszlopy operating in the area of Lake Balaton and was despatched to carry out operations in the area of Székesfehérvár. However, the receipt on 13 August of the news of Bem's defeat at Timişoara and on 18 August of Görgey's surrender caused Klapka to abandon his ideas of further offensive operations, and he withdrew to the safety of the fortress. At the same time the Austrian government had reacted swiftly to Klapka's sortie and sent the Minister of War, Count Gyulai, to take charge of operations in the area. By 16 August Győr had been reoccupied and a huge force of 44 000 assembled which included the Second Corps of General Csorich which had originally been besieging the fortress. Schwarzenberg had no objections to the missions which the Russian officers Isakov and Anichkov were about to undertake with Austrian support, and was hopeful that Grabbe's detachment could be made available to assist the Austrian army in its efforts to bring about the surrender.[81]

After his defeat at Gesztely, Grabbe's detachment had slowly made its way back into north-west Hungary to resume its original task of maintaining order in this mountainous area. By 7 August it had reached Lučenec where a party of Russian soldiers, returning to their units from convalescence in Cracow, had been attacked on 1 August by a group of Hungarian partisans, aided by some of the local population. Paskevich had overruled Grabbe's request to raze the town to the ground in order to deter any further attacks, but on 8 August fire broke out and the town was completely destroyed. Although it could not be proved, it was believed that some of the local inhabitants started the fire.[82] By 18 August Grabbe had reached Banská Bystrica where he had to refuse a request from Gyulai to move south to join the Austrian siege forces, pending the receipt of authority to do so from Warsaw.[83]

On 19 August Klapka rejected an Austrian proposal that he should follow the example of Görgey on the grounds that he had no authentic information about what had happened.[84] The next day Isakov, accompanied by the Austrian Colonel Alcaini, arrived in Komárno from the Austrian headquarters at Ács to show Klapka Görgey's letter to Rüdiger of 11 August. Despite the eloquence of both Alcaini and Isakov, Klapka informed the envoys after a meeting with his War Council that he had no intention of surrendering the fortress unconditionally. In the various conversations that had taken place, the Hungarians had sensed the difference in outlook between Isakov (who spoke only French and no German) and Alcaini and decided that the Russians might well offer them better terms. Accordingly,

Klapka proposed that a fortnight's armistice should be arranged, during which two Hungarian delegations would travel to Haynau's headquarters in Arad and Paskevich's headquarters in Oradea for further discussions. On 21 August there were further talks in Komárno about the implementation of the armistice and after Alcaini had left, Klapka was able to talk privately to Isakov about the likely attitude of the Tsar if he decided to surrender to the Russians. A tearful Isakov did his best to urge Klapka to spare his country further suffering. He was then escorted out of the fortress to make his way north to join Grabbe's detachment, about which Klapka had proved to be disconcertingly well-informed. On 22 August the two Hungarian delegations from Komárno set off for Arad and Oradea.[85]

When Isakov reached Grabbe's headquarters at Banská Bystrica on 22 August, he warned Grabbe that the Hungarians would probably approach him about a surrender to the Russians and also gave him the Tsar's verbal message that his detachment could move south and join the Austrians besieging Komárno. Grabbe immediately gave orders for the detachment to move off the following day. On 24 August Colonel Esterházy arrived in Batovce with a letter from Klapka in which he offered to surrender to the Russians if the Tsar was prepared to respect the political and constitutional rights of Hungary, a proposal which Grabbe inevitably rejected as unacceptable. A disappointed Esterházy returned to Komárno to inform Klapka that he was unlikely to obtain more favourable terms from the Russians.[86] While these negotiations were in progress, the Hungarians made preparations for a lengthy siege. Under the terms of the armistice the units of Mednyánszky and Noszlopy had been allowed to return to the fortress and new battalions were formed from these troops.[87]

On 26 August Colonel Anichkov, accompanied by the Austrian Colonel Jungbauer, arrived with Görgey's letter of 16 August to Klapka written in Oradea in which he explained why he had decided to surrender to the Russians. The letter ended with an exhortation to Klapka to reflect carefully about what he might be able to do.[88] According to one Hungarian emigré source, Anichkov is said to have spoken of the possibility that Russia and Hungary might one day become allies in a future war against 'perfidious Austria'.[89] However, Klapka refused to agree to any surrender until the return of the two delegations from Arad and Oradea, although by this time he had received a first-hand account of Görgey's surrender from an officer who had taken part in it.[90]

At the end of August the two delegations returned. While Görgey advised Klapka to surrender and take advantage of the strategic importance of Komárno in order to gain favourable terms, Haynau warned the garrison that its members would be put to the sword if they failed to surrender. At the same time General Csorich continued to offer to negotiate before the armistice expired on 4 September. By 5 September Grabbe's troops had taken up their positions to the north-east of the fortress near Chotin and the Hungarians were skirmishing with the Cossacks, of whom twelve were taken prisoner.

By this time Klapka was facing serious problems inside the fortress. He had given up the idea of surrendering to the Russians after the failure of Esterházy's mission to Grabbe and realised that all he could do was to seek the best terms he could from the Austrians. Although the fortress could withstand a long siege, there were 4000 sick and wounded inside it. Furthermore, a group of officers led by Colonel Thaly, one of the officers who had visited Haynau's headquarters, and a relative of Kossuth, was opposed to any suggestion of surrender and sought to persuade the garrison to continue the struggle. On 11 September Haynau informed Klapka that the fortress of Petrovaradin had surrendered. It was now clear that Komárno was the last stronghold left in Hungarian hands. Ironically, it was at this time that Klapka received from a French go-between the official proposal made by Manin earlier in the year of an alliance between the Republic of Venice and Hungary.[91] Ultimately, Klapka was compelled to arrest Thaly and the editor of the newspaper *Komáromi Lapok* which still continued to be published inside the fortress, as well as execute a number of soldiers who had attempted to desert.

The negotiations dragged on throughout September. In despair, the Austrians sent in a secret agent to assassinate Klapka, but he was caught and executed on 17 September. Leaflets urging the garrison to surrender were circulated in the Hungarian outposts. The Emperor and Schwarzenberg even agreed that Grabbe could take over the surrender negotiations from General Nugent, who had now replaced Count Gyulai as the commander of the besieging force.[92] However, the Tsar had lost interest in the matter and in the face of pressure from Paskevich, decided that Grabbe's detachment should, after all, be withdrawn. In his view, there was no reason why the Austrians should not be able to conclude the negotiations on their own, nor did they need Russian military assistance, if there were further fighting.[93] By 22 September Grabbe realised that it was unlikely that he would be allowed to remain near Komárno much longer.

However, the end was in sight. On 26 September Haynau arrived in Ács and invited Klapka to visit the Austrian headquarters for further talks. By this time the Austrians were desperately anxious to end the negotiations and at talks the following day surrender terms were soon agreed. The garrison would be allowed to leave unarmed, except for the officers who could retain their swords. Former Habsburg officers would be allowed to emigrate, or return home if they chose not to face a court-martial. All other officers could return home. The rank and file were granted an amnesty, but also allowed to emigrate. Generous financial terms were agreed about payment of arrears of pay, including the allocation of 500 000 gulden in cash in settlement of the paper transactions made during the siege. The sick and wounded were promised full medical treatment and there was to be no confiscation of property. Thus the Komárno garrison received the most generous treatment from the Austrians of all the Hungarian units which had surrendered.[94]

Between 2 and 4 October the Austrians moved back into the fortress. On 5 October Klapka left for Bratislava from where he eventually made his way to Great Britain. Three days earlier in Vidin Kossuth had commissioned Charles Henningsen of the British *Daily News* to travel to Komárno and urge the garrison not to surrender. On 9 October Henningsen's mission came to an end in Belgrade when he learnt that Komárno was no longer in Hungarian hands.[95]

On 28 September a courier from Warsaw brought Grabbe the Tsar's order that his detachment should withdraw from the siege of Komárno and return to winter quarters. After issuing the appropriate orders, Grabbe left on 4 October for Vienna where he was to meet Schwarzenberg and the Emperor who awarded him the Order of Leopold; by 23 October he was back in Warsaw. Somewhat belatedly, on 13 October Schwarzenberg informed Buol, who was now back in Saint Petersburg, that he had no objection to the withdrawal of Grabbe's detachment and the remaining Russian troops in Transylvania.[96]

On 9 October the Tsar received the news of the surrender of Komárno. In his opinion, the terms on which the fortress had been allowed to surrender did Austria no credit and he hoped that Grabbe had not taken part in the final ceremony.[97] Two days later the Tsar was to receive further news about the fate of the Hungarian generals he had handed over to the Austrians which was to cause him even greater irritation with the behaviour of his ally.

10 The Aftermath of the Intervention

Even before the end of the Hungarian revolt the Austrian government had begun a series of courts-martial of those persons who had taken part in it. According to an Austrian official publication, 4628 rebels were tried between 1 November 1848 and the end of 1850. In the absence of accurate information it is difficult to be precise but it appears that about 500 people were condemned to death, of whom 120 were executed, while at least another 1500 were sentenced to long terms of imprisonment, many in extremely harsh conditions. In addition, the Austrians decided in 1851 to try *in absentia* those who had become emigrés. In September of that year Kossuth, several of his former ministers and many others, including Count Gyula Andrássy, a future Prime Minister and Minister of Foreign Affairs, were hanged in effigy in Budapest.[1]

Haynau's decision to bring the negotiations for the surrender of Komárno to a speedy conclusion had been quite deliberate. Once he had been granted authority to carry out executions, he quickly instituted court-martial proceedings against the former Hungarian generals who had surrendered. On 6 October, the day after Komárno had finally been handed over to the Austrians and the anniversary of the murder in Vienna of Count Latour, the former Minister of War, thirteen out of the fourteen Hungarian generals who had been sentenced to death were executed at Arad. Nine of the thirteen (Aulich, Damjanich, Knezich, Lahner, Leiningen-Westerburg, Nagy Sándor, Poeltenberg, Török and Vécsey) who had surrendered to the Russians, were hanged, while the remaining four (Dessewffy, Kiss, Lázár and Schweidel) who had surrendered to the Austrians, were shot. The fourteenth general, András Gáspár, was sentenced to two years' imprisonment and granted an amnesty in 1850. In Budapest, Count Lajos Batthyány, Prime Minister of the Hungarian government in April 1848, who had been arrested in January 1849, was sentenced to be hanged. After he had made an unsuccessful attempt to commit suicide by cutting his throat, the Austrian Commandment in Budapest, General Kempen, altered the sentence to death by a firing-squad, an action which incurred the displeasure of Haynau. Several other executions took place in October 1849, including that of Colonel Kazinczy, who was shot, although he had surrendered to the Russians.²

The Hungarians were never to forget the fate of the thirteen generals executed at Arad and Count Batthyány. Reaction in Europe was, with few exceptions, one of revulsion that Austria had found it necessary to deal so harshly with the Hungarians. Before the executions at Arad had taken place, Palmerston had already written privately to the British ambassador in Vienna that he considered the Austrians to be 'the greatest brutes that ever called themselves by the undeserved name of civilised men'.³ In an effort to counter the reaction in Great Britain, the Austrians mounted an operation from their embassy in London to insert articles in the British press which would attempt to justify their actions.⁴ Palmerston did not have a high opinion of Schwarzenberg's statesmanlike qualities, while Schwarzenberg regarded Palmerston as a trouble-maker. The mutual antipathy was of long standing as Palmerston had been instrumental in rejecting Schwarzenberg as a possible Austrian ambassador in London in the early 1840s.⁵ In France, there was a similar outcry against the executions and Tocqueville, the Minister of Foreign Affairs, had, like Palmerston, been urging the Austrians, as soon as the war had ended, not to treat the Hungarians as if they were traitors and rebels.⁶

The Tsar, who had been feeling unwell at the beginning of October, was outraged when he learnt of the executions at Arad. Batthyány had deserved his fate, but the hanging of the Hungarian generals who had surrendered to the Russian army and for whom the Tsar had interceded with Francis Joseph was 'infamous' and 'insulting' especially when compared with the leniency shown by the Austrians to the garrisons in Venice and Komárno.⁷ The Tsar's sense of outrage was fully shared by Rüdiger and Paskevich⁸ who knew that it was only General Grünne's mission to Arad at the end of August which had prevented the executions taking place much earlier. However, it was typical of Paskevich that he put a large share of the blame for what had happened on Berg and Medem, both of whom, in his opinion, had failed to represent the Tsar's views sufficiently strongly in Arad and Vienna. The Tsar seems to have shared Paskevich's views about Medem, but was prepared to defend Berg, since he considered that there was little that anyone could do to curb Haynau's desire to take revenge on the Hungarians.⁹

A reluctant Nesselrode was instructed to make the Tsar's views known to Buol to whom Nicholas refused to grant an audience after he had returned to Saint Petersburg from Vienna. Although Nesselrode did his best to smooth over the rift in relations between the two countries caused by the executions and referred to the unhappy relationship between Haynau and Paskevich,[10] he was alarmed that the Tsar's anger might cause lasting damage to the Austro-Russian *entente* which he had been so assiduous in fostering.[11] Indeed, it seemed to both the Tsar and Nesselrode that Austria was setting about its task of restoring order in Hungary in completely the wrong way. Instead of adopting a conciliatory policy, Austria was trying to imitate the methods employed by Russia in Poland after the 1830 revolt. In their view, a repressive policy was bound to lead to further trouble, since Hungary formed a major part of the Habsburg Empire, whereas Russian Poland was only a small part of the Russian Empire.[12]

In the event, the Austrian Council of Ministers decided on 26 October to suspend the carrying-out of any further executions of those sentenced to death, thus putting into practice the policy contained in Schwarzenberg's undocumented remark that 'a little bit of hanging' was necessary before the implementation of a policy of reconciliation. Appropriate instructions were sent to Haynau and Wohlgemuth, but no official announcement was made.[13] Early in 1850 Haynau and Schwarzenberg began to differ in their opinions about the treatment of the Hungarians, and later in the year Haynau overreached himself by announcing sentences of death, followed by amnesty, on twenty-three former members of the Hungarian parliament. On 6 July Haynau was dismissed and was ultimately replaced in 1851 by the Archduke Albrecht. On 4 September he was attacked by a mob shouting 'Down with the Austrian butcher' while visiting a brewery in Southwark during a visit to Britain. In Warsaw the Russian army 'from the highest to the lowest' expressed 'the greatest satisfaction' at Haynau's treatment; in Rüdiger's view, a man who hanged the prisoners-of-war of his allies had got what he deserved.[14]

Unaware of the anger he had caused, Schwarzenberg continued to seek the Tsar's aid in settling the differences between Austria and Russia on the problem of the future leadership of Germany, to which he was now able to devote his attention. However, he was to remain unrepentant when he received an account of Buol's meeting with Nesselrode. He had already written a stinging reply to the Austrian ambassador in London, who shared his superior's dislike of Palmerston, about the British offer of mediation in Hungary. Austria had no need of advice from others and did not presume to offer Britain advice about the solution of its problems in Canada, Ireland and the Ionian Islands.[15]

Naturally, he could not write to the Tsar in the same manner. Instead, Schwarzenberg decided to concentrate on the loyalty of the army, a subject which he knew would appeal to the Tsar. He had not forgotten that at his first meeting with Francis Joseph in Warsaw in May, Nicholas, wearing the uniform of the Hungarian hussar regiment of which he was honorary colonel and which had defected *en masse* in December 1848, had presented his respects to the Emperor as the only remaining loyal member of the regiment.[16] Accordingly, in his official reply to Buol, Schwarzenberg pointed out that loyalty was the foundation-stone of a state such as the Habsburg empire which was made up of so many different races. The former Habsburg officers had broken their oath to the Emperor and had ignored repeated appeals to abandon the Hungarian cause. Offended military honour required an 'exemplary expiation' of the crime they had committed, as the Tsar would be the first to appreciate after his experiences during the Decembrist revolt in 1825, of which Schwarzenberg had also been a witness while serving in the Austrian embassy in Saint Petersburg. The lenient surrender terms granted to the garrisons in Komárno and Venice had been a deliberate act which had saved Austria much unnecessary expenditure and bloodshed. Francis Joseph had pardoned Görgey in accordance with the Tsar's request, and there would be no serious consequences for the officers who were about to face a court-martial, as was clear from the decision taken by the Council of Ministers on 26 October. In an accompanying private letter, Schwarzenberg advised Buol to keep calm. Austria would weather the storm. The government had done its duty and as Buol knew only too well, most of the trouble in the relationship between Austria and Russia was due to Paskevich who, as Schwarzenberg had discovered to his chagrin during his visit to Warsaw in August, could do no wrong in the eyes of the Tsar.[17]

On 5 November Nesselrode returned Schwarzenberg's despatch to Buol. The Tsar had read it, but saw no reason to alter his views about the executions at Arad. He still declined to grant Buol an audience, a matter which, in Buol's view, could only serve to increase the dislike for Austria which had developed in the Russian army since the campaign in Hungary.[18]

The executions at Arad were not the only reason for the Tsar's displeasure with the Austrian government. Despite Berg's protest, nothing had been done to correct the misleading impression conveyed in Haynau's victory bulletin of 18 August about the part played by the Russian army in the Hungarian campaign. As a result of Nesselrode's pressure on both Buol and Medem, Schwarzenberg decided that Haynau must be compelled to issue another bulletin in which due recognition would be made of the services rendered by the Russian army. The task was far from easy, and after considerable argument, Haynau issued an Order of the Day from his headquarters in Budapest on 16 December in which a suitably laudatory tribute was made to the cooperation of the Russian army in assisting Austria to defeat the Hungarians. In a private letter to Schwarzenberg, Haynau made it clear that he had issued the order under protest. His praise of Paskevich was nothing short of 'a public lie'.[19] The bulletin was not published in the *Journal de Saint Pétersbourg* until 22 January 1850. According to a note in Paskevich's personal papers, Francis Joseph had personally ordered Haynau to issue the order which had been drafted in Vienna.[20] Despite the fulsome language of the bulletin, according to the British ambassador in Saint Petersburg, there was no reason to believe that this outward show of cordiality between the two governments had done anything to lessen the distaste for the alliance with Austria which was generally felt by the Russian army.[21]

Shortly before the publication of Haynau's bulletin in Russia, Buol was at last granted an audience with the Tsar on 16 January 1850. In his account of the audience Buol referred to the Tsar's continuing displeasure concerning the executions at Arad. However, the Tsar was generous in his praise for the Austrian army which, in his view, had saved the monarchy, and regretted that its relations with the Russian army were unsatisfactory. However, Francis Joseph should not be held responsible for the recent coolness in relations and the Tsar emphasised that he had nothing but the highest regard for his noble character.[22] As Schwarzenberg had predicted, the storm appeared to have blown over, but Buol was not to forgive the Tsar for his decision to keep him at a distance for three months after the cordial relationship the two had enjoyed when they were together in Warsaw.

The Tsar's insistence that Austria should deal leniently with the Hungarians who had surrendered to the Russian army was not matched by his own attitude towards the Poles who had succeeded in escaping to Turkey. Delighted by the final outcome of the campaign, Nicholas was determined not to miss the opportunity of laying his hands on the Polish emigré leaders who had escaped to Turkey and had played such a prominent part in the Hungarian revolt. The Austrians, by contrast, were more concerned with securing the return of the 4000 Hungarians who had sought refuge in the Ottoman Empire. However, both Austria and Russia underestimated the reactions in Great Britain and France to their action, and the eventual refusal of the Turkish government to hand over the refugees was to have serious international repercussions which brought Europe almost to the brink of war. When Windischgraetz began his operations against Hungary at the end of 1848, the Austrian government had raised the problem of members of the Hungarian forces who might cross the border with the Turks. At the same time they sent a detailed description of Kossuth and his wife to Austrian missions in Greece, Serbia and Turkey.[23] In January 1849 the Tsar mentioned the problem briefly to Paskevich[24] and the following month Stratford Canning was also concerning himself with the fate of any Hungarians who might escape into Moldavia and Wallachia as a result of the fighting in Transylvania.[25]

As soon as the news of the surrender of the Hungarian forces became known in Bucharest, General Duhamel gave Fuad Effendi a list of ten Poles whom the Russians wished to extradite, including Bem and Dembiński. In the absence of instructions, Fuad Effendi referred the matter to Constantinople.[26] Shortly afterwards, Nesselrode wrote a letter to Titov, the Russian ambassador in Constantinople, instructing him to seek the extradition not only of Bem and Dembiński, but also Wysocki and Zamoyski, who had served as a colonel in the Hungarian forces. All four were considered to be subjects of the Tsar and had taken part in the 1830 revolt. Titov was instructed to obtain a definite answer to the Russian request and draw attention to the serious consequences that a negative response would entail.[27] The Russian right of extradition was based on Article 2 of the Treaty of Kuchuk-Kainardji signed with Turkey in 1774, which forbade Turkey to grant asylum to rebellious and disaffected Russian subjects. At the same time, the Tsar followed his usual practice of sending a special envoy to Constantinople with a personal letter, in which Nicholas pointedly reminded the Sultan that the Russian intervention in Hungary had been undertaken for exactly the same reasons as the intervention in the Danubian principalities the previous autumn. The bearer of this letter was an officer of Polish origin, Count Leo Radziwill, who arrived in Constantinople from Odessa aboard an Austrian steamer on 4 September.[28]

In a letter written on 24 August to Stürmer, the Austrian ambassador in Constantinople, Schwarzenberg demanded the extradition of all the Hungarians who had fled to Turkey. Among other things, the Austrians claimed that some of the Hungarians had embezzled Austrian official funds. Like the Russians, the Austrians based their right of extradition on articles in two treaties signed with Turkey in the eighteenth century (Article 18 of the Treaty of Belgrade, 1739, and Article 14 of the Treaty of Passarowitz, 1718) which were drafted in similar terms to the relevant article in the Treaty of Kuchuk-Kainardji.[29]

The Turkish government was uncertain about the response it should make to the Austrian and Russian demands, and as usual it sought advice from Stratford Canning. The latter, who felt that he had been out-manoeuvred during Grabbe's visit in April and had been exhorted all summer to ensure that Turkey remained neutral during the fighting in Hungary, considered that he had now been presented with a perfect opportunity to regain some of his lost influence with the Turks. He therefore suggested several amendments to the Turkish draft reply, and stressed in his despatch to Palmerston that both Titov and Stürmer had threatened the Turks with a declaration of war if a single refugee were allowed to escape. Although Nesselrode was subsequently to deny that Titov had made such a remark, the Austrian and Russian threat to declare war was taken very seriously by Palmerston who was to refer to it throughout the ensuing crisis as a justification for the actions of the government. To make matters worse, Titov was also to decide to follow the Austrian example by demanding the extradition of all the Polish refugees (about 1000).[30]

On 6 September Radziwill and Titov presented their case for extradition to the Sultan. The Turkish Council of Ministers remained divided in its opinion about whether it should yield to Russian pressure, with Ali Pasha, the Minister of Foreign Affairs, in favour of handing over the refugees and Reshid Pasha, the Grand Vizier, opposed. Both Canning and his French colleague General Aupick were in no doubt that the Turks should make a firm stand even if this meant war, and used their discreet contact with Czartoryski's diplomatic representative, Czajkowski, to inform the Turks unofficially that they would be prepared to ask their governments to send warships to Turkish waters.[31] As a result of their action Radziwill left for Saint Petersburg on 17 September without having persuaded the Turks to agree to the Tsar's demands and on the same day the

Austrian and Russian envoys broke off diplomatic relations with Turkey. Both Titov and Stürmer had exceeded their instructions and their decision to break off diplomatic relations was to cause their respective governments considerable embarrassment.

As a result of advice from the senior Oriental counsellor in the Austrian Ministry of Foreign Affairs, Schwarzenberg realised that Austria had a poor case in law and in addition, he had no wish to cause Austria further financial problems by embarking on a war with Turkey. However, he was determined, as was the Austrian Council of Ministers, that Turkey should not be used as a base from which the Hungarian and Polish refugees could create further trouble for the Habsburg monarchy. It was therefore agreed on 3 September that the Turks should be asked to move the refugees from the frontier area to the interior of the Ottoman Empire in order to reduce the risk of their harming Austrian interests. In addition, Stürmer was informed on 27 September that diplomatic relations were only to be 'interrupted' and not broken off completely. Meanwhile the Turkish government decided that it would continue its negotiations with Austria on the matter through their diplomatic representative in Vienna, Musurus Effendi.[32]

As the Tsar had sent a special envoy to the Sultan, the Turks decided to return the compliment by sending Fuad Effendi to Warsaw from Bucharest. In the Sultan's reply to the letter he had received from the Tsar, the Turks put forward proposals for settling the refugee problem similar to those made by the Austrians. Making use of a phrase supplied by Canning, they assured the Russians that the refugees would be 'restrained from doing a further mischief' to the Austrian and Russian governments but declined to agree to keep the refugees under surveillance.[33] On 30 September Fuad Effendi arrived in Warsaw and after a brief meeting with the British consul-general, immediately left for Saint Petersburg. In a letter to Canning, Du Plat pointed out that although Nicholas was chivalrous by nature and had finally pardoned Count Załuski, much to the relief of the Austrians, he was unlikely to do the same for Bem whom he regarded as an inveterate troublemaker.[34] Indeed, earlier in the month Baron Brunnow had been reminding the British Prime Minister about the part played in the Hungarian revolt by the Poles, enclosing copies of the correspondence found in Bem's captured papers from the well-known British friend of the Poles, Lord Dudley Stuart. Brunnow's suggestion that the latter should be given 'a sound scolding' was loftily rejected by Russell. In his view, a ruler who had carried out such a praiseworthy act as the prompt withdrawal of the Russian army from Hungary, should be above such petty matters as the contacts between a British member of parliament and a Polish emigré.[35]

Bem himself was under no illusion about his likely fate if he fell into Russian hands. He therefore gladly accepted, along with several others, a Turkish proposal that the refugees should become converts to Islam and thus become exempt from the provisions laid down in article 2 of the Treaty of Kuchuk-Kainardji. However, the majority of the refugees refused the Turkish proposal. Bem's action was to lead to a bitter dispute with his fellow Poles and a quarrel with Kossuth who wrote an impassioned appeal for asylum to Palmerston.[36]

On 17 September, the day on which Radziwill left Constantinople, Canning formally proposed to Palmerston, in accordance with his agreement with Aupick, that part of the British Mediterranean squadron should be sent to Turkish waters to bolster morale. At the same time he gave warning of his proposal to the commander of the squadron, Vice-Admiral Sir William Parker, who agreed to move some of his ships from Malta to Athens, pending the receipt of further orders from the Admiralty.[37] In Saint Petersburg the Tsar, who was by now recovering from the shock of the death of his younger brother, concluded that the failure of Radziwill's mission was due to the actions of his old enemy Stratford Canning, but was still uncertain how he would respond to the proposals which Fuad Effendi was about to put to him.[38]

In Britain, Palmerston was already being criticised by Queen Victoria and Prince Albert about his proposed support for Turkey on the refugee question. In a spirited defence of his policy to the Prime Minister, Palmerston compared the leaders of the Hungarian revolt to those who had carried out the Glorious Revolution of 1688 and the Russian intervention in Hungary to a French intervention in Scotland at the request of England to preserve the union of the two countries.[39] By this time he had received an assurance of support from France and a formal request from the Turkish envoy in London for British moral and material support. He was doubtful whether Austria and Russia would risk a European war over the issue and thus, in his view, all that was required was 'a little manly firmness' to prevent the Tsar 'shooting a cripple like Bem'.[40] Indeed, Palmerston, on his own initiative, responded to Kossuth's impassioned appeal for asylum by authorising Canning on 26 September to offer a safe passage on any British vessel to any prominent Hungarian or

Polish refugee if this would help to bring the crisis to an end.⁴¹

In France, Louis Napoleon was happy to accede to the British request, despite the reservations of Tocqueville who did not consider that 'Kossuth's skin' was worth a general war. Accordingly, French diplomatic representatives abroad were instructed not to associate themselves too closely with their British colleagues, while, at the same time a French squadron consisting of seven ships commanded by Admiral Parseval des Chênes was sent to Turkish waters to act in concert with the British squadron.⁴²

The next day Brunnow, who was becoming alarmed at the way the situation was developing, met Palmerston. He admitted that the Austrian and Russian ambassadors had gone further than intended and that the Russian case was a poor one. However, Brunnow requested Britain and France to take no action. He warned Palmerston that the use of threatening language would probably prevent the Tsar, in his present frame of mind, 'from doing what he might otherwise be disposed to do'.⁴³ This was sound advice given on Brunnow's own initiative and Palmerston was wise enough to accept it. He instructed Canning in a despatch (copies of which were sent by three separate messengers) to be suitably civil and forbearing and in particular, to ensure that the Turks did not ask the British ships to enter the Dardanelles without real necessity, since this would be a breach of the Treaty of London of 1841 and could well cause a Russian reaction.⁴⁴ At the same time Colloredo also admitted to Palmerston that Austria had no legal right to demand extradition. This admission increased Palmerston's conviction that Austria would be unlikely to press its case, unless its 'furious rancour against the Hungarians' caused it to forget its traditional policy towards Turkey and the necessity of keeping the same watchful eye as Great Britain on Russia's continuing presence in the Danubian principalities. However, as Palmerston wrote to Sir Francis Baring, the First Lord of the Admiralty, Schwarzenberg had barely 'a woodcock's allowance' of brains and was notoriously stubborn.⁴⁵ Baring, for his part, was worried that the Russians might capture Constantinople before Parker's ships arrived there.⁴⁶

On 5 October Fuad Effendi arrived in Saint Petersburg from Warsaw and had a preliminary meeting with Nesselrode three days later. At the same time Buol, who had just returned to Saint Petersburg, discussed the situation with Nesselrode, while Lamoricière advised the Foreign Minister that the Tsar's demand for the extradition of the Poles was having an adverse affect on French public opinion.⁴⁷ Shortly afterwards the Tsar received the news of the executions at Arad which, as has been mentioned, shocked him deeply. It appears that at this stage the Tsar had already half made up his mind not to press his demand for the extradition of the Poles, provided the Sultan's reply to his letter was satisfactory.⁴⁸ His wish not to acquire further opprobium by being publicly associated with the Austrian action at Arad doubtless contributed to his decision to adopt a conciliatory attitude. On 16 October Nicholas granted Fuad Effendi an audience and outlined to him the proposals drawn up by Nesselrode that all the Poles considered to be Russian subjects (even if they were naturalised citizens of other countries) should be expelled from Turkey, while those who had become Muslims, like Bem, should be interned in the interior of the Ottoman Empire. An accommodating Fuad Effendi, who denied that the Turkish government had sought British support,⁴⁹ undertook to forward these proposals to Constantinople, while Nesselrode arranged for them to be published in the *Journal de Saint Pétersbourg* and for Buol to submit them to Vienna.

On 22 October Titov was informed of the new proposals and received a list of sixteen Poles to be expelled which included, among others, Czartoryski's unofficial diplomatic envoy in Constantinople who had been specifically mentioned during the Tsar's audience with Fuad Effendi.⁵⁰ Finally, on 19 October Nesselrode had a meeting with Bloomfield who had been pressing for an interview since his return from leave on 13 October. At this meeting, Bloomfield, who had already obtained a copy of the new Russian proposals from Fuad Effendi, handed over to Nesselrode a copy of Palmerston's official despatch of 6 October about the despatch of British ships to Turkish waters. A disconcerted Nesselrode tried vainly to reject the despatch, pointing out that the dispute was now as good as settled. Having finished one war, the Russians had no wish to start another with the Ottoman Empire. They much regretted the executions in Hungary and hoped that their new proposals for settling the dispute with Turkey would be accepted.⁵¹ Three days earlier Brunnow, who had learnt from France of the move of the British squadron, expressed his regrets to Lord John Russell about the government's action in despatching 'these strange messengers of peace', a phrase which he also repeated to Palmerston.⁵²

On 21 October Nesselrode obtained an admission from Lamoricière that he had been aware of the despatch of the French squadron, but had failed to inform the Russian government officially, as he expected the ships to be recalled as a result of the new proposals put forward by Russia for solving the crisis.[53] The Tsar regarded the British and French 'swinish behaviour' as a kind of revenge for Russia's success in Hungary and took the opportunity at a later date to reproach Lamoricière for his lack of sincerity which he had not expected to encounter in 'a well brought-up person'. As far as he was concerned, the crisis was over, unless the Turks decided not to expel the Poles.[54]

In Vienna, Ponsonby, who had openly expressed his disapproval to Schwarzenberg of the British government's policy towards Austria, decided not to submit his copy of Palmerston's despatch of the 6 October to the Austrians until he had learnt of the Russian reaction to the move of the ships.[55] In addition, he wrote on 16 October direct to Canning about his misgivings and suggested that the movements of the British ships should have the 'air of an excursion'. A furious Canning reminded Ponsonby that Austria and Russia had threatened to declare war on Turkey and sent copies of the correspondence to Palmerston.[56]

Ponsonby, who was already engaged in an acrimonious corresponsence with Palmerston about Austria's decision to recall its ambassador from London at his own request,[57] received a private letter from Palmerston informing him quite bluntly that he had no business to oppose the government's policy.[58] Ponsonby's subsequent complaint to the Prime Minister about Palmerston's letters to him met with an unsympathetic reply.[59] Undeterred, he continued to write letters expressing anti-Hungarian and pro-Austrian views to persons who would be more sympathetic such as Baron Stockmar, since he was aware of the dislike felt by Queen Victoria and Prince Albert for Palmerston's anti-Austrian foreign policy.[60]

On 17 October Ponsonby was able to inform Palmerston unofficially that Austria, like Russia, was unlikely to press for extradition. A delighted Palmerston informed Russell that great good had been done at little cost and to Canning he wrote that 'the haughty aristocrat had been forced to retreat, while Austria had been obliged to forego another opportunity of quaffing a bowl of blood'.[61] At the same time he requested Baring (as did the Prime Minister) to order Admiral Parker for a second time not to violate the Treaty of London of 1841 by entering the Dardanelles, unless asked by Canning to defend Constantinople.[62] In jaunty mood, Palmerston remarked to Brunnow that sending the ships had been 'for the Sultan, like giving a bottle of salts to a frightened lady';[63] but Brunnow, who had by now received Nesselrode's despatch about the Tsar's audience with Fuad

Effendi, wrote in a more serious vein to Russell that it was a pity that the British government had not waited until the results of Fuad Effendi's mission were known. Nor did Brunnow approve of the granting of discretionary powers to Canning to act according to circumstances; in his view, the maintenance of peace in the Near East was safer in the hands of the Prime Minister.[64] Brunnow's view was shared by his old friend Lord Aberdeen who was in no doubt that the whole affair had been caused by 'the old rancour of Stratford Canning' and the clamour of the British press. The 'miserable refugees' should have been saved, but it had been quite unnecessary to insult the Tsar at the same time.[65] On 7 November Palmerston congratulated Canning in a peaceful outcome to what Brunnow had called *'une affaire de police et non pas une affaire de politique'*. He was happy to accept the new Russian proposals, but hoped the refugees who had become Muslims would not be kept forever in the interior of the Ottoman Empire. Nor did he propose to take any action about Russian Poles in Turkey who were now naturalised British citizens. As soon as the next despatches were received, the ships would be withdrawn, especially as the French were anxious to withdraw their squadron to deal with disturbances at the other end of the Mediterranean in Morocco.[66]

However, the dispute was not to be resolved quite so easily as Palmerston expected. In Vienna Schwarzenberg was glad to accept a concession offered on 22 October by Musurus Effendi that the leaders of the Hungarian revolt should be interned and subjected to surveillance in order to prevent them carrying out any activities harmful to Austria. The details were immediately sent to London, Paris and Saint Petersburg.[67]

In fact, Schwarzenberg was still hoping for another solution to the problem of making Kossuth less harmful to Austrian interests. Plans had been drawn up for the possible assassination or kidnapping of Kossuth in order that he could stand trial in Austria. For this purpose two agents had been sent to Constantinople to work under the supervision of the newly-arrived Croatian-born consul-general, Anton von Mihanovich. Stürmer had expressed misgivings about the operation which were to be fully justified. After the Turks made their concession to the Austrians about internment and surveillance, Schwarzenberg decided that he could not agree to the abduction of Kossuth while he was still in Turkish custody. On the other hand, if he could be persuaded to make a bid to escape, then the Austrians saw no reason why they should not try to kidnap Kossuth once he had left Turkish custody. Accordingly, it was decided to take advantage of Kossuth's loneliness and depression caused by the absence of his wife, and introduce into his entourage an Austrian female agent, the wife of a Polish officer, in the hope that she could persuade him to try to escape. Unfortunately for the Austrians, an Italian refugee who had served in the Hungarian army learnt of the plot and revealed the details to the Piedmontese minister, who at once informed Canning and the Turkish foreign minister. The arrival of Kossuth's wife in Turkey on 15 January 1850 put an end to the whole scheme and the female agent disappeared from the scene.[68]

In Constantinople, the arrival of the first of Palmerston's three messengers carrying a copy of his despatch of 6 October was joyfully received by Canning. He was determined to follow up the advantage over the Russians which he appeared to have gained, in the hope that this might finally persuade the Sultan to agree to the conclusion of an alliance with Britain about which there had been desultory discussions for some time. Still unaware that both Austria and Russia had no intention of pressing their demands for extradition, Canning had instructed F. W. Calvert, the British vice-consul in the Dardanelles to sound out the local Turkish authorities about the possibility of allowing the British ships actually to enter the Dardanelles and anchor outside the castles which guarded the narrow entrance to the straits. The reply from the local authorities was favourable and Parker was duly informed of it.[69]

Meanwhile on 26 October Admiral Parker's squadron, consisting of seven ships of the line, one frigate, two steam frigates and three steam corvettes, had arrived off the Island of Tenedos, just south of the Dardanelles, in a strong north-east gale which had been blowing for three days. Parker was already worried about the prospect of anchoring his ships in the exposed waters of Besika Bay to the north of Tenedos and also wished to take on supplies of fresh drinking water. On the same day Canning wrote to him officially that Parker might find it advisable to anchor his ships in a less exposed station off the outer castles of the Dardanelles 'on the supposition of its being expedient'.[70] In an accompanying private letter Canning emphasised that Parker was not to pass through the Dardanelles without an invitation from him to do so, as he was still uncertain about the exact interpretation of the terms of the Treaty of London.[71] On 28 October Parker replied from his 120 gun flagship *Queen*, now anchored in Besika Bay, that he would move his ships when the gale blowing from the south-west died down. One of the steam ships

(*Dragon*) had already had her hull damaged. On 31 October Calvert informed Parker that the Porte approved the decision of the local Turkish authorities about anchorage just inside the entrance to the Dardanelles. On the same day Parker decided to move his ships, subject to Canning's agreement. This was readily given, although Canning had by this time come to the conclusion that the Russians would be unlikely to launch a naval operation from Sevastopol at such a late season in the year.[72] On 1 November Parker moved his ships to an anchorage in Barber's Bay just inside the Dardanelles. As he informed Baring, it was a very secure berth which the French squadron would also have liked to occupy.[73] The move was made just in time, as another gale sprang up which was to last for some days.

The move of the British squadron brought an immediate protest to the Turks from the Austrian and Russian ambassadors in Constantinople, which was seconded by their governments in Vienna and Saint Petersburg when they received the news.[74] In Saint Petersburg the Tsar instructed Nesselrode to strengthen the language of a draft despatch to Brunnow. 'This rogue Palmerston' should be told that his threats did not frighten the Russians. Nesselrode himself believed that Palmerston's attempt to provoke a war in the Near East was nothing short of criminal, and was glad that the Tsar had kept calm.[75] In Vienna Schwarzenberg remarked pointedly to Ponsonby that if the Dardanelles was the door to the house, the Bosphorus was the door to the chamber.[76]

Two days after the move Canning learnt that the Austrians and Russians had moderated their demands. He still believed that the 'two Imperial bullies' had been taught a lesson, but admitted privately to Bloomfield and Parker that if he had received this information earlier, he would not have suggested moving the squadron into the Dardanelles. Because of the changed circumstances, it was now essential that the squadron should move back to its original anchorage.[77] However, the continuing bad weather had caused further damage to the British ships, two of which had dragged their anchors. As a result, Parker, despite continuing pressure from Canning who paid him a visit on the steam frigate *Dragon* on 15 November, did not decide to move back into Besika Bay until 16 November. Even then, Canning insisted that the British and French squadrons (whose movements had also been made subject to his discretion by agreement with Louis Napoleon)[78] should remain in Turkish waters, provided there was no further bad weather, until he was satisfied with the outcome of Austria's and Russia's new negotiations with Turkey about the fate of the refugees.

In London, Queen Victoria was predictably displeased with what had happened, and considered that Canning should not encourage the Turks to resist Austrian and Russian demands about the refugees. Her amendments to Palmerston's draft despatch (probably suggested by Prince Albert) reached the Foreign Office too late to be incorporated in the final version which had to be sent urgently to Marseilles where a French ship had been waiting with steam up for a week to take the Queen's messenger to Constantinople.[79] The Prime Minister was also annoyed and wrote to Baring (who had been kept informed by Parker and was also disturbed by his action) that the Russians would not believe that the weather had been bad, 'as we should not believe them in a similar case'.[80] Although Russell admired Canning's ability, he was under no illusion about the ambassador's dislike of the Russians and spoke freely of this, as well as his co-operation with the Turks, to Princess Lieven who made no secret of the fact that she would inform the Tsar in one of her famous letters written on green paper.[81] The belief that the bad weather was only a pretext for the move into the Dardanelles was to persist for some time even in Great Britain.[82]

Parker's decision to move his ships was also the subject of a lengthy discussion between Brunnow and Palmerston at the latter's country estate at Broadlands on 21 and 22 November. On the evening of 21 November Palmerston vigorously defended Parker and stated in a reply to a question from Brunnow that Britain had no intention of sending its army to Turkey. The following morning, however, he admitted that Parker's action had been a mistake, since he realised that, on the basis of the arguments he had used in defending it, Russia could justify the move of its own ships into the Bosphorus. Despite the bad weather Parker should have chosen another anchorage. On the same day Palmerston instructed Canning not to allow Parker to enter the Dardanelles again. In his own words, it had been 'close shaving and nice steerage' proving that being within the straits was not the same thing as entering the straits.[83] In a private letter to Bloomfield written on 25 November Palmerston stated unequivocally that he disapproved of Calvert's interpretation of the local regulations about entering the Dardanelles and had so informed Brunnow. The same statement was made in a letter to Parker from Baring, who, however, admitted that he would have taken the same action as Parker on the basis of the letter sent by Canning. A satisfied Brunnow returned to London to report to Nesselrode about the results of his visit to Broadlands which had produced a result that had exceeded his expectations.[84]

On 14 December, Bloomfield, to whom, like Buol, the Tsar had refused to grant an audience since his return to Saint Petersburg, decided, on his own initiative, to pass an edited version of Palmerston's letter of 25 November to Nesselrode. It was immediately passed to the Tsar who granted Bloomfield an audience three days later. In Bloomfield's own words, Palmerston's apology had 'acted like a charm'. Referring to the refugee crisis, Nicholas reiterated that he had no wish to absorb the Ottoman Empire, but did have certain treaty rights. Much of the conversation was devoted to 'violent abuse' of Canning which Bloomfield omitted from his official despatch. In the Tsar's view, the decision of the British government to send Canning to Constantinople after he had been rejected as ambassador in Saint Petersburg was 'not a friendly act', but not a matter in which Russia had any right to interfere.[85]

Meanwhile throughout November negotiations between Russia and Turkey continued, complicated by the illness of Nesselrode with gout and Fuad Effendi with rheumatism. The Russians and the Turks agreed on the new proposals except for surveillance of the activities of the Poles who were naturalised citizens of other countries, a point which the Russians did not press.[86] On 25 December 1849 an agreement was signed. Under its terms all the Poles on the list submitted by the Russians were to be expelled, with the exception of those who were naturalised citizens of other countries. Complaints about the activities of these people were to be made to the appropriate embassy. Those Poles who had become Muslim converts were to be sent to Aleppo in Syria.[87] On 30 December normal diplomatic relations between Russia and Turkey were resumed and on New Year's Day 1850 Canning informed Admiral Parker and the French admiral that their ships could withdraw from Turkish waters.[88] Parker was naturally worried by all that had happened during the past few weeks and in a private letter informed Canning that he now realised the move should not have taken place. In his reply Canning did his best to reassure Parker by sending him an extract from Palmerston's letter of 22 November. Parker was doubtless relieved to be informed by Baring in a private letter dated 23 December that both the Prime Minister and Palmerston considered that he had had no choice but to follow Canning's instructions which were based on an incorrect interpretation of the Treaty of London of 1841. A subsequent official letter from the Admiralty of 7 January 1850 exonerated the admiral from all blame.[89]

Diplomatic relations between Turkey and Austria were not to be restored as speedily as they were with Russia. As Ponsonby had forecast, Colloredo left London at the beginning of November and was not replaced by a new ambassador. In due course, Palmerston explained to Baron Koller, the Austrian chargé d'affaires, in response to a protest from Schwarzenberg that he disagreed with Calvert's interpretation of the regulations about entry into the Dardanelles.[90] Despite this, Palmerston remained far from satisfied about the Turkish agreement to transfer the Hungarian refugees to the interior of the Ottoman Empire and keep them under surveillance. As he wrote to Ponsonby, he saw no reason why the Sultan should act as a gaoler on behalf of the Austrians. Nor did he understand why the Austrians were so afraid of Kossuth who, after he had been allowed out of Turkey, 'would be the hero of half a dozen dinners in England' and then 'would soon sink into comparative obscurity'. The Austrians should agree to the expulsion of the Hungarians from Turkey as the Russians had done with the Poles.[91] The exchange of correspondence between London and Vienna was to continue until January the following year when Schwarzenberg, after receiving a copy of Palmerston's apology to the Russians, strenuously denied, as Nesselrode had done, that Stürmer had threatened Turkey with a declaration of war, if a single refugee escaped. It was clear that neither side was prepared to give ground and Britain's relations with Austria were to remain at a low ebb. In 1850 Ponsonby left Vienna and it was only in 1851 that Buol was transferred from Saint Petersburg to London as the replacement for Colloredo.[92]

Austrian negotiations with Turkey about the fate of the Hungarian refugees continued until early 1850. By that time, a special Austrian commissioner sent to Turkey had succeeded in persuading some 3000 Hungarians to leave on the promise of an amnesty and further service in the Habsburg army. Discussion then followed about the length of time during which the remaining refugees should be kept in surveillance in the interior of the Ottoman Empire. After several weeks of fruitless negotiations, Schwarzenberg finally agreed not to stipulate a definite period of time, and on 5 April 1850 diplomatic relations between Austria and Turkey were re-established. Subsequently Stürmer was withdrawn from Constantinople, but he remained convinced that he had been justified in breaking off diplomatic relations with

The Aftermath of the Intervention

Turkey in the light of their refusal to agree to extradition.[93]

In February 1850, after the arrival of his wife, Kossuth and several other Hungarians were taken under escort to Kütahya in Anatolia, while the other refugees remained in Shumla. Eventually, in September 1851, as a result of an invitation from the government of the United States, Kossuth, accompanied by his wife and a small staff, left Turkey in the US frigate *Mississipi* in the face of a protest from the Austrians and a polite expression of regret from Nesselrode to the British ambassador in Saint Petersburg.[94] He first visited Great Britain and subsequently the United States where he remained until July 1852. As Palmerston had predicted, he received a hero's welcome in both countries but, on his return to Britain, he did not lapse into total obscurity and remained active in politics. In 1867 he declined to accept the compromise made between Austria and Hungary which he believed would bring about the eventual ruin of his country. Unlike Görgey, he never returned to Hungary, but lived to a ripe old age, dying in Turin on 20 March 1894 at the age of ninety-two.

Conclusion

At his audience with the British Ambassador on 17 December 1849 the Tsar was still feeling pleased by the success of the Russian intervention in Hungary which had succeeded 'beyond his expectations'. It was, however, apparent to Bloomfield that Nicholas remained completely unaware of the political significance of the events of 1848 and 1849. More convinced than ever of the superiority of absolute government and the irresistibility of his vast power, the Tsar clearly believed he could dictate the law to most of Europe.[1] The ambassador's views were shared by others close to the Tsar such as Prince Menshikov, the Minister of the Navy, who considered that after the Hungarian campaign the Tsar was 'drunk with success' and so convinced of his own omnipotence that he would not listen to reason.[2] Others in Russian society were also far from certain of the long-term benefits of the campaign, which appeared to have done little more than flatter the Tsar's vanity.[3] Abroad it seemed to many that Russia had touched 'the pinnacle of greatness' and by seeking no reward for assisting Austria the Tsar had demonstrated that his power 'was wielded in a spirit of austere virtue, ranging high above common ambition'.[4]

Now that order had been restored in the Habsburg monarchy, Nicholas' immediate concern in the field of foreign affairs was the possible unification of Germany under the leadership of the liberally-minded Frederick William IV. He declared to Bloomfield that he was prepared to support Francis Joseph who appeared to him to have 'a natural aptitude for government'.[5] The Tsar was also confident that, as a result of the talks held during his visit to London in June 1844, he had reached a clear understanding, based on a 'gentleman's agreement', with the British government about future action in the event of any further trouble in the Ottoman Empire. Indeed, Bloomfield was optimistic enough to predict that he did not expect any attempt by Russia to subvert the Ottoman Empire 'at all events during the reign of the Emperor Nicholas'.[6]

In the summer of 1850 the Tsar again demonstrated his military power by sending units of the Russian fleet into the Baltic to assist Denmark in the continuing struggle with Prussia about the future of Schleswig-Holstein.[7] On 2 July 1850 a peace treaty was signed between Denmark and Prussia and eventually after lengthy negotiations the

Treaty of London of 8 May 1852, signed by the Great Powers as well as Denmark and Sweden, resolved the dispute in favour of Denmark.

Later in the year the struggle between Austria and Prussia for the future leadership of Germany came to a head when the Elector of Hesse appealed to the reconstituted parliament of the German Confederation in Frankfurt, led by Austria, for support against his own parliament. The Austrians sent federal troops to aid the Elector, while the Prussians also sent troops on the grounds that Hesse's membership of the Prussian Union, established in May 1849, gave them the right to do so. On 8 November Prussian and Bavarian troops clashed in Hesse; both Austria and Prussia mobilised their armies and war seemed inevitable. The Tsar, who had placed the Russian army in Poland on a war footing, came down firmly on the side of Austria and by the Convention of Olomouc signed on 29 November 1850 Prussia was compelled to abandon the Prussian Union and recognise the reconstituted parliament of the German Confederation. The Prussians would not forget the humiliation they had suffered at Olomouc, nor the part played in it by the Tsar, who throughout 1850 had made it clear to Frederick William IV that he wished to see order restored in Germany on the basis of the treaties signed in 1815.[8]

Thus, as 1850 drew to a close, it seemed to many that Russia was invincible, although in his private family circle the Tsar admitted to his daughter that in the eyes of the Almighty, he was but 'a blade of grass'.[9] In the reports presented to Nicholas on the twenty-fifth anniversary of his accession his ministers heaped praise upon him for his achievements. For Nesselrode, the Tsar was 'the representative of the monarchical ideal, the supporter of the principles of order and the impartial defender of the European balance of power'.[10] In 1850 Paskevich celebrated the anniversary of fifty years of service in the Russian army and received awards from the Tsar, the King of Prussia and the Emperor of Austria. In a conversation held in Moscow the following year on the day before the twenty-fifth anniversary of his coronation, Nicholas congratulated Paskevich on his success in crushing 'the hyena of revolt' in Hungary and even expressed the hope that Russia and Poland would merge into a unified Slav state as a result of the work carried out by Paskevich during his rule in Poland.[11]

But it was the Tsar's desire, suppressed since 1829, to advance Russian interests in the Ottoman Empire and liberate the Holy Places in Palestine which was to prove to be his undoing. In 1851 Russia evacuated the Danubian principalities, despite Duhamel's warning that the Act of Balta Liman had provided only a temporary solution to the problems of Moldavia and Wallachia.[12] At the same time Austria was viewing with concern the brutal suppression by Omer Pasha of a revolt in Bosnia in 1850 and a Turkish invasion of Montenegro in 1852. In February 1853 Austria, with the full support of Russia, sent Count Leiningen to Constantinople where he was successful in securing the evacuation of Montenegro and the dismissal of Omer Pasha. Elsewhere, the restless and energetic Louis Napoleon had found an escape for France from the constraints of the treaties of 1815 by demanding from the Sultan of Turkey privileges for the Catholics guarding the Holy Places in Jerusalem which could only be granted at the expense of the rights enjoyed by the Orthodox and their Russian protectors. By the end of 1852 the French were in a stronger position than the Russians, and relations between the two countries had only been made worse by the Tsar's refusal (unlike his fellow European monarchs) to address Louis Napoleon as 'brother' after he had proclaimed himself Emperor in December 1851.

In December 1852 Lord Aberdeen, who had been Foreign Secretary during Nicholas' visit to Britain in June 1844, became Prime Minister of a coalition government. As a mark of his favour, the Tsar decided to yield to repeated British demands emanating from Queen Victoria personally and establish diplomatic relations with Belgium.[13] Towards the end of January 1853 Nicholas, despite the advice of Nesselrode to the contrary, had the first of his conversations with Bloomfield's successor in Saint Petersburg, Sir Hamilton Seymour, about the partition of the Ottoman Empire in the event of its collapse. Shortly before this conversation Nesselrode, who had warned the Tsar that a Catholic Austria would feel bound to support France, wrote a remarkably prescient private letter to Brunnow. In it he forecast that as a result of Louis Napoleon's actions about the custodianship of the Holy Places in Jerusalem, Russia would eventually find itself fighting a war against Turkey and its allies without the support of any other European state. Since no-one would believe that Russia did not desire the collapse of the Ottoman Empire, it was essential that every effort should be made to persuade Britain to oppose France. Unfortunately for Russia and Britain, Lord Aberdeen, who was a reluctant supporter of the integrity of the Ottoman Empire, was not permitted by Brunnow to disclose the contents of this letter to the other members of his cabinet, since it had been written without the knowledge of the Tsar.[14]

Nesselrode's forecast about the likely course of events proved to be entirely accurate. By the end of 1853 Russia and Turkey had failed to settle their differences and were at war. In March 1854 Britain and France, where the memories of the Russian intervention in Hungary were still fresh in the minds of the public, also declared war on Russia. The Crimean War, which was to last until March 1856, was to prove to be a far greater test of the efficiency of the Russian army than the eight-week campaign in Hungary. The deficiencies and shortcomings it revealed were to show up all too clearly the hollowness of the claims made by many contemporary observers about the invincibility of the huge parade-ground army created by Nicholas.[15]

Besides over-estimating Russia's military power, the Tsar also over-estimated his own political influence. It was Nicholas' misfortune that he became the ruler of Russia in an age of change, just as Philip II had become the ruler of Spain in an age of dissolving faiths. He completely failed to understand that ideas could not be kept out of Russia in the era of the railway, the steamship, the telegraph and improved postal communications. It was typical of him that he endorsed Brunnow's judgement that the Great Exhibition held in London in 1851 was nothing more than 'a general gathering of adventurers and industrial revolutionaries' from whom Russia had nothing to learn.[16] Nor could he comprehend the nature of a constitutional monarchy, or that in the Europe which had emerged after the Napoleonic Wars relations between states could no longer be conducted on the basis of personal relationships between sovereigns, as had been possible in the eighteenth century. As Queen Victoria pointed out to him shortly before the outbreak of the Crimean War, the personal qualities of a sovereign, however pure his motives, were 'not sufficient in international transactions by which a state binds itself towards another in solemn engagements'.[17] Even more to the Tsar's dismay, he found that all his eloquent personal appeals to his fellow monarchs to join him in a holy war against the infidel Turk had fallen on deaf ears, so that he wrote despairingly to his sister Anna in Holland that it was doubtful whether England and France could still be regarded as Christian nations when they allied themselves to 'the enemies of Christianity against a nation which is fighting for the privileges of its fellow co-believers'.[18]

In 1839 the Tsar had been warned by Count Adam Rzewuski, who had just returned from a mission to Constantinople, that the Sultan felt humiliated at having had to seek aid from Russia and might show his ingratitude in the future. At that time Nicholas rejected the suggestion on the grounds that only nations, and not sovereigns, could be ungrateful.[19] Fifteen years later the Tsar was to learn once again the bitter lesson that there is no gratitude in international affairs when Francis Joseph, whom he had loved as his son, to quote the words of Alexander II,[20] decided, despite his regard for the Tsar and his assistance to Austria in 1849, not to support Russia in its war with Turkey. As the realistically-minded Emperor, now being advised by his new Foreign Minister Buol, wrote to his mother, it was essential to put Austria's interests first and remember that in the east Russia had always been Austria's 'natural enemy'. The emptiness of the Tsar's boast to Seymour, made a few months earlier, that Austria's and Russia's interests in Turkey were identical was all too apparent. Indeed, Nicholas would have done well to heed the observation made by Napoleon to the young Chernyshev in Fontainebleau in 1811, during an earlier Russian war with Turkey, that by occupying Moldavia and Wallachia, Alexander I had only succeeded in implanting in Austria a permanent suspicion of Russia's intentions.[21] Thus it came about that five years after his intervention in Hungary Nicholas found himself, as Nesselrode had predicted, fighting a war against Great Britain, France, Turkey and Piedmont, while his erstwhile allies Austria and Prussia remained neutral. Even more ironically the Tsar found himself wondering how best he could exploit any disturbances that might break out in Hungary during the war in order to make Austria carry out his wishes.[22]

On 2 March 1855 Nicholas died, after catching a chill, a broken and unhappy man. In the words of a contemporary, it was as if a giant cedar had been blown down by a mighty storm.[23] In his last letter to Paskevich, who was to die a few months later in January 1856, the Tsar wrote that Austria's perfidy exceeded anything ever invented by the 'infernal school of Jesuits'.[24] His wife remained convinced that Francis Joseph 'had been virtually the assassin of her husband' and refused to forgive the Austrian Emperor at the end of her own life in 1868.[25] Even Nesselrode, who was finally to retire from office in April 1856, found it difficult to believe that Russia's 'most intimate ally'[26] would issue an ultimatum in December 1855 which would leave Alexander II and his advisers with no choice but to accept the peace terms of the allies.

The signature of the Treaty of Paris in March 1856 marked a turning-point in European history and the end of the order which had existed since the Congress of Vienna. Russia was never to forget

Conclusion

what it considered to be Austria's treacherous behaviour during the Crimean War. In the years that followed, the rivalry between Austria and Russia, so skilfully exploited by Bismarck, was to lead to the formation of a united Germany and the creation of the tensions in the Balkans which had as their inevitable consequence the First World War, followed by the collapse of the Habsburg, Russian and Ottoman Empires, and the resurrection of the divided Polish state. It was an outcome to his decision to intervene in Hungary which Nicholas could hardly have foreseen as he sat in his study on the first floor of the Grand Palace in the Kremlin, on the evening of 19 April 1849, looking out on the river Moskva.

Notes

The locations of manuscript collections are given in the bibliography.

INTRODUCTION

1. Aberdeen Papers, Add. Mss. 43053, vol. 15.
2. See, for example, Nicholas's letter to his wife of 26 December 1845 written while he was on his way to Vienna. (T. Schiemann, *Geschichte Russlands unter Kaiser Nikolaus I*, vol. IV (Berlin, 1913) p. 376.)
3. *Letters of Queen Victoria* (London, 1908) vol. 2, p. 17.
4. The relationship between Nicholas and Nesselrode is well described by the latter's successor as Minister of Foreign Affairs, A. M. Gorchakov. (See P. K. Men'kov, *Zapiski* (Saint Petersburg, 1898) vol. 1, pp. 19–21.)
5. J. B. Capefigue, *Les Diplomates Européens* (Paris, 1843) vol. 1, p. 357; *Illustrated London News*, 24 August 1844, p. 118.
6. For an early expression of Nicholas' mistrust of Austria, dating from 1816, see the letter of General Miguel de Alava to the Duke of Wellington, 10 October 1829. *Despatches, Correspondence and Memoranda of Field Marshal Arthur, Duke of Wellington, KG*, vol. 6 (London, 1877) pp. 210–11.
7. E. Winter, 'Eine bedeutsame Unterredung zwischen Zar Nikolaus I und Metternich am Neujahrstag 1846', *Zeitschrift für Geschichtswissenschaft*, vol. 9 (Berlin, 1961, 1861–70).
8. Nicholas to Paskevich, 17 February 1847, A. P. Shcherbatov, *General Fel'd-Marshal Knyaz' Paskevich*, vol. 5 (Saint Petersburg, 1888) p. 393.
9. 'Iz Zapisok Barona M. A. Korfa', *Russkaya Starina*, vol. 99 (1899) p. 291.

1 RUSSIAN REACTION TO THE REVOLUTIONS OF 1848

1. Nicholas to Frederick William IV, 18 January 1848. E. Haenchen, *Revolutionsbriefe 1848* (Leipzig, 1930) pp. 20–22.
2. T. Schiemann, 'Eigenhändige Aufzeichung Kaiser Nikolaus I 1848, unmittelbar vor Ausbruch der Februarrevolution', *Zeitschrift für Osteuropäische Geschichte*, no. 2 (1912) pp. 557–60.
3. Metternich to Frederick William IV, 11 January 1848, *Mémoires*, vol. VII (Paris, 1883) pp. 572–3.
4. 'Confession de foi du Prince Metternich à Nikolai I', *Russkaya Starina*, vol. 7 (1873) pp. 783–99.
5. Ponsonby (Vienna) to Palmerston (Private), 19 January 1848. Palmerston Papers, GC/PO/551.
6. Metternich to Nesselrode, 20 January 1848. R. Averbukh, 'Avstriyskaya Revolyutsiya 1848 g. i Nikolay I'. *Krasny Arkhiv*, 89–90 (1938) 164–5.

7. Since the departure of Count Colloredo in November 1847, the Austrian embassy in Saint Petersburg had been without an ambassador, much to the annoyance of Nesselrode who regarded the chargé d'affaires, Baron Eduard Lebzeltern-Collenbach, as a nonentity. In addition, the Tsar had forbidden P. I. Medem, the Russian ambassador to Austria, who was on leave in Russia, to return to Vienna until the dispute about the Bishop of the Old Believers monastery in Bukovina had been settled.
8. Nesselrode to Khreptovich (Naples) 9 March 1848, C. Nesselrode, *Lettres et Papiers*, vol. 9 (Paris, 1911) p. 69. Bloomfield (Saint Petersburg) to Palmerston, 16 February 1848 (FO 65/347).
9. Receiving stations had been built on the roof of the Winter Palace in Saint Petersburg, at Tsarskoe Selo, and Gatchina, so that Nicholas could always be in touch with Paskevich in Warsaw. The optical telegraphs' efficiency was, of course, seriously affected when the weather was bad.
10. N. K. Shil'der, *Imperator Nikolay I*, vol. 2 (Saint Petersburg, 1903) pp. 619–39; and A. S. Nifontov, *Rossiya v 1848 godu* (Moscow, 1949) pp. 45–7.
11. A. F. Filippov, 'Vospominaniya o Knyaze Paskeviche', *Drevnyaya i Novya Rossiya*, vol. 1 (1878) p. 82.
12. *Polny Svod Zakonov*, 2nd edition, vol. XXIII, no. 22017 of 7 March 1848 and no. 22031 of 12 March 1848.
13. Bloomfield (Saint Petersburg) to Palmerston, 6 March 1848 (FO 65/348).
14. Mercier (Saint Petersburg) to Lamartine, 16 March 1848, quoted in De Guichen, *Les Grandes Questions Européennes*, vol. 1 (Paris, 1925) p. 61.
15. A. G. Dement'ev, *Ocherki po istorii russkoy zhurnalistiki 1840–1850 gg.* (Moscow/Leningrad, 1951) pp. 92–7.
16. Nesselrode's memorandum of 7 March 1848 enclosed with his letter to Medem of 9 March 1848 (Averbukh, op. cit., pp. 171–2) and Lebzeltern (Saint Petersburg) to Metternich, 4 and 11 March 1848, quoted in De Guichen, op. cit., vol. 1, p. 58. Nicholas' first choice for the military talks in Vienna was General Duhamel who was sent to the Danubian principalities later in the year. His second choice, General Berg, reached Berlin at the time of the disturbances there and as a result of the overthrow of Metternich in Vienna was ordered back to Russia without having discussed military matters in either capital.
17. Nicholas to Frederick William IV, 7 March 1848 enclosed with Nesselrode to Meyendorff, 7 March 1848 (Averbukh, op. cit., pp. 168–70); and Rochow (Saint Petersburg) to Frederick William IV, 12 March 1849 quoted in A. Stern, *Geschichte Europas*, vol. IV (Stuttgart/Berlin, 1916) pp. 785–7.
18. Brunnow (London) to Palmerston, 26 February 1848. (Palmerston Papers GC/BR/210) and Brunnow (London) to Duke of Wellington, 1 March 1848 (Wellington Papers 2/157/86).
19. Nesselrode to Brunnow (London) 12 and 20 March 1848 (FO 65/357).
20. Palmerston to Bloomfield (Saint Petersburg) 28 March (FO 65/343).
21. F. F. Martens, *Recueil de traités*, vol. XII (Saint Petersburg, 1898) p. 247.

22. King Oskar to Nicholas, 17 April 1848, which was a reply to Nicholas' letter of 1 April 1848 (Swedish State Archives).
23. Bloomfield (Saint Petersburg) to Palmerston, 20 March 1848 (FO 65/348).
24. Nesselrode to Lebzeltern (Saint Petersburg) 22 March 1848. Averbukh, op. cit., p. 177.
25. Paskevich to Nesselrode, 18 March 1848. Averbukh, op. cit., p. 174. A routine telegram was sent to Saint Petersburg from Warsaw every morning which usually read, 'All quiet in Warsaw'. The custom continued even after Paskevich ceased to be Viceroy of Poland.
26. A detailed account of these events can be found in the appropriate extract from Korff's memoirs, *Russkaya Starina*, vol. 10 (1900) pp. 564–7. The full text is in PSV, 2nd edition, vol. XXIII, no. 22087 of 26 March 1848.
27. Nicholas to Paskevich, 27 March 1848. Shcherbatov, op. cit., vol. VI, p. 204.
28. *Journal de Saint Pétersbourg*, 31 March 1848.
29. Bloomfield (Saint Petersburg) to Palmerston, 10 April 1848 (FO 65/348). Nicholas was fond of describing Frederick William IV as a coward; see for example, the remark quoted in A. O. Smirnova's memoirs, *Russky Arkhiv*, no. 9 (1895) p. 84. Some reports of the Russian military representative in Berlin are quoted in the article by A. Savin, 'Nikolay I i Fridrikh Vil'gel'm IV 1840–48', *Rossiya i Zapad* (Petrograd, 1923) pp. 128–34.
30. Nicholas to Paskevich, 25 March 1848 (Shcherbatov, op. cit., vol. 6, p. 203).
31. Lebzeltern (Saint Petersburg) to Ficquelmont, 23 March 1848, quoted in De Guichen, op. cit., vol. I, p. 75.
32. Paskevich to Nicholas (no date quoted) and Nicholas to Paskevich, 28 March 1848 (Shcherbatov, op. cit., vol. 6, pp. 6–7 and p. 207).
33. Polish emigré activities in the western provinces of Russia are discussed in detail in A. Z. Baraboy's 'Pravoberezhnaya Ukraina v 1848 g.', *Istoricheskie Zapiski*, no. 34 (1950) 86–121.
34. V. G. Verzhbitsky, *Revolyutsionnoe Dvizhenie v Russkoy Armii* (Moscow, 1964) p. 228 (footnote).
35. Paskevich assured the British consul-general in Warsaw that Russian military preparations were being made at the request of the King of Prussia. There was no prospect of a European war because the Tsar did not want a war. (Du Plat (Warsaw) to Palmerston, 7 April 1848, FO 65/354.)
36. Nicholas's letters to Paskevich contain numerous questions about the activities of the Poles.
37. Meyendorff (Berlin) to Nesselrode, 29 March 1848. Peter von Meyendorff, *Briefwechsel* vol. II (Berlin, 1923) pp. 55–9; and Canning (Berlin) to Palmerston, 30 March 1848, FO 30/117.
38. Nicholas to Paskevich, 3 April 1848 (Shcherbatov, op. cit., vol. 6, p. 210). The name of the Prussian officer in Königsberg is incorrectly transcribed by Shcherbatov as 'Den'.

39. Nicholas to Prittwitz, 24 May 1848. G. Heinrich, *K. L. von Prittwitz* (Berlin, 1985) p. 448.
40. Meyendorff (Berlin) to Paskevich, 1 April 1848 and Meyendorff (Berlin) to Nesselrode, 8 April 1848 (Meyendorff, op. cit., vol. II, pp. 59–62 and 65–77).
41. Kiselev (Paris) to Nesselrode, 6 April 1848 (Martens, op. cit., vol. XV, p. 240). Nicholas to Paskevich, 25 March 1848 (Shcherbatov, op. cit., vol. 6, p. 203).
42. Nesselrode to Brunnow (London) 29 March 1848, FO 65/357. Palmerston to Bloomfield, 14 April 1848, FO 65/344. Palmerston to Bloomfield (Private) 4 and 11 April 1848, FO 356/259.
43. Nicholas to Victoria, 3 April 1848, *The Letters of Queen Victoria 1837–1861*, vol. II (London, 1907) p. 196. Nicholas to Albert, 18 April 1848, Royal Archives, RA Vic J 69/18.
44. A. S. Nifontov, op. cit., pp. 140–1.
45. J. Pfitzner, *Bakuninstudien* (Prague, 1932) pp. 58–9.
46. The plan dated 11 May 1848 forms the first part of an appendix to Nicholas' letter to Paskevich of 11 July 1848 which also includes a revised version, when Nicholas considered the threat of attack from Prussia had receded (Shcherbatov, op. cit., vol. 6, pp. 231–4).
47. Bloomfield (Saint Petersburg) to Palmerston, 8 and 10 April 1848, FO 65/348. Nesselrode to Meyendorff (Berlin) 27 April 1848, Nesselrode, op. cit., vol. 9, pp. 86–90.
48. Oskar to Nicholas, 4 May 1848, Swedish State Archives.
49. Charlotte to Frederick William IV, May 1848 (drafted by Nicholas), E. Haenchen, op. cit., pp. 92–5.
50. Nordin (Saint Petersburg) to Stierneld, 6 and 20 May 1848, Swedish State Archives. Nicholas' remark is interpreted more fully in Bloomfield (Saint Petersburg) to Palmerston, 23 May 1848, FO 65/349.
51. A. I. Lebedev, 'Uchastie russkago flota v datskoy Kampanii 1840–50 gg.', *Istoriya Russkoy Armii i Flota*, vol. X (Moscow, 1913) pp. 130–3.
52. Nicholas had intended his second son Constantine to adopt a naval career. This was his first diplomatic mission. After visiting Stockholm, he arrived in Copenhagen on 10 June in the company of the Swedish Crown Prince Oskar and was back in Saint Petersburg on 18 June. He was to marry later in the year and took part in the Hungarian campaign in 1849.
53. Denmark rejected a proposal made by Nesselrode and adopted by Palmerston that the Danish-speaking northern part of Schleswig should be incorporated with Denmark, while German-speaking southern Schleswig should be united with Holstein which, while continuing to be a member of the German Confederation, should retain its dynastic link with Denmark. On the grounds that he was under the orders of the Frankfurt Parliament, General Wrangel declined to accept the armistice terms when they were first negotiated, which caused Nicholas to threaten Prussia with war. (Nicholas to Paskevich, 23 July 1848 in Shcherbatov, op. cit., vol. 6, p. 239.)
54. Nesselrode to Ungern-Sternberg (Copenhagen) 25 September 1848, Danish State Archives.

55. Theodor von Bernhardi, *Unter Nikolaus I und Friedrich Wilhelm IV*, vol. 2 (Leipzig, 1893) p. 36.
56. Nesselrode to Meyendorff (Berlin) 10 September 1848, Nesselrode, op. cit., vol. 9, p. 170.
57. Nicholas to Paskevich, 24 and 29 August 1848 (Shcherbatov, op. cit., vol. 6, pp. 246 and 247).
58. Nicholas to Paskevich, 24 August 1848, ibid., p. 246.
59. Nicholas to Frederick William IV, 26 September 1848 (Haenchen, op. cit., pp. 185–7). Nicholas to Paskevich, 27 September 1848 (Shcherbatov, op. cit., vol. 6, pp. 253–4).
60. Ficquelmont to Thun, 21 March 1848 and Ficquelmont to Nesselrode, 21 March 1848, E. Andics, *A Habsburgok és Romanovok szövetsége* (Budapest, 1961) pp. 213–16.
61. F. I. Tyutchev, 'Rossiya i Revolyutsiya', *Russky Arkhiv*, no. 11 (1873) 895–912.
62. Thun (Saint Petersburg) to Ficquelmont, 5 April 1848, De Guichen, op. cit., p. 79.
63. Fonton (Vienna) to Nesselrode, 21 March 1848 (Andics, op. cit., p. 211).
64. Nicholas to Paskevich, 28 March 1848 (Shcherbatov, op. cit., vol. 6, p. 206).
65. Nesselrode to Ficquelmont, 5 April 1848 (Andics, op. cit., p. 219).
66. Nicholas to Paskevich, 10 April 1848 (Shcherbatov, op. cit., vol. 6, p. 213); Paskevich to Bibikov, 19 April 1848 (Baraboy, op. cit., p. 114). The correspondence of the governors-general of the Baltic provinces, Lithuania and the western provinces about Polish affairs was always copied to Paskevich in Warsaw.
67. Nesselrode to Meyendorff (Berlin) 11 April 1848 (Nesselrode, op. cit., vol. 9, p. 82); Thun (Saint Petersburg) to Ficquelmont, 1 April 1848, quoted in C. Grunwald, *La vie de Nicolas 1er* (Paris, 1945) p. 246; G. Berti, *Russia e gli stati italiani nel Risorgimento* (Turin, 1957) p. 591.
68. Nicholas to Paskevich, 10 May 1848 (Shcherbatov, op. cit., vol. 6, p. 219).
69. Ficquelmont to Nesselrode, 20 June 1848 (Nesselrode, op. cit., vol. 9, p. 115).
70. Palmerston to Wessenberg, 20 June 1848, A. Arneth, *Johann Freiherr von Wessenberg*, vol 2 (Vienna/Leipzig, 1898) p. 230.
71. Canning (Vienna) to Palmerston, 30 April 1848, FO 181/215.
72. Nesselrode to Medem (Innsbruck), 27 May 1848, enclosing Nicholas to Ferdinand, 21 May 1848 (Averbukh, op. cit., p. 189); Medem (Innsbruck) to Nesselrode, 19 June 1848 (Andics, op. cit., p. 235); Ponsonby (Innsbruck) to Palmerston, 20 June 1848, FO 7/350.
73. Blackwell (Pest) to Ponsonby, 25 April 1848 and Blackwell (London) to Palmerston, 14 July 1850, *South-Eastern Affairs* vol. 3 (1933) 115–20 and 127–31.
74. F. Deák to his brother-in-law, 28 March 1848, quoted in *Österreichisch-Ungarische Revue*, vol. 4 (1887) 7. Ponsonby (Vienna) to Palmerston, 3 May 1848, FO 7/349.
75. Gaj had been in touch with the Third Department's representative in

the Russian Embassy in Vienna since 1838. His attempts to persuade Nicholas, whom he regarded as the protector of the Principality of Serbia in the Ottoman Empire, to support the southern Slavs in their fight against Magyarisation and develop their own national consciousness, met with no success, despite a visit to Russia in 1840. The matter is discussed fully in P. E. Mosely, 'A Pan-Slavist Memorandum of Ljudevit Gaj in 1838', *American Historical Review*, vol. 40 (1938) 704–16.
76. In a letter to Ponsonby Blackwell had reported the Hungarian view that the despatch of Hungarian troops to Italy to assist Vienna in the suppression of Italian independence would be 'a national crime'. Ponsonby (Vienna) to Palmerston, 15 April 1848, FO 7/348.
77. 'František Palacký's letter to Frankfurt, 11 April 1848', *Slavonic and East European Review*, vol. 26 (1948) 303–8.
78. V. A. Frantsev, 'Priglashenie russkikh na Slavyansky S'ezd v Prage v 1848', *Golos minuvshago*, no. 5 (1914) 238–40.
79. Meyendorff (Berlin) to Nesselrode, 7 July 1848 (Meyendorff, op. cit., vol. II, pp. 109–11).
80. Leo Thun to Pillersdorf, 29 June 1848, O. Odložilik, 'Slovanský sjezd a svatodušní bouře v r. 1848', *Slovanksý Přehled*, vol. 20 (1928) 412.
81. Nicholas to Windischgraetz, 1 July 1848, Andics, op. cit., p. 240.
82. Tolstoy (Paris) to Orlov, 20 July 1848, *Revolyutsiya 1848 g. vo Frantsii* (Leningrad, 1925) pp. 93–5.
83. Nesselrode's comments, dated 27 June 1848, in an unpublished memorandum of Nicholas, Averbukh, op. cit., 190–2.
84. Moscow and Saint Petersburg were especially badly affected by the epidemic. In Saint Petersburg it was estimated that out of a population of 445 000 one in every twenty fell ill and one in every thirty-six died. The Third Department report for 1848 recorded 1 784 000 cases of illness and 707 000 deaths, but the true figures were probably higher, A. S. Nifontov, op. cit., pp. 23–5.
85. Ibid., pp. 19–21 and pp. 25–6.
86. Danilevsky (Belgrade) to Nesselrode, 15 May 1848, I. I. Leshchilovskaya, *Obshchestvenno–politicheskaya bor'ba v Khorvatii 1848–49* (Moscow, 1977) p. 127.
87. Fonton (Vienna) to Nesselrode, 23 July 1848, ibid., pp. 213–14.
88. Ibid., pp. 215–16.
89. Fonton (Vienna) to Nesselrode, 29 June 1848, Andics, op. cit., p. 83.
90. J. Thim, *A magyarországi 1848–49 iki Szerb fölkelés története*, vol. 1 (Budapest, 1940) pp. 143, 239, 249, 255–6, 267, 363–4.
91. Nicholas' comment on Danilevsky (Belgrade) to Nesselrode, 10 May 1848, S. Damyanov, *Frenskata politika na Balkanite 1829–53* (Sofiya, 1977) pp. 232–3.
92. D. M. Pavlović, *Srbija i Srpski Pokret u Južnoj Ugarskoj 1848 i 1849* (Belgrade, 1904) pp. 38–40.
93. Nicholas to Paskevich, 17 July 1848, Shcherbatov, op. cit., vol. 6, p. 238.
94. Nicholas to Paskevich, 23 July 1848, ibid., p. 240; Windischgraetz to Nicholas, 8 July 1848, Andics, op. cit., pp. 246–7.

95. Medem (Innsbruck) to Nesselrode, 24 July 1848, ibid., pp. 251–2. Ponsonby (Innsbruck) to Palmerston, 24 July 1848 (Private) Ponsonby Papers.
96. Medem (Innsbruck) to Nesselrode, 18 June 1848, Andics, op. cit., p. 74. Unlike Medem, Ponsonby did not disclose his conversations with the Empress on this subject until much later. Ponsonby (Vienna) to Palmerston, 8 November 1848, Palmerston Papers, GC/PO 584/2.
97. Medem (Innsbruck) to Nesselrode, 5 August 1848, Andics, op. cit., pp. 252–3.
98. Nicholas to Paskevich, 10 June 1848, Shcherbatov, op. cit., vol. 6, pp. 224–5; Nesselrode to Khreptovich (Naples) 22 June 1848, Nesselrode, op. cit., vol. 9, p. 115.
99. Nesselrode to Kiselev (Paris) 25 July 1848, Martens, op. cit., vol. XV, pp. 235–7.
100. Nicholas to Paskevich 14 and 24 August 1848, Shcherbatov, op. cit., vol. 6, pp. 245–6.
101. Radetzky to Nicholas, 10 September 1848, Andics, op. cit., pp. 255–6.
102. Jelačić to Rajačić, 28 August 1848, Thim, op. cit., vol. II, pp. 651–2.
103. Nicholas to Paskevich, 13 September 1848, Shcherbatov, op. cit., vol. 6, p. 250.
104. Paskevich to Nicholas, 16 September 1848, ibid., p. 28–9.
105. Nicholas to Paskevich, 20 September 1848, Shcherbatov, op. cit., vol. 6, p. 252; Bloomfield (Saint Petersburg) to Palmerston, 22 September 1848, FO 65/350.
106. Nesselrode to Medem (Vienna) 18 September 1848, Averbukh, op. cit., pp. 198–200. A copy of the memorandum can be found in the Austrian State Archives (hereafter HHStA) PAX 27 (Varia 1849).
107. Medem (Vienna) to Nesselrode, 27 September 1848, Averbukh, op. cit., p. 200.
108. Medem (Vienna) to Nesselrode, 5 September 1848, R. Averbukh, 'Nikolay I i evropeyskaya reaktsiya 1848–49 gg', *Krasny Arkhiv*, vol. 47–8 (1930) 25.

2 THE RUSSIAN INTERVENTION IN THE DANUBIAN PRINCIPALITIES

1. The activities of the Polish emigration in Moldavia and Wallachia are treated in a number of books and articles. See, *inter alia*, the following: K. Dach, *Polsko-rumuńska współpraca polityczna w latach 1831–1852* (Warsaw, 1981); S. Łukasik, *Pologne et Rumanie* (Paris, 1938); V. Ya Grosul, 'Pol'skaya politicheskaya emigratsiya na Balkanakh v 40 – nachale 50-kh godov XIX veka', *Balkansky Istorichesky Sbornik*, II (Moscow, 1970); P. P. Panaitescu, 'Revoluţia romănă de la 1848 şi alianţa Polonă', *Romanoslavica*, VIII (Bucharest, 1963) 59–77; V. Popovici, 'Despre activitatea emigraţilor poloni in Moldova in ani 1846–1848', *Ştudie şi cercatori ştiintificie istorie/filologei*, Anul IX, fasc. 1/2, (Jassy, 1958).
2. Ivan S. Aksakov, brother of the Slavophile Konstantin S. Aksakov, was sent by the Russian Ministry of the Interior to investigate the

activities of the Old Believers in Bessarabia at the end of 1848. He commented unfavourably about the Poles in his letters to his family and expressed surprise at their employment in administrative posts. *I. S. Aksakov v ego pis'makh 1848–1851*, vol. II (Moscow, 1888) pp. 47–75, *passim*.
3. S. Łukasik, op. cit., p. 89.
4. V. Ya Grosul, op. cit., pp. 55–6.
5. Nesselrode to Brunnow (London), 29 March 1848, enclosing copy of Nesselrode to Titov (Constantinople), 28 March 1848 (FO 65/357).
6. Gardner (Jassy) to Palmerston, 14 April 1848, enclosing copy of Nesselrode to Kotzebue (Bucharest), 28 March 1848 (FO 78/745).
7. Brunnow (London) to Nesselrode, 13 March 1848 (FO 65/357).
8. Ponsonby (Vienna) to Palmerston, 30 March 1848 enclosing copy of Blackwell (Pest) to Ponsonby, 28 March 1848 (FO 7/347), and Fonblanque (Belgrade) to Palmerston, 27 March 1848 (FO 78/739).
9. A detailed account of the events of 1848 in Moldavia and Wallachia is to be found in G. Georgescu-Buzău, *The 1848 Revolution in the Rumanian lands* (Bucharest, 1965).
10. The universal dislike of Sturdza is reflected in the report written by two French officers for the French ambassador in Constantinople after they had toured Moldavia and Wallachia at the end of 1848. E. Georgescu, 'Un mémoire inédit sur les Principautés Danubiennes au XIXème siècle', *Revue historique du Sud-Est*, vol. 14 (1937) 147. I. S. Aksakov, op. cit., p. 47, in a letter dated 22 November 1848 referred to Sturdza as a 'first–class swine, a robber and usurer'.
11. R. R. Florescu, 'Stratford Canning, Palmerston and the Wallachian Revolution of 1848', *Journal of Modern History*, XXV (1963) 230.
12. Gardner (Jassy) to Palmerston, 14 April 1848 enclosing copy of Sturdza's proclamation of 12 April 1848 published in the local newspaper. (FO 78/745).
13. Chapter XII of Duhamel's autobiography published in *Russky Arkhiv*, II (1885) 371–98, gives a detailed account of his experiences in the principalities during 1848 and 1849.
14. The text of Nesselrode's instructions to Duhamel is given in R. A. Averbukh's 'Avstriyskaya Revolyutsiya 1848 i Nikolay I', *Krasny Arkhiv*, vol. 89–90 (1938) 183–187.
15. Nicholas to Paskevich, 18 April 1848. (Shcherbatov, op. cit., vol. 6, I, p. 215). Kiselev to Bibescu, 22 April 1848. *Prince Georges Bibesco*, vol. I (Paris, 1894) pp. 320–3.
16. In 1845 the Fifth Infantry Corps was at half its normal strength. See Nicholas to I. V. Vasil'chikov, 5 February 1845, *Starina i Novizna*, XVI (1913) 44.
17. Nicholas to Paskevich, 18 April 1848, Shcherbatov, op. cit. vol. 6, p. 215. The detailed orders from Nicholas are reproduced in P. K. Men'kov, *Zapiski*, Vol. III (SPB, 1898) pp. 224–5. See also FO 65/354 (reports from the British consul in Odessa), for further details of Russian troop movements at this time.
18. This claim is made in the memoirs of Czartoryski's representative in Constantinople, 'Zapiski Mikhaila Chaykovskago', *Russkaya Starina*,

vol. 95 (1898) 439.
19. Nicholas to Paskevich, 10 May 1848. Shcherbatov, op. cit., vol 6, p. 220.
20. Nesselrode to Meyendorff (Berlin), 24 May 1848. Nesselrode, op. cit., vol. 9, p. 104.
21. Duhamel, op. cit., p. 373. Duhamel was also worried about Kotzebue's gambling and addiction to cards. There is a reference to this habit of Kotzebue in the 'Soldatskaya Pesnya' attributed to P. K. Men'kov, *Vol'naya Russkaya Poeziya XVIII–XIX vv.* (Leningrad, 1970) p. 695.
22. A copy of the memorandum is enclosed with Colquhoun (Bucharest) to Palmerston, 20 June 1848 (FO 195/281).
23. G. Georgescu-Buzău, op. cit., *passim*.
24. Before the revolution started, Duhamel had tried to persuade Bibescu to exile Heliade Rădulescu, *Prince Georges Bibesco*, II, pp. 255–356.
25. N. V. Bereznyakov, *Revolyutsionnoe i natsional'no – osvoboditel'noe dvizhenie v Dunayskikh Knyazhestvakh v 1848–1849*, (Kishinev, 1955) pp. 44 and 47.
26. On 24 May a group of Moldavian revolutionaries drew up a programme at Braşov in Transylvania which was influenced by the petition which had been drawn up at Blaj on 5 May. After moving to Bukovina, the Moldavians kept in touch with the Wallachians. A further programme of action drawn up at the end of August was influenced by the events at Islaz.
27. Details of Talat Effendi's correspondence with the Austrian Commander-in-Chief in Transylvania can be found in E. Horváth, *Origins of the Crimean War* (Budapest, 1937) p. 1.
28. J. Thim, *A Magyarországi 1848–1849 iki Szerb Fölkelés Története*, vol. I, p. 63, and vol. II, p. 277 (Budapest, 1930); Fonblanque (Belgrade) to Palmerston, 1 July 1848 (FO 78/739), also confirms the Serbian refusal of the Russian offer of military aid.
29. Nicholas to Paskevich, 22 June 1848, Shcherbatov, op. cit., vol. 6, p. 228.
30. Bereznyakov, op. cit., p. 46.
31. Gardner (Jassy) to Palmerston, 6 July 1848 (FO 78/745).
32. On 6 July Nesselrode had sent a further circular on non-intervention to Russian missions in Germany. Bloomfield (Saint Petersburg) to Palmerston, 18 July 1848 (FO 65/350).
33. See Duhamel, op. cit., pp 374–6 for his account of the confusion. Nicholas' reaction to Duhamel's proposals is given in his letters to Paskevich. Shcherbatov, op. cit., vol. 6, pp. 231, 237–8. On 11 July Nicholas was still under the impression that the Russian intervention force had not crossed the Pruth. Nesselrode comments on the annoyance in Saint Petersburg in the postscript of his letter to Meyendorff (Berlin) of 15 July 1848. Nesselrode, op. cit., IX, p. 130. For Nicholas' fear of being taxed with inconsistency in his actions see Bloomfield (Saint Petersburg) to Palmerston of 18 July 1848 (FO 65/350).
34. Sturdza's accusation about Duhamel's failure to consult him is reported in Gardner (Jassy) to Palmerston of 27 July 1848 (FO 78/745). The Turkish Minister of Foreign Affairs, Rifat Pasha, did not believe this

denial. Stratford Canning (Constantinople) to Palmerston of 4 August 1848 (FO 78/734). I can find no evidence to support the assertion made in Canning's letter of 17 July 1848 (FO 78/333) that Duhamel received a bribe of 6000 ducats from Sturdza before agreeing to intervention. In a later interview with Gardner on 5 September, Sturdza asserted that Wallachia had been the cause of the Russian intervention, Gardner (Jassy) to Palmerston, 4 October 1848 (FO 78/745). Nicholas' phrase 'extremely imprudently' is mentioned in his letter to Paskevich of 17 July 1848, Shcherbatov, op. cit., vol. 6, p. 237.

35. Kotzebue to Bibescu, 8 July 1848, *Prince Georges Bibesco*, I, pp. 327–8.
36. The subject is treated in detail in D. Berindei, 'La politique extérieure de la Valachie pendant la révolution bourgeoise-démocratique de 1848', *Nouvelles études d'histoire* (Bucharest, 1965) 285–97.
37. The *hospodar* of Wallachia had an official envoy in Constantinople, Aristarchi, who did his best to prevent Ghica from gaining access to the appropriate Turkish authorities. Ghica was much helped by Michał Czajkowski, the representative of Prince Czartoryski in Constantinople.
38. Brunnow (London) to Nesselrode, 28 July 1848, R. Averbukh, 'Nikolay I i evropeyskaya reaktsiya v 1848–49 gg.', *Krasny Arkhiv*, vol. 47 (1930) 20–4.
39. Brunnow (London) to Palmerston, 17 July 1848 (FO 65/357). The details of Brunnow's exchange with Palmerston are also summarised in R. Averbukh, *Tsarskaya interventsiya v bor'be s vengerskoy revolutsiey* (Moscow, 1935) pp. 60–1.
40. The full text of the British government's reply to the Wallachian provisional government is in *Anul 1848 în Principatele Române*, II (Bucharest, 1902) p. 91.
41. Averbukh, op. cit., pp. 57–8.
42. Nesselrode to Brunnow (London) 17 July 1848 (FO 65/357). Bloomfield (Saint Petersburg) to Palmerston, 18 July (FO 65/350). Nesselrode stressed the reluctance with which the occupation had been carried out. *'Nous l'avons fait à notre corps défendant'* were his words to Bloomfield.
43. Canning (Vienna) to Palmerston, 30 April 1848 (FO 78/733).
44. Canning (Trieste) to Palmerston, 22 May 1848 (FO 78/733).
45. Ghica (Constantinople) to Voinescu, 22 July 1848. *Anul 1848*, op. cit. II, p. 686.
46. S. Damyanov, op. cit., pp. 235–6.
47. See Endre Kovács, *Szabadságharcunk és a francia Közvélemény* (Budapest, 1976) pp. 62–70, for a discussion of French reaction to events in Moldavia and Wallachia. Ya N. Tolstoy's report of 20 July 1848 on the subject is in *Revolyutsiya vo Frantsii*, op. cit., pp. 89–95.
48. T. Ionescu, 'Misiunea lui Al. Gh. Golescu la Paris in 1848', *Revista de istorie*, 12 (1974), 1727–46.
49. Bastide's exchanges with Palmerston are summarised in Paul Henry, 'La France et les nationalités en 1848', *Revue historique*, CLXXXVIII (April–June 1940) 247–8; and L. C. Jennings, *France and Europe in 1848* (Oxford 1973) pp. 218–19.
50. Austria's reaction to events in the principalities is documented in

Averbukh, *Tsarskaya interventsiya* pp. 58–9 and her article in *Krasny Arkhiv*, vol. 89–90 (1938) 194–5.
51. Ponsonby (Vienna) to Palmerston, 19 April 1848 (FO 7/348); and Palmerston to Ponsonby (Vienna), 28 April 1848 (FO 7/343).
52. Hungary's attitude to Russia is discussed in Andics, *Szövetsége*, pp. 55–60. (This part of her introductory essay is omitted in the German edition of her book.) The correspondence with Medem can be found in Averbukh, *Krasny Arkhiv*, vol. 89–90 (1938) 193–7; and E. V. Waldapfel, *A Forradalom és a szabadságharc levelestára*, I (Budapest, 1950) pp. 348–50.
53. Fonton (Vienna) to Nesselrode, 11 July 1848. Andics, op. cit., pp. 247–8.
54. Canning (Constantinople) to Palmerston 1 July 1848 (FO 78/733); and Nesselrode to Meyendorff, 22 June 1848 and 29 July 1848. Nesselrode, op. cit., vol. 9 (1901) pp. 122 and 136.
55. Kotzebue to Nesselrode, 22 July 1848, *Formirovanie natsional 'nykh nezavisimykh gosudarstv na Balkanakh* (Moscow, 1986) p. 299; Nesselrode to Duhamel, 10 August 1848, *Anul 1848*, op. cit., III, p. 30. A distorted version of the right-wing boyars' plans suggesting that Russia wished to take over the principalities reached General Puchner in Transylvania and was duly reported to the Hungarian government on 2 August 1848. See '1848 and Rumanian unification', *Slavonic and East European Review*, vol. 26 (April 1948) 390–421. The text of the provisional government's petition is in G. F. Martens, *Nouveau Recueil Général de Traités*, XIII (Göttingen, 1855) pp. 562–4.
56. Canning (Constantinople) to Palmerston, 15 July 1848. (FO 78/733).
57. Sir A. Henry Layard, *Autobiography and Letters*, vol. II, (London, 1903) p. 127.
58. Duhamel. op. cit., p. 378.
59. Proclamation of 31 July 1848. Martens, op. cit., XIII, pp. 569–71.
60. Nesselrode's circular of 31 July 1848. Martens, op. cit., XIII, pp. 564–9.
61. 'Iz Zapisok Senatora K. N. Lebedeva (1846–1849)', *Russky Arkhiv*, 10 (1910) 239.
62. Palmerston to Bloomfield (Saint Petersburg) 2 August 1858 (FO 65/345); and Palmerston to Bloomfield (Saint Petersburg) (private) of 18 August 1848 (FO 356/29).
63. Brunnow to Wellington, 31 July 1848 and Wellington to Brunnow, 2 August 1848, Wellington Papers 2/159/45.
64. Nicholas to Paskevich, 23 July 1848 and August 1848, Shcherbatov, op. cit., vol 6, pp. 240 and 242; see also Nesselrode to Meyendorff (Berlin), 12 August 1848, Nesselrode, op. cit., vol 9, p. 144. There is no indication of Ponsonby's views in either his official or his private correspondence despite Medem's assertion that Ponsonby would be expressing his approval to Palmerston.
65. *Revolyutsiya yo Frantsii*, op. cit., letter of 15 August 1848, pp. 95–8, reporting a conversation with John Delane, editor of *The Times* during a visit to London.
66. Duhamel, op. cit., p. 376.

67. S. Golescu to A. G. Golescu, 24 July 1848, *Annul 1848*, op. cit., vol. VI, pp. 12–13.
68. The Russian assertion about the bribery of Suleiman was made by Nicholas to Bloomfield at a farewell audience on 21 September 1848 before he went on leave, (Bloomfield to Palmerston, 22 September 1848, (FO 65/350)). See also Brunnow (London) to Palmerston, 19 September 1848 (FO 65/357).
69. Łukasik, op. cit., pp. 88–9.
70. See Colquhoun to Palmerston, 1 August 1848, enclosing a copy of a report from a secret agent about Poles in the Russian occupation force (FO 78/742). The Polish democrats' representative also wrote to the Wallachian government on the same subject. Filanowicz's letter of 3 July 1848, *Anul 1848*, op. cit. II, pp. 270–2. In her book, Andics states (p. 157) that Gardner, the British consul in Jassy, informed the Russians about Polish activities in the Russian occupation force. There is no reference to this in the consul's official reports in the Public Record Office.
71 The two French officers arrived in Bucharest on 10 August. Their information on the Russian army was given to the British in mid-October, Canning to Palmerston 14 October 1848 (FO 78/736). For the text of their official report see n. 10 above.
72. Aupick (Constantinople) to Bastide, 6 September 1848, *Anul 1848*, op. cit., vol. III, pp. 656–9.
73. Martens, op. cit., vol. XIII, pp. 574–5.
74. Bloomfield to Palmerston, 22 September 1848 (FO 65/350), and Bloomfield to Palmerston, 24 January 1848 (FO 65/347).
75. General Aleksandr Nikolaevich Lüders was one of the few Russian officers to emerge from the Russian campaign in 1849 with an enhanced reputation. Born in 1790, he entered the Russian army at the age of fifteen and took part in the wars against France and Turkey during the reign of Alexander I. Under Nicholas he fought against Turkey in 1828–9 and against the Poles in 1831. In 1837 he replaced General N. N. Murav'ev as commanding officer of the Fifth Infantry Corps.
76. A copy of Nicholas' letter to the Sultan of 16 September 1848 and Nesselrode's despatch to Titov of the same date were sent as enclosures to Canning's despatch to Palmerston of 29 September 1848 (FO 78/735). Nesselrode summed up the reasons for the Russian action in his Annual Report for 1848 and his Silver Jubilee Report of 1850. As extract from the 1848 report can be found on p. 70 of V. Ya. Grosul and E. E. Chertar, *Rossiya i Formivovanie Rumynskogo Mezhdunarodnogo Gosudarstva* (Moscow, 1969). The relevant extract from the 1850 report can be found in Nesselrode, op. cit., vol. 9, p. 9.
77. Martens, op. cit., vol. XIII, pp. 597–8.
78. Palmerston to Brunnow (Brighton) 15 September 1848, and Brunnow (Brighton) to Palmerston 19 September 1848 (FO 65/357).
79. Lüders to Fuad Effendi, 25 September 1848, Barbara Jelavich, 'The Russian Intervention in Wallachia and Transylvania', *Rumanian Studies*, 4, (Leiden, 1979) 40. The appendix to this article consists of a valuable selection of Luders' diplomatic correspondence with the Turkish and

Wallachian authorities during the occupation drawn from the private papers of the Russian MFA official attached to his staff, N. K. Giers, who later became Minister of Foreign Affairs.

80. Yeames (Odessa) to Palmerston, 28 August 1848 and 29 September 1848 (FO 65/354); and Gardner (Jassy) to Palmerston of 4 September 1848 and 2 October 1848 (FO 78/745).
81. Martens, op. cit., vol. XIII, pp. 575–6.
82. Canning (Constantinople) to Palmerston, 16 October 1848 enclosing Fuad Effendi to Duhamel, 28 September 1848 and Duhamel to Fuad Effendi, 29 September 1848 (FO 78/736).
83. Nicholas in conversation with Rochow, the Prussian ambassador, in Saint Petersburg on 23 October 1848, quoted in A. Stern, *Geschichte Europs*, vol. VII (Stuttgart and Berlin, 1916) p. 630. See also Nicholas to Paskevich, 24 October 1848, Shcherbatov, op. cit., vol. 6, p. 260; and Buchanan (Saint Petersburg) to Palmerston 17 October 1848 (FO 65/351).
84. N. Iorga, 'Un complot militaire polonais en Valachie en 1848', *Revue historique du Sud-Est européen*, 11 (1934) 7–9; D. Gh. Ionescu, 'Date noi despre "Episodul Polonez" in revoluția munteana din 1848', *Romanoslavica*, VIII (Bucharest, 1963) 79–85; K. Dach, op. cit., pp. 204–14. Evidence of Nicholas' personal interest in this operation is contained in Buchanan (Saint Petersburg) to Palmerston, 17 October 1848 (FO 65/351).
85. Martens, op. cit., vol. XIII, p. 576.
86. Colquhoun reported in detail to Palmerston and Stratford Canning about the Russian measures and the inability of the Turks to prevent them being carried out (see his letters for this period in FO 78/743 and 195/321). The subject is also discussed in Barbara Jelavich's article (see n. 79 above).
87. This episode is discussed in Grosul, op. cit., pp. 58–9; and Jelavich, op. cit., pp. 38–9.
88. Brunnow (London) to Nesselrode, 9 December 1848, Averbukh, *Tsarskaya interventsiya*, p. 64; and Brunnow to Palmerston, 31 December 1848, Palmerston Papers, GC/BR 215/1 and 2.
89. Ségur (Bucharest) to Bastide, 30 November 1848, *Anul 1848*, op. cit., vol. V, pp. 454–6.
90. Nesselrode to Khreptovich (Naples), 22 November 1848, Nesselrode, op. cit., p. 192.
91. Nesselrode to Bibescu, 29 December 1848, Bibescu, op. cit., vol. I, pp. 328–30.
92. Segur (Bucharest) to Bastide, 18 November 1848 and 15 December 1848, *Anul 1848*, op. cit., vol. V, pp. 456 and 577–80.
93. Canning (Constantinople) to Palmerston, 4 November 1848 quoting the British consul in Odessa (FO 78/736).
94. Palmerston to Lord John Russell, 16 March 1849 (PRO 3/22/7F).
95. Colquhoun was later to be accused of having arranged for money from the Wallachian treasury to be sent to Paris. See R. R. Florescu, op. cit., p. 237.
96. Canning (Constantinople) to Palmerston, 3 November 1848 (FO 78/736).

97. Canning (Constantinople) to Palmerston, 4 December 1848 (FO 78/737).
98. Buchanan (Saint Petersburg) to Palmerston, 10 November and 20 November 1848 (FO 65/351).
99. Palmerston to Buchanan (Saint Petersburg), 31 October 1848, enclosing a copy of Palmerston to Normanby (Paris) 27 October 1848 (FO 65/346).
100. Nesselrode to Brunnow (London) 8 November 1848, Averbukh, *Krasny Arkhiv*, vol. 47 and 48 (1938) 203–4.
101. Buchanan (Saint Petersburg) to Palmerston, 20 November 1848 and 4 December 1848 (FO 65/352).
102. Canning (Constantinople) to Palmerston, 11 December 1848, enclosing a summary of a despatch from Nesselrode to Titov (FO 78/737).
103. Colquhoun (Bucharest) to Canning, 13 December 1848 (FO 195/321).
104. Palmerston to Canning, 7 November and 10 November 1848 (FO 78/732).
105. Delahante (Jassy) to Bastide, 9 October 1848, *Anul 1848*, op. cit., vol. IV, pp. 551–3.
106. Canning to Palmerston, 4 January 1849 (FO 78/772). The Russian ambassador in Constantinople handed the Turkish Foreign Minister a copy of the draft convention on 27 December 1848.

3 THE OCTOBER REVOLUTION IN VIENNA AND ITS AFTERMATH

1. Nicholas to Paskevich, 4 October 1848, Shcherbatov, op. cit., vol. 6 p. 255.
2. Born in Tarnów (Galicia) in 1794, Józef Bem was to play an important part in the Hungarian revolt. He was a member of the Polish force which fought with Napoleon during the invasion of Russia in 1812. An artillery specialist, he served in the independent Polish army in Russian Poland until 1826. During the 1830 revolt he fought against the Russians and after its collapse, emigrated to France. Always anxious to fight the Russians, he was given command of the Hungarian forces in Transylvania at the end of 1848. After the Hungarian defeat in 1848, he became a Muslim and entered Turkish service. He died in Aleppo (Syria) in 1850.
3. Because Medem was uncertain of the Emperor's destination, he travelled first to Salzburg (via Bad Ischl) and from there was ordered to Olomouc where he was to remain with the court until March 1849. On this occasion, contrary to Medem's expectation, the British ambassador chose to remain in Vienna with the diplomatic corps.
4. On the basis of papers in the Windischgraetz archive, Andics has demonstrated that Windischgraetz began to make his plans in July by agreement with the *camarilla* in Innsbruck (E. Andics, *Das Bündnis Habsburg-Romanow* (Budapest, 1963) pp. 88–9). This information is omitted from the Hungarian edition of her book.
5. Schwarzenberg to Windischgraetz, 8 October 1848, F. Walter, *Die Österreichische Zentralverwaltung*, part 3, vol. 1 (Vienna, 1964) p. 224;

Jelačić also wrote to Windischgraetz urging him to take charge, Fonton (Vienna) to Nesselrode, 6 November 1848, Andics, op. cit., p. 273.
6. Schwarzenberg to Radetzky, 22 October 1848, Radetzky to Schwarzenberg, 31 October 1848, ibid. pp. 228–30.
7. Nicholas to Paskevich, 24 October 1848, Shcherbatov, op. cit., vol. 6, p. 259.
8. F. Reinöhl, 'Aus dem Tagebuch der Erzherzogin Sophie', *Historische Blätter*, 4 (1931) p. 125.
9. Nicholas to Paskevich, 4 November 1848, Shcherbatov, op. cit., vol. 6, p. 256 where the letter is given the incorrect date of 5 October.
10. Korff, op. cit., vol. 101 (1900), p. 588.
11. Nicholas to Ferdinand, 10 November 1848, Andics, op. cit., pp. 277–8.
12. Charlotte to William, 28 October 1848, T. Schiemann, op. cit., vol. 4, p. 396; Charlotte to Meyendorff (Berlin), 1 November 1848, Meyendorff, op. cit., vol. III, p. 360. Meyendorff had accompanied Nicholas' wife to Italy in 1845. Nicholas to Dohna, 19 October 1848, E. Corti, *The Downfall of Three Dynasties* (London, 1934) p. 58.
13. Nicholas to Paskevich, 16 November 1848, Shcherbatov, op. cit., vol. 6, p. 261. Lebzeltern (Saint Petersburg) to Wessenberg, 18 November 1848, J. Helfert, *Geschichte Oesterreichs vom Ausgange des Wiener Oktober-Aufstandes 1848*, vol. IV/2 (Prague, 1886) p. 540.
14. Medem (Olomouc) to Nesselrode, 4 November 1848, Andics, op. cit., pp. 271–2.
15. Fonton (Vienna) to Nesselrode, 27 November 1848, Andics, op. cit., pp. 287–9.
16. Ponsonby (Vienna) to Palmerston, 5 November 1848 (FO 7/353) and Palmerston to Ponsonby (Vienna), 12 November 1848, Ponsonby Papers (PO 819/2).
17. Medem (Olomouc) to Nesselrode, 4 and 6 November 1848, Andics, op. cit., pp. 271–2 and 275–6.
18. Paskevich to Nesselrode, 9 November 1848, Averbukh, op. cit., pp. 204–5.
19. Fonton (Hietzing) to Nesselrode, 26 October 1848, Andics, op. cit., p. 265. Windischgraetz had taken part in Russian manoeuvres at Voznesensk in 1838, where he had been told by the Tsar that he could look upon the Russian army as his reserve (Helfert, op. cit., vol. I, p. 69).
20. Medem (Olomouc) to Nesselrode, 4 November 1848, ibid., p. 271.
21. Nesselrode to Medem (Olomouc), 22 November 1848, ibid., pp. 283–4.
22. Nesselrode to Fonton (Vienna), 10 November 1848, ibid., pp. 279–80.
23. Medem (Olomouc) to Nesselrode, 30 November 1848, ibid., p. 290.
24. Nicholas to Paskevich, 16 November 1848, Shcherbatov, op. cit., p. 262.
25. Nesselrode to Medem (Olomouc), 22 November 1848, ibid., pp. 281–3. Nicholas to Paskevich, 27 December 1848, Shcherbatov, op. cit., vol. 6, p. 265.
26. Two examples of such requests are: Puchner (Sibiu) to Windischgraetz, 1 November 1848, Horváth, op. cit., p. 2; and Hammerstein (L'vov) to

Windischgraetz, early November 1848, H. Kerchnawe, 'Feldmarschall Alfred Fürst Windischgraetz und die Russenhilfe 1849', *Mitteilungen des oesterreichischen Instituts für Geschichtsforschung*, vol. 43 (1929) 332.
27. Windischgraetz to Schwarzenberg, 22 November 1848, Helfert, op. cit., vol. IV/2, p. 331.
28. Medem (Olomouc) to Nesselrode, 17 November 1848, Andics, op. cit., p. 280.
29. Lebzeltern (Saint Petersburg) to Wessenberg, 3 October 1848, Helfert, op. cit., vol. IV/3, pp. 421–2.
30. Nicholas to Pope Pius IX, January 1849. Nesselrode to Butenev (Gaeta), January 1849, Andics, op. cit., pp. 308–10.
31. Nesselrode to Kiselev (Paris), 30 August 1848, F. F. Martens, op. cit., vol XV, p. 237.
32. E. Bapst, *Les origines de la Guerre de Crimée*, (Paris, 1892), pp. 27–33.
33. Nicholas to Paskevich, 27 December 1848 and 14 January 1849, Shcherbatov, op. cit., vol. VI, pp. 265 and 268. Tolstoy (Paris) to Orlov, 31 October 1848, *Revolyutsiya vo Frantsii*, op. cit., pp. 117–19.
34. Nesselrode to Meyendorff (Berlin), 17 November 1848, Nesselrode, op. cit., vol. 9, p. 194.
35. Nicholas to Paskevich, 5 December 1848 and 27 December 1848, Shcherbatov, op. cit., vol. 6, p. 262 and p. 265.
36. Helfert, op. cit., vol. IV/2, p. 331.
37. Fonton (Vienna) to Nesselrode, 25 November 1848, Andics, op. cit., pp. 286–7.
38. A. Hübner, *Ein Jahr Meines Lebens 1848–1849* (Leipzig, 1891) p. 293.
39. Nicholas to Paskevich, 18 December 1848, Shcherbatov, op. cit., vol. 6, p. 264.
40. Ferdinand, Francis Joseph and Sophie to Nicholas, all three letters dated 2 December 1848, Andics, op. cit., pp. 291–4.
41. V. A. Abaza, 'Vzglyad na revolyutsionnoe dvizhenie v Evrope s 1815 p. 1848 g', *Russky Arkhiv*, no. 5 (1887), 106–7.
42. Medem (Olomouc) to Nesselrode, 17 December 1848, Andics, op. cit., pp. 295–6.
43. Bernhardi, op. cit., vol. 2, p. 41.
44. Nesselrode to Medem (Olomouc), 18 December 1848, Andics, op. cit., pp. 300–1. There was a bitter exchange of letters between Schwarzenberg and Palmerston on the subject. A further consequence of the strained relationship existing between the two countries was the Austrian decision not to send a special envoy to Great Britain to announce the accession of Francis Joseph, an event which increased the disagreement between Palmerston and Queen Victoria about the conduct of Britain's foreign policy, especially towards Austria.
45. Lebzeltern (Saint Petersburg) to Schwarzenberg, E. Andics, *A Nagybirtokos Arisztokrácia Ellenforradalmi Szerepe 1848–49 ben*, vol. I (Budapest, 1981) p. 370. E. Corti, *Vom Kind zum Kaiser* (Graz, 1950) p. 115.
46. Nicholas to Paskevich, 27 December 1848, Shcherbatov, op. cit., vol. 6, p. 265.

47. Nicholas to Paskevich, 18 December 1848, ibid., p. 264.
48. Francis Joseph to Nicholas, 28 December 1848, Andics, op. cit., p. 304.
49. Schwarzenberg to Buol (Saint Petersburg), 31 December 1848, HHStA PAX 27.
50. Ibid.
51. Buchanan (Saint Petersburg) to Palmerston, 1 February 1849 (FO 65/363); and Rochow (Saint Petersburg) to Prussian Minister of Foreign Affairs, 9 January 1849 and 14 February 1849, G. Becker, 'Oppozitsionnoe Dvizhenie v Rossii v 1848 g.', *Novaya i Noveyshaya Istoriya*, no. 1 (1968), 74.
52. HHStA PAX 27 contains the relevant correspondence on the negotiations between Vienna and Saint Petersburg, which finally ended on 16 June 1849 shortly before the Russian military intervention in Hungary began.
53. HHStA, Diary of Buol-Schauenstein, vol. IV (1848–49) p. 319.
54. Buol (Saint Petersburg) to Schwarzenberg, 3 January 1849, HHStA, PAX 26. A private letter of the same date is in PAX 27.
55. Ponsonby (Vienna) to Palmerston, 25 November 1848, Palmerston Papers, GC/80/586.
56. Eddisbury to Szalay, 13 December 1848, C. Sproxton, *Palmerston and the Hungarian Revolution* (Cambridge, 1919) pp. 45–6.
57. S. Szilassy, 'America and the Hungarian Revolution of 1848–49', *Slavonic and East European Review*, vol. 44 (1965–6), 180–4.
58. Görgey's feelings about Hungary are expressed very clearly in letters written to his brothers from Prague in 1847, I. Görgey, *Görgey Arthur ifjusága es féjlödése a forradalomig* (Pest, 1916) pp. 290 and 302.
59. Görgey's views on the problems facing him at this time are well expressed in his memoirs. A. Görgey, *My Life and Acts in Hungary*, vol. 1 (London, 1852) pp. 101–2.
60. Kossuth to Görgey, 27 November 1848, L. Kossuth, *Összes Munkái* (hereafter referred to as KLÖM), vol. XIII (Budapest, 1952) pp. 568–9.
61. The stretch of line from Budapest to Szolnok (sixty-eight miles) had been opened on 1 September 1847. The first steam railway in Hungary from Budapest to Vác had opened the previous year.
62. Although Duschek moved to Debrecen and Szeged, he surrendered to the Austrians with his staff at the end of the war. He was released after a short term of imprisonment. It is virtually certain that he kept the Austrian government informed about Hungary's financial affairs while he was employed in the Hungarian Ministry of Finance.
63. F. Reinöhl, op. cit., pp. 127–8.
64. D. Angyal, *Az ifjú Ferenc József* (Budapest, n.d.) p. 66.
65. Nicholas to Paskevich, 14 January 1849, Shcherbatov, op. cit., vol. 6, pp. 267–8.

4 THE RUSSIAN INTERVENTION IN TRANSYLVANIA AND ITS CONSEQUENCES

1. K. Hitchins, *The Rumanian National Movement in Transylvania, 1780–1849* (Cambridge, Mass., 1969) pp. 244–7.
2. I. Lupaş, 'Un Martyr Transylvain: Le Pasteur Stefan L. Roth', *Revue de Transylvanie*, vol. v (1939) 224–30.
3. J. Gyalokay, 'Báró Puchner Antal altábornagy jelentése az erdélyi állapatokról', *Levéltári Közlemények*, vol. 1 (1923) 334–41.
4. J. Horváth, op. cit., pp. 4–5.
5. F. Pulszy, *Meine Zeit, Mein Leben*, vol. 2 (Pressburg/Leipzig, 1881) pp. 266–8.
6. E. Kovács, 'Bem József és a Magyar Szabadságharc', *Századok*, vol. 84 (1950) 12.
7. J. Czetz, *Bems Feldzug in Siebenbürgen in den Jahren 1848 und 1849* (Hamburg, 1850) pp. 96, 365–70.
8. Hammerstein (L'vov) to Schwarzenberg, 8 January 1849, HHStA PAX 29.
9. Shcherbatov, op. cit., vol. 6, pp. 38–9 which quotes Nicholas' letter to Paskevich of 17 January 1849. On p. 38 Shcherbatov inadvertently refers to Veselitsky as the Chief of Staff of the Third Infantry Corps. M. D. Likhutin, *Zapiski o pokhode v Vengriyu v 1849 godu* (Moscow 1875) pp. 9–10. Likhutin was a staff officer in the Fourth Infantry Corps.
10. Averbukh, *Tsarskaya interventsiya*, op. cit., p. 88 footnote.
11. Horváth, op. cit., pp. 12–13.
12. Ibid., pp. 11, 14–18.
13. A. A. Nepokoychitsky, *Opisanie voennykh deystviy v Transilvanii v 1849 godu* (Saint Petersburg, 1866) pp. 7–8.
14. Windischgraetz to Francis Joseph, 10 January 1849, Andics, op. cit., pp. 111–12.
15. Horváth, op. cit., p. 17.
16. Helfert, op. cit., vol. IV/2, pp. 337–8.
17. Medem (Olomouc) to Nesselrode, 17 January 1849, Shcherbatov, op. cit., vol. 6, pp. 39–40.
18. Medem (Olomouc) to Nesselrode, 21 January 1849, Andics, op. cit., p. 314.
19. P. Mueller, *Feldmarschall Fürst Windischgraetz* (Vienna, 1938) p. 224.
20. Horváth, op. cit., pp. 19–21.
21. Nicholas to Paskevich, 30 January 1849, Shcherbatov, op. cit., vol. 6, p. 270.
22. Schwarzenberg to Windischgraetz, 20 January 1849, HHStA, KA GA 12. Schwarzenberg to Buol, 25 January 1849, Andics, op. cit., pp. 314–15.
23. Schwarzenberg to Puchner, 20 January 1849, Andics, op. cit., pp. 312–14.
24. J. Gyalokay, 'Az első orosz megszállás Erdélyben (1849 jan 31–márcz 28)', *Századok*, vol. 51 (Budapest, 1922) pp. 637–9.
25. B. Jelavich, op. cit., pp. 62–3.
26. Ibid., pp. 64–5.

27. E. Hurmuzaki, *Documente privitoare la Istoria Românilor*, vol. 18 (Bucharest, 1916) pp. 106–7; Horváth, op. cit., pp. 27–30, 32–3.
28. Colquhoun (Bucharest) to Canning (Private), 26 January 1849 (FO 78/772).
29. Canning (Constantinople) to Palmerston, 5 February 1849 (FO 78/768).
30. Palmerston to Canning (Constantinople), 26 February 1849 (FO 78/768).
31. Gyalokay, op. cit., *passim*.
32. Medem (Olomouc) to Nesselrode, 16 February 1849, Andics, op. cit., p. 317.
33. Schwarzenberg to Buol (Saint Petersburg), 21 February 1849, HHStA PAX 28.
34. Schwarzenberg (Olomouc) to Puchner, 16 February 1849, ibid., pp. 318–19.
35. Puchner to Schwarzenberg, 8 February 1849 and 19 March 1849, HHStA PAX 29.
36. Nesselrode to Meyendorff (Berlin), 21 February 1849, Nesselrode, op. cit., vol. 9, p. 222.
37. G. F. Martens, op. cit., vol. XIII, pp. 577–8.
38. Wellington to Brunnow, 11 March 1849 (Wellington Papers, 2/161/118). Canning (Constantinople) to Palmerston, 12 March 1849, FO 78/773.
39. KLÖM, op. cit., vol. 14, pp. 533–7.
40. Jelavich, op. cit., pp. 65–8.
41. Nicholas to Paskevich, 19 March 1849, Shcherbatov, op. cit., vol. 6, p. 275.
42. D. I. Daragan, *Zapiski o voyne v Transilvanii v 1849 godu* (Saint Petersburg, 1859) p. 25.
43. J. Mezei, 'Visszaemlékezések a szabadságharcra', *Vasárnapi Újság*, no. 18 (1880) 287.
44. J. Horváth, 'Bem Tábornok és a Bukaresti külképviseletek, 1849 március – juniusban'. *Hadtörténelmi Közlemények*, vol. 28 (1927) 375–86.
45. Colquhoun (Bucharest) to Palmerston, 8 April 1849 and Palmerston to Colquhoun (Bucharest), 21 April 1849, (FO 78/787).
46. Horváth, op. cit., pp. 93–4 and 282.
47. Hurmuzaki, op. cit., vol. 18, p. 142.
48. Horváth, op. cit., pp. 107–8.
49. Colquhoun (Bucharest) to Palmerston, 8 April 1849 (FO 78/787).
50. Nicholas to Paskevich, 1 April 1849, Shcherbatov, op. cit., vol. 6, pp. 276–7.
51. Nesselrode to Meyendorff, 1 April 1849, Nesselrode, op. cit., vol. 9, pp. 226–7.
52. A. F. Danzer, *Dembinski in Ungarn*, vol. I (Vienna, 1873) *passim*.
53. I. Kovács, 'The Polish Legion in the War of Independence in 1848–49', in Béla Király (ed.), *East Central European Society and War in the Era of Revolutions* (New York, 1984).
54. Andics, op. cit., pp. 100–1.
55. Buol (Saint Petersburg) to Schwarzenberg, 6 April 1849 HHStA PAX 26.
56. Nesselrode to Medem (Olomouc), 28 March 1849, Andics, op. cit., pp. 335–6.

57. Nicholas to Paskevich, 5 April 1849, Shcherbatov, op. cit., vol. 6, p. 278; Nicholas' note of 24 March 1849 in 'Sobstvennoruchnye Pis'ma Imperatora Nikolaya I', *Russkaya Starina*, vol. 86 (1896) 518–19.
58. 'Appendix: Die Banknotenfabrik' in *Die Magyarische Revolution im Jahre 1848 und 1849* (Pest, 1852) pp. 277–304.
59. *Tagebücher des Carl Friedrich Freiherrn Kübeck*, vol. 2 (Vienna, 1909) p. 42; *Aus dem Nachlass des Freiherrn Carl Friedrich Kübeck von Kübau* (Graz/Cologne, 1960) p. 21. The text of Francis Joseph's letter of appointment for Kübeck's mission to Budapest dated 12 March 1849 is printed on pp. 203–4.
60. Kerchnawe, op. cit., pp. 353–4.
61. Hübner, op. cit., p. 377; H. Friedjung, *Österreich von 1848 bis 1860* vol. 1 (Vienna, 1908) pp. 215–16.
62. Schwarzenberg to Buol (Saint Petersburg), 25 March 1849, HHStA PAX 28; Windischgraetz to Schwarzenberg, 17 March 1849, Müller, op. cit., p. 225.
63. Schwarzenberg to Buol (Saint Petersburg), 28 March 1849, HHStA BAX 161.
64. Medem (Olomouc) to Nesselrode, 25 March and 28 March 1849, Andics, op. cit., pp. 330 and 332–5.
65. Schwarzenberg to Hammerstein, 28 March 1849, Hammerstein to Schwarzenberg, 28 March 1849, HHStA PAX 29.
66. Hammerstein to Schwarzenberg, 10 April 1849, Andics, op. cit., p. 343; Kerchnawe, op. cit., pp. 360–1.
67. Kübeck to his wife, 22 March 1849, *Aus dem Nachlass*, op. cit., p. 184; Kübeck to Schwarzenberg, 23 March 1849, Andics, op. cit., pp. 327–8; Windischgraetz to Francis Joseph, 24 March 1849, Kerchnawe, op. cit., p. 339; Windischgraetz to Schwarzenberg, 24 March 1849, Andics, op. cit., pp. 325–6.
68. *Aus dem Nachlass*, op. cit., pp. 185–9, contains Kübeck's letters to his wife on this subject. Kübeck's official reports to Schwarzenberg are to be found in Andics, *A Nagybirtokos*, op. cit., vol. 3, pp. 119–20 and pp. 151–3.
69. Kerchnawe, op. cit., pp. 356–7, Müller, op. cit., pp. 227–8. Andics, *A Nagybirtokos*, op. cit. vol. 3, pp. 121–2.
70. M. Szapáry, unpublished thesis, 'Carl Graf Grünne, Generaladjutant des Kaisers Franz Joseph 1848–1859' (Vienna, 1935) pp. 33–7.
71. Müller, op. cit., pp. 232–3.
72. Windischgraetz to Grünne, 30 March 1849, Windischgraetz to Schwarzenberg, 31 March and 1 April 1849, Andics, *A Nagybirtokos*, op. cit. vol. 3, pp. 121–2 and 137–9.
73. Kübeck to his wife, 2 April 1849, *Aus dem Nachlass*, op. cit., p. 190.
74. Kerchnawe, op. cit., pp. 357–61.
75. Medem (Olomouc) to Nesselrode, 4 April 1849, Averbukh, *Nikolay I*, op. cit., pp. 32–3.
76. Schwarzenberg to Buol (Saint Petersburg), 6 April 1849, Andics, op. cit., pp. 337–8.
77. Medem (Vienna) to Nesselrode, 9 and 10 April 1849, Andics, op. cit., pp. 340–2.

78. Kiselev (Paris) to Nesselrode, 10 March 1849, K. F. Miziano, 'Podgotovka Kontrrevolyutsionnoy interventsii protiv Rimskoy Respubliki' in *K Stoletiyu Revolyutsii 1848 goda* (Moscow, 1949).
79. B. E. No'lde, *Yuriy Samarin i ego vremya* (Paris, 1926) pp. 47–9.
80. I. S. Aksakov, op. cit., vol. 2, pp. 154–60.
81. 'Iz Dnevnika i Zapisnoy Knizhki Grafa P. Kh. Grabbe', *Russky Arkhiv*, no. 11 (1888), p. 402.
82. 'Iz Zapisok N. V. Isakova', *Russkaya Starina*, vol. 157 (1914), pp. 53–8.
83. Nesselrode to Meyendorff (Berlin), 1 April 1849, Nesselrode, op. cit., vol. 9, pp. 225–6.
84. Kübeck to his wife, 27 March 1849, *Aus dem Nachlass*, op. cit., p. 186.
85. Nesselrode to Meyendorff (Berlin), 1 April 1849, Nesselrode op. cit., vol. 9, pp. 227–8.
86. Nicholas to Paskevich, 5 April 1849, Shcherbatov, op. cit., vol. 6, pp. 277–9; Nesselrode to Medem (Vienna) 6 April 1849, Andics, op. cit., pp. 339–40; Buol (Saint Petersburg) to Schwarzenberg, 6 April 1849, HHStA PAX 28.
87. Buol (Saint Petersburg) to Schwarzenberg, 14 and 28 March 1849, HHStA PAX 26; Shcherbatov, op. cit., vol. 6, p. 46.

5 THE RUSSIAN DECISION TO INTERVENE IN HUNGARY

1. *Aus dem Nachlass* . . ., op. cit., p. 26; Kerchnawe, op. cit., pp. 362–4; Szapáry, op. cit., pp. 35–6.
2. Kerchnawe, op. cit., pp. 356–67.
3. Medem (Vienna) to Nesselrode, 13 April 1849; Schwarzenberg to Buol (Saint Petersburg), 14 April 1849; Andics, op. cit., pp. 344–7. An account of the unrest in Cracow and the surrounding area in April 1849 can be found in D. B. Katsnel'son, 'K istorii uchastiya slavyan v vengerskoy revolyutsii 1848–1849 gg.' in Yu. A. Pisarev, *Tsentral'naya i Yugo-vostochnaya Evropa v novoe vremya* (Moscow, 1974).
4. Medem (Vienna) to Nesselrode, 13, 15 and 17 April 1849, Andics, op. cit., pp. 348–50, 352–3.
5. Schwarzenberg to Hammerstein, 15 and 19 April 1849, ibid., pp. 351–2 and 354.
6. Paskevich to Nicholas (two letters, no date quoted), Shcherbatov, op. cit., vol. 6, pp. 51–5.
7. Nicholas to Paskevich, 13 April 1849, ibid., pp. 279–81; undated memorandum from Nicholas to Chernyshev, I. Oreus, *Opisanie vengerskoy voyny 1849 g.* (Saint Petersburg, 1880), appendix to Chapter 1, pp. 5–6.
8. Adlerberg to Lüders, 20 April 1849, Nepokoychitsky, op. cit., pp. 283–4 and pp. 36–40.
9. Schiemann, op. cit., vol. 4, pp. 188–9; Yu. Oksman, 'Mery Nikolaevskoy tsenzury protiv Fur'erizma i Kommunizma', *Golos Minuvshago*, vol. 3 (1917) 69–71.

10. Nifontov, op. cit., p. 276, quoting the diary of the Grand Duke Constantine; M. P. Fabricius, *Le Kremlin de Moscou* (Moscow, 1883) p. 286.
11. Nicholas to Paskevich, 20 and 25 April 1849, Shcherbatov, op. cit., vol. 6, pp. 281–2 and 283–5.
12. Ibid. Nicholas' remarks to Paskevich about the Poles are echoed in his words to Alexander of Hesse that if the revolution in Hungary were allowed to continue, it would have to be fought eventually in Poland (E. Corti, *Mensch und Herrscher* (Vienna, 1952) pp. 26–7). A similar view was expressed by Sir Hamilton Seymour three years later (Seymour (Saint Petersburg) to Malmesbury, 8 April 1852, FO 65/408).
13. The number of Poles who fought with the Hungarians was between 2000 and 3000, rather than the official Austrian estimate of 20 000. Schwarzenberg's tactics in using his information on the Poles is discussed in Bernhardi, op. cit., vol. 2, p. 62.
14. Welden to Schwarzenberg, 20 April 1849, Andics, op. cit., pp. 358–9.
15. R. Kiszling, *Die Revolution im Kaisertum Osterreich 1848–1849*, vol. 2 (Vienna, 1948) pp. 110–16.
16. Thim, op. cit., vol. 1, pp. 363–4, and vol. 3, pp. 620–2; Pavlović, op. cit., p. 149; Fonblanque (Belgrade) to Palmerston, 4 May 1849, FO 78/785.
17. Thim, op. cit., vol. 3, p. 680; Damyanov, op. cit., pp. 232–3.
18. Kerchnawe, op. cit., pp. 368–72.
19. Schwarzenberg to Medem, 21 April 1849; Medem (Vienna) to Nesselrode, 21 April 1849; Schwarzenberg to Buol (Saint Petersburg), 21 April 1849, Andics, op. cit., pp. 360–5.
20. Paskevich to Medem (Vienna), 24 April 1849, ibid., pp. 365–6.
21. Paskevich to Hammerstein, 25 April 1849, ibid., pp. 366–7.
22. Medem (Vienna) to Nesselrode, 26 April 1849, ibid., pp. 368–9.
23. Medem (Vienna) to Paskevich and Nesselrode, 27 April 1849, ibid., pp. 369–72.
24. Welden to Schwarzenberg, 23 April 1849, L. Steier, *Az 1849iki trónfosztás előzményei és következményei* (Budapest, n.d.) p. 355.
25. Kerchnawe, op. cit., p. 375.
26. Francis Joseph to Nicholas, 1 May 1849, Andics, op. cit., pp. 373–4. Grünne's note of 25 April 1849 makes it clear that Schwarzenberg took the decision to make a formal request for Russian aid with great reluctance, a point which was fully appreciated by Francis Joseph (Andics, *A Nagybirtokos*, op. cit., vol. 3, p. 211).
27. Du Plat (Warsaw) to Palmerston, 27 April 1849, FO 65/369.
28. Paskevich to Nicholas, 1 May 1849 (not 10 April as printed) Oreus, op. cit., pp. 104–5; Du Plat (Warsaw) to Palmerston, 30 April and 1 May 1849, FO 65/369. The Austrians had been forewarned of a possible rising in Bohemia and arrested the ringleaders on 9 and 10 May 1849. For further details see Stanley Z. Pech, *The Czech Revolution of 1848* (Raleigh, North Carolina, 1969) pp. 246–7.
29. Paskevich to Berg (Vienna) 1 May 1849. 'Pokhod v Vengriyu v 1849 godu', *Voenny Sbornik*, vol. 14 (1860) pp. 11–12.
30. Nicholas to Paskevich, 30 April 1849, Shcherbatov, op. cit., vol. 6,

pp. 286–7.
31. E. Kovács, op. cit., pp. 31–2; R. Gelich, *Magyarország Függetlenségi Harcza 1848–49 ben*, vol. 3 (Budapest, 1889) pp. 379–82.
32. Nicholas to Paskevich, 5 May 1849, Shcherbatov, op. cit., vol. 6, pp. 288–9. I have included in this letter part of the text of another letter dated 18 July printed on pp. 308 and 309, since it is clear that the events mentioned relate to early May.
33. Schwarzenberg to Paskevich, 1 May 1849, Andics, op. cit., pp. 375–6.
34. The text of the relevant documents can be found in Andics, op. cit., pp. 377–9. See also Schwarzenberg to Caboga, 1 May 1849, HHStA PAX 29.
35. Berg to Paskevich and Schwarzenberg to Paskevich, 3 May 1849, Oreus, op. cit., appendix to Part 2, pp. 7–8.
36. Steier, op. cit., pp. 363–4; J. K. Mayr, *Das Tagebuch des Polizeimeisters Kempen von 1848 bis 1859* (Vienna/Leipzig, 1931) p. 134.
37. Du Plat (Warsaw) to Palmerston, 10 May 1849, FO 65/369.
38. Schwarzenberg to Paskevich, 4 May 1849, Andics, op. cit., pp. 380–1.
39. Medem (Vienna) to Nesselrode, 5 May 1849, Andics, op. cit., pp. 382–3. See Radetzky's letter to Schwarzenberg of 17 April 1849, quoted in A. Filipuzzi, *La Pace di Milano (6 Agosto 1849)* (Rome, 1955) p. 107.
40. Caboga (Warsaw) to Schwarzenberg, 6 and 8 May 1849, HHStA PAX 29; Oreus, op. cit., pp. 108–9; Shcherbatov, op. cit., vol. 6, pp. 64–6 and 353–6.
41. Paskevich to Nicholas, 7 May 1849, Oreus, op. cit., appendix p. 9; Men'kov, op. cit., vol. 3, pp. 237–8.
42. Nicholas to Paskevich, 9 May 1849, Shcherbatov, op. cit., vol. 6, pp. 68 and 290.
43. Men'kov, op. cit., vol. 2, pp. 198–9.
44. *Pokhod v Vengriyu*, op. cit., pp. 17–18; M. Annenkov, 'Voennaya sluzhba zheleznykh dorog', *Voenny Sbornik*, no. 3 (1876) 115–16; 'Iz vospominaniy o pokhode v Vengriyu v 1849 godu', *Zhurnal dlya chteniya vospitannikam voenno-uchebnykh zavedeniy*, vol. 122 (1856) 152–3; A. Alekseenko, 'Vospominaniya starago sluzhaki', *Russky Arkhiv*, no. 10 (1890) 162.
45. 'K istorii dela Petrashevskago', *Byloe* no. 2 (1906) 244–7; 'Zapiski I. P. Liprandi', *Russkaya Starina*, vol. 6 (1872) 71.
46. Diary of Buol-Schauenstein, pp. 311–12, HHStA (277c, vol. 4).
47. Lobkowitz (Saint Petersburg) to Schwarzenberg, 9 May 1849, Andics, op. cit., pp. 385–6.
48. Nicholas to Francis Joseph, 10 May 1849, ibid., pp. 388–9.
49. Nicholas to Frederick William IV, 10 May 1849, Meyendorff, op. cit., vol. 2, pp. 196–8; Buol (Saint Petersburg) to Schwarzenberg, 16 May 1849, HHStA PAX 26; Nicholas to Paskevich, 9 May 1849, Shcherbatov, op. cit., vol. 6, p. 291.
50. Zapiski, op. cit., *Russkaya Starina*, vol. 102 (1900) 40–3. Korff's account of his conversation with Nicholas makes it clear that the possible spread of the Hungarian revolt to Russian Poland was uppermost in the Tsar's mind at the time he drafted the manifesto.
51. *Vysochayshie Manifesty i Prikazy Voyskam i Izvestiya iz Armiy v*

prodolzhenie voyny protiv myatezhnykh Vengrov v 1849m godu (Saint Petersburg, 1849); a French version of the manifesto can be found in G. F. Martens, op. cit., vol. XIII, pp. 559–60.
52. Ibid., pp. 560–2.
53. M. Polovtsev, 'Glagol Vremen', *Severnaya Pchela*, no. 96, 15 May 1849.
54. 'Zametki Generala L.V. Dubel'ta', *Golos Minuvshago*, no. 3 (1913) 162.
55. Nifontov, op. cit., p. 287.
56. Du Plat (Warsaw) to Palmerston, 8 May 1849, FO 65/369.
57. Lebedev, op. cit., no. 11 (1910) 362.
58. Buchanan (Saint Petersburg) to Palmerston, 5 May 1849, FO 65/364.
59. De Guichen, op. cit., vol. 1, p. 317.
60. Buol (Saint Petersburg) to Schwarzenberg, 11 May 1849, HHStA PAX 26; Nesselrode to Khreptovich (Naples) 16 May 1849, Nesselrode, op. cit., vol. 9, p. 237.
61. E. Bapst, op. cit., pp. 56–8.
62. Magenis (Vienna) to Palmerston, 22 May 1849, FO 7/367; Buchanan (Saint Petersburg) to Palmerston, 1 June 1849, FO 65/365.
63. Kiselev (Paris) to Nesselrode, 18 June 1849, Andics, op. cit., pp. 405–6.
64. *Souvenirs de Alexis de Tocqueville* (Paris, 1893) pp. 394–5.
65. Nesselrode, op. cit., vol. 9, p. 237.
66. Palmerston to Lord John Russell, 16 March 1849, Russell Papers, PRO 3/22/7F.
67. Palmerston to Lord John Russell, 9 April 1849, ibid.
68. Palmerston to Buchanan (Saint Petersburg) 17 May 1849, FO 65/361; Palmerston to Du Plat (Warsaw) 24 May 1849, FO 65/359.
69. Canning (Constantinople) to Palmerston, 25 April 1849, FO 78/775. Vass reached Paris, but then left for the United States without travelling to London. The British consul in Galaţi informed his Austrian colleague of Vass' peace mission, and for reasons which are not clear suggested to Canning that Vass might be a Russian agent (Cunningham to Canning, 21 April 1849, ibid.).
70. An account of Pulszky's conversation with Palmerston at this time is given in his memoirs (F. Pulszky, op. cit., vol. 2, p. 322).
71. See for example, Andics, op. cit., pp. 156 *et seq.*
72. Brunnow (London) to Nesselrode, 11 and 19 May 1849, Averbukh, *Nikolay I*, op. cit., pp. 40–5.
73. F. F. Martens, op. cit., vol. 12, p. 255.
74. Aberdeen to Princess Lieven, 18 April 1849, E. Jones Parry (ed.) *The Correspondence of Lord Aberdeen and Princess Lieven 1832–54*, Camden 3rd Series, vol. 62 (1930) p. 309.
75. Guichen, op. cit., vol. 1, pp. 302–3.
76. A Russian translation of the Act of Balta Liman is published in T. Yuzefovich, *Dogovory Rossii s Vostokom: politicheskie i torgovye* (Saint Petersburg, 1869) pp. 103–7.
77. Canning (Constantinople) to Palmerston, 25 April 1849, FO 78/775.
78. Grabbe to A. P. Ermolov, 17 November 1849, *Russkaya Starina*, vol.

88 (1896) 113–14.
79. Damyanov, op. cit., p. 233.
80. Grabbe, op. cit., p. 405.
81. Canning (Constantinople) to Palmerston, 28 April 1849, FO 78/775.
82. Palmerston to Buchanan (Saint Petersburg) 19 May 1849, FO 65/361.
83. Palmerston to Canning (Constantinople) 1 June 1849, FO 78/769.
84. Nicholas to Abdul Mejid, 13 May 1849, enclosed in Canning (Constantinople) to Palmerston, 5 June 1849, FO 78/776.
85. Duhamel, op. cit., pp. 389–94; Buol (Saint Petersburg) to Schwarzenberg, 8 April 1849, HHStA PAX 26.

6 RUSSIAN PREPARATIONS FOR WAR

1. Three of Nicholas' orders to the Minister of War from this period are reproduced in 'Imperator Nikolay Pavolovich v ego voennykh rasporyazheniyakh 1849 i 1854 gg', *Russkaya Starina*, vol. 9 (1886) 571–5.
2. A decree about a further levy of recruits in the western provinces had been issued on 31 March 1849 (*PSZ, vol. XXIII, no. 23108*).
3. For further details of Polish involvement in Lithuania at this time see 'Doneseniya L. Dubel'ta Kn.A.I. Chernyshevu', *Golos Minuvshago* no. 4 (1914) 222–3 and Chernyshev's letter of 9 May 1849 to Nicholas, *SIRIO*, vol. 122, p. 406.
4. The guards left Saint Petersburg on 10 June and remained in Lithuania until the end of August. N. K. Imeretinsky, 'Iz zapisok starago preobrazhentsa – 1849 god', *Russkaya Starina*, vol. 80 (1893) 253–79.
5. Nicholas' decree to the Minister of War of 14 May 1849, *Russkaya Starina*, vol. 91 (1884) 159. Alexander and his wife lost their first child, Alexandra, after a long illness shortly before her seventh birthday on 16 June 1849.
6. Shcherbatov, op. cit., vol. VI, p. 288.
7. Paskevich to Chernyshev, 10 May 1849, *SIRIO*, vol. 122, p. 526.
8. Francis Joseph to Sophie, 21 May 1849, F. Schnuerer, *Briefe Kaiser Franz Joseph an seine Mutter 1838–1872* (Munich, 1930) p. 98.
9. Nicholas to Charlotte, 21 May 1849, Schiemann, op. cit., vol. IV, footnote p. 196. A copy of the order to the Russian fleet can be found in the enclosure of Nesselrode to Brunnow (London) 16 May 1849, FO 65/374.
10. Nicholas to Charlotte, 2 June 1849, Schiemann, op. cit., vol. IV, footnote p. 172.
11. Du Plat (Warsaw) to Palmerston, 2 June 1849, FO 65/369.
12. The full text of the convention with appendices can be found in F. Zatler, *O gospitalyakh v voennoe vremya* (Saint Petersburg, 1861) appendix 21.
13. Nicholas to Charlotte, 23 May 1849, Schiemann, op. cit., vol. IV, footnote p. 207.
14. Conversation with General Berg, the Russian liaison officer with the Austrians, quoted in *Denkwürdigkeiten des Fursten Chlodwig*

zu Hohenlohe-Schillingsfürst, vol. 1 (Stuttgart/Leipzig, 1906) p. 387. Nicholas' proposal was bound to be rejected as Francis Joseph had become Commander-in-Chief of all the Austrian armed forces on 30 April 1849.
15. Conversation with Rochow quoted in Du Plat (Warsaw) to Palmerston, 29 May 1849, FO 65/369.
16. Grünne to Cordon, 22 May 1849, quoted in Corti, op. cit., pp. 30–1 and Nesselrode to Khreptovich, 16 May 1849, Nesselrode, op. cit., vol. 9, pp. 236–7.
17. It is indicative of the Austrian attitude to the Russian intervention that in official correspondence the Russian army was always referred to as 'auxiliary troops'.
18. Paskevich to Schwarzenberg, 23 May 1849, HHStA, PA X 28 and Diary of Buol-Schauenstein, pp. 323–4, HHStA, PA XL—277e.
19. Kiszling, op. cit., vol. 2, p. 164.
20. Shcherbatov, op. cit., vol. 6, pp. 357–60.
21. Nepokoychitsky, op. cit., pp. 45–9. There is a detailed discussion of Jelačić's plans in J. Gyalokay, 'Jellachich hadmüveletei tervei majus havában', *Hadtörténelmi Közlemények*, XXV (1924) 60–89.
22. Nepokoychitsky, op. cit., pp. 49–50.
23. Nepokoychitsky, op. cit., pp. 50–1.
24. Nicholas to his wife, 21 May 1849, Schiemann, op. cit., vol. IV, p. 195.
25. Paskevich to Chernyshev, 1 June 1849, SIRIO, vol. 122, p. 521.
26. Du Plat (Warsaw) to Palmerston, 24 May 1849, FO 65/369.
27. Nicholas to Francis Joseph, 31 May 1849, and Francis Joseph to Nicholas, 8 June 1849, L. Steier, *Haynau és Paskievics*, vol. 2 (Budapest, n.d.) pp. 402–4.
28. Prokesch-Osten to Schwarzenberg, 21 May 1849, D. Jánossy, 'Die Russische Intervention in Ungarn im Jahre 1849', *Bécsi Magyar Intézet Évkönyve*, vol. I (Budapest, 1931) p. 239.
29. Schwarzenberg to Paskevich, 28 May 1849, HHStA PAX 28.
30. Berg to Paskevich, 22 May 1849, Men'kov, op. cit., vol. III, p. 247.
31. Adlerberg to Berg, 24 May 1849, Shcherbatov, op. cit., vol. 6, pp. 356–7.
32. Nesselrode to Schwarzenberg, 25 May 1849, HHStA PAX 28. See also Nicholas' note (n.d.) about Hammerstein's forces in Shcherbatov, op. cit., vol. 6, p. 353.
33. On 11 July 1852 Francis Joseph unveiled a memorial to Hentzi during a visit to Buda. After the compromise of 1867 it was moved to a less conspicuous position in the courtyard of an infantry cadet school.
34. L. Welden, *Episoden aus meinem Leben* (Graz, 1855) pp. 180–5. In a letter written before Schwarzenberg visited Warsaw on 16 May 1849, Caboga had warned of Paskevich's sensitivity about the role of Panyutin's division which could be the source of future disagreement, HHStA PAX 29.
35. Schwarzenberg to Paskevich, 28 May 1849, HHStA PAX 28.
36. Schwarzenberg to Paskevich, 31 May 1849, HHStA PAX 28. The text of the proclamation can be found in *Sammlung der für Ungarn erlassenen Allerhöchsten Manifeste und Proklamationen, dann der Kundmachungen*

der Oberbefehlshaber der Kaiserlichen Armee in Ungarn (Buda, 1849) pp. 86–7.
37. Schwarzenberg to Nesselrode, 28 May 1849, HHStA PAX 28.
38. Nesselrode to Schwarzenberg, 1 June 1849, HHStA PAX 28.
39. O. Regele, *Feldzeugmeister Benedek* (Wien/München, 1960) p. 75.
40. Nesselrode to Meyendorff, 6 June 1849, Nesselrode, op. cit., vol. 9, pp. 248–9.
41. Shcherbatov, op. cit., vol. 6, pp. 75–6.
42. A detailed account of the occupation of Eastern Galicia by the Fourth Infantry Corps can be found in the following two works: M. D. Likhutin, *Zapiski o pokhode v Vengrii v 1849 godu* (Moscow, 1875) pp. 16–51; P. V. Alabin, *Chetyre Voyny* (Samara, 1888) pp. 1–26. Cheodaev's order of the day of 5 May 1849 is reproduced in Alabin, pp. 4–5.
43. Likhutin, op. cit., p. 24 and Hammerstein to Schwarzenberg, 23 May 1849, HHStA PAX 29.
44. Nifontov, op. cit., p. 305; and K. A. Varnhagen von Ense, *Tagebücher*, vol. VI (Leipzig, 1862) p. 202, entry for June 1849.
45. General Fedor Vasilyevich Rüdiger was to play a prominent part in the Russian intervention in Hungary. Born in 1784 in the Baltic province of Kurland, he entered the Semenovsky Guards Regiment at the age of fifteen. After fighting in the wars against Napoleon, he became a lieutenant-general in 1826 and took part in the wars against Turkey and Poland in 1829 and 1831. In November 1831 he became Commander of the Third Infantry Corps, a post he was to hold until 1850. In 1846 he commanded the detachment of Russian troops which moved into Cracow during the Galician revolt. A Lutheran who remained a poor Russian speaker, he enjoyed the complete confidence of Paskevich. After the Hungarian campaign he wrote several reports for Nicholas about the state of the Russian army. He died in 1856.
46. *Opisanie voennykh deystviy rossiyskikh voysk protiv vengerskikh myatezhnikov v 1849 godu* (Saint Petersburg, 1851) p. 14.
47. A detailed account of these patrols can be found in the diary of Men'kov. Men'kov, op. cit., vol. II, pp. 138–45.
48. A. K. Baumgarten 'Dnevnik 1849 goda', *ZhIRVIO*, vol. 4 (1910) 17.
49. Ibid., pp. 17–18. There is also a reference to this episode in the memoirs of Rüdiger's adjutant F. Grigorov, 'Iz Vospominaniy o Vengerskoy Kampanii 1849 goda', *Russkaya Starina*, vol. 94 (1898) 494.
50. Ibid., pp. 18–19.
51. A. Fateev, 'Iz Vospominaniy o Vengerskom pokhode 1849 goda', *Den'*, no. 24 (1864).
52. Shcherbatov, op. cit., vol. 6, pp. 16–17. According to the British consul-general in Warsaw, officers were sent to Germany, Italy, Bohemia and Hungary. Du Plat (Warsaw) to Palmerston, 22 July 1848, FO 65/354.
53. Shcherbatov, op. cit., vol. 6, pp. 364–6.
54. Paskevich's use of the Kurds is mentioned in C. J. Walker, *Armenia* (London, 1980) p. 54.
55. The correspondence between Paskevich, Berg and Schwarzenberg on this subject can be found in HHStA PAX 28. Nesselrode's exchanges

with Medem are reproduced in Andics, *Szövetsege*, pp. 400–2. Many of the Austrian documents are also printed in D. Rapant, *Slovenské Povstanie Roku 1848–9*, part IV (2) (Bratislava, 1961) and L. Steier, *A tót nemzetiségi kérdés 1848–49 ben*, vol. 2 (Budapest, 1937).

56. Schwarzenberg to Berg, 1 June 1849, HHStA PAX 28.
57. Ibid., and Medem to Nesselrode, 2 June 1849, Andics, *Szövetsége*, pp. 401–2.
58. Medem to Nesselrode, 6 June 1849, Andics, *A Nagybirtokos*, vol. 3, pp. 294–6.
59. P. Luzsenszky to Kossuth, 24 May 1849, L. Steier, op. cit., vol. 2, pp. 507–8.
60. Rapant, op. cit., vol. IV (2), pp. 112–17.
61. Shcherbatov, op. cit., vol. 1, p. 235.
62. Shcherbatov, op. cit., vol. 6, p. 5.
63. Shcherbatov, op. cit., vol. 6, p. 73. In a note written after the end of the campaign Paskevich, in a curious echo of a phrase used by Palmerston, referred to the Austrian promises of assistance as being those of a drowning man. 'Materialy dlya istorii Vengerskoy Voyny v 1849 godu', *Voenny Sbornik*, vol. 103 (1875) 195.
64. F. K. Zatler, *Zapiski o prodovolstvii voysk v voennoe vremya* vol. 1 (Saint Petersburg, 1865) p. 163; and V. Aratovsky, 'Rasporyazheniya po prodovolstviyu deystvuyushchey armii v 1849 godu', *Voenny Sbornik*, no. 1 (1872) 201.
65. Aratovsky, op. cit., p. 195.
66. Pechy letter to Vienna, 8 June 1849, Andics, *A Nagybirtokos*, vol. 3, pp. 297–9.
67. Paskevich to Chernyshev, 1 June 1849, *SIRIO*, vol. 122, p. 527.
68. Du Plat (Warsaw) to Palmerston, 8 May 1849, FO 65/369.
69. 'Vospominaniya o pokhode v Vengriyu v 1849 godu', *Inzehenerny Zhurnal*, no. 6 (1863) 231.
70. Aratovsky, op. cit., pp. 205–14.
71. F. K. Zatler, *O gospitalyakh v voennoe vremya* (Saint Petersburg, 1861) pp. 147–61.
72. Du Plat (Warsaw) to Palmerston, 8 May 1849, FO 65/369.
73. Zatler, *Zapiski*, vol. 1, pp. 166–7.
74. Buol-Schauenstein (Saint Petersburg) to Schwarzenberg, 11 June 1849, HHStA PAX 28.
75. Nepokoychitsky, op. cit., pp. 51–2; D. I. Daragan, op. cit., pp. 261–6.
76. Nesselrode to Schwarzenberg, 1 June 1849 and Schwarzenberg to Nesselrode, 5 June 1849, HHStA PAX 28.
77. Adlerberg to Lüders, 2 June 1849, Nepokoychitsky, op. cit., pp. 285–7.
78. Men'kov, op. cit., vol. III, pp. 238–43.
79. Ibid., pp. 243–6.
80. Nepokoychitsky, op. cit., pp. 70–4. Lüders referred to the intercepted correspondence in conversation with the French consul in Bucharest. E. Poujade, *Chrétiens et Turcs* (Paris, 1859) pp. 305–6.
81. *Materialy*, op. cit., pp. 200 and 205.
82. *Opisanie*, op. cit., pp. 3 and 19.

83. P. N. Miller, 'Okhranenie russkikh ofitserov ot pol'skago dukha (1831–1846)', *Minuvshie Gody*, no. 12 (1908) 132–4.
84. This episode was reported to Palmerston by Buchanan (Saint Petersburg) on 10 May 1849, FO 65/364 and Du Plat (Warsaw) on 20 May 1849, FO 65/369.
85. Colquhoun (Bucharest) to Palmerston, 29 May 1849, FO 78/788.
86. D. B. Katsnel'son, op. cit., pp. 176–7.
87. Item 3292, *Katalog Voenno-uchenago Arkhiva Glavnago Shtaba*, vol. 1 (Saint Petersburg, 1905).
88. Buol-Schauenstein (Warsaw) to Schwarzenberg, 9 June 1849, HHStA PAX 27, supplemented by entries in his diary for June 1849, HHStA 277c.
89. Adlerberg to Berg, 11 June 1849, Shcherbatov, op. cit., vol. 6, pp. 366–7.
90. Nicholas to Charlotte, 12 June 1849, Schiemann, op. cit., vol. IV, footnote p. 202.
91. Schwarzenberg to Hammerstein, 14 June 1849, Andics, *Szövetsége*, pp. 408–9.
92. Schwarzenberg to Buol-Schauenstein, 10 June 1849, HHStA PAX 27.
93. Ibid.
94. Du Plat (Warsaw) to Palmerston, 12 and 14 June 1849, FO 65/369.
95. Francis Joseph to Nicholas, 13 June 1849, Andics, *Szövetsége*, pp. 407–8.
96. Zichy to Schwarzenberg, 15 June 1849, Andics, *A Nagybirtokos*, vol. 3, p. 304.
97. Hammerstein to Schwarzenberg, 20 June 1849, HHStA PAX 27.
98. It is characterstic of Nicholas that he had already made up his mind to commute the death sentence and hand Załuski back to the Austrians at the time of his arrest. See Nicholas to Paskevich, 27 June 1849, Shcherbatov, op. cit., vol. 6, p. 293. Załuski was subsequently exiled to Merano in the South Tyrol.
99. Likhutin, op. cit., p. 47.
100. L. Steier, op. cit., vol. 1 (Budapest, 1926) p. 49.
101. The full text is printed in the collection *Vysochayshie Manifesty*, op. cit.
102. D. Solntsov, 'Iz Vospominaniy o Vengerskoy Kampanii', *19 vek*, book 1 (Moscow, 1872) 260.

7 THE FIRST HALF OF THE CAMPAIGN

1. Oreus, op. cit., p. 141.
2. 'Dnevnik Barona L. P. Nikolai', *Russkaya Starina*, vol. 20 (1877) 115; Likhutin, op. cit., p. 63; Grigorov, op. cit., p. 498; Solntsov, op. cit., p. 261.
3. Shcherbatov, op. cit., vol. 6, p. 94.
4. Solntsov, op. cit., p. 262.
5. Grabbe, op. cit., pp. 416–20.
6. Oreus, op. cit., p. 166.

7. Shcherbatov, op. cit., p. 97.
8. Aratovsky, op. cit., p. 225; Zatler, *Zapiski*, op. cit., pp. 172–81.
9. A detailed account of the temporary occupation of Debrecen can be found in Likhutin, op. cit., pp. 116–37.
10. The shortage of small change is mentioned in many of the memoirs written by Russian officers after the campaign. See, for example, Solntsov, op. cit., pp. 262–3; and A. Bobrenev, 'Zametki Russkago ofitsera na puti iz Varshavy v Glavnuyu Kvartiru Armii v 1849 godu', *Russkaya Beseda*, vol. 4 (1858) p. 16.
11. Andics, *A Nagybirtokos*, op. cit., vol. 3, pp. 337–8.
12. Oreus, op. cit., pp. 161–3; Zatler, *O gospitalyakh*, op. cit., pp. 147–60.
13. The more fortunate cavalry were able to make improvised shelters from a horse blanket stretched out over their sabres, scabbards and carbines. They also used their saddle blankets as raincoats by putting their hands through the stirrup-holes. Fateev, op. cit., *Den'*, no. 25 (1864).
14. A. L. Vernikovsky, 'Vengerskiy Pokhod 1849 goda', *Russky Arkhiv*, no. 12 (1885) 515–34; Solntsov, op. cit., pp. 263–4.
15. Zatler, op. cit., p. 157.
16. Nepokoychitsky, op. cit., pp. 77–8.
17. Daragan, op. cit., p. 69.
18. Nicholas to Paskevich, 22, 26 and 28 June 1849, Shcherbatov, op. cit., vol. 6, pp. 291–7; Nicholas to Paskevich, 24 June 1849, Averbukh, *Tsarskaya Interventsiya*, op. cit., pp. 314–15.
19. P. Bogatyrev, 'Iz pisem Ljudvit Shtur k Izmailu Sreznevskomu', *Slavyane*, no. 4 (1944) 20–3.
20. I. I. Pervol'f, 'Avstriyskie Slavyane v 1848–49', *Vestnik Evropy*, April 1879, pp. 535–6.
21. M. Faragó, *A Kossuthbankók Kora* (Budapest n.d.), pp. 252–5.
22. Steier, *Haynau*, op. cit., vol. 1, pp. 25–6.
23. Kossuth to Bem (no date), quoted in L. Kővari, *Okmánytár az 1848–9 ki Erdélyi eseményekhez* (Kolozsvár, 1861), pp. 190–3.
24. V. P. Bykova, *Zapiski Staroy Smolyanki* (Saint Petersburg, 1898) p. 190.
25. Oreus, op. cit., appendix, pp. 74–5.
26. Guichen, op. cit., vol. 1, p. 373.
27. Baumgarten, op. cit., p. 26.
28. Ibid., p. 28; *Iz vospominaniy*, op. cit., p. 173; Alekseenko, op. cit., p. 180.
29. R. Kiszling, op. cit., vol. 2, pp. 185–6.
30. Steier, *Haynau*, op. cit., vol. 2, pp. 405–7.
31. Meyendorff (Warsaw) to his wife, 3 July 1849, Meyendorff, op. cit., vol. 3, pp. 377–8. Meyendorff had left Berlin on leave on 25 June and did not return to his post until 20 September.
32. Steier, *Haynau*, op. cit., vol. 1, pp. 135–6.
33. S. Vukovics, *Visszaemlékezései 1849 re* (Budapest, 1982), pp. 155–6.
34. Francis Joseph to Panyutin, 14 July 1849, *Vysochayshie Manifesty*, op. cit., no. 6.
35. Schwarzenberg to Paskevich, 19 June 1849 and Schwarzenberg to Buol

(Warsaw), 27 June 1849, HHStA PAX 28.
36. The exchange of letters on this subject between Berg, the Tsar, Adlerberg and Paskevich can be found in 'Russko-Vengerskaya Voyna 1849g.', *Russkaya Starina*, vol. 58 (1888) 583–9. See also Nicholas to Paskevich, 1 July 1849, Shcherbatov, op. cit., vol. 6, pp. 297–300.
37. Buol (Warsaw) to Schwarzenberg, 2 July 1849, HHStA PAX 28.
38. Shcherbatov, op. cit., vol. 6, p. 103.
39. Francis Joseph to Nicholas, 29 June 1849, Andics, *A Nagybirtokos*, op. cit., vol. 3, pp. 312–13.
40. Nicholas to Paskevich, 4 July 1849, Shcherbatov, op. cit., vol. 6, pp. 300–1.
41. Steier, *Haynau*, op. cit., vol. 1, pp. 166–7. Two copies of Paskevich's letter to Haynau were sent by hand of two Slovaks who travelled by separate routes. A Russian translation of Haynau's letter of 10 July 1849 is to be found in Men'kov, op. cit., vol. 3, pp. 254–5. It was sent back by the same method.
42. Haynau to Paskevich, 10 July 1849, Shcherbatov, op. cit., vol. 6, pp. 374–5.
43. Nicholas to Paskevich, 9 July 1849, ibid., p. 302.
44. Nikolai, op. cit., p. 124; Andics, *A Nagybirtokos*, op. cit., vol. 3, pp. 318, 336, 339–40; Grabbe, op. cit., p. 424.
45. Men'kov, op. cit., vol. 3, pp. 256–7. Gorchakov's note to Paskevich of 16 July pressing for an attack to be made is given in P. K. Men'kov, 'Materialy dlya Istorii Vengerskoy Voyny', *Voenny Sbornik*, vol. 103 (1875), 199. Paskevich's relationship with Gorchakov was far from cordial, and this doubtless contributed to his decision to ignore the note. For Rüdiger's criticism of Paskevich at Vác see Baumgarten, op. cit., p. 49.
46. Ibid., vol. 2, pp. 151–3 and 159.
47. Langenau to Schwarzenberg, 14 July 1849, HHStA PAX 29. The letter was one of a series written by Langenau to Schwarzenberg full of complaints about the Russians. Before being attached to Rüdiger, Langenau had been attached to Panyutin and had been equally unhappy. (See, for example, his letter to Schwarzenberg of 17 May 1849, ibid.)
48. Men'kov, *Materialy*, op. cit., p. 201.
49. Alabin, op. cit., p. 97 *et seq*.
50. Shcherbatov, op. cit., vol. 6, pp. 115–16.
51. Ibid., p. 123. Men'kov, *Zapiski*, op. cit., vol. 3, pp. 261–2.
52. Shcherbatov, op. cit., vol. 6, pp. 368–70; Steier, *Haynau*, op. cit., vol. 1, p. 220 and 229; Grabbe, op. cit., p. 425.
53. Shcherbatov, op. cit., vol. 6, pp. 372–4.
54. *Russko-Vengerskaya Voyna*, op. cit., pp. 589–90.
55. Steier, *Haynau*, op. cit., vol. 1, pp. 223–4.
56. Grabbe, op. cit., pp. 424–6.
57. Men'kov, *Materialy*, op. cit., pp. 198–9.
58. Steier, *Haynau*, op. cit., vol. 1, pp. 220–40; Shcherbatov, op. cit., vol. VI, pp. 108–16; Averbukh, *Tsarskaya interventsiya*, op. cit., p. 144.
59. Oreus, op. cit., pp. 233–4.
60. Daragan, op. cit., pp. 114–15.

Notes

61. Nepokoychitsky, op. cit., p. 119 footnote.
62. Ibid., p. 157.
63. J. Gyalokay, 'Bem Moldvaországi Hadmüveletei', *Történeti Szemle*, vol. 7 (1918) pp. 251–2.
64. Nicholas to Paskevich, 9 July 1849, Shcherbatov, op. cit., vol. 6, p. 304. In a letter to the Tsarina written on 6 July Nicholas had delivered himself of a homily on the need to do one's duty and made no reference to a visit, although he himself was as saddened as his wife, son and daughter-in-law by Alexandra's death. (Schiemann, op. cit., vol. 4, pp. 208–9 and the telegrams given in 'Depeshi Imperatora Nikolaya I Imperatritse Aleksandre Feodorovne i Nasledniku Tsesarevichu v 1849 godu', *Russkaya Starina*, vol. 86 (1896) 587–96.)
65. Volkonsky to Zakrevsky, 13 July 1849, SIRIO, vol. 73 (1890) pp. 88–9.
66. Vronchenko to Baring Brothers, 19 July 1849, Baring Brothers Archives, HC.10.14; Decree No. 23445 of 22 August 1849, PSV.
67. Averbukh, *Tsarskaya interventsiya*, op. cit., pp. 311–14; Shcherbatov, op. cit., vol. 6, p. 308.
68. Schiemann, op. cit., vol. 4, p. 198 footnote.
69. Nicholas to Paskevich, 25, 28 and 31 July 1849, ibid., pp. 310–19.
70. Buol (Warsaw) to Schwarzenberg, 31 July 1849, HHStA PAX 28.
71. Du Plat (Warsaw) to Palmerston, 30 July 1849, FO 65/370; Nikolai, op. cit., p. 231; V. A. Dokudovsky, *Trudy Ryazanskoy Uchenoy Arkhivnoy Komissii*, vol. 13 (Ryazan', 1898) p. 4.
72. The texts of Rüdiger's memorandum and Görgey's replies of 21 and 22 July can be found in Steier, *Haynau*, op. cit., vol. 2, pp. 106–12. An account of the Khrulev episode was issued as a supplement to the official Russian army bulletin of 21 July 1849 (*Vysochayshie Manifesty*, op. cit.).
73. Baumgarten, op. cit., p. 49.
74. A. Wacquant, *Die Ungarische Donauarmee 1848–49* (Breslau, 1900) pp. 233–40.
75. István Görgey, *1848 és 1849 ból Élmények és Benyomások*, vol. 3 (Budapest, 1888), pp. 230–1.
76. Steier, *Haynau*, op. cit., vol. 2, p. 11; A Görgey, op. cit., vol. 2, pp. 291–4.
77. I. Görgey, op. cit., vol. 3, p. 239; A. Görgey, op. cit., vol. 2, p. 295.
78. Neither Görgey nor Kossuth could have known that the Duke of Leuchtenberg was already seriously ill and that Nicholas had already authorised him to travel to Madeira on doctor's orders, where he died in 1852 (see Nicholas' telegram of 28 May 1849 in *Depeshi*, op. cit., p. 585).
79. A. Seherr Thoss, *Erinnerungen aus meinem Leben* (Berlin, 1881) pp. 49–56.
80. Shcherbatov, op. cit., vol. 6, pp. 130–1.
81. Steier, *Haynau*, op. cit., vol. 2, pp. 113–14.
82. Shcherbatov, op. cit., vol. 6, pp. 125–8; Oreus, op. cit., appendices, pp. 98 and 101; Averbukh, *Tsarskaya interventsiya*, op. cit., pp. 166–9.

83. Nicholas to Paskevich, 28 July 1849, Shcherbatov, op. cit., vol. 6, pp. 314–17.
84. Korff, op. cit., *Russikaya Starina*, vol. 102 (1900) 272. The text given in the printed version of Korff's memoirs, which were censored by Alexander II before publication, differs somewhat from the text of the same paragraph taken from the original manuscript of vol. I of A. M. Zaionchkovsky, *Vostochnaya Voyna* (Saint Petersburg, 1908).
85. Grunwald, op. cit., p. 248.

8 THE SECOND HALF OF THE CAMPAIGN

1. *Vospominaniya o pokhode v Vengriyu*, op. cit., p. 252.
2. After serving with the Polish Legion, Rulikowski gave himself up in Oradea at the end of the war, claiming that he had been taken prisoner. In the face of evidence from a captured Hungarian officer and Görgey about his treacherous conduct, he was sentenced to death by a field court martial and executed on 28 August 1849. The Rulikowski cemetery in Oradea contains a monument erected in 1872 which commemorates his action. The incident is mentioned in several of the memoirs written by Russian officers. For further details see V. G. Verzhbitsky, 'Sochuvstvie peredovykh ofitserov i soldat Russkoy armii Vengerskoy revolyutsii 1848–9', *Istoricheskyi Arkhiv*, no. 4 (1962) p. 250 and Baumgarten, op. cit., p. 50.
3. Nicholas to Paskevich, 31 July 1849, Shcherbatov, op. cit., vol. 6, p. 317.
4. Grabbe, op. cit., pp. 427–8, 430; N. V. Isakov, 'Vengerskaya Kampaniya 1849 g.', *Istoricheskyi Vestnik*, no. 3 (1913), pp. 821–5.
5. Paskevich's anxieties about Görgey at this time are revealed in a letter he wrote to the Tsar on 27 July 1849 (Oreus, op. cit., Appendix p. 101). See also Solntsov, op. cit., pp. 271–2. The Tsar was also worried that Görgey might attack Galicia and ordered Shabel'sky's force to move to Stryj (Shcherbatov, op. cit., vol. 6, p. 317).
6. Görgey's order to the First, Third and Seventh Corps of 28 July 1849, quoted in J. Gyalokaj, 'A Debreceni ütközetről', *Hadtörténelmi Közlemények*, vol. 28 (1927) p. 75.
7. Nikolai, op. cit., p. 243.
8. The scene at the bridge is vividly described in A. I. Del'vig, *Polveka Russkoy Zhizni* (Moscow/Leningrad, 1930) pp. 495–8. The Grand Duke Constantine's disagreement with Paskevich about the use of cavalry is mentioned in Bernhardi, op. cit., p. 54.
9. Grabbe, op. cit., pp. 430–1. Grabbe's criticism of Paskevich's actions at this time are echoed in the memoirs of other Russian officers, e.g. Solntsov, op. cit., pp. 272–3.
10. Nicholas to Paskevich, 6 August 1849, Shcherbatov, op. cit., vol. 6, p. 319.
11. 'General-leytenant David Osipovich Bebutov', *Voenny Sbornik*, no. 7 (1867) 125–6.
12. A. O. Streng, 'Voyna protiv Vengertsev', *Russkaya Starina*, vol. 61

(1889) pp. 475–6.
13. After the battle was over, the unfortunate commander of this cavalry division, Lieutenant-General Glazenap, was much criticised for his inactivity and reluctance to display any initiative (Del'vig, op. cit., p. 500; Alabin, op. cit., p. 500).
14. Kupriyanov was given a pension and replaced by Panyutin. The Grand Duke Constantine received a Russian and Austrian decoration for his bravery. He kept one of the Hungarian cannon-balls which fell between him and a member of his suite on this occasion as a paperweight on his desk (A. F. Grimm, *Alexandra Feodorowna*, vol. 2 (Edinburgh, 1870) pp. 330–1).
15. A. M. Fateev, 'Rasskaz otstavnago soldata', *Russkaya Beseda*, vol. 2 (1860) p. 61; Solntsov, op. cit., p. 275.
16. Nikolai, op. cit., p. 393; Solntsov, op. cit., p. 275; Fateev, op. cit., p. 62; Del'vig, op. cit., p. 490.
17. Nicholas to Paskevich, 10 August 1849, Shcherbatov, op. cit., vol. 6, p. 321.
18. Oreus, op. cit., appendix, pp. 107–8.
19. Z. Varga, *Debrecen az orosz megszállás alatt* (Sárospatak, 1930) pp. 38–40.
20. Solntsov, op. cit., p. 276; Alabin, op. cit., p. 111.
21. Men'kov, op. cit., vol. 3, p. 265.
22. Steier, *Haynau*, op. cit., vol. 2, pp. 162–3.
23. Del'vig, op. cit., pp. 501–3.
24. Aratovsky, op. cit., pp. 248–50.
25. Daragan, op. cit., pp. 124–5.
26. J. Gyalokay, 'A segesvári ütközet, 1849 julius 31', *Hadtörténelmi Közlemények*, vol. 32 (1932) 187–235; Oreus, op. cit., pp. 408–14.
27. *Vasárnapi Ujság*, no. 41 (1881) 654.
28. Nepokoychitsky, op. cit., pp. 187–9.
29. Daragan, op. cit., pp. 203–5.
30. Oreus, op. cit., p. 443.
31. The previous commander, General Wohlgemuth, had been appointed Governor of Transylvania.
32. V. Zelenetsky, 'Srazhenie pod Segedinym', *Severnaya Pchela*, 18 December 1858, pp. 1171–2.
33. Kiszling, op. cit., vol. 2, p. 248.
34. G. Klapka, *Memoirs of the War of Independence in Hungary* (London, 1850) vol. 1, pp. 225–7, and vol. 2, pp. 1–2.
35. *Zapiski Mikhaila Chaykovskago*, op. cit., p. 655.
36. Kiszling, op. cit., vol. 2, p. 260.
37. Baumgarten, op. cit., pp. 40–5.
38. Kiszling, op. cit., vol. 2, p. 262.
39. *Zhurnal dlya chteniya*, op. cit., pp. 286–91.
40. Steier, *Haynau*, op. cit., vol. 2, pp. 175–8.
41. Francis Joseph to Nicholas, 6 August 1849, HHStA PAX 27.
42. Schiemann, op. cit., vol. 4, p. 212.
43. Nicholas to Paskevich, 10 and 13 August 1849, Shcherbatov, op. cit., vol. 6, p. 323 and 327.

44. Nicholas to Francis Joseph, 9 August 1849, Steier, *Haynau*, op. cit., vol. 2, pp. 407–8.
45. Men'kov, op. cit., vol. 3, pp. 266–71.
46. Shcherbatov, op. cit., vol. 6, pp. 378–9.
47. Nesselrode (Warsaw) to Schwarzenberg, 15 August 1849, HHStA PAX 27.
48. *KLÖM*, vol. 14, pp. 820–1.
49. Steier, *Haynau*, op. cit., vol. 2, pp. 154–5.
50. A. Görgey, op. cit., vol. 2, pp. 350–4.
51. Grigorov, op. cit., pp. 500–5; I. Drozdov, 'Sdacha Vengerskoy armii Russkim voyskam pod Vilagoshem 1go Avgusta 1849 g.', *Voenny Sbornik*, no. 9 (1870) p. 133; T. Katona (ed.) *Az Aradi Vértanuk* (Budapest, 1971) vol. 1, pp. 233–40.
52. I. Görgey, op. cit., vol. 3, pp. 548–9; *Az Aradi Vértanuk*, op. cit., vol. 1, pp. 12–14.
53. All these letters are quoted in Steier, *Haynau*, op. cit., vol. 2, pp. 101–2, 164–9. Rüdiger also informed Haynau of Poeltenberg's mission (ibid., p. 99).
54. Nicholas to Paskevich, 13 August 1849, Shcherbatov, op. cit., vol. 6, pp. 328–9.
55. Steier, *Haynau*, op. cit., vol. 2, pp. 17–18.
56. J. K. Mayr, op. cit., pp. 145–6.
57. Steier, *Haynau*, op. cit., vol. 2, p. 154.
58. *Az Aradi Vértanuk*, op. cit., vol. 2, pp. 14–17.
59. I. Görgey, op. cit., vol. 3, pp. 569–70.
60. *Az Aradi Vértanuk*, op. cit., vol. 2, p. 19.
61. Grigorov, op. cit., p. 509.
62. Drozdov, op. cit., pp. 134–5; *Az Aradi Vértanuk*, op. cit., vol. 2, pp. 243–6; I. Görgey, op. cit., vol. 3, pp. 578–84; Wacquant, op. cit., pp. 251–2.
63. Grigorov, op. cit., pp. 510–11.
64. *Russko-Vengerskaya Voyna*, op. cit., pp. 593–4; Grigorov, op. cit., pp. 508–9. See also Zs.P. Pach, 'Kiadatlan Görgey iratok 1849 Augusztusából', *Századok*, vol. 1–4 (1957) pp. 206–7.
65. Oreus, op. cit., p. 490 footnote. The same extract from Paskevich's letter to the Tsar forms part of the Russian official communique No. 18 of 20 August 1849.
66. Steier, *Haynau*, op. cit., pp. 345–7.
67. Men'kov, op. cit., vol. 3, pp. 273–4.
68. Oreus, op. cit., pp. 461–3.
69. Fateev, op. cit., *Den'*, no. 26 (1864) p. 11.
70. Oreus, op. cit., pp. 491–2; Wacquant, op. cit., pp. 255–7; Drozdov, op. cit., p. 13.
71. Wacquant, op. cit., pp. 256–7 footnote; Averbukh, *Tsarskaya Interventsiya*, op. cit., p. 319.
72. For two slightly differing versions of this episode see A. M. Fateev, 'Den' Sdachi Vengrov', *Russkaya Beseda*, no. 4 (1859) 104 and Fateev, op. cit., *Den'*, no. 26 (1864).
73. Shcherbatov, op. cit., vol. 6, p. 171; Men'kov, op. cit., vol. 2, pp. 157–

8; L. Islavin, 'Documents – Nicolas 1er et François Joseph', *Le Monde Slave* (1929) 455–6.
74. Baumgarten, op. cit., p. 49.
75. Steier, *Haynau*, op. cit., vol. 2, pp. 344–5.
76. Parrot (Oradea) to Schwarzenberg, 18 August 1849, HHStA PAX 29.
77. Steier, *Haynau*, op. cit., vol. 2, pp. 232–3; Reinöhl, op. cit., p. 132; Ponsonby (Vienna) to Palmerston, 18 August 1849, FO 7/369.
78. Steier, *Haynau*, op. cit., vol. 2, p. 349.
79. Shcherbatov, op. cit., vol. 6, p. 388.
80. Steier, *Haynau*, op. cit., vol. 2, pp. 348–9.
81. Shcherbatov, op. cit., vol. 6, p. 173. The fortress was located on an island in the river Mureş.
82. Men'kov, op. cit., vol. 3, pp. 275–6.
83. Oreus, op. cit., pp. 497–502. Buturlin was later to refute accusations made in István Görgey's memoirs (vol. 3, p. 660) that he had assured the Hungarians that they would never be handed over to the Austrians (*La Patrie* (Paris) 6 March 1850; a Hungarian translation is to be found in *Pesti Napló*, 30 March 1850).
84. *Materialy dlya istorii*, op. cit., pp. 208–12.
85. Steier, *Haynau*, op. cit., vol. 2, pp. 281–4. Schlick recommended mercy for Duschek because of his co-operation with the Austrians, but he was sentenced to a short term of imprisonment after the war was over.
86. Men'kov, op. cit., vol. 3, pp. 281–2.
87. Adlerberg (Warsaw) to Schwarzenberg, 25 August 1849, HHStA PAX 29; Shcherbatov, op. cit., vol. 6, p. 332; Buol (Warsaw) to Schwarzenberg, 19 August 1849, HHStA PAX 28.
88. Steier, *Haynau*, op. cit., vol. 2, pp. 105–12 and 261.
89. Ibid., pp. 376–7.
90. Men'kov, op. cit., vol. 3, pp. 281–6.
91. Shcherbatov, op. cit., vol. 6, p. 175.
92. Steier, *Haynau*, op. cit., vol. 2, p. 356. Rüdiger also gave a dinner for Schlick after the surrender of Arad in an effort to cement relations with the Austrian army.
93. Grigorov, op. cit., p. 54.
94. 'Istoricheskaya Popravka', *Russky Arkhiv*, no. 2 (1886) 224–5.
95. Oreus, op. cit., appendix, pp. 110–11.

9 AFTER THE SURRENDER

1. Isakov, op. cit., p. 827.
2. Lieven to Aberdeen, 25 August 1849, quoting a letter from her nephew, Count Benckendorff, who was one of the Tsar's ADCS (Aberdeen papers, Add. MSS 43053, vol. 15).
3. Schiemann, op. cit., vol. 4, p. 213; Shcherbatov, op. cit., vol. 6, pp. 329–30 and 392–3.
4. Steier, *Haynau*, op. cit., vol. 2, pp. 408–10.
5. Buol (Warsaw) to Schwarzenberg, 16 August 1849, HHStA PAX 28.
6. Steier, *Haynau*, op. cit., vol. 2, pp. 385–9; Men'kov, op. cit., vol. 3,

pp. 278–80.
7. Steier, *Haynau*, op. cit., vol. 2, pp. 390–2.
8. *Russko-vengerskaya Voyna*, op. cit., pp. 594–5; Shcherbatov, op. cit., vol. 6, pp. 172–3. Zichy's letters to Schwarzenberg of 8 and 20 August 1849 are to be found in Steier, *Haynau*, op. cit., pp. 367–80.
9. Men'kov, op. cit., vol. 3, pp. 286–90.
10. Nicholas to Paskevich, 19 August 1849, Shcherbatov, op. cit., vol. 6, p. 331. In 1896 Nicholas II returned Görgey's sword to Hungary during the Millenary celebrations. In March 1941 Stalin returned the captured banners and standards to Hungary, after two prominent Communists, Mátyás Rákosi and Zoltán Vas, had been released from prison in Hungary and allowed to travel to the Soviet Union in November 1940.
11. Steier, *Haynau*, op. cit., vol. 2, pp. 416–17.
12. Isakov, op. cit., pp. 828–31.
13. Steier, Haynau, op. cit., vol. 2, pp. 392–3.
14. Ibid., p. 394.
15. A. Schmidt-Brentano, *Die Armee in Oesterreich*, (Boppard am Rhein, 1975) p. 360.
16. *Aradi Vértanuk*, op. cit., vol. 2, pp. 27–34; Steier, *Haynau*, op. cit., vol. 2, p. 272.
17. Andics, *A Nagybirtokos*, vol. 3, pp. 390–2. There was further discussion about the Emperor's decision to pardon Görgey in the Council of Ministers on 22 August. Despite the opposition of some ministers, it was finally decided that the circumstances in which Görgey had surrendered to the Russians made it impossible for the Emperor not to pardon him, despite his responsibility for the execution of Count Ödön Zichy in September 1848 (See *Aradi Vértanuk*, op. cit., vol. 2, pp. 59–60.)
18. Steier, *Haynau*, op. cit., vol. 2, pp. 384–5.
19. Ibid., pp. 352–4; Shcherbatov, op. cit., vol. 6, pp. 175–6.
20. *Aradi Vértanuk*, op. cit., vol. 2, pp. 55–6; Szapáry, op. cit., pp. 44–6.
21. Steier, *Haynau*, op. cit., vol. 2, pp. 417–28.
22. Andics, *A Nagybirtokos*, vol. 3, pp. 402–9; *Aradi Vértanuk*, op. cit., vol. 2, pp. 77–82; A. Károlyi (ed.): *Némétujvári Gróf Batthyány Lajos Első Magyar Miniszterelnök főbenjáró pöre*, vol. 1 (Budapest, 1932) pp. 549–52.
23. Du Plat (Warsaw) to Palmerston, 19 August 1849, FO 65/371; E. Keller, *Le Général de Lamoricière*, vol. 2 (Paris, 1891) pp. 194–5.
24. E. Bapst, *L'Empereur Nicolas Ier et la Deuxième République Française* (Paris, 1898) p. 82.
25. D. D. Akhsharumov, *Iz moikh vospominaniy* (Saint Petersburg, 1905) pp. 61–2.
26. A. Nevakhovich, 'Na pobedy v Vengrii', *Severnaya Pchela*, 20 August 1849.
27. The text of both these items can be found in *Vysochayshie Manifesty*, op. cit.
28. Buol (Warsaw) to Schwarzenberg, 31 August 1849, HHStA PAX 28.
29. Steier, *Haynau*, op. cit., pp. 412–14; Shcherbatov, op. cit., vol. 6, pp. 333–4.

30. Kiszling, op. cit., vol. 2, p. 283. A notable exception to Francis Joseph's generosity on this occasion was General Rüdiger.
31. Alabin, op. cit., appendix 2.
32. Steier, *Haynau*, op. cit., vol. 2, p. 412; I. Görgey, op. cit., vol. 3, pp. 680–1.
33. Shcherbatov, op. cit., vol. 6, pp. 391–4.
34. At Paskevich's request Görgey wrote a brief *résumé* of the operations of his army (See *Voenny Sbornik*, no. 3 (1859) 242–8 for a Russian translation).
35. Ibid., p. 177, footnote; Wacquant, op. cit., p. 264; I. Görgey, op. cit., vol. 3, pp. 684–5.
36. A. Alekseenko, op. cit., p. 196.
37. Grigorov, op. cit., pp. 514–20.
38. Steier, *Haynau*, op. cit., vol. 2, pp. 427–8.
39. Kempen, op. cit., p. 151.
40. I. N. Bozheryanov, *Pervy Tsarstvenny General-Fel'dtseykhmeyster Veliky Knyaz' Mikhail Pavlovich 1798–1849* (Saint Petersburg, 1898) pp. 111–12.
41. Schiemann, op. cit., vol. 4, p. 215; V. A. Zhukovsky, *Polnoe Sobranie Sochineniy*, vol. 11 (Saint Petersburg, 1902) p. 42.
42. Steier, *Haynau*, op. cit., vol. 2, pp. 341–3.
43. Grosul, op. cit., p. 63. The crown was later retrieved by the Austrians and used at Francis Joseph's coronation in Budapest in 1867.
44. I. Hajnal, 'A lengyel légió utolsó napjai Magyarországon 1849', *Hadtörténelmi Közlemények*, vol. 26 (1925) 91–9; Kiszling, op. cit., vol. 2, p. 279.
45. Buol (Warsaw) to Schwarzenberg, 24 August 1849, HHStA PAX 28; Daragan, op. cit., p. 222.
46. E. Poujade, op. cit., pp. 305–6.
47. Daragan, op. cit., pp. 230–6; Nepokoychitsky, op. cit., pp. 245–7; P. Szathmáry Károly, 'Hogyan bántak velünk a Muszkák Erdélyben 1849 ben', *Vasárnapi Ujság*, vol. 38, no. 1 (1891) 316.
48. Kiszling, op. cit., vol. 2, pp. 277–8.
49. Nikolay, op. cit., p. 404.
50. Nepokoychitsky, pp. 264–5.
51. *Aradi Vértanuk*, op. cit., vol. 2, p. 226.
52. Ibid., pp. 258–64.
53. Kiszling, op. cit., vol. 2, pp. 279–80; *Aradi Vértanuk*, op. cit., vol. 2, p. 76.
54. A. Shepelev, 'Sdacha Kosinchi', *Istorichesky Vestnik*, no. 7 (1904) 135–6.
55. Oreus, op. cit., pp. 462–3; Adlerberg (Warsaw) to Schwarzenberg, 9 September 1849 (HHStA PAX 29).
56. N. Bogdanovsky, 'Iz Vospominaniy o Vengerskoy i Krymskoy Kampaniyakh', *Russkaya Starina*, vol. 77, (1893) 244–5. Mezösy was, however, not hanged, as stated by Bogdanovsky, but sentenced to 18 years' imprisonment. He was pardoned in 1850.
57. I. O. Panas, 'Karpato-russkie otzvuki Russkogo pokhoda v Vengrii 1849 g.', *Karpato-russky Sbornik* (Uzhgorod, 1930) pp. 214–23.

58. Nicholas to Paskevich, 25 August 1849, Shcherbatov, op. cit., vol. 6, p. 335.
59. Shcherbatov, op. cit., vol. 6, pp. 336–7; Schwarzenberg's correspondence with Lebzeltern, the Austrian chargé d'affaires in Saint Petersburg, on this subject can be found in HHStA PAX 28.
60. Oreus, op. cit., appendix 115–16. For an account of the Guards' stay in Lithuania, see N. K. Imeretinsky, 'Iz zapisok starago Preobrazhentsa 1849 god', *Russkaya Starina*, vol. 80 (1893) 253–79.
61. The text of the Tsar's order of 7 September 1849 is to be found in *Russkaya Starina*, vol. 49 (1886) 574–5.
62. The relationship between the two armies is discussed in many of the memoirs written by Russian officers. See, *inter alia*, Alabin, op. cit., pp. 124–9; Del'vig, op. cit., pp. 516–17; and Likhutin, op. cit., p. 247. For a semi-official view (written after the Crimean War) see 'Pochemu Gergey polozhil oruzhie pered Russkimi, a ne pered Avstriytsami?', *Voenny Sbornik*, no. 2 (1869) 163–8. The remarks about the army having carried out the Tsar's orders and not hating the Hungarians are taken from Benckendorff's letter of 30 August 1849 to his aunt, Princess Lieven (Aberdeen Papers, Add. MSS 43053, vol. 15).
63. For a comprehensive survey of this subject see the appropriate section in V. G. Verzhbitsky, *Revolyutsionnoe dvizhenie v Russkoy armii* (Moscow, 1964) pp. 245–9. It is of interest that the author was unable to find any documents in Soviet archives to substantiate the account of the case of Captain A. Gusev, after whom a Budapest street is named, contained in the book by B. Illés, *A Guszev ügy* (Budapest, 1948).
64. D. B. Katsnel'son, op. cit., p. 77.
65. Baumgarten, op. cit., p. 50.
66. V. Zherve, 'Pis'ma P. E. Gol'mana', *ZhIRVIO*, no. 5 (1910) p. 21; Canning (Constantinople) to Palmerston, 4 November 1848, quoting a letter from the British consul in Odessa, FO 78/736; Du Plat (Warsaw) to Palmerston, 1 July 1849, FO 65/370.
67. Aratovsky, op. cit., pp. 254–8.
68. Shcherbatov, op. cit., vol. 6, pp. 187–90, 347–50, and 386–7.
69. Z. Varga, op. cit., p. 38.
70. Oreus, op. cit., appendix, pp. 117–18.
71. Nepokoychitsky, op. cit., pp. 267–71.
72. Du Plat (Warsaw) to Palmerston, 26 June 1850, FO 65/383.
73. Shcherbatov, op. cit., vol. 7, p. 2.
74. Shcherbatov, op. cit., vol. 6, p. 345.
75. Averbukh, *Tsarskaya interventsiya*, op. cit., pp. 322–6. For details of Austria's financial difficulties see De Guichen, op. cit., vol. 1, p. 428.
76. Aratovsky, op. cit., pp. 260–1.
77. Du Plat (Warsaw) to Palmerston, 17 February and 1 April 1850, FO 65/383.
78. Correspondence from the Baring Brothers archives.
79. Nifontov, op. cit., p. 39.
80. Bloomfield (Saint Petersburg) to Palmerston, 30 January 1850, FO 65/376.
81. Kiszling, op. cit., vol. 2, pp. 286–8.

82. Grabbe, op. cit., p. 432; Oreus, op. cit., pp. 504–6.
83. Grabbe, op. cit., p. 438.
84. Klapka, op. cit., vol. 2, pp. 22–4.
85. Isakov, op. cit., pp. 833–44; P. Szillányi, *Komorn im Jahre 1851* (Leipzig, 1851) pp. 176–265; Klapka, op. cit., vol. 2, pp. 31–6, 42.
86. Grabbe, op. cit., pp. 440–1. On 26 August Grabbe received written confirmation of the Tsar's verbal message.
87. Szillányi, op. cit., p. 194.
88. Klapka, op. cit., pp. 42–3.
89. D. Irányi and C. Chassin, *Histoire politique de la révolution de Hongrie* (Paris, 1859) p. 595.
90. D. Kászonyi, *Magyarhon négy Korszaka* (Budapest, 1977) p. 268.
91. Klapka, op. cit., vol. 2, p. 63.
92. Grabbe, op. cit., pp. 448–51; Schwarzenberg to Gablenz, 12 September 1849, HHStA PAX 29.
93. Nicholas to Paskevich, 18 and 20 September 1849, Shcherbatov, op. cit., vol. 6, pp. 336–7; Lebzeltern (Saint Petersburg) to Schwarzenberg, 30 September 1849, HHStA PAX 28.
94. Kiszling, op. cit., vol. 2, p. 291.
95. I. Hajnal, *A Kossuth emigráció Törökországban* (Budapest, 1927) vol. 1, pp. 495 and 502.
96. Schwarzenberg to Buol (Saint Petersburg), 13 October 1849, HHStA PAX 28.
97. Nicholas to Paskevich, 9 October 1849, Shcherbatov, op. cit., vol. 6, p. 341.

10 THE AFTERMATH OF THE INTERVENTION

1. I. Deak, *The Lawful Revolution* (New York, 1979) pp. 330–7.
2. Kiszling, op. cit., vol. 2, pp. 292–3; Kempen, op. cit., pp. 154–5.
3. Palmerston to Ponsonby (Vienna), 9 September 1849 (Private), Palmerston Papers, GC/PO/836.
4. The Austrians posted two officials to their London embassy to carry out this task, one from the Ministry of the Interior and one who was a close acquaintance of Metternich. The ambassador was not in favour of the operation (Andics, *A Nagybirtokos*, op. cit., vol. 2, 410–11 and E. Andics, *Metternich und die Frage Ungarns* (Budapest, 1973) pp. 315–16). For the ambassador's views see Hajnal, op. cit., pp. 815–16.
5. See n. 3 above and Palmerston to Russell, 20 December 1851, Palmerston papers, GC/RU/109.
6. *Némutujvári Gróf Batthyány*, op. cit., vol. 1, pp. 547–8.
7. Schiemann, op. cit., vol. 4, footnote p. 217. For details of the Tsar's ill health see Shcherbatov, op. cit., vol. 6, p. 340.
8. Du Plat (Warsaw) to Palmerston, 15 October 1849, FO 65/371.
9. Shcherbatov, op. cit., vol. 6, pp. 183–4, 337, 342–4. In order to avoid a meeting with Paskevich in Warsaw, Berg returned to Saint Petersburg from Arad through Prussia. He spoke about Paskevich's anger with Haynau to Buol at the end of October (*Aradi Vértanuk*, op. cit., vol.

2, pp. 256–7). Medem was recalled from Vienna in May 1850 and replaced by Meyendorff from Berlin.
10. Buol (Saint Petersburg) to Schwarzenberg, 20 October 1849, HHStA PAX 26. After his return to Warsaw, Paskevich spoke to Buol about Austria's mistake in using Haynau to pacify Hungary, and forecast that the Austrian government would live to regret this decision (HHStA, Diary of Buol-Schauenstein, entry for 14 September 1849.)
11. Nesselrode, op. cit., vol. 9, pp. 272–5.
12. Buol (Saint Petersburg) to Schwarzenberg, 1 November 1849, HHStA PAX 27; Nesselrode, op. cit., vol. 9, pp. 275–7.
13. *Aradi Vértanuk*, op. cit., vol. 2, p. 257.
14. Du Plat (Warsaw) to Palmerston, 17 September 1850, FO 65/3831.
15. C. Sproxton, op, cit., pp. 108–9; Horváth, op. cit., pp. 222–4.
16. F. W. H. Cavendish, *Society, Politics and Diplomacy (1820–1864)* (London, 1913) p. 170.
17. Schwarzenberg to Buol (Saint Petersburg) 28 October 1840, HHStA PAX 27 (both the official and private letter bear the same date).
18. Buol (Saint Petersburg) to Schwarzenberg, 5 and 15 November 1849, HHStA PAX 26.
19. Haynau (Budapest) to Schwarzenberg, 18 December 1849, HHStA KA GA 10 III.
20. Averbukh, *Tsarskaya Interventsiya*, op. cit., p. 324.
21. Bloomfield (Saint Petersburg) to Palmerston, 12 January 1850, FO 65/376. Bloomfield's views were echoed by Du Plat in Warsaw (see, for example, his letter to Palmerston of 7 January 1850, FO 65/383).
22. Hajnal, op. cit., pp. 885–8.
23. Hajnal, op. cit., pp. 699–700.
24. Shcherbatov, op. cit., vol. 6, pp. 267–8.
25. Canning (Constantinople) to Palmerston, 14 February 1849, FO 78/772; Canning to Colquhoun (Bucharest), 12 February 1849, Canning Papers PRO 352/32 A.
26. Hajnal, op. cit., pp. 861–2.
27. Nesselrode to Titov (Constantinople), 25 August 1849, Palmerston Papers, GC/NE/2. Wysocki and Zamoyski had also taken part in the Galician revolt of 1846.
28. E. Bapst, op. cit., p. 85; Canning (Constantinople) to Palmerston, 5 September 1849, FO 78/779.
29. Bapst, op. cit., p. 88.
30. Canning (Constantinople) to Palmerston, 3 and 5 September 1849, FO 78/779; Palmerston to Russell, 30 December 1849, Russell Papers, PRO 30/22/8c; Bapst, op. cit., p. 88.
31. *Zapiski Mikhaila Chaykovskgagu*, op. cit., pp. 659–63.
32. Hajnal, op. cit., pp. 721, 737–8, 54–5, 830. A copy of the Sultan's letter to Francis Joseph of 6 September 1849 is attached to Canning's letter to Palmerston of 25 September 1849, FO 78/779.
33. See n. 30.
34. Du Plat (Warsaw) to Canning, 1 October 1849, copy enclosed with Canning (Constantinople) to Palmerston, 20 October 1849 FO 78/780.
35. Brunnow to Russell of 9 September 1849 and Russell to Brunnow of

12 September 1849, Russell Papers, PRO 30/22/8A. For copies of Lord Dudley Stuart's letters to Bem, see Palmerston Papers, GC/BR/223 and 224.
36. Hajnal, op. cit., pp. 482–6; *Zapiski Mikhaila Chaykovskago*, op. cit., pp. 665–8.
37. A. Phillimore, *The Life of Admiral of the Fleet Sir William Parker*, vol. 3 (London, 1880) pp. 556–7; Canning (Constantinople) to Palmerston, 17 September 1849, FO 78/779.
38. Shcherbatov, op. cit., vol. 6, pp. 338–9. It should be borne in mind that much of the diplomatic business between foreign embassies and the Turkish government was, for linguistic reasons, transacted by dragomans (often of Greek origin) who were notoriously venal and were often related to one another, although employed by different missions. Canning had little difficulty in acquiring copies of Russian diplomatic correspondence with Turkey, and there seems no reason to suppose that the Russians were not just as successful in acquiring copies of the diplomatic correspondence of other foreign missions, including the British.
39. Palmerston to Russell, 14 September 1849, Royal Archives, RA. Vic. J103/4.
40. Palmerston to Russell, 29 September 1849, Russell Papers, PRO 30/22/8A; E. Ashley, *Life of Henry John Temple, Viscount Palmerston*, vol. 1 (London, 1876) pp. 144–7.
41. Palmerston to Canning (Constantinople), 26 September 1849, FO 78/770.
42. Bapst, op. cit., pp. 95–8; *Souvenirs de Tocqueville*, op. cit., pp. 405–7.
43. Ashley, op. cit., vol. 1, pp. 144–47. Brunnow's advice was echoed by Princess Lieven, who wrote to Lady Palmerston at this time that the vanity of success and sorrow for his brother had turned the Tsar's head (T. Lever, *The Letters of Lady Palmerston*, London 1957, p. 308). Compare also Brunnow's words to Charles Greville about the Tsar's sensitivity to articles in the British press, suggesting that the refugee question was merely a pretext to be used by Russia for attacking Turkey (Viscountess Enfield (ed.), *Leaves from the Diary of Henry Greville*, London 1883, p. 349).
44. Ashley, op. cit., vol. 1, pp. 150–3. The copies of Palmerston's despatches for Canning were sent by messengers travelling by three different routes, one of which was the famous ride of the Queen's Messenger Captain Charles Townley. (For further details see S. Lane-Poole, *Life of Stratford Canning*, vol. 2, London 1888, p. 194.)
45. Palmerston to Ponsonby (Vienna), 6 October 1849, FO 7/364; Palmerston to Bloomfield (Saint Petersburg), 6 October 1849, Bloomfield Papers, PRO 356/29; Palmerston to Baring, 4 October 1849, Northbrook Papers, N.13/10/291.
46. Baring to Grey, 4 October 1849, ibid., N.13/10/93. Baring estimated that Parker's ships would take seven days to reach Constantinople, whereas the Russian ships from Sevastopol would require only two days.
47. Bapst, op. cit., p. 108.

48. The Grand Duchess Olga, on her return to Württemberg from Saint Petersburg, informed the King, her father-in-law, that the Tsar had 'no intention of pushing matters to extremities in Turkey'. Cowley (Frankfurt) to Palmerston, 9 October 1849, FO 30/130.
49. Bloomfield (Saint Petersburg) to Canning, 19 October 1849, Canning Papers, PRO 352/32/A; *Aberdeen/Lieven Correspondence*, op. cit., vol. 1, p. 342.
50. Averbukh, *Tsarskaya Interventsiya*, op. cit., pp. 251–3; Shcherbatov, op. cit., vol. 6, p. 342; Buol (Saint Petersburg) to Schwarzenberg, 14 October 1849, HHStA PAX 27; *Zapiski Mikhaila Chaykovskago*, op. cit., p. 668.
51. Bloomfield (Saint Petersburg) to Palmerston, 19 October 1849, FO 65/367; private letter to Palmerston of same date, Bloomfield Papers, PRO 356/29; Bloomfield to Canning, private, same date, ibid.
52. Brunnow (London) to Nesselrode, 21 October 1849, FO 65/374; Brunnow to Russell, 16 October 1849, Russell Papers PRO 30/22/8B.
53. Bapst, op. cit., p. 118.
54. Ibid., p. 127; Shcherbatov, op. cit., vol. 6, p. 343.
55. The evidence for this is contained in a private letter to the Belgian Minister of Foreign Affairs from O'Sullivan, the Belgian Minister in Vienna, dated 6 November 1849. The information in this letter was passed (via the French Embassy in Brussels) to Louis Napoleon, who subsequently informed the British ambassador in Paris (Normanby to Palmerston, 26 November 1849, Royal Archives RA.Vic. J. 103/42).
56. Canning (Constantinople) to Palmerston, 26 October 1849, FO 78/780.
57. Hajnal, op. cit., pp. 801–2, 807–8.
58. Ashley, op. cit., vol. 1, pp. 157–8.
59. Ponsonby (Vienna) to Russell, 4 December 1849 and Russell to Ponsonby, 29 January 1850, Ponsonby Papers.
60. Ponsonby (Vienna) to Stockmar, 10 November 1849, Ponsonby Papers; ditto, 14 November 1849, Royal Archives RA.Vic. J.103/35.
61. Palmerston to Russell, 23 October 1849, Russell Papers, PRO 30/22/8/B; Lane-Poole, op. cit., vol. 2, p. 202.
62. Palmerston to Baring, 23 and 24 October 1849, Northbrook Papers, N.13/10/315; Russell to Baring, 27 October 1849, ibid., N.13/11/145.
63. Ashley, op. cit., vol. 1, pp. 155–7.
64. Brunnow to Russell, 27 October and 1 November 1849, Russell Papers, PRO 30/22/8B; Russell to Baring, 29 October 1849, Northbrook Papers, N.13/11/153; Palmerston's memorandum of 21 October 1849, Palmerston Papers, MM/TU 42/1/9; Averbukh, *Tsarskaya Interventsiya*, op. cit., pp. 292–9.
65. *Aberdeen/Lieven Correspondence*, op. cit., vol. 1, pp. 339–40.
66. Ashley, op. cit., vol. 1, pp. 158–64; Averbukh, *Tsarskaya Interventsiya*, op. cit., p. 254.
67. Hajnal, op. cit., pp. 758–62, 833–4.
68. H. von Srbik, 'Ein Mordanschlag Felix Schwarzenbergs auf Ludwig Kossuth', *Archiv für Oesterreichische Geschichte*, no. 117 (1949) 127–75; Canning (Constantinople) to Palmerston, 26 December 1849, FO 78/783; Kossuth's wife was interviewed in the Piedmontese Consulate

in Belgrade by the British consul-general who issued her with a British passport in the name of Bloomfield (also used by Kossuth). Fonblanque (Belgrade) to Palmerston, 19 December 1849, FO 78/786.
69. Phillimore, op. cit., vol. 3, p. 562.
70. Canning (Constantinople) to Palmerston, 26 October 1849, enclosing a copy of his letter to Parker, FO 78/780.
71. Canning to Parker, 26 October 1849, Canning Papers, PRO 352/32/B. One of Parker's ships, the steam frigate *Odin*, was being used by Canning and Parker to convey messages rapidly to and from Constantinople. It had been detached from the main squadron at the beginning of October (Phillimore, op. cit., vol. 3, p. 559).
72. Phillimore, op. cit., vol. 3, pp. 569–73.
73. Parker to Baring, 3 November 1849, Northbrook Papers, N.13/12/639.
74. Hajnal, op. cit., pp. 768–70, 775–6.
75. Martens, op. cit., vol. XV, p. 257; *Arkhiv Vorontsova*, vol. 40, Saint Petersburg 1895, p. 356.
76. Ponsonby (Vienna) to Palmerston, 4 December 1849, FO 7/370.
77. Canning to Parker, 2, 3 and 7 November (all private); Parker to Canning, 7 November 1849; Canning to Bloomfield, 5 November 1849, Canning Papers, PRO 352/32/A and 352/32/B. Canning's official letter to Parker of 4 November 1849 is given in Phillimore, op. cit., vol. 3, pp. 578–9.
78. Phillimore, op. cit., vol. 3, pp. 580–5; Palmerston to Russell, 16 November 1849, Russell Papers, PRO 30/22/8B.
79. Victoria to Palmerston, 17 and 24 November 1849; Palmerston to Victoria, 24 November 1849, Royal Archives, RA. Vic. J.103/20 and J.103/27. Palmerston's reluctance to allow Queen Victoria to amend his despatches before they were sent abroad was to be the subject of repeated complaints by the Queen and Prince Albert to the Prime Minister. Palmerston's justification was that the delay involved slowed up the speedy conduct of official business.
80. Russell to Baring, 21 November 1849, Northbrook Papers, N.13/11/177.
81. *Aberdeen/Lieven Correspondence*, op. cit., vol. 1, pp. 333–5.
82. M. E. Chamberlain, *Lord Aberdeen* (New York, 1983) p. 409.
83. Ashley, op. cit., vol. 1, pp. 165–7.
84. Palmerston to Bloomfield (Saint Petersburg), 25 November 1849, Bloomfield Papers, PRO 356/29; Averbukh, *Tsarskaya Interventsiya*, op. cit., pp. 299–305; Baring to Parker, 24 November 1849, Northbrook Papers, N.13/12/683.
85. Bloomfield (Saint Petersburg) to Palmerston, 18 December 1849, FO 65/367; ditto, private letters of 14, 19 and 28 December 1849, Bloomfield Papers, PRO 356/29. Nesselrode also wrote to Brunnow on 2 January 1850 expressing his satisfaction with Palmerston's apology, see Sproxton, op. cit., p. 141.
86. Hajnal, op. cit., pp. 819–20.
87. Ibid., pp. 787–9.
88. Canning (Constantinople) to Palmerston, 31 December 1849, FO 78/783; Phillimore, op. cit., vol. 3, p. 597.
89. Parker to Canning, 12 December 1849 and Canning to Parker, 15

December 1849, Canning Papers, PRO 352/32/B; Baring to Parker, 23 December 1849, Northbrook Papers, N.13/12/755; Phillimore, op. cit., vol. 3, p. 599.
90. Hajnal, op. cit., pp. 819–20.
91. Palmerston to Ponsonby (Vienna), 27 and 30 November 1849, Palmerston Papers, GC/PO/842 and 843.
92. W. Heindl, *Graf Buol-Schauenstein in Sankt Petersburg und London*, 1848–52 (Vienna, 1970) p. 59.
93. Hajnal, op. cit., pp. 776–8, 792–3, 796–8.
94. Deak, op. cit., p. 337; Seymour (Saint Petersburg) to Palmerston, 15 October 1851, FO 65/395.

CONCLUSION

1. Bloomfield (Saint Petersburg) to Palmerston, 19 December 1849, Bloomfield Papers, PRO 356/29.
2. P. A. Zaionchkovsky, *Pravitel'stvenny Apparat Samoderzhavnoy Rossii v XIX veke* (Moscow, 1978) p. 181.
3. Lebedev, op. cit., pp. 371–3.
4. A. W. Kinglake, *The Invasion of the Crimea* (London, 1877) vol. 1, p. 15.
5. Bloomfield (Saint Petersburg) to Palmerston, 18 December 1849, FO 65/367.
6. See n. 1 above and Bloomfield (Saint Petersburg) to Palmerston, 24 January 1850, FO 65/376. The ambassador's optimism was not shared by Buchanan, who had acted as *chargé d'affaires* during Bloomfield's absence on leave in the summer of 1849. During his own leave in the autumn Buchanan informed Palmerston that he thought there would be further trouble among the Christian subjects of the Ottoman Empire which would be bound to affect Russia's relations with Turkey (Ashley, op. cit., vol. 1, p. 161).
7. N. A. Epanchin, 'Datskaya Ekspeditsiya 1850 g.', *Russkaya Starina*, vol. 148 (1911) 112–27.
8. Martens, op. cit., vol. 8, p. 382.
9. 'Zapiska Grafini A. D. Bludovoy', *Russky Arkhiv* (1893) 89.
10. Nesselrode, op. cit., vol. 10, pp. 1–11.
11. Men'kov, op. cit., vol. 2, pp. 169–70.
12. P. V. Bezobrazov, 'O snosheniyakh Rossii s Palestinoy v XIX veke', *Soobscheniya Imperatorskago Pravoslavnago Obshchestva*, vol. 22 (1911) 179; Duhamel, op. cit., pp. 389–94.
13. Brunnow to Aberdeen, 24 and 31 January 1853, Aberdeen Papers, Add. Mss 43144.
14. Nesselrode to Brunnow (London), 2 January 1853 and Brunnow to Aberdeen (undated, possibly 25 January 1853), ibid.
15. See, for example, Bloomfield (Saint Petersburg) to Palmerston, 4 March 1850, enclosing a detailed report on the Russian army prepared by the French ambassador, General de Lamoricière, FO 65/376.
16. Martens, op. cit., vol. 12, p. 269.

17. Ibid., vol. 15, p. 334.
18. S. W. Jackman, *Romanov relations* (London, 1969) p. 341.
19. 'Otryvok iz memuarov Grafa A. Rzhevuskago', *Istorichesky Vestnik*, vol. 82 (1913) 849–50.
20. J. Redlich, *Emperor Francis Joseph of Austria* (London, 1929) p. 159.
21. Schnürer, op. cit., p. 232; Seymour (Saint Petersburg) to Russell, 21 February 1853, FO 65/424; *SIRIO*, vol. 122, p. 19.
22. E. Tarle, *Krymskaya Voyna* (Moscow, 1941) vol. 1, p. 468.
23. V. P. Bykova, op. cit., p. 313.
24. Shcherbatov, op. cit., vol. 7, p. 249.
25. Seymour (Vienna) to Clarendon, 1 April 1857, FO 7/514; Grunwald, op. cit., p. 308 footnote. According to the wife of F. P. Fonton of the Russian embassy in Vienna, Francis Joseph was extremely distressed by his inability to prove to the Tsar that he was not ungrateful, and shut himself up in his study for three days when he received the news of Nicholas' death (N. Sollohub, 'The Death of Nicholas I', *Oxford Slavonic Papers*, vol. 16 (1983) p. 174). In February 1874 Francis Joseph visited Saint Petersburg, and on that occasion laid a wreath on Nicholas' tomb, as well as being shown the Tsar's rooms in the Winter Palace.
26. Martens, op. cit., vol. VIII, pp. 430–1.

Select Bibliography

ARCHIVAL SOURCES

Haus-, Hof- und Staatsarchiv, Vienna
Public Record Office, London
Rigsarkivet, Copenhagen
Riksarkivet, Stockholm

PRIVATE PAPERS

Aberdeen Papers, British Library, London
Baring Brothers & Co. Ltd., London
Bloomfield Papers, Public Record Office, London
Buol-Schauenstein Diary, Haus-, Hof- und Staatsarchiv, Vienna
Stratford Canning Papers, Public Record Office, London
Northbrook Papers, Baring Brothers Archives, London
Palmerston Papers, University of Southampton
Ponsonby Papers, University of Durham
Russell Papers, Public Record Office, London
Correspondence of Queen Victoria and Prince Albert, Royal Archives, Windsor
Wellington Papers, University of Southampton

BOOKS AND ARTICLES

Many articles in pre-Revolutionary publications were unsigned, as the responsibility for publication rested with the periodical editor. Such items are listed here alphabetically under the first *full* word of the title e.g. 'Aksakov'. The same procedure has been followed with other anonymous works.

Abaza, V. A., 'Vzglyad na revolyutsionnoe dvizhenie v Evrope s 1815 po 1848g.', *Russky Arkhiv*, No. 5 (1887) 82–109.
I. S. Aksakov v ego pis'makh 1848–1851, vol. 2 (Moscow, 1888).
Aksharumov, D. D., *Iz moikh vospominaniy* (Saint Petersburg, 1905).
Alabin, P. V., *Chetyre Voyny* (Samara, 1888).
Alekseenko, A., 'Vospominaniya starago sluzhaki', *Russky Arkhiv*, no. 10 (1890) 161–98.
Andics, E., *A Habsburgok és Romanovok szövetsége* (Budapest, 1961).
Andics, E., *A Nagybirtokos Arisztokrácia Ellenforradalmi Szerepe 1848/49ben*, vols 1 to 3 (Budapest, 1952–81).
Andics, E., *Das Bündnis Habsburgok-Romanow* (Budapest, 1963).

Andics, E., *Metternich und die Frage Ungarns* (Budapest, 1973).
Angyal, D., *Az ifjú Ferenc József* (Budapest, n.d.).
Annenkov, M., 'Voennaya sluzhba zheleznykh dorog', *Voenny Sbornik*, no. 3 (1876) 112–43.
Aratovsky, V., 'Rasporyazheniya po prodovol'stviyu deystvuyushchey armii v 1849 godu', *Voenny Sbornik*, no. 1 (1872) 117–265.
Arneth, A., *Johann Freiherr von Wessenberg*, vols. 1 and 2 (Vienna/Leipzig, 1898).
Ashley, E., *Life of Henry John Temple, Viscount Palmerston*, vols 1 and 2 (London, 1876).
Averbukh, R. A., 'Avstriyskaya Revolyutsiya 1848g. i Nikolay I', *Krasny Arkhiv*, vol. 89/90 (1938) 155–207.
Averbukh, R. A., 'Nikolay I i Evropeyskaya Reaktsiya 1848/49 gg.', *Krasny Arkhiv*, vol. 47/48 (1930) 3–49.
Averbukh, R. A., *Tsarskaya Interventsiya v Bor'be s Vengerskoy Revolyutsiey* (Moscow, 1935).
'Die Banknotenfabrik' in *Die Magyarische Revolution im Jahre 1848 und 1849* (Pest, 1852).
Bapst, E., *Les Origines de la Guerre de Crimée* (Paris, 1892).
Bapst, E., *L'Empereur Nicolas Ier et la Deuxième République Française* (Paris, 1898).
Barabay, A. Z., 'Pravoberezhnaya Ukraina v 1848 g.', *Istoricheskie Zapiski*, no. 34 (1950) 86–121.
Baumgarten, A. K., 'Dnevnik 1849 goda', *Zhurnal Imperatorskago Russkago Voennago Istoricheskago Obshchestva*, vol. 4 (1910) 1–56.
Bebutov, D. O. 'General-Leytenant David Osipovich Bebutov', *Voenny Sbornik*, vol. 7 (1867) 109–40.
Becker, G., 'Oppozitsionnoe Dvizhenie v Rossii v 1848 g.', *Novaya i Noveyshaya Istoriya*, no. 1 (1968) 68–75.
Benson, A. C. and Viscount Esher (eds), *Letters of Queen Victoria 1837–61*, vol. 2 (London, 1908).
Bereznyakov, N. V., *Revolyutsionnoe i Natsional'no-osvoboditel'noe Dvizhenie v Dunayskikh Knyazhestvakh v 1848–1849* (Kishinev, 1955).
Berindei, D., 'La politique extérieure de la Valachie pendant la révolution bourgeoise-démocratique de 1848', *Nouvelles Études d'Histoire* (Bucharest, 1965) 285–97.
von Bernhardi, T., *Unter Nikolaus I und Friedrich Wilhelm IV*, vol. 2 (Leipzig, 1893).
Berti, G., *Russia e gli Stati Italiani nel Risorgimento* (Turin, 1957).
Bezobrazov, P. V., 'O snosheniyakh Rossii s Palestinoy v XIX veke', *Soobshcheniya Imperatorskago Pravoslavnago Obshchestva*, vol. 22 (1911) 173–91.
Prince Georges Bibesco, vols 1 and 2 (Paris, 1894).
Bludova, A. D., 'Zapiska Grafini A. D. Bludovoy', *Russky Arkhiv*, no. 1 (1893) 89–96.
Bobrenev, A., 'Zametki Russkago Ofitsera na Puti iz Varshavy v Glavnuyu Kvartiru Armii v 1849 godu', *Russkaya Beseda*, vol. 4 (1858) 15–34.
Bogatyrev, P., 'Iz pisem Ljudovit Shtur k Izmailu Sreznevskomu', *Slavyane*, no. 4 (1944) 20–23.

Select Bibliography

Bozheryanov, I. N., *Pervy Tsarstvenny General-Fel'dtseykhmeyster Veliky Knyaz' Mikhail Pavlovich (1798–1849)* (Saint Petersburg, 1898).
Bratianu, I. C., (ed.) *Anul 1848 în Principatele Române*, vols 1–6 (Bucharest, 1902).
Capefigue, J. B., *Les Diplomates Européens*, vol. 1 (Paris, 1843).
Cavendish, F. W. H., *Society, Politics and Diplomacy (1820–1864)* (London, 1913).
Chamberlain, M. E., *Lord Aberdeen* (New York, 1983).
'Zapiski Mikhaila Chaykovskago', *Russkaya Starina*, vol. 95 (1898) 197–231, 435–64, 651–85.
'Arkhiv Knyazya Chernysheva', *Soobshcheniya Imperatorskago Rossiyskago Istoricheskago Obshchestva*, vol. 122 (Saint Petersburg, 1905).
Corti, E., *The Downfall of Three Dynasties* (London, 1934).
Corti, E., *Vom Kind zum Kaiser* (Graz, 1950).
Corti, E., *Mensch und Herrscher* (Vienna, 1952).
Czetz, J., *Bems Feldzug in Siebenbürgen in den Jahren 1848 und 1849* (Hamburg, 1850).
Dach, K., *Polsko-rumuńska współpraca polityczna w latach 1831–1852* (Warsaw, 1981).
Damyanov, S., *Frenskata Politika na Balkanite 1829–53* (Sofia, 1977).
Danzer, A. F., *Dembinski in Ungarn*, vol. 1 (Vienna, 1873).
Daragan, D. I., *Zapiski o Voyne v Transilvanii v 1849 godu* (Saint Petersburg, 1859).
Deak, I., *The Lawful Revolution* (New York, 1979).
De Guichen, Comte, *Les Grandes Questions Européennes*, vols 1 and 2 (Paris, 1925).
Del'vig, A. I., *Polveka Russkoy Zhizni* (Moscow/Leningrad, 1930).
Dement'ev, A. G., *Ocherki po Istorii Russkoy Zhurnalistiki 1840–1850 gg.* (Moscow/Leningrad, 1951).
Dokudovsky, V. A., 'Vospominaniya', *Trudy Ryazanskoy Uchenoy Arkhivnoy Komissii*, vol. 13 (Ryazan', 1898) 3–36.
Dostyan, I. (ed.), *Formirovanie Natsional'nykh Gosudarstv na Balkanakh* (Moscow, 1986).
Drozdov, I., 'Sdacha Vengerskoy Armii Russkim Voyskam pod Vilagoshem 1-go Avgusta 1849g.', *Voenny Sbornik*, no. 9 (1870) 133–38.
Dubel't, L. V., 'Zametki Generala L. V. Dubel'ta', *Golos Minuvshago*, no. 3 (1913) 127–71.
Dubel't, L. V., 'Doneseniya L. V. Dubel'ta Kn. A. I. Chernyshevu', *Golos Minuvshago*, no. 4 (1914) 222–3.
Duhamel, A. O., 'Avtobiografiya A. O. Dyugamelya', *Russky Arkhiv*, vol. 2 (1885) 371–98.
Enfield, Viscountess (ed.) *Leaves from the Diary of Henry Greville* (London, 1883).
'England and the Hungarian Revolution, 1 March/13 May 1848', *South-East Affairs*, vol. 3 (1933) 91–132.
Epanchin, N. A., 'Datskaya Ekspeditsiya 1850 g.', *Russkaya Starina*, vol. 148 (1911) 112–27.
'Aleksey Petrovich Ermolov', *Russkaya Starina*, vol. 88 (1896) 97–119.
Fabricius, M. P., *Le Kremlin de Moscou* (Moscow, 1883).

Faragó, M., *A Kossuthbankók Kora* (Budapest, n.d.).
Fateev, A. M., 'Den' Sdachi Vengrov', *Russkaya Beseda*, no. 4 (1859) 99–106.
Fateev, A. M., 'Iz Vospominaniy o Vengerskom Pokhode 1849 goda', *Den'* nos. 24/29 (1864).
Fateev, A. M., 'Rasskaz Otstavnago Soldata', *Russkaya Beseda*, no. 2 (1860) 21–70.
Filippov, A. F., 'Vospominaniya o Knyaze Paskeviche', *Drevnyaya i Novaya Rossiya*, vol. 1 (1878) 81–4.
Filipuzzi, A., *La Pace di Milano (6 Agosto 1849)* (Rome, 1955).
Florescu, R. R., 'Stratford Canning, Palmerston and the Wallachian Revolution of 1848', *Journal of Modern History*, XXV (1963) 227–44.
Frantsev, V. A., 'Priglashenie Russkikh na Slavyansky S'ezd v Prage v 1848', *Golos Minuvshago*, no. 5 (1914) 238–40.
Friedjung, H., *Osterreich von 1848 bis 1860*, vol. 1 (Vienna, 1908).
Gelich, R., *Magyarország Függetlenségi Harcza 1848–49ben*, vols 1 to 3 (Budapest, 1889).
Georgescu, E., 'Un mémoire inédit sur les Principautés Danubiennes au XIXème siècle', *Revue Historique du Sud-Est Européen*, vol. 14 (1937) 125–50.
Georgescu-Buzáu, G., *The 1848 Revolution in the Rumanian Lands* (Bucharest, 1965).
Görgey, A., 'Kratky Obzor Voennykh Deystviy v Verkhney Vengrii', *Voenny Sbornik*, no. 3 (1859) 242–8.
Görgey, A., *My Life and Acts in Hungary*, vols. 1 and 2 (London, 1852).
Görgey, A., 'Pochemu Gergey polozhil oruzhie pered Russkimi, a ne pered Avstriytsami', *Voenny Sbornik*, no. 2 (1869) 163–8.
Görgey, I., *Görgey Arthur Ifjusága es Féjlödése a Forradalomig* (Pest, 1916).
Görgey, I., *1848 es 1849ból Élmények és Benyomások*, vols 1–3 (Budapest, 1888).
Grabbe, P. Kh., 'Iz Dnevnika i Zapisnoy Knizhki Grafa P.Kh.Grabbe', *Russky Arkhiv*, no. 11 (1888) 414–32 and No. 12 (1888) 433–64.
Grigorov, F., 'Iz vospominaniy o Vengerskoy Kampanii 1849 goda', *Russkaya Starina*, vol. 94 (1898) 492–522.
Grimm, A. F., *Alexandra Feodorovna*, vols 1 and 2 (Edinburgh, 1870).
Grosul, V. Ya, 'Pol'skaya Politicheskaya Emigratsiya na Balkanakh v 40-nachale 50kh godov XIX veka', *Balkansky Istorichesky Sbornik*, II (Moscow, 1970).
Grosul, V. Ya., and E. E. Chertar, *Rossiya i Formirovanie Rumynskogo Mezhdunarodnogo Gosudarstva* (Moscow, 1969).
Grunwald, C., *La Vie de Nicolas 1er* (Paris, 1945).
Gyalokay, J., 'A Debreceni ütközetről', *Hadtörténelmi Közlemények*, XXVIII (1927) 48–82.
Gyalokay, J., 'A Segesvári ütközet, 1849 július 31', *Hadtörténelmi Közlemények*, XXXII (1932) 187–235.
Gyalokay, J., 'Az első orosz megszállás Erdélyben (1849 jan 31–márcz. 28)', *Századok*, vol. 51 (1922) 626–62.
Gyalokay, J., 'Báró Puchner Antal altábornagy jelentése az erdélyi állapotokról', *Levéltári Közlemények*, vol. 1 (1923) 334–41.

Gyalokay, J., 'Bem Moldvaorszagi Hadmüveletei', *Történeti Szemle*, vol. 7 (1918) 237–53.
Gyalokay, J., 'Jellachich hadmüveleti tervei majus havában', *Hadtörténelmi Közlemények*, XXV (1924) 60–89.
Haenchen, E., *Revolutionsbriefe 1848* (Leipzig, 1930).
Hajnal, I., *A Kossuth Emigráció Törökországban*, vol. 1 (Budapest, 1927).
Hajnal, I., 'A Lengyel légió utolsó napjai Magyarországon 1849', *Hadtörténelmi Közlemények*, vol. 26 (1925) 91–9.
Heindl, W., *Graf Buol-Schauenstein in Sankt-Petersburg und London (1848/52)* (Vienna, 1970).
Heinrich, G., *K. L. von Prittwitz* (Berlin, 1985).
Helfert, J., *Geschichte Oesterreichs vom Ausgange der Wiener Oktober-Aufstandes 1848*, vols I to IV (Prague, 1886).
Henry, P., 'La France et les Nationalités en 1848', *Revue Historique*, vol. CLXXXVIII (April/June 1940) 234–58.
Hitchins, K., *The Rumanian National Movement in Transylvania, 1780–1849* (Harvard, 1969).
Horváth, J., 'Bem Tábornok es a Bukaresti Külképviseletek, 1849 március-juniusban', *Hadtörténelmi Közlemények*, vol. 28 (1927) 375–86.
Horváth, J., *Origins of the Crimean War* (Budapest, 1937).
Hübner, A., *Ein Jahr meines Lebens 1848–1849* (Leipzig, 1891).
Hurmuzaki, E., *Documente privitoare la Istoria Românilor*, vol. 18 (Bucharest, 1916).
Imeretinsky, N. K., 'Iz Zapisok Starago Preobrazhentsa – 1849 god', *Russkaya Starina*, vol. 80 (1893) 253–79.
Ionescu, D. Gh., '"Date noi despre "Episodul Polonez" in revoluția munteana din 1848', *Romanoslavica*, VIII (1963) 79–85.
Ionescu, T., 'Misiunea lui Al. Gh. Golescu la Paris in 1848' *Revista de Istorie*, 12 (1974) 1727–46.
Iorga, N., 'Un complot militaire polonais en Valachie en 1848', *Revue Historique du Sud-Est Européen*, vol. 11 (1934) 7–9.
Irányi, D., and C. Chassin, *Histoire Politique de la Révolution de Hongrie* (Paris, 1859).
Isakov, N. V., 'Vengerskaya Kampaniya 1849 g.' *Istorichesky Vestnik*, no. 3 (1913) 814–46.
Isakov, N. V., 'Iz Zapisok N. V. Isakova', *Russkaya Starina*, vol. 157 (1914) 52–71.
Islavin, L., 'Documents – Nicolas Ier François Joseph', *Le Monde Slave* (1929) 446–57.
'Istoricheskaya Popravka', *Russky Arkhiv*, no. 2 (1886) 224–5.
Jackman, S. M., *Romanov Relations* (London, 1969).
Jánossy, D., 'Die Russische Intervention in Ungarn im Jahre 1849', *Bécsi Magyar Intézet Évkönyve*, vol. 1 (Budapest, 1931) 314–35.
Jelavich, B., 'The Russian Intervention in Wallachia and Transylvania (September 1848 to March 1849)', *Rumanian Studies*, 4 (1979) 16–74.
Jennings, L. C., *France and Europe in 1848* (Oxford, 1973).
Károlyi, A., *Németujvári Gróf Batthyány Lajos Első Magyar Miniszter-elnök Főbenjáró Pöre*, vol. 1 (Budapest, 1932).
Kászonyi, D., *Magyarhon Négy Korszaka* (Budapest, 1977).

Katona, T. (ed.), *Az Aradi Vértanuk*, vol. 1 (Budapest, 1971).
Katsnel'son, D. B., 'K istorii uchastiya Slavyan v Vengerskoy revolyutsii 1848–1849 gg.' in Yu. A. Pisarev, *Tsentral'naya i Yugo-vostochnaya Evropa v Novoe Vremya* (Moscow, 1974).
Keller, E., *Le Général de Lamoricière*, vol. 2 (Paris, 1891).
Kerchnawe, H., 'Feldmarschall Alfred Fürst Windischgraetz und die Russenhilfe 1849', *Mitteilungen des Oesterreichischen Instituts für Geschichtsforschung*, vol. 43 (1929) 325–75.
Kinglake, A. W., *The Invasion of the Crimea* (London, 1877).
Kiszling, R., *Die Revolution im Kaisertum Oesterreich 1848–1849*, vols 1 and 2 (Vienna, 1948).
Kiszling, R., *Fürst Felix zu Schwarzenberg* (Graz, 1952).
Klapka, G., *Memoirs of the War of Independence in Hungary*, vols 1 and 2 (London, 1850).
von Klinkowstroem, M. A. (ed.), *Mémoires de Metternich*, vol. VII (Paris, 1883).
Korff, Baron M. A., 'Iz Zapisok Barona M. A. Korfa', *Russkaya Starina*, vols 99–102 (1899/1900).
Kossuth, L., *Összes Munkái*, vols XI to XV (Budapest, 1951/55).
Kovács, E., *Szabadságharcunk és a Francia Közvélemény* (Budapest, 1976).
Kovács, E., 'Bem József és a Magyar Szabadságharc', *Századok*, vol. 84 (1950) 1–36.
Kovács, I., 'The Polish Legion in the War of Independence in 1848–49', in B. Király (ed.), *East Central European Society and War in the Era of Revolutions* (New York, 1984).
Kővári, L., *Okmánytár az 1848–9ki Erdélyi Eseményekhez* (Kolozsvár, 1861).
von Kübeck, Max (ed.), *Tagebücher des Carl Friedrich Freiherrn Kübeck von Kübau*, vol. 2 (Vienna, 1909).
Lane-Poole, S., *Life of Stratford Canning*, vols 1 and 2 (London, 1888).
Layard, Sir A. Henry, *Autobiography and Letters*, vol. 2 (London, 1903).
Lebedev, A. I., 'Uchastie Russkago Flota v Datskoy Kampanii 1848–50 gg.' in *Istoriya Russkoy Armii i Flota*, vol. X (Moscow, 1913).
Lebedev, K. N., 'Iz Zapisok Senatora K. N. Lebedeva (1846–1849)', *Russky Arkhiv*, no. 10 (1910) 185–253 and 353–76.
Leshchilovskaya, I. I., *Obshchestvenno-politicheskaya Bor'ba v Khorvatii 1848–49* (Moscow, 1977).
Lever, T., *The Letters of Lady Palmerston* (London, 1957).
Likhutin, M. D., *Zapiski o Pokhode v Vengriyu v 1849 godu* (Moscow, 1875).
Lincoln, W. Bruce, *Nicholas I* (London, 1978).
Liprandi, I. P., 'Zapiska I. P. Liprandi', *Russkaya Starina*, vol. 6 (1872) 71.
Łukasik, S., *Pologne et Roumanie* (Paris, 1938).
Lupaş, I., 'Un Martyr Transylvain: le Pasteur Stefan L. Roth', *Revue de Transylvanie*, vol. V (1939) 224–30.
Martens, F. F., *Recueil de Traités et Conventions*, vols IV, VIII, XII and XIV (Saint Petersburg, 1898).
Martens, G. F., *Nouveau Recueil Général de Traités*, vol. 13 (Göttingen, 1855).

Mayr, J. K. (ed.), *Das Tagebuch des Polizeimeisters Kempen von 1848 bis 1859* (Vienna/Leipzig, 1931).
Men'kov, P. K., 'Materialy dlya Vengerskoy Voyny v 1849 godu', *Voenny Sbornik*, vol. 103 (1875) 191–212.
Men'kov, P. K., *Zapiski*, vols 1 to 3 (Saint Petersburg, 1898).
Metternich, Prince, 'Confession de Foi du Prince Metternich à Nikolai I', *Russkaya Starina*, vol. 7 (1873) 783–99.
von Meyendorff, P., *Ein Russischer Diplomat an den Höfen Berlin und Wien*, vols. 1 to 3 (Berlin/Leipzig, 1923).
Mezei, J., 'Visszaemlékezések a Szabadságharcra', *Vasárnapi Újság*, no. 18 (1880).
Miller, P. N., 'Okhranenie Russkikh Ofitserov ot Pol'skago Dukha (1831–1846)', *Minuvshie Gody*, no. 12 (1908) 132–4.
Miziano, K. F., 'Podgotovka Kontrrevolyutsionnoy Interventsii protiv Rimskoy Respubliki' in *K Stoletiyu Revolyutsii 1848 goda* (Moscow, 1949).
Mosely, P. E., 'A Pan-Slavist Memorandum of Ljudevit Gaj in 1838', *American Historical Review*, vol. 40 (1938) 704–16.
Mueller, P., *Feldmarschall Fürst Windischgraetz* (Vienna, 1938).
Nepokoychitsky, A. A., *Opisanie Voennykh Deystviy v Transilvanii v 1849 godu* (Saint Petersburg, 1866).
Nesselrode, C., *Lettres et Papiers du Chancelier*, vols 1 to 11 (Paris 1904/11).
Nevakhovich, A., 'Na Pobedy v Vengrii', *Severnaya Pchela*, 20 August 1849.
Nifontov, A. S., *Rossiya v 1848 godu* (Moscow, 1949).
Nikolai, Baron L. P., 'Dnevnik Barona L. P. Nikolai', *Russkaya Starina*, vol. 20 (1877) 101–26, 223–51, 393–406.
'Depeshi Imperatora Nikolaya I Imperatritse Aleksandre Feodorovne i Nasledniku Tsesarevichu v 1849 godu', *Russkaya Starina*, vol. 86 (1896) 587–96.
'Imperator Nikolay Pavlovich i ego Vremya 1831/1849', *Russkaya Starina*, vol. 41 (1884) 135–60.
'Imperator Nikolay Pavlovich v ego voennykh rasporyazheniyakh 1849 i 1854 gg.', *Russkaya Starina*, vol. 49 (1886) 571–75.
'Sobstvennoruchnye Pis'ma Imperatora Nikolaya I', *Russkaya Starina*, vol. 86 (1896) 518–19.
'Zapisochki Imperatora Nikolaya I k Knyazyu Ilarion Vasil'chikovu', *Starina i Novizna*, vol. XVI (1913) 34–45.
Nol'de, B. E., *Yuriy Samarin i ego Vremya* (Paris, 1926).
Odložilik, O., 'Slovanský Sjezd a Svatodušní Bouře v r. 1848', *Slovanský Přehled*, vol. 20 (1928) 408–25.
Oksman, Yu., 'Mery Nikolaevskoy Tzenzury protiv Fur'erizma i Kommunizma', *Golos Minuvshago*, vol. 3 (1917) 69–71.
Opisanie Voennykh Deystviy Rossiyskikh Voysk protiv Vengerskikh Myatezhnikov v 1849 godu (Saint Petersburg, 1851).
Oréus, I., *Opisanie Vengerskoy Voyny 1849 g.* (Saint Petersburg, 1880).
Pach, Zs. P., 'Kiadatlan Görgey Iratok 1849 Augusztusából, *Századok*, vols 1–4 (1957) 198–226.
'František Palacký's Letter to Frankfurt, 11 April 1848', *Slavonic and East European Review*, vol. 26 (1948) 303–8.
Panaitescu, P. P., 'Revoluţia Română de la 1848 şi Alianţa Polonă',

Romanoslavica, vol. VIII (1963) 59–77.
Panas, I. O., 'Karpato-russkie otzvuki Russkago Pokhoda v Vengrii 1849 g.', *Karpato-russky Sbornik* (Uzhgorod, 1930) 209–29.
Parry, E. Jones (ed.), 'The Correspondence of Lord Aberdeen and Princess Lieven 1832–54', *Camden 3rd Series*, vol. 62 (1930).
Pavlović, D. M., *Srbija i Srpski Pokret u Južnoy Ugarskoj 1848 i 1849* (Belgrade, 1904).
Pech, S. Z., *The Czech Revolution of 1848* (Raleigh, North Carolina, 1969).
Pervol'f, I. I., 'Avstriyskie Slavyane v 1848–49', *Vestnik Evropy* (April, 1879) 491–542.
'K Istorii Dela Petrashevskago', *Byloe*, No. 2 (1906) 244–7.
Pfitzner, J., *Bakuninstudien* (Prague, 1932).
Phillimore, A., *The Life of Admiral of the Fleet Sir William Parker*, vol. 3 (London, 1880).
'Pokhod v Vengriyu v 1849 godu', *Voenny Sbornik*, vol. 14 (1860) 3–70
Polny Svod Zakonov (2nd edition), vol. XXIII (Saint Petersburg, 1873).
Polovtsev, M., 'Glagol Vremen', *Severnaya Pchela*, 15 May 1849.
Popovici, V., 'Despre Activitatea Emigraţilor Poloni in Moldova in ani 1846–1848', *Studie şi Cercatori Stiintificie Istorie/filologei*, anul IX, fasc. 1/2 (Jassy, 1958).
Poujade, E., *Chrétiens et Turcs* (Paris, 1859).
Pulszky, F., *Meine Zeit, Mein Leben*, vols 1 and 2 (Pressburg/Leipzig, 1881).
Rapant, D., *Slovenské Povstanie roku 1848–49*, vol. IV (2) (Bratislava, 1961).
Redlich, J., *Emperor Francis Joseph of Austria* (London, 1929).
Regele, O., *Feldzeugmeister Benedek* (Vienna/Munich, 1960).
Reinöhl, F., 'Aus dem Tagebuch der Erzherzogin Sophie', *Historische Blätter*, no. 4 (1931) 109–36.
Reiser, S. A. (ed.) *Vol'naya Russkaya Poeziya XVIII–XIX vv.* (Leningrad, 1970).
Riasanovsky, N., *Nicholas I and Official Nationality in Russia, 1825–1855* (Berkeley, 1959).
'1848 and Rumanian Unification', *Slavonic and East European Review*, vol. 26 (1948) 390–421.
Russian Ministry of War, *Katalog Voenno-uchenago Arkhiva Glavnago Shtaba*, vol. 1 (Saint Petersburg, 1905).
'Russko-vengerskaya Voyna 1849 g.', *Russkaya Starina*, vol. 58 (1888) 583–9.
Rzhevusky, Graf A., 'Otryvok iz Memuarov Grafa A. Rzhevuskago', *Istorichesky Vestnik*, vol. 82 (1913) 849–50.
Sammlung der für Ungarn erlassenen Allerhöchsten Manifeste und Proklamationen, dann der Kundmachungen der Oberbefehlshaber der Kaiserlichen Armee in Ungarn (Buda, 1849).
Savin, A., 'Nikolay I i Fridrickh Vil'gel'm IV 1840–48' in *Rossiya i Zapad* (Petrograd, 1923) 128–34.
Schiemann, T., 'Eigenhändige Aufzeichnung Kaiser Nikolaus I 1848, unmittelbar vor Ausbruch der Februarrevolution', *Zeitschrift für Osteuropäische Geschichte*, no. 2 (1912) 557–60.
Schiemann, T., *Geschichte Russlands unter Kaiser Nikolaus I*, vols 1 to 4 (Berlin, 1913).

Schmidt-Brentano, A., *Die Armee in Oesterreich* (Boppard-am-Rhein, 1975).
Schnuerer, F., *Briefe Kaiser Franz Joseph an seine Mutter 1838–1872* (Munich, 1930).
Seherr-Thoss, A., *Erinnerungen aus meinem Leben* (Berlin, 1881).
Shcherbatov, A. P., *General Fel'dmarshall Knyaz' Paskevich*, vols 1 to 7 (Saint Petersburg, 1888/1904).
Shepelev, A., 'Sdacha Kosinchi', *Istorichesky Vestnik*, no. 7 (1904) 135–6.
Shil'der, N. K., *Imperator Nikolay I*, vols 1 and 2 (Saint Petersburg, 1903).
Sminova, A. O., 'Iz Zapisok A. O. Smirnovoy', *Russky Arkhiv*, No. 9 (1895) 84.
Sollohub, N., 'The Death of Nicholas I', *Oxford Slavonic Papers*, vol. 16 (1963) 164–81.
Solntsov, D., 'Iz Vospominaniy o Vengerskoy Kampanii', *19 Vek*, book I (1872) 256–81.
Spira, G., *A Magyar Forradalom 1848/49ben* (Budapest, 1959).
Sproxton, C., *Palmerston and the Hungarian Revolution* (Cambridge, 1919).
von Srbik, H., 'Ein Mordanschlag Felix Schwarzenbergs auf Ludwig Kossuth', *Archiv für Oesterreichische Geschichte*, no. 117 (1949) 127–75.
Steier, L., *A Tót Nemzetiségi Kérdés 1848/49ben*, vols 1 and 2 (Budapest, 1937).
Steier, L., *Az 1849iki Trónfosztás Előzményei és Következményei* (Budapest, n.d.).
Steier, L., *Haynau és Paskievics*, vols 1 and 2 (Budapest, n.d.).
Steinbach, G., 'Franz Deák', *Oesterreichisch-Ungarische Revue*, vol. IV (1887) 7.
Stern, A., *Geschichte Europas*, vols IV to VII (Stuttgart/Berlin, 1916).
Streng, A. O., 'Voyna protiv Vengertsev', *Russkaya Starina*, vol. 61 (1889) 459–78.
Szapáry, M., 'Carl Graf Grünne, Generaladjutant des Kaisers Franz Joseph 1848–59' (unpublished thesis, University of Vienna 1935).
Szathmáry Károly, P., 'Hogyan Bántak velünk a Muszkák Erdélyben 1849ben', *Vasárnapi Újság*, vol. 38 (1891) 3–6.
Szilassy, G., 'America and the Hungarian Revolution of 1848–49', *Slavonic and East European Review*, vol. 44 (1965–6) 180–4.
Szillányi, P., *Komorn im Jahre 1849* (Leipzig, 1851).
Tarle, E., *Krymskaya Voyna*, vol. 1 (Moscow, 1941).
Thim, J., *A Magyarországi 1848–49iki Szerb Fölkelése Története*, vols 1 and 2 (Budapest, 1940).
de Tocqueville, A., *Souvenirs de Alexis de Tocqueville* (Paris, 1893).
Tyutchev, F. I., 'Rossiya i Revolyutsiya', *Russky Arkhiv*, vol. 11 (1873) 895–912.
Varga, Z., *Debrecen az Orosz Megszállás alatt* (Sárospatak, 1930).
Varnhagen von Ense, K. A., *Tagebücher*, vol. VI (Leipzig, 1862).
Vernikovsky, A. L., 'Vengersky Pokhod 1849 goda', *Russky Arkhiv*, no. 12 (1885) 515–34.
Verzhbitsky, V. G., *Revolyutsionnoe Dvizhenie v Russkoy Armii* (Moscow, 1964).
Verzhbitsky, V. G., 'Sochuvstvie Peredovykh Ofitserov i Soldat Russkoy Armii Vengerskoy Revolyutsii 1848–9', *Istorichesky Arkhiv*, no. 4 (1962) 121–33.

'Pis'ma Knyazya P. M. Volkonskago k A. A. Zakrevskomu', *Soobshcheniya Imperatorskago Rossiyskago Istoricheskago Obshchestva*, vol. 73 (Saint Petersburg, 1890).
Arkhiv Vorontsova, vol. 40 (Saint Petersburg, 1895). 'Iz Vospominaniy o Pokhode v Vengriyu v 1849 godu', *Zhurnal dlya Chteniya Vospitannikam Voenno-uchebnykh Zavedeniy*, vol. 122 (1856) 145–96 and 273–319.
'Vospominaniya o Pokhode v Vengriyu v 1849 godu', *Inzhenerny Zhurnal*, no. 6 (1863) 209–25 and 227–72.
S. Vukovics, *Visszaemlékezései 1849re* (Budapest, 1982).
Vysochayshie Manifesty i Prikazy Voyskam i Izvestiya iz Armiy v Prodolzhenie Voyny protiv Myatezhnykh Vengrov v 1849m godu (Saint Petersburg, 1849).
Wacquant, A., *Die Ungarische Donauarmee 1848–49* (Breslau, 1900).
Waldapfel, E. V., *A Forradalom és a Szabadságharc Levelestára*, vol. 1 (Budapest, 1950).
Walker, C. J., *Armenia* (London, 1980).
Walter, F. (ed.) *Aus dem Nachlass des Freiherrn Carl Friedrich Kübeck von Kübau* (Graz/Cologne, 1960).
Walter, F., *Die Oesterreichische Zentralverwaltung*, vol. 1 (Vienna, 1964).
Welden, L., *Episoden aus meinem Leben* (Graz, 1855).
Wellesley, A. R. (ed.) *Despatches, Correspondence and Memoranda of Fieldmarshal Arthur, Duke of Wellington, K.G.*, vol. 6 (London, 1877).
Winter, E., 'Eine bedeutsame Unterredung zwischen Zar Nikolaus I und Metternich am Neujahrstag 1846', *Zeitschrift für Geschichtswissenschaft*, vol. 9 (1961) 1861–70.
Yuzefovich, T., *Dogovory Rossii s Vostokom: Politicheskie i Torgovye* (Saint Petersburg, 1869).
Zaionchkovsky, A. M., *Vostochnaya Voyna*, vols 1 and 2 (Saint Petersburg, 1908).
Zaionchkovsky, P. A., *Pravitel'stvenny Apparat Samoderzhavnoy Rossii v XIX veke* (Moscow, 1978).
Zajdel' E. (ed.) *Revolyutsiya 1848 vo Frantsii* (Leningrad, 1925).
Zarek, O., *Kossuth* (London, 1937).
Zatler, F. K., *O Gospitalyakh v Voennoe Vremya* (Saint Petersburg, 1861).
Zatler, F. K., *Zapiski o Prodovol'stvii Voysk v Voennoe Vremya*, vol. 1 (Saint Petersburg, 1865).
Zelenetsky, V., 'Srazhenie pod Segedinym', *Severnaya Pchela*, 18 December 1858.
Zherve, V., 'Pis'ma P. E. Gol'mana', *Zhurnal Imperatorskago Russkago Voennago Istoricheskago Obshchestva*, no. 5 (1910) 1–22.
Zhukovsky, V. A., *Polnoe Sobranie Sochineniy*, vol. 11 (Saint Petersburg, 1902).

Index

Abdul Mejid I, Sultan of Turkey (1821–61), 31, 45–8, 50–1, 96, 104, 117, 210–12, 215–16, 218, 222, 226
Aberdeen, Earl of (1784–1860), 3, 55, 115, 217, 226
Abrud, 103
Ács, 180, 201, 204
Adlerberg, Captain Aleksandr Vladimirovich (1818–88), 151
Adrianople, Treaty of (1829), 5
Aksakov, Ivan Sergeevich (1823–86), 96
Alba Julia, 87, 137–8, 171, 193–5
Albert, Prince Consort (1819–61), 18, 25, 213, 216, 220
Albrecht, Archduke of Austria (1817–95), 207
Alcaini, Colonel Kajetan (1792–1854), 201–2
Aleksandriya, 159
Aleppo, 221
Alexander I, Emperor of Russia, elder brother of Nicholas I (1777–1825), 3–5, 124, 228
Alexander II, Emperor of Russia, eldest son of Nicholas I (1818–81), 8, 97, 159, 171, 185, 187–90, 192
Alexander, Prince of Serbia, *see* Alexander Karadjordjević
Alexandra Aleksandrovna, Grand Duchess, daughter of Alexander II (1842–49), 159
Alexandra Fyodorovna, Empress of Russia, wife of Nicholas I, (1798–1860), 159
Algeria, 32, 113
Ali Pasha (1815–71), 49, 211
Alsózsolca, 162
amnesty for Hungarians, 133, 163, 182, 185–9, 191
Anatolia, 223
Andrássy, Count Gyula (1823–90), 104, 205

Anichkov, Colonel, 187, 201–2
Anichkov Palace, Saint Petersburg, 11
Anna Pavlovna, Queen of Holland, sister of Nicholas I (1795–1865), 227
Anrep, General Iosif Romanovich (1798–1860), 191–2
April Laws, 13, 26–7, 34, 74, 77
Apuşeni mountains, 103, 139
Arad, 103, 137, 152, 170, 173–5, 177–80, 182–4, 186, 189, 191, 196, 202; executions at, 205–9, 215
Ártánd, 177
Árav river, 138, 143
Asprea, Dimitrios, 54
Auersperg, Count Karl (1786–1859), 58
Aulich, Lajos (1793–1849), 151, 205
Aupick, General Jacques (1789–1851), 45, 49, 84, 116, 211, 213
Austria, 3–9, 11–12, 14–15, 21–33, 45–51, 57–70, 76–7, 82, 85, 90–2, 95–7, 99, 101–17, 122–7, 132–3, 139–40, 147, 160, 163, 170, 176, 180, 186–8, 190–6, 199, 202, 206–10, 212–18, 220, 222–9; 'bestowed' constitution of 1849, 90; committee of public safety of, 24, 28, 33; constituent assembly of, 24–5; council of ministers of, 62, 81, 91, 94–5, 99, 104–5, 128, 188–9, 195, 207–8, 212; council of state of, 7, 22, 200
Austro-Russian military convention of 10 June 1849, 123–4, 186

Bach, Alexander (1813–93), 61
Bácska, 98, 103, 151
Baden, Grand Duchy of, 122
Bad Gastein, 192
Bad Ischl, 182, 188
Bakunin, Mikhail Aleksandrovich (1814–76), 19, 28, 122

Index

Balassagyarmat, 155, 161
Balaton, Lake, 201
Bălcescu, Nicolae (1819–52), 38, 40–1, 48, 158
Balmazújváros, 167
Balta Liman, Act of (1 May 1849), 116, 226
Baltic Germans, 96
Baltic Sea, 20, 123, 224
Bánát, the, 98, 103, 126, 137, 147, 173
Banská Bystrica, 153, 201–2
Banská Stiavnica, 153
Barber's Bay, 219
Bardejov, 125, 143
Baring Brothers (London), 159, 200
Baring, Sir Francis (1796–1866), 214, 216, 219–21
Barrot, Odilon (1791–1873), 113
Bastide, Jules (1800–79), 18, 55, 70
Batovce, 202
Batthyány, Count Kázmér (1807–54), 176–7
Batthyány, Count Lajos (1806–49), 26, 34, 69–74, 205–6
Baumgarten, Colonel Aleksandr Karlovich (1815–83), 175
Bavaria, Kingdom of, 10, 12, 14
Bavarian Palatinate (Rhineland), 122
Bayer, Colonel József (1821–64), 148
Bebutov, General David Iosifovich (1793–1867), 154, 167–8
Beke, Colonel József (1812–96), 194
Belgium, Kingdom of, 5, 8, 13, 226
Belgrade, 31, 36, 42, 103–4, 204; Treaty of (1739), 211
Bem, General Józef (1794–1850), 58, 60, 62, 73, 76, 79–89, 92–3, 95, 98, 103, 107, 131, 137, 139–40, 145–8, 157–60, 170–9, 185–6, 192–6, 201, 210–15
Benckendorff, Colonel Konstantin Konstantinovich (1817–58), 16–17, 21, 149–50, 153
Benedek, General Ludwig (1804–81), 129
Berettyóújfalu, 166
Berg, General Fyodor Fyodorovich (1793–1874), 101, 105–9, 115, 125–9, 132, 140–2, 149, 152–7, 163, 173, 176, 180–4, 206, 208
Berlin, 14, 17–18, 22, 62–3, 123, 130, 192
Besika Bay, 218–19
Bessarabia, 39, 43, 52
Bethlen, Colonel Gergely (1810–67), 179
Biala Krinitsa, 10
Bibescu, Gheorghe (1804–73), 40–1, 50, 54
Bibikov, General Dmitriy Gavrilovich (1789–1870), 23, 112
Bicske, 74
Bihar, 176
Bîrlad, 42–3
Bismarck, Prince Otto von (1815–98), 229
Bistriţa, 79–80, 87, 146, 158, 196
Blackwell, Joseph Andrew (1798–1886), 26
Blaj, 27, 40, 77–8
Bloomfield, Lord Arthur (1802–79), 12, 18, 48, 200, 209, 215, 219–24
Blum, Robert (1807–48), 60, 63
Bochnia, 199
Bohemia, 24–8, 71
Bohus, Baron János, 179
Bolliac, Cezar (1813–81), 158
Bory, Baroness Karolina, 161–2
Bosnia, 104, 226
Bosphorus, 6, 219–20
Brăila, 38
Brandenburg, 62
Brandenburg, General Friedrich von (1792–1850), 62
Braşov, 79, 81–6, 146, 158, 170
Brassier, Count Joseph (1798–1872), 22
Brătianu, Dumitrie (1818–92), 44
Bratislava, 13, 28, 60, 75, 79, 106, 108, 122, 128, 137–8, 148–9, 178, 204
Brescia, 128
Brezovica, Pass, 88
Britain, Great, 4, 6, 8, 12–13, 18, 20, 33, 37, 44, 48, 51, 55, 66, 70,

Index

Britain, Great – *continued*
87–8, 96, 104, 113–16, 123, 136, 200, 204–14, 218, 220–8
Broadlands, 220–1
Brody, 80
Bruck, Baron Karl (1798–1860), 61
Brüneck, General, 111
Brunnow, Baron Filipp Ivanovich (1797–1875), 12–13, 18, 37, 44–5, 48, 51, 54–5, 85, 115, 212–20, 226–7
Brussels, 17, 197
Buchanan, Sir Andrew (1807–82), 55–6, 116
Bucharest, 37–45, 50–5, 81–8, 95, 101, 126, 136, 195, 210, 212
Buda, *see also* Budapest, 98, 102, 110, 137–8; fortress of, 128
Budapest, 13, 26–30, 33–4, 44, 58, 73–5, 80–1, 88–93, 97–102, 125, 138, 143–59, 172–4, 178, 192, 205, 209
Bukovina, 10, 42, 79–81, 93, 95, 97, 100–2, 105, 121, 129, 134, 138–9, 146, 158–9
Bulgaria, 52, 104, 116
Bułharyn, Colonel Jerży (1798–1885), 89
Buol-Schauenstein, Count Karl von (1797–1865), 68–9, 82, 85, 90, 92, 95, 97, 100, 105, 111, 117, 140, 152–3, 160, 175, 185, 192, 204, 206–9, 214–15, 221–2, 228
Butashevich-Petrashevsky, Mikhail Vasil'evich (1821–66), 101, 110, 190, 198
Buturlin, General Sergey Petrovich (1803–73), 180, 183

Caboga, Count Bernhard (1785–1855), 107–9, 123, 125, 186
Calvert, F. W., 218–22
camarilla, 26
campaign accounts, settling of, 199
Canada, 208
Canning, Sir Stratford (1786–1880), 17, 25, 37, 45, 49, 55–6, 84–5, 87, 116, 210–21
Cantacuzino, Constantine, 50–53

Caranşebes, 103, 193
Carlist War, 66
Carlos, Don (1788–1855), 66
Carpathian mountains, 125, 128, 130, 134–7, 142
Catherine II, Empress of Russia, grandmother of Nicholas I (1729–96), 4, 96
Caucasian irregular cavalry, 147, 154, 167–9
Caucasus, 4, 39, 154, 159
Cavaignac, General Louis (1802–57), 32–3, 45, 65, 70, 113, 190
Cegléd, 150, 172
Chain Bridge, Budapest, 75, 128, 150–1
Charles X, King of France (1757–1836), 8
Charles Albert, King of Piedmont (1798–1849), 10, 14, 22, 90
Chartists, 52
Cheodaev, General Mikhail Ivanovich (1785–1859), 80, 105, 129, 144, 162, 165, 170, 176
Chernovtsy, 80
Chernyshev, Prince Aleksandr Ivanovich (1785–1857), 97, 121, 126–7, 135, 228
Chişineu, Criş, 179, 181
chloroform, 136
cholera, 5, 21, 30, 42–3, 85, 191; effects of during campaign, 145, 148, 158, 170
Chotin, 203
Christian VIII, King of Denmark (1786–1848), 10
Chrzanowski, General Wojciech (1788–1861), 90
Cuicea, 79, 195
Città Vecchia, 113
Clam-Gallas, General Eduard von (1805–91), 137, 158, 170–1, 195
Cluj, 79–80, 171, 193, 195
Colloredo, Count Franz (1799–1859), 207, 214, 222
Colomb, General Friedrich von (1775–1854), 17–18
Colquhoun, Sir Robert (1803–70), 44, 48–50, 54–5, 84–8

Index

committee of 14 April (2 April o.s.), 12
Constantine Nikolaevich, Grand Duke, second son of Nicholas I (1827–92), 20, 67, 97, 141, 163–4, 167–8, 186, 191
Constantine Pavlovich, Grand Duke, elder brother of Nicholas I (1778–1831), 3–4, 30
Constantinople, 5, 37–8, 40, 44–5, 48–50, 55–6, 85, 96, 104, 114, 116–17, 210, 213–21, 226–7
Copenhagen, 20
Cordon, Field-Marshal Franz (1796–1869), 108
Cossacks, 52, 83, 130, 147, 151, 155, 161, 171, 203; Ataman of, 162
Cracow, 6, 23, 29, 34–5, 58, 61, 64, 100, 110, 122, 130–2, 134–8, 141–2, 161, 198–201
Craiova, 41
Crimean war, 3, 6, 47, 56, 112, 199, 227, 229
Croatia, 26–7, 33–4
Csányi, László (1790–1849), 74, 86–7
Csorich, General Anton (1795–1864), 152–3, 157, 174, 201, 203
Custozza, 33
Czajkowski, Michał (1804–86), 45, 174, 211, 215
Czartoryski, Prince Adam (1770–1861), 17, 31, 36, 40, 45, 49
Czech national committee, 28–9

Daily News, 304
Damjanich, General János, (1804–49), 98, 110, 179, 182–3, 205
Dannenberg, General Pyotr Andreevich (1792–1872), 126, 170
Danube river, 5, 47, 72–5, 98, 102–3, 108, 126, 128, 137–8, 148, 151, 154–6, 193
Danubian principalities, *see also* Moldavia and Wallachia, 5, 36–7, 39, 44–7, 51–6, 65, 78, 84, 95–7, 100–1, 112, 114–17, 121, 126, 185, 210, 214, 226

Dardanelles, 6, 214, 216, 218–20, 222
Deák, Ferenc (1803–76), 33, 74
Debrecen, 74–5, 84–5, 88, 93–4, 104, 110, 131, 138, 143–4, 147, 159, 165–70, 177, 180, 196–8
Decembrist Revolt (1825), 3, 61, 96, 112, 208
Dej, 195–6
Dekonsky, Captain, 193
Dembiński, General Henryk (1791–1864), 80, 88–9, 131, 137, 139, 140–3, 149–50, 173–4, 193, 210
Denmark, Kingdom of, 10, 19, 20, 85, 111, 123, 224–5
Dessewffy, General Arisztid (1802–49), 193, 205
Deva, 193–4
Diebitsch, Field Marshal Ivan Ivanovich (1785–1831), 5, 30
Doblhoff-Dier, Anton (1800–72), 25, 58
Dohna-Schlobetten, General Karl (1784–1859), 17, 62, 111
Dolný Kubín, 138
Dorsner, Colonel Franz (1795–1852), 146
Dostoevsky, Fyodor Mikhailovich (1821–81), 101
Dragoș, Ioan, 103
Drava river, 34
Dubel't, General Leontiy Vasil'evich (1792–1862), 112
Duhamel, General Aleksandr Osipovich (1801–80), 38–43, 47–55, 83–7, 103, 117, 210, 226
Dukla, 141–2; pass of, 106, 108, 111, 125, 135–6, 138, 142
Du Plat, Colonel Gustave, 200, 212
Durando, General Giovanni (1805–69), 32
Duschek, Ferenc (1797–1872), 74, 183
Dyck, General, 170, 193, 195

East Prussia, 8, 111
Eider river, 19

Engelhardt, Major-General Nikolay Fyodorovich (1799–1856), 79, 83–4, 86
Epanchin, Rear-Admiral Ivan Petrovich (1791–1875), 20
Esterházy, Colonel Pál (1806–77), 202–3
Esterházy, Pál (1786–1866), 26, 46, 59
Făgăraş, 158, 170, 195
Ferdinand, Emperor of Austria (1793–1875), 7, 13, 16, 23–5, 31–2, 62, 66–7, 71, 77
Ferdinand II, King of the Two Sicilies (1810–59), 10, 32, 115
Ficquelmont, Count Ludwig von (1777–1857), 22–5, 31
Filanowicz, Faustyn, 36
Filaret field, 41
Filippescu, G., 46, 50
Fischhof, Dr Adolf (1816–93), 24
Florence, 115
Focşani, 41
Fonton, Feliks Petrovich (1801–?), 23, 31, 46, 59, 63–4, 66, 90
Fourier, Charles (1772–1837), 101
France, 4–6, 9, 11–13, 16–19, 22, 30–3, 37–8, 40, 45, 65–6, 88, 97, 101, 104, 113–16, 121, 206, 210, 213–15, 227–8
French National Assembly, 113
Francis, Emperor of Austria (1768–1835), 4, 6, 186
Francis Charles, Archduke of Austria, brother of Ferdinand (1802–75), 24, 32
Francis Joseph, Emperor of Austria (1830–1916), 32, 62, 66–9, 71, 75, 81, 94, 99, 106, 109, 111, 121–9, 137, 140–1, 149, 151–3, 160, 169, 175–8, 180–9, 191–9, 203–9, 224, 228; meeting with Nicholas I in Warsaw, 122–7, 208
Frankfurt-am-Main, 14, 21, 28, 225; parliament of, 18, 21, 28, 32, 34, 44, 60, 70, 91, 122
Frederick VII, King of Denmark (1808–63), 19

Frederick William III, King of Prussia (1770–1840), 22
Frederick William IV, King of Prussia, brother-in-law of Nicholas I (1795–1861), 7, 8, 14, 16, 18–20, 22, 62, 69, 91, 111, 122–3, 224–5
Freiligrath, Ferdinand (1810–76), 14
Freytag, General Robert Karlovich (1802–51), 156–7, 168
Frolov, General Il'ya Stepanovich (1808–79), 177, 179–81
Frummer, Colonel Antal (1818–82), 194
Fuad Effendi (1815–69), 50–3, 81, 84, 87, 103, 210–7, 221

Gaeta, 65
Gaj, Ljudevit (1809–72), 27
Gál, Colonel Sándor (1817–66), 195
Galaţi, 38, 50
Galicia, 6, 12, 16, 23–4, 29–30, 35, 57, 63, 74, 78, 80–1, 87–9, 92–3, 95, 97, 100–2, 105–7, 111–12, 121–9, 131–46, 152–9, 167–9, 176, 185, 192, 197–8
Găneşti, 83
Garibaldi, Giuseppe (1807–82), 113
Gáspár, General András (1804–84), 205
Germany, 6, 8, 9, 12, 14, 20–1, 30–1, 65, 85, 91, 109, 111, 121–4, 139, 160, 207, 224–5, 229; Confederation of, 18, 19, 21, 61, 68, 82, 91–2, 96, 225
Gerstenzweig, General Daniil Aleksandrovich (1790–1848), 42–3, 51
Gesztely, 166–7, 174, 187, 201
Ghica, Grigore, 116
Ghica, Ion (1816–97), 44–5
Giurgiu, 47, 50
Gödöllő, 97, 151
Golescu, Alexandru (1819–81), 44
Golescu, Nicolae (1810–78), 48
Goluchowski, Count Agenor (1812–75), 93
Gorchakov, Prince Mikhail Dmitrievich (1793–1861), 165, 168

Görgey, General Artúr (1818–1916), 3, 71–5, 80, 88–9, 97–8, 104, 110, 128, 131, 137, 143, 146–51, 154– 203 *passim*
Görgey, Johann, 131, 161, 208
Gorlice, 142
Grabbe, General Pavel Khristoforovich (1787–1875), 96, 115–16, 138, 143, 146, 152–7, 165– 7, 174, 187, 196, 201–4, 211
Graebe, Captain, 178
Grant, Effingham, 50, 87, 95
Great Britain, *see* Britain, Great
Greece, Kingdom of, 10, 210
Grotenhjelm, General Maksim Maksimovich (1789–1867), 139, 145–6, 157–9, 170–1, 193, 195–6
Grünne, General Karl (1808–84), 68, 94, 99, 122, 189, 206
Grybów, 142
Guizot, François (1787–1874), 11
Guyon, General Richard (1812–56), 178, 193
Gyöngyös, 154
Győr, 73, 75, 108, 148–50, 153, 174, 188, 200–1
Gyula, 192
Gyulai, Count Ferenc (1798–1868), 201, 203

Habsburg Empire, *see* Austria
Hammerstein-Equord, General Wilhelm von (1785–1861), 61, 80– 2, 93, 100, 105, 125, 127, 130, 134– 5, 139–41
Hanover, Kingdom of, 12, 14
Hasford, General Gustav Khristianovich (1794–1874), 170– 2, 194
Hatvan, 154
Haţeg, 194
Haynau, General Julius (1786– 1853), 128–9, 142, 147–57, 160–4, 170–7, 180–9, 191–6, 202–8
Hegyes, *see* Mali Idos
Henningsen, Charles (1815–77), 204
Hentzi, General Heinrich (1785– 1849), 102, 128

Herzinger, General Anton (1798– 1868), 149
Hesse, Grand Duchy of, 12, 225
Hilfferding, Fyodor Ivanovich (1798–1864), 106
Hodonin, 109
Holstein, Duchy of, 19, 85, 123, 224
Holy Alliance, 6
honvéd, *see* Hungarian army
Hübner, Count Josef (1811–92), 59
Hungary, 3, 8, 13, 22–7, 30, 33–5, 39, 46, 57–8, 61, 66–77, 80–99 *passim*, 101–15, 121–30, 133–49 *passim*, 151–4, 158–69, 174–77, 180–9, 191–8, 201–8, 210–16, 223
Hungarian army, 71–2, 88, 149; committee of national defence, 34, 69, 71, 74–5, 78, 104; constitution of 1848, 161–2, 186; council of ministers, 173; declaration of independence, 104, 131, 147; national guard, 72; parliament, 13, 34, 74, 104, 172, 179; partisans, 137–8, 154, 201; standards captured by Russian army, 187, 195; war council, 178– 9

Iancu, Avram (1842–72), 103, 139, 194
Inczédy, Colonel László (1809–82), 194
Ineu, 179, 193
Innsbruck, 24–5, 27–31, 33
information about Hungarian army, lack of, 94–5, 132
Ionian islands, 54–5, 208
Ireland, 12, 208
Isabella II, Queen of Spain (1833– 68), 66
Isakov, Colonel Nikolay Vasil'evich (1821–91), 167, 187–8, 201–2
Isaszeg, 97
Islaz, 40–1
Italian legion in Hungary, 193
Italy, 8–10, 12, 14, 22, 25–7, 30–3, 45, 57, 61, 72, 91, 97, 101–2, 109, 112, 115, 123, 128

Jassy, 36–40, 42–3, 54, 56
Jelačić, Baron Josip (1801–59), 27, 30, 33–4, 58–60, 62, 72, 75, 94, 97, 102, 104, 126, 137, 151–2, 157, 160, 173, 196
Jibou, 195
John, Archduke of Austria (1782–1859), 21, 25, 32
Jordanów, 130, 135
Jósika, Baron Samu (1805–60), 99
Journal de Saint Pétersbourg, 16, 47, 112, 209, 215
Jungbauer, Colonel, 202
Jutland, 19–20

Kaliningrad, 17, 62
Kalisz, 142
Kalliány de Kallian, General Joseph (1786–1859), 86
Kápolna, 89
Karadjordjević, Alexander, Prince of Serbia (1806–85), 31, 42, 104
Karcag, 166
Karlovac, 27
Karlovich, General Anton Mikhailovich (1785–1861), 180, 196
Kazinczy, Colonel Lajos (1820–49), 195–6, 206
Kecskemét, 172
Kempen, General Johann (1793–1863), 178, 205
Kerecsend, 165
Khrulev, Colonel Stepan Aleksandrovich (1807–70), 141, 160–4, 176, 183
Kiel, 19–20
Kiev, 23, 136
Kiselev, Nikolay Dmitrievich (1800–69), 18
Kiselev, General Pavel Dmitrievich (1788–1872), 39
Kismarja, 166
Kiss, General Ernő (1800–49), 205
Klagenfurt, 188, 191
Klapka, General György (1820–92), 74, 88, 98, 110, 151, 173–4, 178, 187, 200–4

Kmety, General György (1813–65), 174
Knezich, General Károly (1808–49), 205
Koller, Baron August (1805–83), 222
Kolowrat, Count Franz von (1778–1861), 22
Kolta, 102
Komárno, 73, 93–4, 97, 102, 110, 125, 128, 137, 149–57, 163, 172–4, 178, 186–9, 196, 200–8
Komáromi Lapok, 203
Korff, Baron Modest Andreevich (1800–76), 15, 111
Košice, 74, 88, 138, 143, 145, 156–7
Kossuth, Lajos (1802–94), 13, 26, 30, 34, 46, 59–60, 68–75, 79–80, 85–91, 95–8, 103–4, 107, 110, 114, 131, 134, 144–51, 158, 162–6, 173–9, 191–2, 203–5, 210, 213–14, 217–18, 222–3
Kossuth bank notes, 91, 99, 136, 144, 148, 169, 196
Kotlyarov, Captain, 160–2
Kotzebue, Karl Evstaf'evich, 36–8, 40–1, 52–5
Kremlin, Great Palace of, 96, 101, 229
Kroměříž, 60, 67, 90
Kübeck von Kübau, Baron Karl Friedrich (1780–1855), 91, 93–4, 97–9
Kuchuk Kainardji, Treaty of (1774), 210–11, 213
Kupriyanov, General Pavel Yakovlevich (1789–1874), 130, 168
Kütahya, 223
Kuznetsov, General Mikhail Mikhailovich, 162

Lahner, General György (1795–1849), 205
Lamartine, Alphonse de (1790–1869), 12–13, 16, 18, 40, 44
Lamberg, General Franz (1791–1848), 34

Index

Lamoricière, General Christophe de (1806–65), 113–14, 190, 192, 214–16
Langenau, Colonel Ferdinand (1818–81), 155
Latour, Count Theodor Baillet von (1780–1848), 58, 205
Lázár, Colonel Vilmos (1815–49), 193, 205
Lazarev, Admiral Andrey Petrovich (1788–1849), 21
Łazienki palace, Warsaw, 122, 185
Lebzeltern-Collenbach, Baron Edward (1812–67), 16, 25
Le Flô, General Adolphe (1804–87), 33, 55–6, 65
Legeditsch, General Ignaz (1790–1866), 131, 134
Leiningen-Westerburg, General Christian (1812–56), 103, 226
Leiningen-Westerburg, General Károly (1819–49), 205
Leitha river, 59
Leményi, Bishop János, 78
Leopold II, Grand Duke of Tuscany (1794–1870), 10, 115
Leopold I, King of Belgium (1790–1865), 4
Leovo, 39–43
Leuchtenberg, Duke of, son-in-law of Nicholas I (1817–52), 86, 162
Liechtenstein, Prince Franz (1802–87), 172, 175, 189, 193
Lieven, Princess Darya Khristoforovna (1785–1857), 3, 115, 220
Lieven, Baron Vilgel'm Karlovich (1800–80), 62, 64, 66
Liptovský Mikuláš, 27, 143
Lithuania, 16, 121, 197
Lobkowitz, Prince Joseph (1803–75), 106, 111, 131
Lombardy, 14, 23
London, 46, 70, 114, 159, 200, 206, 216–17, 220–22; Treaty of (1841), 6, 214–18, 221
Louis Napoleon, later Emperor Napoleon III (1808–73), 56, 65–6, 113, 214, 219, 226

Louis Philippe, King of France (1773–1850), 5, 8, 11, 14
Löwenhagen, General Pyotr Petrovich (1805–58), 194
Lučenec, 155, 160, 201
Lüders, General Aleksandr Nikolaevich (1790–1874), 51–2, 56, 79, 81–7, 101, 103, 117, 126, 138–9, 145–6, 157–60, 170–2, 185, 193–6
Ludwig, Archduke of Austria (1784–1864), 22
Ludwig I, King of Bavaria (1786–1868), 10, 14
Luga, 159
Lugoj, 103, 174–5, 179, 193
Lutița, 78
L'vov, 49, 61, 63–4, 130, 134, 138

Madarász, László (1811–1909), 70
Magheru, Gheorghe (1804–80), 41, 50
Magyaróvár, 149
Maiorescu, Ioan (1811–64), 44
Mali Idos, 152, 160
Malkovsky, General Ignaz (1784–1854), 103
Malmö, 21, 123
Manin, Daniele (1804–57), 14, 203
Maria Anna, Empress of Austria, wife of Ferdinand (1803–84), 26, 32
Maros river, 149, 194
Maximilian II, King of Bavaria (1811–64), 14
Medem, Pavel Ivanovich (?–1854), 12, 25, 32, 35, 46, 63–4, 67, 90, 92, 95, 100, 105, 109, 186, 206, 209
Mediaş, 86, 171, 193, 195
Mediterranean naval squadrons, British and French, 55, 84, 213–19
Mednyánszky, Colonel Sándor (1816–75), 200, 202
Mel'nikov, Colonel, 195
Mercurea, 171–2
Menshikov, Prince Aleksandr Sergeevich (1787–1869), 20, 224

Messenhauer, Wenzel (1813–48), 58, 60
Mészáros, General Lázár (1796–1858), 72, 74, 150
Metternich, Prince Clemens von (1773–1859), 4, 6, 9–10, 13, 15, 22, 25, 68, 70
Meyendorff, Baron Peter Kazimirovich (1796–1863), 17–18, 29, 46, 97
Mezőkövesd, 154–6, 166–7
Mezösy, Colonel Pál (1801–?), 196
Michael Pavlovich, Grand Duke, younger brother of Nicholas I (1798–1849), 190, 192, 196
Miercurea-Ciuc, 170
Mierosławski, Ludwik (1814–78), 16, 18
Mihanovich, Anton, 217
Milan, 10, 14, 22, 33, 59–60
military frontier of Habsburg Empire, 26–7, 34
military intelligence, collection of by Russian missions abroad, 132
Miloradovich, Lieutenant, 176–7
Miskolc, 143–5, 153–6, 161–6
Mnichovo Hradiště, 6, 64
Modena, Grand Duchy of, 14
Móga, General János (1785–1861), 59–60, 71
Moldavia, 36–49 *passim*, 51–6, 64, 96, 116–17, 146, 158–60, 170, 197, 210, 226–8
Montenegro, Principality of, 226
Montenuovo, General Wilhelm (1821–95), 192
Mór, 73
Moravia, 24, 28, 106, 108–10, 128, 157
Moscow, 30, 95, 97, 100–9, 225
Muenchengraetz, *see* Mnichovo Hradiště
Mukachevo, 180, 196
Musurus Effendi (1807–91), 212, 217

Nagy Sándor, General József (1802–49), 150, 160, 162, 166, 168–9, 174, 181, 205
Naples, 10, 32
Napoleon I, Emperor of France (1769–1821), 4, 24, 88, 109, 111, 228
Napoleonic Wars, 3, 5, 6, 8–9, 17, 33, 78, 109, 124, 199, 227
Năsăud, 79
Neofit, Metropolitan, 41, 50
Nepokoychitsky, Colonel Artur Adamovich (1813–81), 81
Nesselrode, Count Karl Vasil'evich (1780–1862), 4, 10, 12, 15, 22–4, 29–30, 32, 35–8, 44–7, 53–5, 64–9, 85, 88, 90, 97, 100, 112–15, 122–9, 132, 144, 152, 175–6, 190–2, 206–11, 214–19, 221–8
Netherlands, Kingdom of, 8
Nicholas I, Emperor of Russia (1796–1855),
succession to throne, 3; character of, 3–4; relations with ministers, 4; relationship with Paskevich, 5; visit to London in 1844, 4, 6, 224, 226; foreign policy in early 1848, 8–9; authorises extra military expenditure in March 1848, 15; reaction to Prussian invasion of Denmark in April 1848, 19–20; views on German unification, 21; cancels loan to Austria in March 1848, 22; reception of Ficquelmont's envoy Thun-Hohenstein, 23; approves Medem's move to Innsbruck in May 1848, 25; congratulates Windischgraetz on suppression of Prague revolt in June 1848, 29; views on activities of Serbs in Hungary and Principality of Serbia, 31, 103; congratulates Cavaignac on suppression of revolt in Paris in June 1848, 33; congratulates Radetzky on victory at Custozza on 23 July, 33; views on possible disturbances in Danubian principalities in early 1848, 37; criticism of Duhamel for occupying Moldavia, 43; circular of 31 July 1848 about occupation of Moldavia, 47–8; orders

Nicholas I, Emperor of
Russia – *continued*
occupation of Wallachia in
September 1848, 50–1;
congratulates Windischgraetz on
suppression of Vienna revolt in
October 1848, 62; views on
restoration of order in Prussia in
November 1848, 63; hesitation
about aiding Austria at end of
1848, 64; refuses to restore
diplomatic relations with Spain at
end of 1848, 66; declines Austrian
offer of rank of Field Marshal in
their army, 67; refuses Austrian
request for loan in early 1849, 69;
authorises limited intervention in
Transylvania in early 1849, 82;
disapproves of Austrian
'bestowed' constitution of March
1849, 90; visits Moscow at Easter
1849, 96; uneasiness about internal
situation in Russia in early 1849,
96; annoyance at Austrian request
to send Russian troops to
Transylvania in April 1849, 100–
1; decides to intervene in
Hungary, 101–2; returns from
Moscow at end of April 1849, 106;
disapproves of Paskevich's
decision to send Panyutin's
division to Moravia, 109; orders
arrest of members of Petrashevsky
group, 110; urges King of Prussia
to end war with Denmark, 111;
manifesto about intervention in
Hungary in May 1849, 111–12;
decides to restore diplomatic
relations with France, 113; moves
to Warsaw for duration of
campaign, 121–2; meeting with
Francis Joseph in Warsaw in May
1849, 127–8, 208; accepts Lüders'
plan for operations in
Transylvania, 137; anxiety about
security situation in Galicia, 139–
40; inspects Russian troops near
Hungarian frontier, 142; order of
the day to Russian army of 13
June, 142; returns to Warsaw after
troop inspection, 142; awards
decoration to Francis Joseph, 149;
displeasure with General Berg,
152–3; travels to Peterhof for
wife's 51st birthday, 159; breaks
off negotiations for loan with
Baring Brothers, 159; does not
wish Russian troops to advance
south of Oradea, 160; rejects offer
of Hungarian crown and bribery
of Görgey, 163; questions
Paskevich about failure to defeat
Görgey, 167–9; approves
Paskevich's rejection of
Hungarian offer of surrender,
177–8; reaction to news of
Görgey's surrender, 185; views on
granting amnesty to Hungarians,
185–7; grief at death of Grand
Duke Michael, 192; wishes
Russian army to leave Hungary,
196; concern about views of
Russian officers left in Hungary,
198; settles financial accounts for
campaign, 199; seeks loan from
Baring Brothers, 200; orders
withdrawal of Grabbe's forces,
203; reaction to executions at
Arad, 206, 215; sends Radziwill
to Constantinople, 211; views on
Stratford Canning, 221; views on
success of Hungarian intervention,
224; supports Denmark in
summer of 1850, 224; supports
Austria against Prussia in 1850,
225; views on 25th anniversary
reports in 1850, 225; evacuates
Danubian principalities in 1851,
226; establishes diplomatic
relations with Belgium, 226;
refuses to address Louis Napoleon
as 'brother', 226; declares war on
Turkey, 227; over-estimation of
his own political influence, 227;
failure to understand nature of
constitutional monarchy, 227;
death on 2 March 1855, 228; views
on Austria's perfidy, 228

Index

Noszlopy, Gaspar (1822–53), 200, 202
Novara, 90, 92, 115
Nowy Targ, 138
Nugent, General Laval (1777–1862), 203
Nyiregyháza, 166

Obrenović, Michael (1823–68), 31
Ocna, 158
Odessa, 30, 54, 96, 117, 126, 198, 210
Odobescu, Colonel Ioan (1793–1857), 41
Odorheiul Săcuiesc, 170–1
Oituz Pass, 158, 170
Olga Nikolaevna, Grand Duchess, daughter of Nicholas I (1822–92), 10
Olomouc, 58–63, 66–9, 75, 81, 85, 92–5, 99, 101, 106, 122; convention of (1850), 225
Omer Pasha (1806–71), 47, 50, 53–4, 126, 226
optical telegraph, 11
Oradea, 88, 146, 148, 157, 160, 166–70, 177, 180, 191, 195–8, 202
Orăștie, 194
Organic statute, 40–1, 47, 50–1
Orlov, Count Aleksey Fyodorovich (1787–1861), 11, 53, 101, 110, 112, 141
Orşova, 103, 126, 193
Osijek, 126
Oskar I, King of Sweden (1799–1859), 14, 20
Osten-Sacken, General Dmitriy Erofeevich (1798–1881), 138, 154, 156, 159, 165–7, 170, 178
Otto, King of Greece (1815–67), 10
Ottoman Empire, *see* Turkey
Oudinot, General Nicolas (1791–1863), 113
Ozora, 34, 72
Ozun, 158

Pacification Committee, *see* Rumanian National Committee
Pacifico, Don, 54

Pákozd, 34, 59
Palacký, František (1798–1876), 28–9
Palatine, *see* Stephen, Archduke of Austria
Palermo, 10, 115
Pálffy, Count Móric, 75
Palmerston, Viscount Henry John Temple (1784–1865), 9, 13, 18, 20, 25, 37, 44–8, 51, 54–6, 61, 63, 70, 84–5, 87, 114–17, 127, 206–7, 211–23 *passim*
Pančevo, 103
Panyutin, General Fyodor Sergeevich (1790–1865), 109–10, 122, 125, 128, 137, 140, 149–52, 156, 160, 172, 175, 182–4, 198
Papal States, 14, 113
Paris, 11–13, 32, 38–42, 45, 55, 70, 88, 113–14, 217; Treaty of (1856), 228
Parker, Vice-Admiral Sir William (1781–1866), 213–14, 216, 218–21
Parma, Grand Duchy of, 14
Parrot, General Jakob von (1797–1858), 125, 152, 177
Parseval des Chênes, Admiral Alexandre (1790–1860), 214, 221
Paskevich, Prince Ivan Fyodorovich (1782–1856), 3–5, 11, 15–17, 21, 23, 30, 33–5, 39, 43, 60, 63, 76, 80, 82, 88, 97, 100–11, 117, 122, 125–9, 132–9, 141–8, 151–99 *passim*, 201–10, 225, 228; attempt by Schwarzenberg to remove as commander, 175–6; celebrates 50 years of service in Russian army, 225; criticism of, in Warsaw, 160; disagreements with Haynau, 152–3, 157; dislike of Berg, 153; letters to Berg and Nicholas about surrender terms for Görgey, 163–4; modification of original operational plan, 137–8; views on importance of adequate supplies, 134
Passarowitz, Treaty of (1718), 211
Paul I, Emperor of Russia, father of Nicholas I (1754–1801), 3, 192

Index

Peace party in Hungary, 70, 104, 147
Péchy, Imre (1789–1864), 135
Peel, Sir Robert (1788–1850), 13, 55
Perczel, General Mór (1811–99), 73–4, 98, 102–3, 137, 155–6, 172
Pered, *see* Tešedikovo
Persia, 4–5
Pest, *see* Budapest
Peter III, Emperor of Russia, grandfather of Nicholas I (1728–62), 19
Petőfi, Sándor (1823–49), 13, 80, 171
Petrashevsky, *see* Butashevich-Petrashevsky
Petrovaradin, 102, 196, 203
Pezinok, 148
Pfersmann, General Alois (1781–1854), 81, 83
Pfuel, General Ernst von (1779–1866), 62
Piedmont, Kingdom of, 9, 32, 59, 65, 90, 96, 115, 228
Pillersdorf, Baron Franz (1786–1862), 24–5
Pius IX, Pope (1792–1878), 10, 32, 65, 113
Podolia, 16, 23, 197
Poeltenberg, General Ernő (1813–49), 161, 177, 179, 188, 205
Poland, Russian, 3, 8, 14, 16, 20, 23, 64, 66, 80, 87, 92, 102, 108, 111–12, 121, 134–5, 138, 143, 146, 154, 164, 185, 197–9
Polish emigrés, activities of, 8, 16, 23–4, 29, 35–8, 49, 51, 53, 67, 95, 100, 103–4, 112, 122, 193, 210, 213
Polish legion in Hungary, 89, 107, 139, 193
Polish revolt (1830–1), 5, 7, 39, 89, 140, 142, 186, 207, 210
Ponsonby, Viscount John (1770–1865), 9, 25, 32, 46, 48, 70, 206, 216, 219, 222
Pope, *see* Pius IX
Poroszló, 165
Portugal, Kingdom of, 6, 66
Posen, Grand Duchy of, 14, 16–20, 23, 29

Pott, General Gustav von (1792–1850), 153
Prague, 28–31, 106
Predeal Pass, 146
Prešov, 88, 125, 143, 156, 165–6, 197
printing press for Hungarian banknotes, 74, 148, 150, 183
Prittwitz, General Karl von (1790–1871), 17
Prokesch-Osten, Count Anton von (1795–1876), 127
Prussia, Kingdom of, 4, 6–9, 12, 14–17, 20–3, 35, 46, 82, 85, 91–2, 101, 108, 110–11, 114, 122–3, 157, 160, 196, 224–5, 228; parliament of, 22
Pruth river, 42–3
Puchner, General Anton (1779–1852), 77–88 *passim*, 93, 103, 126, 137
Pulszky, Ferenc (1814–97), 59, 70, 114
Putnok, 166

Quadrilateral, fortresses of, 14

Rába, river, 102
Radetzky, Field Marshal Johann (1766–1858), 14, 33–4, 59–60, 75, 90, 92, 109, 115, 129, 175, 189, 192
Radowitz, Joseph Maria von (1797–1853), 122
Rădulescu, Ion Heliade (1802–72), 41, 48
Radziwill, Count Lyov Lyudvigovich (1808–84), 210–13
Rajačić, Josif (1785–1861), 27, 31, 33, 103
Ramberg, General Georg (1786–1855), 151, 172, 194–5
Rauch, General Friedrich Wilhelm (1790–1850), 111, 122
Reghin, 158
Reischach, General Sigmund (1809–78), 192
Reshid Pasha (1802–58), 40, 49, 211
Richthofen, Baron (1810–?), 46
Rimavská Sobota, 160

Rîureni, 50
Rochow, General Theodor von (1794–1864), 17, 122, 192
Rome, 10, 65
Roman republic, 113, 115
Rönne, General Vasiliy Egorovich (1787–1864), 123
Roth, General Karl (1784–1864), 72
Roth, Stephan (1796–1849), 78
Rucăr, 41
Rüdiger, General Fyodor Vasil'evich (1784–1856), 125, 130–5, 138, 141, 143, 154–6, 160–2, 170, 176–89, 193, 197, 201, 206–7
Rüdiger, Lieutenant Fyodor (1829–90), 160–2
Rulikowski, Cornet, 165
Rumania, 48, 56
Rumanian legion, 158; national committee, 77–8; national guard, 77
Rumanians, activities of, 27, 46, 56, 77–8, 81, 87, 139, 146, 158, 178, 193–4
Ruse, 47
Rusovce, 108
Russell, Lord John (1792–1878), 114–15, 212, 215–17, 220–1
Russia, 3–10, 15–21, 24, 26, 30–7, 42–8, 51–8, 61–9, 76, 80–5, 92–7, 101–6, 109–17, 121–6, 138, 147, 161–3, 182, 185–90, 196–9, 202–10, 213–18, 220–22
Russian Baltic fleet, 20; Baltic provinces, 17; casualties in campaign, 198–9; council of ministers, 4; council of state, 4, 11, 97; field postal service, inefficiency of, 198; finances in 1848–9, 68–9, 200; Holy Synod, 31; military council, 4; western provinces, see also Podolia and Volhynia, 66, 80, 102, 105, 121, 146, 197
Rusul-Bîrgaului, 146
Ružomberok, 143
Rzewuski, Count Adam Adamovich (1801–88), 227

Şaguna, Bishop Andreiu (1809–73), 78, 81
Saint Peter and Saint Paul, fortress of, 190
Saint Petersburg, 3, 8, 13, 15, 18, 20–3, 30–4, 39–44, 47, 54, 58, 61, 63–8, 75, 80–6, 92, 95–7, 100–6, 111–16, 121–2, 131, 136, 159, 170, 187, 190–2, 197–200, 204–8, 211–19, 221–22
Saint Stephen, crown of, 74, 161–3, 176, 178, 183, 193
Sajó, river, 161
Samarin, Yuriy Fyodorovich (1819–76), 96
Şapcă, Father Radu, 41
Sardinia, see Piedmont, Kingdom of
Sarim Pasha (1801–54), 40
Sarkad, 191
Sass, General Grigoriy Khristoforovich (1797–1833), 130, 133, 154–5, 160, 162, 176
Sattler, Colonel Fyodor Karlovich (1805–76), 134, 156
Saxons, activities of in Transylvania, 77–8, 81, 86–7, 103, 146, 158, 194
Saxony, Kingdom of, 12, 14, 60, 122
Schleswig, Duchy of, 19, 85, 123, 224
Schleswig-Holstein, see Holstein and Schleswig
Schlick, General Franz (1789–1862), 74–5, 88, 150, 157, 172–4, 182–3, 186
Schobeln, Colonel Eduard (1902–80), 99, 105–6
Schönbrunn palace, Vienna, 60, 188
Schurtter, General Josef (1787–1857), 83
Schwarzenberg, Prince Felix (1800–52), 33, 59–65, 68–9, 71, 80–5, 91–100, 102, 105–9, 122–30, 133–7, 140–1, 147–9, 152–3, 155, 160, 169–70, 175–8, 184–9, 191, 199, 201–9, 211–19, 222
Schwechat, 60, 69, 71–2
Schweidel, General József (1796–1849), 205
Sebeş, 193

Seleuş, 180–1
Sel'van, General (?–1854), 154
Serbia, Principality of, 5, 27, 31, 36, 42, 46, 103, 126, 193, 210
Serbs, activities of in Hungary, 30–1, 34, 103
Sevastopol, 219
Seymour, Sir Hamilton (1797–1880), 226, 228
Sfîntul, Gheorghe, 158
Shabel'sky, General Ivan Petrovich (1796–1784), 146, 159
Shumla, 223
Sibiu, 77, 81–7, 92, 158–9, 170–2, 185, 193–5
Sicilies, Kingdom of the Two, 14
Sicily, 10, 32, 115
Sighişoara, 86, 170–2
Silesia, Austrian, 28
Siliesia, Prussian, 108, 157
Simbschen, General Karl (1794–1870), 193
Simonich, General Ivan Osipovich (1793–1851), 162
Simunich, General Balthasar, (1785–?), 74
Şiria, 3, 179–80, 182, 194
Skaryatin, Colonel Yuriy Yakovlevich (?–1849), 52, 83–4, 86–7, 171
Slavonia, 26
Slavonic Congress, June 1848, 28–9
Slavophiles, activities of, 29, 96, 101
Slovakia, 74, 88
Slovak militia, Rüdiger's proposal to re-create, 133
Slovaks, activities of in Hungary, 27–8, 133, 147, 197
small change, shortage of during campaign, 144, 169
Soltyk, Captain, 182
Sophie, Archduchess of Austria (1805–72), 26, 32, 67
Spain, Kingdom of, 6, 66
Spirei hill, 50
Srbobran, 103
Stadion, Count Franz (1806–53), 61, 90
Stará L'ubovňa, 141

Stein, Colonel Maximilian (1811–60), 171, 193
Stephen, Archduke of Austria, Palatine of Hungary (1817–67), 33–4, 68, 78
Stiles, William, 70, 74
Ştirbei, Barbu, 116
Stockmar, Baron Christian (1787–1863), 216
Stratimirović, Djordje (1822–1908), 27
Strengberg, 188
Stryj, 138
Stuart, Lord Dudley (1803–54), 51, 212
Sturdza, Michael, 36, 38, 40, 43–5, 50, 53
Stürmer, Count Bertholomaus (1787–1863), 211–12, 217, 222
Stutterheim, Colonel Johann (1803–70), 79
Styria, 128, 152
Subotica, 172
Suleiman Pasha (1807–64), 47–51, 83
Sultan of Turkey, see Abdul Mejid I
Šupljikać, Stevan (1786–1848), 27
Sweden, Kingdom of, 14, 20, 225
Switzerland, Confederation of, 9
Szalay, László (1813–88), 70
Széchenyi, Count István (1791–1860), 26, 71
Szeged, 126, 150–1, 158, 164, 172–3
Székesfehérvár, 201
Széklers, activities of in Transylvania, 77–9, 81–5, 138, 158
Szemere, Bertalan (1812–69), 89, 172, 176–8
Szikszó, 162
Szolnok, 74, 166–7
Szőreg, 173

Talat Effendi (?–1854), 40, 42, 47, 49
Tata, 148, 173
Teleki, László (1811–61), 70, 88, 113
Tell, Christian (1807–84), 41, 48
Tenedos, Island of, 218
Tešedikovo, 148

Thaly, Colonel Zsigmond (1814–86), 203
Third Department of His Majesty's Chancery, 11, 36, 53, 111–12; representative in Paris, 45, 66
Thun-Hohenstein, Count Friedrich (1810–81), 22–3
Times, The, 48
Timişoara, 103, 137, 151, 173–4, 178, 183, 192, 201
Tîrgu Mureş, 171, 193
Tisza river, 72–4, 89, 126–7, 137–8, 143–4, 149, 155–6, 165–7, 170, 173
Tiszacsege, 166–7
Tiszafüred, 165, 168
Titov, Vladimir Pavlovich (1805–91), 37, 47, 210–12, 215
Tocqueville, Alexis de (1805–59), 113, 114, 206, 214
Todorović, General Cosman (1787–1858), 102
Tokaj, 138, 143–4, 165–7
Tolstoy, General Aleksey Petrovich (1798–1864), 156
Tolstoy, Yakov Nikolaevich (1791–1867), 45, 66
Török, General Ignác (1795–1849), 205
Trajan's Field, 50
Transylvania, 26–7, 38, 40–2, 45–6, 56, 60, 64, 76–89, 92–107, 112, 117, 126, 136–9, 145–9, 157–60, 170–8, 185, 193–9, 204, 210
Trei Scaune, 79
Tumansky, Fyodor Antonovich (?–1853), 38
Tura, 155
Turkey, 4–6, 20, 27, 36–40, 44–8, 51–6, 76, 83–4, 96–7, 104, 116–17, 121, 126, 193–4, 209–28
Turkish council of ministers, 134, 211
Turn Roşu pass, 86, 170–2
Twelve Points, the 13
Tyutchev, Fyodor Ivanovich (1803–73), 23

Uherské Hradiště, 108, 110
United States of America, 70, 223
Unkiar-Skelessi, Treaty of (1833), 5
Urban, Colonel Karl (1802–77), 79, 84, 146, 195–6
Uzon, *see* Ozun

Vác, 75, 98, 151, 154–5, 159; manifesto of, 75, 89
Váh river, 106, 111, 125, 128, 138, 143, 149, 152–3
Vámospércs, 166, 176
Varna, 50
Vass, Samu (1814–79), 114
Vatra Dornei, 79
Vatta, 166
Vay, Baron Miklós (1802–94), 77
Vécsey, General Károly (1809–49), 174, 193, 205
Venice, 14
Venetian Republic, 65, 104, 123, 189, 203, 206, 208
Veselitsky, Colonel Sergey Gavrilovich (1804–66), 80
Vetter, General Antal (1803–82), 89, 172–3
Victor Emmanuel II, King of Piedmont (1820–78), 90
Victoria, Queen of Great Britain (1819–1901), 4, 18, 25, 63, 213, 216, 220, 226–7
Vidin, 193, 204
Vienna, 12–13, 15, 22–9, 32–4, 44–5, 58–67, 71, 75–6, 80–2, 86, 93–9, 100–10, 115, 122, 127–8, 131–8, 160, 174, 176, 182, 185–92, 204–9, 215–22; Congress of (1815), 6, 228
Viennese Academic Legion, 24; national guard, 24, 58, 60
Világos, *see* Şiria
Vilnius, 121
Vintilă-Vodă, 52
vojvodina, 27
Volhynia, 16, 23, 129, 197
Volkonsky, Prince Pyotr Mikhailovich (1776–1852), 121, 159
Vorparlament, 14, 28

Wallachia, 37–8, 40–56, 86–7, 103, 116–17, 139, 146, 158, 170–1, 197, 210, 226–8
Wallmoden, General Karl (1792–1883), 193
Warsaw, 5, 15, 17, 30, 39, 63, 66, 68–9, 92, 95, 100–7, 111–17, 121–37 *passim*, 140–2, 150–60, 165–7, 175, 180–99 *passim*, 201–9, 212, 214
Welden, General Ludwig (1782–1853), 94–5, 99–100, 102, 104–5, 108, 125, 128–9, 147
Wellington, Arthur, Duke of (1769–1852), 9, 12, 48, 85, 115
Wessenberg, Baron Johann von (1773–1858), 25, 35, 58–9
Wieliczka saltmines, 132, 199
Wiener Zeitung, 106
William, Archduke of Austria (1827–94), 67, 141
William II, King of Holland, brother-in-law of Nicholas I (1792–1849), 13, 95
William I, King of Württemberg (1781–1864), 10, 16
William, Prince of Prussia (1797–1888), 22, 62

Windischgraetz, Prince Alfred (1787–1862), 29, 31–4, 59–67, 71–8, 80–9, 91–100, 124, 136, 147, 175, 210
Winter Palace, Saint Petersburg, 96
Wohlgemuth, General Ludwig (1789–1853), 102, 148–9, 195, 207
Wrangel, General Friedrich (1784–1877), 19
Wrocław, 19
Württemberg, Kingdom of, 12, 14
Wysocki, Józef (1809–73), 89, 143, 193, 210

Załuski, Count Józef (1786–1866), 140–1, 212
Zamość, 141, 185
Zamoyski, Colonel Władysław (1803–68), 210
Zărand, 180–1
Zichy, Count Ferenc (1811–97), 136, 141, 144, 156, 169, 177, 184, 186, 198–9
Zichy, Count Ödön (1809–48), 72
Žihárec, 148
Żmigród, 141–2
Zsigárd, *see* Žihárec

Walewska, Maria, 38–40, 56, 58–9, 60, 146–17, 150, 156, 158, 150–1, 197–200, 274–8

Washington, General Karl (1752–1803), 93–4

Wawrzecki, Tomasz, General, 65, 82, 90, 92, 93, 94, 100–5, 112, 151, 171–5, 179, passim, 140–3, 154–6, 181–3, 176–, 280 Bonaparte, 204–7, 214

Weimar, General, Ludwig (1757–1858), 94–5, 99, 100, 102, 110, 124, 198, 125, 128–9, 137

Wellington, Arthur, Duke of (1769–1852), 9, 16, 18, 85, 175

Werculbek, Baron Johann von (1775–1854), 29, 35, 38–70

Wenceslas, summer, 12, 196

Werona, Ronne, 106

Wilhelm, Archduke of Austria (1827–96), 65, 142, 197

Willbrett, King of Holland, brother-in-law, Nicholas, I (1792–1849), 18, 95

Wilhelm I, King of Wurttemberg (1781–1864), 105–4

William, Prince of Prussia (1797–1888), 22, 67

Windischgrätz, Prince Alfred (1787–1862), 29, 38–41, 69, 70–71, 8, 80–5, 91–4, 112, 124–5, 136, 147, 175, 210

Winter-Palace, saint-Petersburg, 96

Wittgenstein, General Ludwig (1769–1843), 1002, 3, 9, 195, 207

Wrangel, General (1784–1877), 79

Wrocław, 19

Wysocki, Josef (1809–73), 86, 142, 193, 210

Zamoyski, Count Jozef (1789–1866), 140–1, 231

Zamoyski, Jan, 157

Zamoyski, Colonel Władysław (1803–68), 210

Zamość, 150–1

Zaliwski, Count Pierre (1811–87), 135, 141, 143, 156, 169, 177, 183, 185, passim

Zboy, Edmund Odo (2504–6), 35, Zaharov, 138

Zaria nad, 111,

Żaługa, see Zaliwski